RATIONALIZED
EPISTEMOLOGY

SUNY Series in Logic and Language
John T. Kearns, Editor

RATIONALIZED EPISTEMOLOGY

Taking Solipsism Seriously

BY ALBERT A. JOHNSTONE

State University of New York Press

Published by
State University of New York Press, Albany

© 1991   State University of New York

For information, address State University of New York
Press, State University Plaza, Albany, N.Y. 12246

Production by Marilyn P. Semerad
Marketing by Theresa A. Swierzowski

Library of Congress Cataloging-in-Publication Data

Johnstone, Albert A., 1927–
    Rationalized epistemology : taking solipsism seriously / Albert A.
Johnstone.
        p. cm. — (SUNY series in logic and language)
    Includes index.
    ISBN 0–7914–0787–X — ISBN 0–7914–0788–8 (pbk.)
    1. Skepticism. 2. Knowledge, Theory of. I. Title. II. Series.
BD201.J64 1991
121' .2—dc20
                                                                    90–49126
                                                                    CIP

10 9 8 7 6 5 4 3 2 1

To Maxine
true believer

CONTENTS

PREFACE

The present work has two principal aims, both somewhat ambitious. The first of these is to resolve three long-standing skeptical problems in epistemology. Each of these problems is traceable in its modern form to the writings of Descartes. The central issue in each is that of the warrant one has for endorsing cherished everyday beliefs in the independence and reality of the world and for rejecting a solipsistic scenario that ties the everyday world to one's own self and to one's awareness of it. The first problem (the one commonly associated with Descartes) is whether the world is real rather than a dream or personal illusion, or the conjuration of a devious demon bent upon deceit. The second problem is whether things in the world (and indeed the world itself) continue to exist when not perceived by oneself. The third is the classical problem of the existence of a world external to one's sensations, that is, whether there does in fact exist a world similar to one's own private representations of it. Each raises one form of a question which would have made an appropriate title for this work, "Does the World Exist?"

The second aim of the book is to help lay the groundwork for a reorientation of Anglo-American epistemology back toward the foundational investigations of Husserl and Russell, investigations into the warrant that the evidence of the senses provides for everyday beliefs about the world. The past fifty years have seen Husserl's work largely ignored, and Russell's heritage in epistemology too often reduced to subtle and painstaking analyses of incurably imprecise everyday concepts. Meanwhile, the linguistic turn and an attendant cultural relativism have, despite their valuable insights, deflected philosophical interest and effort from examination of fundamental philosophical issues, issues that are both pancultural and independent of language. While a redressment of the error is inevitable in the long run of philosophical trends, nevertheless the swifter the treatment, the sooner the cure.

The two aims pursued are inextricably linked. Indeed, one of the conclusions imposed by a careful sifting of the evidence is that Cartesian skeptical theses can be satisfactorily answered only by a return to a foundationalist epistemology. Precisely because this conclusion is so much at odds with current philosophical mythology, a fair portion of the book is devoted to establishing it. An auxiliary conclusion strongly supported by the extensive critical analysis of modern Western philosophy is that the foundationalist solution proposed is not simply one solution, but the only possible one.

Of the three skeptical problems considered, only the third admits of a solution (a partial one) through currently popular methods. The two others, those concerning the reality of the world and its unperceived continuation over time, remain obdurately recalcitrant to treatment by the wide variety of currently employed strategies for answering skepticism. Beginning chapters show the inefficacy of the appeal to commonsense claims, to reasonableness, to pragmatic considerations, to consistency, to normal perceptual procedures and the criterion of coherence, and to the conditions for meaningful utterance. A Cartesian account of meaning is sketched, one that properly ties linguistic meaning and reference to particular individuals with their epistemological limitations. Subsequent chapters show in detail the futility of charging a solipsistic thesis with parasitism, i.e., with denying a truth the thesis itself presupposes as a condition of its own truth or meaning. In particular, they show that, despite the widespread popularity of linguistic parasitism arguments since Wittgenstein and Strawson first used them against solipsism, such arguments rely generally on no less than three mistaken assumptions: that language presupposes a public world in the sense of a nonsolipsistic one; that language cannot be private, and that conceptualization is impossible (or insignificant) apart from language. The Cartesian skeptical problems are found to be prelinguistic in the sense that in principle they can arise for an individual prior to the acquisition of language. They are consequently pancultural.

In the later chapters the skeptical problems are reconsidered from the perspective of the radical skeptic, which is to say, on the terrain of the scanty, ephemeral, sensuous materials to which radical skepticism reduces the world. A careful examination of these materials leads to a number of significant finds with regard to tactual space—its primacy as a model for three-dimensionality and its absence of perspective. The ever-present occupant of tactual space, the tactile-kinesthetic body, is recognized to be an indispensable constituent of the willing, feeling, thinking subject—whence it may be concluded that Descartes's view of the self as a thinking being immune to skeptical attack is mistaken. Freedom to choose is found to provide a randomizer sufficient to yield quasi-random observations of items in the world, and hence samples to which inverse probability considerations may be cogently applied. As a result rational warrant may be provided for the claims that objects continue to exist unperceived, and that sense fields are so correlated as to form a world of common objects. Free will is thus found to be an indispensable prerequisite for rational belief in the everyday world of common sense. The conjunction of these results—the spatiality and phenomenal nature of the self, the nonperspectival nature of tactual space, and the continued existence of unobserved phenomena—also yields rational grounds for the claim that the world is not some form of personal illusion. The central role played by the tactile-kinesthetic body in the epistemological constitution of the commonsense world is validation of the need for what Maxine Sheets-Johnstone in her book, *The Roots of Thinking*, has termed "the corporeal turn" in philosophy.

In view of the detailed nature of the investigations and analyses it contains, *Rationalized Epistemology* is obviously appropriate as a text for graduate courses, whether in epistemology, skepticism, or Cartesian studies. It should be added, however, that much of the interest of Cartesian skeptical problems lies in the collateral examinations their resolution necessitates—examinations in semantics, the philosophy of language, and metaphysics. More precisely, it proves necessary not only to probe the concept of knowledge, the nature of perceptual experience and the perceptual given, but also to undertake in-depth analyses of the nature of meaning generally and linguistic meaning in particular, analyses of both verbal and nonverbal thinking, of the structures of the various sense fields, of the nature of feeling, of the nature of thinking and of the self or the thinking, feeling subject, of spontaneity, the freedom of the individual to do or not do. On these grounds, there is good reason to hope that the work will be stimulating as well as useful, not only to graduate students but to undergraduates as well as to a wider public interested in philosophical issues.

ACKNOWLEDGMENTS

I should like to express my deepest appreciation to the countless thinkers, past and present, without whose prior struggles these present reflections, whatever their worth, would never have been.

PERSONAE ARGUMENTI

In order of disappearance

Internal World Solipsists:

The Sensa Solipsist, for whom what exists is the private world of one's own sensations or representations.

The Lingua-Sensa Solipsist, or the Sensa Solipsist as portrayed by Wittgenstein.

Observed World Solipsists:

The Ephemerata Solipsist, for whom any portions of the world not actually perceived by oneself do not exist.

The Monopsyche Solipsist, an Ephemerata Solipsist whose sole concern is to deny the existence of other minds.

The Sense Data Solipsist, a radical Ephemerata Solipsist who also denies the existence of all properties and relations not actually perceived.

Unreal World Solipsists:

The Demoniac Solipsist, for whom the world is a hoax conjured up by a demon.

The Phantasmata Solipsist, for whom the world is a personal illusion.

The Oneirata Solipsist, for whom the world is but a dream the solipsist is having.

The Non-Sensa Solipsist, who parts company with the Sensa Solipsist after the latter's conviction on a charge of parasitism.

CHAPTER ONE

CARTESIAN SOLIPSISM

THE CHALLENGE OF SOLIPSISM

The skeptical scenarios entertained some centuries ago by the French philosopher, René Descartes, have lost nothing of their power to shake complacency. Their unsettling effect may be judged first-hand from a reading of the following passage:

> How can you be certain that your life is not a continuous dream, and that everything you think you learn through the senses is not false now, just as much as when you are asleep? In particular, how can you be certain of this when you have learned that you were created by a superior being who, being all-powerful, would have found it no more difficult to create us just as I am describing, than to create us as you think you are?[1]

How indeed? The least that may be said is that no reassuring answer is immediately forthcoming. Descartes himself devoted a considerable portion of his philosophical writings to an attempt (ultimately unsuccessful) to put to rest the skeptical questions he raised. Lest one be prompted in self-defence to dismiss the questions as the pointless preoccupations of an otherworldly intellectual, it should be noted that Descartes was a quite normal human being—at least to the extent that there is such a thing. By modern psychiatric standards he would be judged neither schizoid nor seriously paranoid. Moreover, when a young man, he fought duels, served in the army, travelled to Italy to see the investiture of the pope, and participated in the social whirl of Paris. Later when he withdrew to the quiet of the Dutch countryside to devote himself to more intellectual pursuits, his interests were neither otherworldly nor wildly theoretical: they ranged over optics, physics, physiology, astronomy, and encompassed possible practical applications such as eyeglasses, fireplaces, and wheelchairs. As a result the above queries may lay serious claim to be those of an eminently practical and sane human being.

The issue raised is whether this world, which certainly appears solid, independent, and real enough, is in fact but a dream from which one will some day awake, perhaps at the prompting of a playful divinity. A scenario of the sort, when promoted into a serious account of the nature of the world, is one possible form of a particular skeptical thesis, solipsism. Solipsism may be loosely characterized as the terminal stage of eliminative egocentricity. The etymology of the term (Latin, *solus* and *ipse*), rightly suggests the doctrine that the self alone exists. Here, the self must be understood to encompass not only the solipsist but also those things of which the solipsist is aware. Thus, solipsism might be described alternatively as the thesis that a necessary condition for the existence of anything in the world is one's own awareness of it. Consequently, to qualify as a solipsist it suffices to make the claim that the everyday world exists only to the extent that one is aware of it.

The aim of the present book is to take up Descartes's failed enterprise and to show that the various forms of solipsism traceable to Descartes's writings are mistaken accounts of the world. Otherwise stated, the aim is to provide rational foundations for the belief that the everyday world does in fact exist independently of oneself. It might be wondered how such an undertaking could possibly be thought worthwhile. Solipsism clearly is an account that contradicts the everyday knowledge claims that all sensible individuals are inclined to make, and one that clearly has to be mistaken even if its falsity is not readily established. In addition it contradicts the claims most professional epistemologists are disposed to defend and hardly figures as a serious contender in present day heated debates. Hence, one might ask, why bother with solipsism? A brief word should be said on both points.

First with regard to everyday knowledge, the question is why one should bother to attempt to refute an account of the world so clearly mistaken. The answer lies in the tantalized exasperation provoked by solipsistic scenarios. Despite one's firm conviction that solipsism is absurd, all attempts to show its absurdity tend to have rather the contrary result of making it less preposterous. The upshot of even a modest number of valiant but fruitless sallies in defence of common sense is that one finds oneself concurring with the sentiments voiced by Immanuel Kant on the issue:

It still remains a scandal to philosophy and to human reason in general that the existence of things outside us...must be accepted merely on *faith*, and that if anyone thinks good to doubt their existence, we are unable to counter his doubts by any satisfactory proof.[2]

The point here, of course, is not merely that one's belief in the existence of the everyday world has no rational foundation. If it were, the moral to be drawn might simply be that one must resign oneself to living irrationally, to making an irrational leap of faith into comforting arms the existence of which one has never seriously doubted. The scandal has deeper implications. Could it be that the everyday view of the world is mistaken? In the absence of good reasons for thinking the view to be true, as far as one can tell it may in fact be false. Conversely, could it be that there is some truth to solipsism? In the absence of good reasons for thinking the doctrine false, as far as one can tell, it may be true. Perhaps the world does in fact reduce to oneself and to those things one now actually perceives.

What then of the second point above, that present-day epistemologists do not take solipsism seriously? For the sake of accuracy it should be observed that if it is not taken seriously, it by no means follows that it has been ignored. This particular variety of skepticism is as familiar to professional philosophers in their quasi totality as are Platonic forms. It has elicited myriad negative responses. It has been castigated as a sophomoric frivolity, dismissed as irrelevant to practical concerns, or relegated to the role of the *absurdum* in *reductio ad absurdum* arguments. It has been characterized as an irrational demand for the impossible, or the deformed fruit of a misconceived epistemology. Alternatively, it has been condemned as a semantically aberrant and hence meaningless thesis arising from a linguistic confusion acting as a philosophical fly-trap. It has also been accused of covert self-contradiction, or of denying its own factual and conceptual presuppositions. On the most flattering estimate, it has been compared to an impregnable fortress and judged logically sound, indeed irrefutable, although incapable of being sincerely believed. With careful examination of the evidence, however, all these assessments of solipsism turn out to be mistaken in their near totality. The considerations on which they are based yield a few local successes but leave the doctrine essentially unscathed. When properly formulated, solipsism is found to be neither frivolous nor irrelevant nor absurd nor self-contradictory, nor senseless nor irrational. The challenge it poses to everyday beliefs is in fact still with us.

There would seem, then, to be serious reasons for taking solipsism seriously. In view of the widespread prevalence of the contrary opinion in philosophical circles, it will be necessary in a first step to show that solipsism still constitutes an unresolved problem for any serious thought about the world as well as any serious epistemology. To borrow a phrase from Ludwig Wittgenstein, the first step will be to show that the fly is still captive in the fly-bottle.

The second step will be to resolve the problem in the light of various lessons learned from the failure endemic to presently dominant trends in western philosophy. One important lesson, as we shall see, is the need to return to the epistemology practiced by Bertrand Russell and Edmund Husserl, where the attempt is made to meet skepticism on its own terrain. The latter task should in principle be achievable. In this regard Kant's characterization of solipsism is reassuring. For a particular epistemological position to be literally a "scandal to human reason," it must be profoundly unreasonable or irrational. As such it must be in conflict with some rational principles or procedures of human reason—and that despite the awkward circumstance that it is not immediately obvious what the principles or procedures may be. The explanation of their apparent absence must be not that they do not exist but that they have been overlooked, or better still, that they were once used but now lie forgotten somewhere, buried deep among the layers of past cognitive successes. On this initially not implausible view of the situation, the task of refuting solipsism reduces to an archeological one of excavating the long-buried rational foundations of human cognition.

INTRODUCING SEVEN CARTESIAN SOLIPSISTS

The ancestry of present-day formulations of solipsism is traceable to Descartes's philosophical meditations, albeit often with an important detour through the British empiricism of Locke, Berkeley, and Hume. In Descartes's enterprise of methodical doubt, solipsistic theses serve as a foil to set off naively accepted opinions and as a prod to find unshakable foundations on which to erect knowledge of the world. Each of a number of distinct skeptical scenarios envisaged by Descartes in his quest for certainty may plausibly be judged to qualify as solipsistic. To complicate the situation further, many of the additional doubts entertained, if properly mothered, might be made to lead to skeptical positions also characterizable as solipsistic. Let us look at these two sources in turn.

Two solipsistic theses in particular figure very prominently in

Descartes's *Meditations on First Philosophy*. One is introduced with Descartes's attempt to reassure himself that some of the things he perceives must be true. Surely he would have to be mad, Descartes tells himself, to doubt that he is sitting by the fire with a piece of paper in his hands, and yet, he reflects, he has often been convinced of just such things in dreams, when in fact he was lying asleep in bed. After thinking the matter over, he is astounded to realize that there are "never any sure signs" for distinguishing waking from dreaming.[3] For all he can tell with any assurance, the world might be one vast dream he is having. The theme of the second solipsistic thesis is first quietly introduced with a reflection on God's goodness: it is perhaps not enough to appeal to God's benevolence for reassurance that one is not constantly deceived, Descartes muses, since God certainly allows one to be deceived at least some of the time. Shortly thereafter, the theme breaks in with full force. Descartes resolves to assume that the world with all its shapes and sounds, earth and sky, are not the creations of a benevolent God, but are mere delusions devised by "some malicious demon of the utmost power and cunning" who devotes all his energy and talent to deceiving Descartes.[4] He needs to entertain resolutely this fantastic scenario, he finds, in order to counterbalance the skewing of his judgment by the weight of past beliefs.

Both the above scenarios are powerfully skeptical. Both qualify as solipsistic in that according to each the world has no existence independently of the solipsist's awareness of it. They might be termed *Oneirata Solipsism* and *Demoniac Solipsism*, respectively. Descartes reasons that even if the world is solipsistic and hence does not exist, the solipsist at least must exist. On the supposition that what he now perceives arises like a dream through some inner faculty, it must nevertheless be the case that he exists as the dreamer. On the supposition that the world is the work of an archdeceiver bent on deceiving him, he, the intended target of the deception, nevertheless must exist. Likewise, in order for him to wonder whether anything exists, to have doubts, and entertain solipsistic scenarios, he must exist.

In Descartes's skeptical probing a third doubt inspired by perceptual illusion plays an important albeit secondary role. Early in the *Meditations* after declaring his intention to seek indubitable foundations, Descartes observes that he has sometimes found that the senses deceive, a circumstance he esteems suitable for the application of the maxim, "it is prudent never to trust completely those who have deceived us even once."[5] Later in the course of an ostensibly autobiographical confession, he expands his case somewhat by admitting the prevalence of sense error, and its extension into the most intimate of matters, as is evident in the phenomenon of the phantom limb.[6] Descartes repeatedly brings up the theme of sense illusion in the context of skeptical doubt, but tends to find it somewhat wanting for his purposes. The reason is that sensory illusion is a localized and recognizable phenomenon, a point he has his character, Polyander, bring out in *The Search after Truth*, and which he voices himself in the *Meditations*.[7] He seems nevertheless to think that sense illusions do provide some cause for a general skeptical doubt which envisions the possibility that all sensory appearances are illusory. Such is implied by the fact that he speaks of 'adding' the two more powerful skeptical scenarios to the case already made by sense illusions, rather than of substituting the former two for the latter.

The hypothesis that the world is a generalized illusion is, properly speaking, not solipsistic as it stands. The concept of an illusion is that of something which is not really where it appears to be; thus, there is no inconsistency in the notion of an illusion continuing to be present to someone else when the solipsist is not perceiving it. Some further argumentation is required if the hypothesis of a generalized illusion is to lead to a properly solipsistic conclusion in which the illusion is the solipsist's personal illusion rather like an hallucination. Supposing this supplementary manoeuvre effectuated, we might term the resulting form of solipsism, *Phantasmata Solipsism*.

Yet another solipsistic doubt emerges in the *Meditations* in reflections subsequent to the above formulations of skeptical scenarios.[8] Descartes reasons that in perception he does not clearly and distinctly perceive (as he had formerly assumed he did) that there are things outside him in an independent world, things that affect his senses and give rise to 'ideas' or images resembling their originals in the world. On reflection he finds himself compelled to endorse the more modest claim that he perceives merely that there are ideas present in himself. Descartes goes on to discuss the reasons he had for thinking there is an external world behind the sensuous copies of it. Of the two reasons he considers, the first, that nature teaches him as much, he dismisses as a mere natural desire to believe; the second, the fact that ideas do not depend upon his will, he judges insufficient to show any likeness between ideas and their presumed originals. He finds nothing to show that ideas do not arise like dreams, through the operation of some unknown faculty in himself. His conclusion is that it is only by blind impulse that he has believed that there exists an external world resembling his ideas of it.

The possible state of affairs envisaged in the above skeptical reflections may also be characterized as solipsistic. On the proposed hypothesis, what is perceived of the everyday world is demoted to the status of a mere idea bearing no resemblance to an external source; the everyday world is construed to be an aggregate of the solipsist's private impressions or ideas or private representations or images. Since the latter were called *sensa* in the literature of some years back, the resulting solipsistic thesis might be termed *Sensa Solipsism*.

These four forms of solipsism constitute the four solipsistic theses more or less explicitly entertained by Descartes. They do not, however, exhaust the possibilities for deriving solipsistic positions from Descartes's skeptical reflections. The latter contain a variety of interesting doubts. In his discussion of the role of judgment in perception, Descartes appeals to a quite striking example: on his looking from a window at men crossing a square, he finds himself inclined to say he sees men in the street, whereas what he sees in fact are mere hats and coats which might well cover automatons.[9] This notion of vestimentary ambulation may easily be expanded to yield a quite general skeptical doubt. It suggests the possibility that perceived objects become something quite different when unperceived, or better still, that they cease to exist altogether. A like suggestion is implicit in the analogy Descartes draws between dreams and paintings, which, given the perceptual context of the remark, comes down to likening perceived objects to colored façades.[10] If the implications of such an analogy are vigorously pursued, then the assumption that an object visibly present has an inside and an unperceived far side is called into question, as is the assumption that things continue to exist when unperceived.

Such a general skeptical doubt must await the arrival of David Hume for its more explicit formulation. Hume thinks the doubt unanswerable, and proposes rather to examine the question, "Why we attribute a CONTINU'D existence to objects, even when they are not present to the senses."[11] Later still, it is given colorful formulation by Bertrand Russell with his hypothesis "that tables, whenever no one is looking, turn into kangaroos."[12] Not surprisingly, it figures among the skeptical scenarios to be found in Ludwig Wittgenstein's later musings: "'The chair is the same whether I am looking at it or not'—that *need* not have been true. People are often embarrassed when one looks at them."[13] As noted earlier, a generalized doubt of the sort is nowhere explicitly entertained by Descartes. Indeed no suggestion of it may be found among the doubts to which an answer is proposed in the final section of the *Meditations*. As a result, it is best considered but second-generation Cartesian.

The skeptical thesis that things cease to exist altogether when unobserved by oneself clearly qualifies as solipsistic. It states that the world is composed only of those things or parts of things actually perceived by the skeptic. Hence, it limits what exists to that of which the solipsist is aware. Since this variant of solipsism states the sole constituents of the world to be the ephemeral aspects of objects perceived by the solipsist, it might be termed *Ephemerata Solipsism.*

Consider a moment the import of the thesis. If one were a solipsist in this mode, one would hold that the world which now exists consists of the following items: the two white rectangles lined with print which are the surfaces of two pages of this book, the collection of indefinite outlines and shapes beyond the borders of the two white surfaces, perhaps a snatch of desktop or wallpaper; the rough bottom of the book pressing against one's hand, the benign voluminous mass of one's felt body of which the salient points are perhaps a contracted brow, a gently heaving chest, a protesting elbow and a shaking fitful foot; then behind oneself and to the left a soft and relentless ticking and, beyond that, an occasional muffled roar. Such would be the meager furniture of the world: the other pages of the book have ceased to exist, one's face has shrunk to a vague hovering heaviness, the desk to an unyielding prop and nebulous reddish-tan horizon, while the world outside the sparse remnants of the room is but a distant and capricious hum.

While the world may appear appallingly meager on this view, it is nevertheless susceptible to further erosion from skeptical doubt. Ephemerata Solipsism limits skeptical scrutiny to the existence of unobserved portions of the world, and takes no stand on an array of further issues. Among these are the possible illusory nature of the observed phenomena (Is the desktop really reddish tan?), the dispositional properties automatically attributed but not actually observed at the time (Would the white pages burn?), the correlation of facets in one sense modality with those in another (Are the printed pages and the felt heaviness two aspects of one material object?). These various characteristics of observed partial objects (or ephemerata) would be called into question with a strict application of the general Cartesian rule of withholding assent where doubt is possible and hence casting a skeptical eye on all characteristics not actually observed. Descartes's hedged claim simply to seem to see and hear, as opposed to really seeing and hearing, is a first firm step in this direction. What is observed may be illusory; hence, there is cause to suspend judgment on any claim that what is perceived is really where it seems to be.

This first firm step breaks into a sprightly trot only with David Hume's skeptical scrutiny of causal connections.[14] As Hume points out, causal relations are discoverable only through experience. No analysis of the cause, no reasoning could ever conclude what a stone will do when left unsupported in the air, or what will happen when one billiard ball meets another. Experience shows that a number of cases of an event of one kind are followed by an event of another kind. From these observations it is inferred that in unobserved cases events of the first kind are followed by events of the second. Yet, Hume asks, what rational grounds do the observed cases provide for concluding that the unobserved ones will behave in like fashion? Hume's own answer is that they provide none, and that habit alone is the motor for drawing the conclusion. A solipsist who denies the existence of anything unperceived, might with equal rigor at this point agree that there are no rational grounds for any extrapolations from observed regularities to unobserved ones.

In a final step it might be denied that there is any correlation between visual phenomena and tactual or auditory ones. The world would consequently be reduced to an assembly of colored façades and concomitant but otherwise unrelated sounds and feelings. These radicalized ephemeral items answer to one description of what are termed "sense data" in the literature. The radicalized version of Ephemerata Solipsism might be termed *Sense Data Solipsism.*

Sense Data Solipsism so defined has much in common with the earlier encountered thesis of Sensa Solipsism. The sensa, or images or representations that make up the world of the Sensa Solipsist are presumably equally lacking in the various nonostensible properties denied to sense data. Sensa and sense data differ, however, in one important respect. To say that a thing is a sensum is to imply that it is an image, that it is sensed, that it is 'in the mind' and consequently a constituent in a private world. To say that an item is a sense datum is to imply nothing of the sort. A sense datum is an object stripped of all but its ostensible characteristics and, as such, may conceivably exist unsensed. It is important to note that the skeptical problems arising in connection with each are different problems. The point was noticed by Hume who distinguishes two skeptical questions,[15] that of why we attribute continued existence to objects (the question of Ephemerata and Sense Data Solipsism) and the question of why we suppose objects to have an existence independent of the mind (the question of Sensa Solipsism).

The skeptical doubt as to whether other people have minds may likewise take two closely related forms. One of these coincides with Sensa Solipsism. The Sensa Solipsist, shut up in a private world of sensations, asks not only whether there is a public world but also whether there are other private worlds, worlds similar to that made up of the solipsist's sensations and private to other people. For this reason, the issue of solipsism is sometimes found to coincide with the issue of the existence of other minds. Now, to complicate matters, a skeptical doubt as to the existence of other minds may also arise on the terrain of Ephemerata or Sense Data Solipsism. Just as it may be asked whether unobserved tables and chairs continue to exist when one turns away from them, so also it may be asked whether the private experiences of other people—their feelings, pains, dreams, and imaginings, all unobserved by oneself—exist in fact. The denial that they do is one of the denials contained in Ephemerata Solipsism. Since the issue of unobserved private items such as feelings is a somewhat different issue from that of unobserved public objects such as tables and chairs, it may be convenient to distinguish it. Consequently, that part of the thesis of Ephemerata Solipsism that denies the existence of the private experiences of other people could be given a special name, *Monopsyche Solipsism.*

Thus, seven forms of Cartesian solipsism can be distinguished. Each states that the world, or what is commonly considered to be the world, exists only to the extent that the solipsist is aware of it. The four first-generation forms of Cartesian solipsism—Oneirata, Demoniac, Phantasmata, and Sensa Solipsism—characterize the world as the solipsist's personal world, a dream, a demon-induced fiction, a personal illusion, or an aggregate of sense impressions. Of the three second-generation forms of solipsism, Ephemerata Solipsism restricts membership in the world community to those portions of things of which the solipsist is actually aware; Sense Data Solipsism advocates an identical ontological restriction while denying in addition any putative unobserved characteristics to the chosen few admitted by Ephemerata Solipsism; and Monopsyche Solipsism pursues the one issue of the experiences of other minds and denies the existence of any alleged private entities such as pains, feelings, or dreams experienced by other persons.

PRECURSORS IN ANTIQUITY

A word of commentary is perhaps not misplaced on the characterization of these seven forms of solipsism as Cartesian. It may plausibly be argued that many of the forms are based on doubts entertained by various Greek philosophers of antiquity and that consequently it is somewhat incorrect to use terminology which attributes the resulting forms of skepticism to Descartes. The issue merits the opening of a short parenthesis.

It is undeniable that the majority of the doubts entertained by Descartes and leading to solipsism are very similar to doubts entertained previously by the Greeks. Perhaps the clearest instance of such precedence is to be found in the doubt leading to Oneirata Solipsism. In the course of a discussion of Protagoras's views on perception, Plato has Socrates raise Descartes's question of how we may determine whether we are now awake or merely dreaming.[16] Significantly enough, Socrates characterizes the question as a familiar one. In this particular passage Plato uses it to provoke doubt regarding the existence of objects of sense perception. If Cicero's reports are accepted as accurate, then the skeptics of the New Academy in their disputes with the Stoics likewise presented a number of the points made later by Descartes in formulating his doubts. According to Cicero, they argued that it is quite possible in principle for dreams and waking states to be indistinguishable, and that at the time of actual dreaming, dreams are undistinguished (even indistinguishable) from waking states.[17] It would clearly be mistaken to view the dream hypothesis as a Cartesian invention.

The skeptical doubts elicited by the phenomenon of perceptual illusion are even less of a Cartesian innovation. The above-mentioned passage in which Socrates raises the possibility of a dream world is part of a broader discussion of dreams, hallucinations, and illusions and their implications for perception as a source of knowledge. At another point Plato has Socrates declare the senses to be "inaccurate witnesses" that invariably mislead and are best ignored in the search for truth.[18] The particular notion that sense illusion makes the senses deceptive witnesses to be mistrusted is a notion found even more clearly in the thought of Epicurus, although with implications inversely construed. According to Cicero, Epicurus emphatically denied that there is such a thing as sense illusion at all, his reasoning being that "if one sense has told a lie once in a man's life, no sense must ever be believed."[19] The declaration finds a familiar echo in Descartes's above-noted claim that one instance of sense illusion is sufficient to raise the issue of the reliability of any of the senses at any time. Sense illusion leads Pyrrho to declare (reportedly) in a still more skeptical vein that "things are by nature equally undeterminable, admitting of neither measure nor discrimination," a conclusion endorsed and defended by Sextus Empiricus, particularly in his Seventh Mode.[20]

Sensa Solipsism would also seem to have been anticipated in its essential lines by Greek philosophy. It was a common view that perception is representational. Empedocles' theory of effluences which emanate from bodies and enter the pores of sense organs giving rise to percepts is echoed in its main lines by Leucippus and Democritus as well as Plato. The supplementary view that in perception sensations are transmitted from the senses to the brain is apparently even more ancient, since Theophrastus attributes it to Alcmaeon, a pupil of Pythagoras.[21] A representational theory of perception is also presupposed by both sides in the debate between Stoics and Academic skeptics over the Stoic thesis of cataleptic impressions. The latter are defined by Zeno to be faithful impressions that guarantee their own truth in that they are molded from their objects in a form that they could not have if they had come from some different object. The Academics, for their part, contend that there are no such impressions and that any true impression could have a false one exactly like it.[22] From the latter contention it follows, of course, that insofar as it can be judged from the impression itself, the impression may be the effect of nothing in the world. The Academics refrain from drawing anything approaching a solipsistic conclusion and are content to substitute the likelihood and presumption of truth for the certainty defended by the Stoics. Sextus Empiricus naturally draws the more sanguine conclusion that there is no way of determining whether appearances are similar to external realities, or even whether there are any real objects or not—to which he appends the corollary that it cannot be known whether sensation apprehends anything.[23] Such a skeptical position is remarkably close to that of Sensa Solipsism.

Of the skeptical hypotheses which Descartes entertains in the *Meditations*, only one appears not to have been entertained by the ancients, the hypothesis of a wily demon addicted to deception. Indeed, it would seem that the envisaged skeptical scenario must be attributed squarely to Descartes. Its main character, interestingly enough, is the moral antithesis of the one who ultimately manages to put Descartes's doubts to rest. The scenario is absent from the earlier work, *Discourse on the Method*, in which the key role is played solo by the dream hypothesis. It must have been conceived by Descartes some time between 1637, when the *Discourse* was published, and 1641, the date of publication of the *Meditations*. God's goodness is for Descartes the ultimate guarantee of the existence of the world in the *Discourse* as in the *Meditations*. Hence, one might almost say that after finding the answer to his question, Descartes discovered what the question was.

The three second-generation forms of Cartesian solipsism, Ephemerata, Monopsyche, and Sense Data Solipsism, would both seem to have been anticipated to a not insignificant degree by Greek philosophers. The Pyrrhonean resolve, as stated by Sextus Empiricus, not to assent to anything non-evident, might be considered an ancestor of sorts to both these forms of solipsism, particularly since the doubt, as Sextus notes, "does not concern the appearance itself but only the account given of that appearance."[24] The concept of an appearance itself is, of course, not too far removed from that of a sense datum. Furthermore, to the extent that any belief in continued existence or in unobserved characteristics generally might be considered to depend in some way on inductive generalization, it is possible to consider skepticism about induction to be a precursor of sorts to the doubt leading to Ephemerata and Sense Data Solipsism. Sextus does indeed voice such skepticism with his enunciation of the following dilemma: "If only some instances are reviewed, the induction will be insecure; if all are reviewed the task is impossible since the instances are infinite."[25] Consequently, he might lay some claim to be rightfully listed in the direct ancestry of those two forms of solipsism. In fairness to Descartes, however, it should be noted that the skepticism of Sextus is a general one regarding the possibility of determining how things really are, as distinct from how they merely seem to be now. Sextus presents nothing to vie with Descartes's striking hypothesis of hats and coats covering machines, that is, nothing to suggest doubts regarding things or events in places hidden from observation. Thus, if Descartes's claim is one of second-generation ancestry to Sense Data Solipsism, Sextus might reasonably claim to be ranked as showing among the great-grandparents.

Despite the numerous anticipations of Descartes's skeptical doubts and lines of argument, his solipsistic theses differ from the corresponding positions entertained by Greek philosophers in one notable respect: their resolute egocentricity as opposed to the egalitarianism of the latter. Where Descartes asks if *he* is dreaming, Socrates asks if *we* are dreaming; and where Descartes speaks of *his* impressions, his Greek precursors speak merely of impressions. The difference often amounts merely one of emphasis, yet because of it, the theses entertained by the Greeks are more aptly characterized as skeptical, while those of Descartes are solipsistic. The deliberately personal approach taken by Descartes to epistemological problems would seem to be quite absent from ancient philosophy prior to Augustine. For this reason, the solipsistic versions of the skeptical theses are perhaps best characterized as Cartesian.

On circumstantial evidence alone the Augustinian influence on Descartes must be judged to be sizeable. Descartes's methodical doubt leads him to the rock of certainty of his own existence, an existence that cannot be doubted as long as he doubts or otherwise thinks. Descartes's discovery echoes the following passage from Augustine's work, *On the Trinity*:[26]

> Yet who ever doubts that he himself lives, and remembers, and understands, and wills, and thinks, and knows, and judges? Seeing that even if he doubts, he lives; if he doubts, he remembers why he doubts;...whoever doubts about anything else ought not to doubt of all these things, which if they were not, he would not be able to doubt of anything.

Depicted here is a Cartesian egocentric island of certainty immune to skeptical doubt. It would suffice to add perceiving or sensing to the list of intellectual operations envisaged and to entertain the skeptical notion that nothing else is known in order to reach a position akin to Sense Data Solipsism or to Sensa Solipsism. If Pyrrho, Plato, or Alcmaeon had read the church fathers, Cartesian solipsism might have preceded Descartes by two thousand years. As matters stand, however, there remains good cause to characterize the solipsistic theses as Cartesian. In virtue of the striking family resemblance between solipsistic and more general skeptical theses, the task of answering Cartesian solipsistic doubts will on occasion be found to coincide with that of answering some more ancient skeptical doubt.

THE EPISTEMOLOGICAL TASK

The seven forms of Cartesian solipsism come close to dividing into two tidy groups of theses; those that deny the reality of observed things and their characteristics, and those which deny the existence of unobserved things and their characteristics. Phantasmata, Oneirata, and Demoniac Solipsism each clearly belong in the first group. Ephemerata Solipsism belongs squarely in the second group along with Sense Data and Monopsyche Solipsism. The troublemaker is Sensa Solipsism. This particular form of solipsism might with good reason lay claim to membership in both groups. Insofar as it denies that the representations present in perception resemble their unobserved originals, it denies the reality of the world that figures in the representations, and consequently, it qualifies for membership in the first group. Insofar as it denies the existence of the originals, it denies the existence of something unobserved and hence qualifies for membership in the second group. The bivalence of membership suggests that Sensa Solipsism might best be classed in neither group, and left rather to form a group of its own. On this line of thinking we have three types of Cartesian solipsism describable as follows:

1. *Unreal World Solipsism,* which states that the world is unreal in that it is one's personal illusion or dream, or demon-conjuration.

2. *Observed World Solipsism,* which states that the world exists only in as much as it is perceived by oneself.

3. *Internal World Solipsism,* which states that the world of one's own representations is all that exists.

In place of the commonsense view, each type of solipsism proposes a metaphysical thesis that is a revised account of the nature and structure of the world. In each case, it implies that the everyday world does not exist. Thus, each of the three types of Cartesian solipsism raises in its own way the metaphysical question of whether the everyday world exists. The resulting three questions run as follows:

1. Is the world real, or is it only an illusion, or a dream, or a hoax?

2. Does that part of the world unperceived by oneself cease to exist?

3. Is there any external world corresponding to one's representations?

To each of these metaphysical questions there corresponds one of the following three epistemological problems:

1. *The Problem of Reality:* What rational grounds are there to think that the things one perceives are real rather than unreal in some way?

2. *The Problem of Unobserved Existence:* What rational grounds are there to think that anything exists other than what one now actually perceives?

3. *The External World Problem:* What rational grounds are there to think there is an external world resembling the world such as one perceives it to be?

The solipsistic claim in each case is that there are no good grounds to support the commonsense view of the world and that, consequently, belief in the truth of that view is not rational. The solipsist's case could in principle take the form of a positive argument in favor of the solipsistic thesis, or more modestly, it might simply consist in pointing out the apparent absence of grounds for the everyday view. The general procedure in the latter case is simply to throw the solipsistic theses up for consideration and to ask for reasons for thinking that the commonsense view is any more likely to be true. This course is more or less the one followed by Descartes. It is also the one we shall take.

Our task in what follows will be to find some way of showing that there are rational grounds for thinking that the world of our everyday assumptions does exist, and that the various solipsistic scenarios are inaccurate accounts of the nature of the world. Ideally, these grounds will provide a conclusive proof, but failing such a proof, a demonstration of high probability or likelihood would be most welcome. Failing both of these, a demonstration that solipsistic theses are less likely to be true than the commonly held views would still be a positive result. Ironically enough, much contemporary discussion of the issue begins at the latter point, that is, by assuming the greater plausibility of the everyday view to be obvious.

It should be noted that in principle a skeptical challenge to commonsense claims may take any of at least two forms. One of these forms voices the complaint that the evidence is insufficient to warrant a claim to absolute certainty. Skepticism that questions or denies such absolute certainty might be labeled *certainty skepticism*. A second form of skepticism doubts or denies that the evidence provides any warrant whatever for commonsense claims. This form might be called *warrant skepticism*. An intermediate form of skepticism affirms that there is as much evidence for as against commonsense tenets and consequently might be termed *equipollent skepticism*. This latter form, which is the one pursued by Sextus Empiricus, will be ignored in what follows so as not to complicate further an already complicated discussion.

Clearly, Cartesian skeptical scenarios may in principle be so presented as to support a skeptical thesis in either of the two modes, certainty or warrant skepticism. The dream hypothesis, for instance, may be used to draw either of two conclusions: that the reality of the world is never absolutely certain or that there is no reason whatever to think that the world is not a dream. The skeptical doubts entertained by Descartes tend to veer rather toward warrant skepticism. It is true enough that Descartes's enterprise of systematic doubt involves a withholding of assent from "opinions which are not completely certain and indubitable"[27] and, as such, certainly seems to qualify for inclusion in the category of certainty skepticism. On the other hand, later in the course of the investigation Descartes speaks of his doxastic plight in the following dramatic terms: "It feels as if I have fallen unexpectedly into a deep whirlpool which tumbles me around so that I can neither stand on the bottom nor swim up to the top."[28] The suggestion is clearly of a deeper deficiency than a mere lack of absolute certainty. The situation is similar when he examines the reasons he has for believing a world exists external to his mind and concludes, "all these considerations are enough to establish that it is not reliable judgement but merely some blind impulse that has made me believe up till now that there exist things distinct from myself which transmit to me ideas or images of themselves."[29] His realization is not that he is less than absolutely certain but that he has no warrant at all.

With David Hume too, skepticism is clearly a matter of warrant. Hume asks for rational grounds or reasons for thinking there is any causal connection whatever in a particular succession of events.[30] His question is not that of whether one may be absolutely certain of such a connection. In more recent times, in contrast, the tendency has been to construe the skeptical challenge in terms of certainty. The trend has been encouraged both by Bertrand Russell's skeptical reflections together with Moore's widely discussed discussion of them, and by Peter Unger's influential modern version of Cartesian demonology featuring an evil scientist stimulating captive, electrode-studded brains.[31] In what follows, we shall be concerned with solipsistic theses primarily in the mode of warrant skepticism. For reasons that will be discussed later, certainty skepticism cannot properly be considered to constitute a genuine epistemological problem.

It will be assumed throughout what follows that the various solipsists are eminently rational beings. The convictions or doubts of an irrational skeptic are of no more interest for our purposes than is the skeptic's personal taste in culinary or vestimentary matters. It is a mistake to conceive of a skeptic as a cantankerous and obdurate individual, whom one has to convince somehow of the truth of beliefs held by all 'normal' human beings. The skeptic is oneself, oneself in one's more thoughtful moments, and hence presumably in a rational frame of mind.

To avoid possible misunderstanding, it should be noted that rationality of frame of mind is a matter of being concerned with evidence. The evidence in question may be anything that lends support to the belief and so makes it more likely to be true. A concern with rationality is thus ultimately a concern with truth. The term 'rational' should be confused neither with 'sensible' nor even with 'reasonable'. A rational skeptic is clearly not a sensible person, nor even necessarily a reasonable person in the everyday sense. The skeptic Hume, as one might point out, was both an eminently sensible and reasonable person, but in being reasonable he espoused the various beliefs his skepticism called into question. Likewise, a sensible belief need not be a rational one. Hume considered a belief in the existence of the familiar everyday world to be sensible enough but far from rational; he thought it to be based on habit with no possible rational foundation, and whatever Hume's errors on the issue, they were not conceptual. On the other hand, a reasonable belief may on occasion coincide with a rational one. Such is the case when what is meant by 'a reasonable belief' is a belief supported by sound evidence or good reasons. Very often, however, by 'a reasonable belief' is meant a belief that fits in well with the body of generally accepted beliefs about the world. Since it is not immediately clear how such a fit makes the belief likely to be true, it is best for our purposes to suspend judgment on the issue of whether such beliefs qualify as rational.

To facilitate future reference to the point, let us set up a principle which may be termed the *Rational Assertion Truism*, or RAT for short.

RAT: A rational affirmation is a function of supporting evidence.

The principle is simply a partial explication of what is meant by 'rational'. Translated into more concrete terms, what the principle states is that for it to be a rational assertion that P is true, P must be true on the evidence. Likewise, for it to be a rational affirmation that P is more likely to be true than Q, the evidence must make P more likely than Q to be true.

Serious difficulties arise on the issue of what constitutes supporting evidence. For the present, let it be said merely that the criterion to be used is the old-fashioned one of 'seeing' that the evidence does actually make the statement in question more likely to be true. This is the criterion used by Descartes when he finds that the alleged evidence of his senses provides no sure sign that he is not dreaming or by Hume when he argues "that there is nothing in any object consider'd in itself, which can afford us a reason for drawing a conclusion beyond it," and hence that we have no reason to draw inferences from experience.[32] Unless there is a graspable truth-conferring connection between datum and hypothesis, the datum is not to be considered evidence for the hypothesis. In particular, a datum is not to be considered evidence on the mere ground that it counts as evidence in the practice of the community. To accept a datum as evidence on such a ground would be analogous to laughing at a joke simply because everyone else is laughing.

As noted earlier, current philosophical literature contains a wealth of discussion and argument purporting to refute solipsism in general or, more modestly, some particular variant of the thesis. Consequently, our first task is the review and evaluation of this profusion of views. Since the vast majority of these discussions and arguments endorse or presuppose a nonfoundationalist account of knowledge, a word on the distinction between this type of account and a foundationalist one is perhaps in order.

A foundationalist epistemology, the conception of which is imputable to a considerable extent to Descartes, in its traditional form sees its task as that of tracing the origin of all knowledge to the data of experience in conjunction with a set of indubitable or self-evident rational or necessarily true principles including rules of inference. The contradictory or denial of the foundationalist approach is the view that the traditional foundationalist enterprise is quite misconceived, and that the correct account must recognize that any cognitive enterprise presupposes in some manner or other the existence of everyday objects, full-blown material things such as envelopes, pigs, hands, and spruce trees. This latter epistemological position is termed "coherentism" in current philosophical jargon, but the label is somewhat inappropriate. While it is true enough that the criterion of coherence does and must play a crucial role in such a view, the terminology nevertheless has two serious enough defects: it incorrectly suggests that foundationalism must reject the criterion of coherence, and it obscures the essential distinction between the two positions which is that one attempts to base knowledge of the world on awareness of something less than full-fledged objects, whereas the other denies the feasibility of any such attempt. In what follows, we shall use the more appropriate term, *objectualism,* to designate the view that any cognitive enterprise must assume the existence of at least some everyday objects and hence also knowledge of, or warranted belief in, the existence of these objects. *Foundationalism* may be said to be the view that no such assumption is necessary and that any knowledge of, or warranted belief in, the existence of everyday objects is to be justified ultimately in terms of more fundamental experiential evidence.

Epistemic objectualism should obviously not be confused with the semantic theory of objectualism to the effect that actual individuals may be constituents in propositions.[33] Interestingly enough, epistemic objectualism entails the view that there is no problem of solipsism. If objectualism is true, and any correct account of cognition must assume the existence of everyday objects, then the falsity of solipsistic theses follows more or less as a corollary of a correct account of cognition. From the point of view of objectualism, any difficulty there may appear to be in answering solipsistic doubts arises only within the context of the mistaken foundationalist enterprise. From the point of view of solipsism, the assumption of existence is unwarranted, and furthermore false. While the existence assumption makes objectualism appear in a strong position with regard to skepticism, it is also the great weakness of the approach. An assumption of existence is vulnerable to challenge; it implies a factual claim that certain items exist in the world, a claim which, if not defended, is gratuitous.

Our examination of the purported refutations of solipsism will begin with the commonsense view of G. E. Moore and of his plethora of later-day witting and unwitting disciples to the effect that commonsense truths are known and are much more certain than any skeptical considerations that may be marshalled against them. Moore's response to skepticism is a good point of departure, not simply because it so closely adheres to an everyday point of view or because it contains, as it were, the first green sprouts of modern versions of both the objectualist and the foundationalist positions. The great merit of the commonsense claim to know the everyday truths denied by skeptical theses is that it quite effectively (albeit unintentionally) underscores the impressive strength of the skeptical challenge and the futility of the attempt to answer the skeptic by an appeal to everyday knowledge claims. Given the quasi-universal assumption in present-day epistemology that such claims are warranted, the point is an excellent one from which to begin.

Having brought the problem into clearer focus, we shall in subsequent chapters examine proposed solutions. We shall first turn briefly to three unsuccessful strategies for a summary dismissal of solipsism, strategies featuring the charges that solipsism is pragmatically irrelevant, self-referentially self-destructive, and unreasonably overdemanding. We shall then undertake a review and assessment of the wealth of proposed coherentist answers to skepticism. Certain of these appeal to actual perceptual procedures and experience (chapter 4). Others purport to establish that skepticism is self-destructively parasitic in that its theses presuppose factual data denied by the theses themselves (chapter 5). Yet others appeal to the conditions of linguistic meaningfulness (chapter 6). Others again maintain that skepticism is parasitic on a conceptual scheme of which it denies some of the conditions, and that its theses deny the conditions of their own meaningful enunciation (chapter 8). We shall find one of these to provide an answer to the External World Problem. An adequate treatment of the linguistic approach to skeptical problems will require an investigation into meaning generally (chapter 7), as well as into the possibility of thinking outside a public language (chapter 9).

As we shall see, the repeated failure of the various coherentist attempts allows many deep-rooted and pervasive misconceptions regarding the nature of skeptical problems to be exposed. It equally clearly demonstrates the necessity of adopting a foundationalist approach if any rational resolution of such problems is to be achieved. In subsequent chapters, we shall turn to a foundationalist exploration of the world admitted by the radical skeptic, and to the uncovering of rational rebuttals of each of the remaining variants of Cartesian solipsism. This exploration constitutes the enterprise of *Rationalized Epistemology*.

CHAPTER TWO

THE CLAIM TO KNOW

THE CHARGE OF ABSURDITY

When Cartesian solipsistic theses are first encountered, in those tender times prior to the numbing of sensibilities by philosophical argumentation, the response most likely to be elicited is an indignant imputation of absurdity. The source of indignation cannot be simply that the proposed scenarios are fantastic or unbelievable. Tales of ancient interplanetary graffiti or of egg-bearing Easter rabbits are no less implausible and yet provoke no reaction of outrage. The reason is rather that the skeptical theses are felt to call into question cherished and firmly held beliefs in the permanence and reality of our everyday surrounds. The charge of absurdity is thus not solely an assessment of implausibility. It is in addition an emphatic assertion of the certainty of everyday truths about the world. Each of the two estimates is the negative image of the other. The absurdity imputed to skeptical scenarios is a direct reflection of the absolute certainty accorded commonsense assertions about the world. Conversely, any plausibility granted such scenarios can only be at the expense of a weakening of commonsense certainty.

The driving force of the unsophisticated view is clearly the emphatic assertion of commonsense certainty in the face of skeptical doubt. In more recent years this element of the view has acceded to a position of considerable philosophical respectability. The promotion is due in large part to the influence of G. E. Moore and his commonsense philosophy, the central pillar of which is the claim that statements of banal everyday facts are "obvious truisms" known "with certainty."[1] The strength accorded this certainty would be difficult to overestimate.

According to Moore, he would be "guilty of absurdity" to express uncertainty about such matters as the fact that he is now standing fully clothed in a room with papers in his hand.[2] His famous proof of the existence of an external world is essentially an appeal to a fact of the sort—the fact indicated with certain gestures and the remark, "Here is one hand and here is another," a fact so certain as to warrant the comment, "How absurd it would be to suggest that I did not know it, but only believed it, and that perhaps it was not the case!"[3]

Moore's emphatic endorsement of everyday knowledge is repeatedly echoed in more recent philosophical writings. One such echo is J. L. Austin's claim that everyday statements of fact are *"in fact* incorrigible—in the sense that when they are made, the circumstances are such that they are quite certainly, definitely, and un-retractably *true."*[4] Another is Anthony Quinton's declaration that after half an hour spent repairing the sparking plug of his lawn mower, he would have to be a fool to doubt its existence.[5] Yet another is John L. Pollock's claim that a skeptical argument that denies everyday knowledge "can only be construed as a *reductio ad absurdum* of its premises."[6] Most present-day epistemologists follow Moore's lead in taking everyday knowledge to be a given fact, one requiring analysis certainly, but not proof.

From an unshakable tenet of the sort it is plausible to conclude that skeptical doubts regarding such matters are absurd or patently false. The outraged neophyte does so in responding to skeptical scenarios with the earlier-noted imputation of absurdity. Moore himself does likewise and claims furthermore to know that he is not dreaming and that what he perceives is not produced by a malicious demon.[7] The reasoning of the novice no less than that of his or her more sophisticated counterpart might be fairly represented by the following *Common Sense Argument*, where 'Q' states some Cartesian skeptical thesis and 'P' states its commonsense alternative.

Premiss 1: P is absolutely certain (known).

Premiss 2: If P is absolutely certain (known), then Q is absurd (patently false, known to be false).

Conclusion: Q is absurd (patently false, known to be false).

The argument mirrors a very common skeptical argument advanced by various philosophers, notably by Descartes, more recently by Unger, and attributed to Russell by Moore.[8] The second argument is an argument for certainty skepticism, and might be termed the *No Knowl-*

edge Argument. It has the same second premiss as the former, while its first premiss is the negation of the former's conclusion, and its conclusion is the negation of the former's first premiss. This second argument has roughly the following structure:

Premiss 1:   Q is not absurd (patently false, known to be false).

Premiss 2:   P is absolutely certain (known) only if Q is absurd (patently false, known to be false).

Conclusion: P is not absolutely certain (known).

The first premiss of each of the two arguments is the negation of the other's conclusion. Since each has an air of plausibility when considered independently, the understandable result is the generation of some discomfort among epistemologists—discomfort which in point of fact falls far short of that warranted by the situation. If it is assumed (rightly enough, as we shall see later) that Premiss 2 is true, then the first premiss of one of the two arguments must be false. The disturbing fact is that when the two premisses are scrupulously and impartially weighed against each other with an eye to their supporting evidence, the scales are found to lean heavily against the commonsense knowledge claim. Worse still, the disposition of the scales remains essentially unchanged even when the alleged absolute certainty of commonsense knowledge is watered down to some less pretentious degree of likelihood. Present-day epistemology apparently not only has no answer to the challenge of skepticism, but is often quite unaware that a serious challenge exists. As we shall see, the above indictment cannot rightly be dismissed as alarmist.

Operations will start with an examination of the skeptical first premiss, the thesis that skeptical scenarios are not absurd, or not patently false. The skeptic's main defence of the premiss is that the skeptical scenario cannot rightly be judged absurd on any of the evidence offered against it. To test this claim, let us place the skeptical scenarios in some concrete context. Any sentiment of unfairness to common sense may be avoided by taking the terrain of Moore's proof as our test site, and the statement, "here's a hand," as the commonsense truth allegedly known with certainty. The question to be answered is whether in this context the various Cartesian solipsistic scenarios should be judged absurd.

One skeptical thesis is the hypothesis that things cease to exist when one ceases to observe them. In the present instance, it translates into the scenario that the hand reduces to what one actually perceives of it. Now, is the scenario absurd on the evidence? One's first inclination may well be to agree with Moore, and to declare that it is. If one does as Moore did, that is, hold up a hand and declare it to be a hand, one is making the claim that the hand presented is a full-fledged material object, part of a living organism in its everyday surrounds. The claim is in clear contradiction with the skeptical scenario and, if obviously true, would make the latter absurd.

Yet the question posed by the skeptic concerns the evidence one has for a claim of the sort. Consider first the evidence provided by what is now actually perceived—let us say, to concretize matters—by a visible grooved palm with five appendages and a felt three-dimensional heaviness. Taken by itself, this evidence is not in contradiction with the skeptical scenario. It is certainly conceivable that the palm visibly there may have in fact no far side—or more precisely, no visual far side, since a tactual far side continues to be felt. Quite conceivably, the nails, veins, and wrinkles of the back of the hand, perhaps all visible an instant before, may have ceased to exist altogether on passing out of sight. Indeed, one might ask, what warrant does the evidence of what is actually perceived, considered solely on its own merits, provide for the claim that the hidden side still exists, that the vanished visual back of the hand is still there a short distance behind the palm. The answer to come bouncing back is that it apparently provides none whatever; taken by itself, the palm presents no demands at all to be fleshed out with its familiar far side; its presence militates in no way whatever against the skeptical thesis, since it neither contradicts nor refutes nor even challenges that hypothesis. In these circumstances, it can hardly be said to show that the latter is absurd.

Undoubtedly, the claim of absurdity is also based in part on evidence additional to what is now actually perceived, evidence such as common knowledge, the weight of past experience, the accumulated wisdom of our forebears. And yet, can one rightly claim that the skeptical hypothesis is made absurd by the addition of this further evidence? The latter cannot consist of an array of alleged past and present instances of continued unobserved existence. The skeptical doubt is a general one, so if appeal is made to other cases of unobserved existence, it must be said on what evidence the claim of unobserved existence is based in these cases. Otherwise, the appeal is question-begging, somewhat like defending one's present belief in tree spirits by an appeal to instances of such past belief in oneself and others. What counts as evidence in the present context is evidence that addresses the skeptic's request for warrant, not evidence that simply voices the everyday assumptions called into question by the skeptic. With this in mind, let us return to the issue: can one calmly contemplate one's palm and, on the basis of the alleged further evidence, impartially declare absurd the thesis that the now unperceived visual far side has ceased to exist? Apparently one cannot, at least not on the basis of any evidence to which appeal may readily be made.

The test results are no less favorable for the skeptical premiss when the thesis considered is that the world is unreal in some way, a dream or the conjuration of a devious demon. The evidence of what one actually perceives, the hand and its surrounds (fleshed out or not) in no way contradicts the truth of the skeptical thesis; everything seen, heard, and felt might apparently remain exactly as it is and without contradiction nevertheless be part of a dream or vast hoax. On executing Moore's gesture some three centuries earlier,[9] Descartes likewise concluded that an outstretched hand possesses no features or characteristics allowing one to claim with assurance that it is not unreal in some way. The experiential evidence apparently provides no warrant for the claim that the dream hypothesis is absurd or patently false.

The situation is hardly improved by the addition of evidence from the past. First of all, any accumulation of such evidence cannot be inconsistent with the hypothesis, since apparently each past experience may without inconsistency be considered part of the dream. Furthermore, it apparently cannot establish the more modest claim that the dream hypothesis is patently false. What possible evidence could ever achieve this result? Peter Unger quite convincingly bases his argument for universal ignorance on the analogous premiss, that "no one *can or could know*"[10] that one's experiences are not the deceptive product of electrode manipulation by an evil scientist. To make matters worse still, the evidence apparently fails to support even the more modest assessment that the dream hypothesis is implausible or unlikely to be true. What data qualifies as evidence that the world is real? Indeed, where should one begin in arguing the point? In these circumstances, it hardly seems warranted to claim that the dream hypothesis is absurd or patently false.

There remains the Cartesian skeptical thesis that there is in fact no external world at all corresponding to one's private representations. As might be expected, the test results in this case are not significantly different from those in the two preceding ones. It is quite unclear how the solipsistic thesis that there is no external world could be in any way weakened or challenged, let alone refuted, by a Moorean gesture and accompanying statement. Furthermore, even with the addition of the evidence of past experience, it remains quite unclear how the thesis might be shown to be false. A charge of absurdity thus appears to be gratuitous.

Analogous results would undoubtedly grace any attempt to replace the example of the hand with illustrations featuring telephones, lawn mowers, or escaped cows. The most persistent scrutiny of an object at an optimum distance and in ideal visual, tactual, and/or olfactory conditions apparently contributes nothing toward refuting the thesis that the body has no underside or that it is not some complicated mirage or dream. Furthermore, it is unclear how various manipulations might show that the parts manipulated do not immediately pass out of existence when abandoned to their own devices, and equally unclear how skeptical reservations about the reality of the object are to be dispelled by an intimate half-hour spent in its company.

The test results might be summed up aptly enough as follows: where Q is some Cartesian-type scenario, and where the evidence is not question-begging, then apparently it is true that

1. Q is *data-consistent*, i.e., the evidence one has does not contradict Q;

2. Q is *data-unfalsified*, i.e., the evidence one has does not conclusively confirm the claim that Q is false;

3. Q is *data-unchallenged*, i.e. the evidence one has provides no support whatever for the claim that Q is false. Otherwise stated, Q is *data-impervious*.

Skeptical Premiss 1 must be esteemed to have passed its test, at least until such time as more telling evidence is disclosed. The conclusion follows from finding 2 above, the fact that the skeptical scenarios are data-unfalsified. Finding 2 corroborates the estimate of the strength of skepticism proffered in Nozick's remark, "the skeptic's possibilities make us uneasy because, as we deeply realize, we do not know that they don't obtain; it is not surprising that attempts to show that we do know these things leave us suspicious, strike us even as bad faith."[11] The finding stated in 3 takes us quite beyond any premiss required by certainty skepticism.

THE CHARGE OF IRRELEVANCE

The above test results present what certainly appears to be a serious challenge to claims to know everyday matters of fact. In present-day epistemological discussion, it is often felt that the skeptical challenge reduces to the task of reconciling the obvious fact of knowledge of everyday matters of fact with the apparent failure of the charge of absurdity. The general strategy for effectuating a reconciliation is to appeal to certain alleged features of knowledge. G. E. Moore may plausibly claim responsibility for the first attempt in this direction. In discussing Hume's denial of knowledge of causal conjunction, Moore retorts that the argument is fallacious in that "we may quite well *know* many things which do not follow logically from anything else which we know."[12] Similarly, in discussing Russell's advocacy of the Cartesian demon hypothesis, Moore comments as follows: "Where, therefore, I differ from him is in supposing I do know for certain things which I do not know immediately and which do *not* follow logically from anything which I do know immediately."[13] In both cases, Moore is advocating the view that the truth of a knowledge claim need not follow logically from the evidence on which it is based, which is to say, that knowledge is *evidentially unentailed.*

On such a view a skeptical hypothesis can be quite consistent with all the available evidence without invalidating knowledge claims based on that evidence. If the knowledge claim P were entailed by the evidence, the denial of P would have to be inconsistent with the evidence. So would any alternative of P, such as Q, since it entails the denial of P. However, if P is evidentially unentailed by the evidence, it is no longer necessary that a denial of P be inconsistent with the evidence. In these circumstances, the data consistency of Q does not exclude the possibility that P is known. By the same token, it becomes possible to parry effectively any antiknowledge argument based on the mere fact that skeptical scenarios are conceivable. The view finds support in everyday practice in knowledge assessments, since in everyday situations it is certainly not the case that for a knowledge claim to be rightly made, the evidence must entail the truth of the claim, or alternatively, the falsity of every data-consistent alternative. In everyday situations it would seem I may rightly claim to know without showing every conceivable alternative to be inconsistent with the evidence—to know, for instance, who the culprit is in a pie theft, even though the evidence does not logically exclude interplanetary visitors.

However, the alleged feature is clearly insufficient in itself to account for the further findings that the evidence apparently neither confirms nor even supports the falsity of skeptical hypotheses. Knowledge must possess some additional feature if such facts are to be accommodated. At the very least, it must be *confirmationally autonomous,* i.e., it must be such that the truth of what is known is conclusively established by evidence which need neither establish the falsity of rival hypotheses nor even support a claim of falsity. In the absence of a feature of the sort, the above test results remain unexplained.

Before considering whether knowledge does indeed have this feature, let us first examine yet a further feature that is sometimes attributed to knowledge in the literature and that would explain the alleged evidential unentailment of knowledge. Such otherwise differing epistemologists as Alvin I. Goldman, Peter Klein, Douglas Odegard, Nicholas Rescher, and Robert Nozick all argue that in everyday knowledge situations only relevant alternatives need be excluded by the evidence. Cartesian skeptical scenarios simply are not and need not be among those alternatives.[14] Actual practice certainly bears out the claim, since in everyday situations numerous conceivable alternative accounts (including skeptical hypotheses) are regularly dismissed from serious consideration, when indeed they are considered at all. In recognition of this practice everyday knowledge may be said to be *relevance-structured*. Such a feature holds considerable prima facie promise. Not only does it provide grounds for rejecting skeptical hypotheses, but it gives plausibility to the claim that knowledge is evidentially unentailed and in addition offers an explanation of sorts as to how rival skeptical hypotheses may be data-unfalsified and data-unchallenged. Certainly, if the possibility that I am now dreaming is irrelevant to my knowing that I am now sitting in my armchair reading, then it does not matter that the evidence I have that I am actually reading neither falsifies nor weakens the hypothesis that I am merely dreaming.

To avoid undue elation, however, it should be immediately recognized that only a very world-weary skeptic would be persuaded by considerations of the sort. The claim is that the skeptical case may rightly be rejected, since skeptical hypotheses are discounted as irrelevant in everyday knowledge claims. While this latter observation may very well be accurate, in the absence of further elaboration it cannot pretend to be more than an interesting sociological and perhaps even anthropological fact, the relevance of which to present concerns remains to be established. Some justification must be given for the practice of discounting skeptical hypotheses, a justification in the form of reasons convincing to the skeptic or any other rational thinker. These reasons must provide good grounds for thinking the skeptical hypotheses are unlikely to be true, or wanting that, they must show why the practice in question must be adopted. An account of everyday knowledge procedures accompanied with the simple comment that this is what we do, is quite insufficient. An analogous response might with equal warrant be given in defence of explanations featuring pixies and evil spells or of divination procedures involving chicken entrails.

A favorite line of thinking on irrelevance would have it that hypotheses are irrelevant if they are merely compatible with the evidence and derive no positive support from it. On this view, to count as a genuine alternative a hypothesis must have positive, case-specific support or be backed by counterevidence unabsorbed by its rival. It cannot be simply a purely hypothetical possibility, one based solely on conjecture and logical possibility. Rescher, Odegard, Klein, and Rorty all dismiss skeptical theses on the ground that they fail to qualify as genuine alternatives.[15] Yet if this line of thinking is to be convincing, it will require the backing of a considerably more probing analysis than any effectuated to date. The difficulty to be faced is a serious one. What must be explained is how a lack of supporting evidence for a hypothesis manages to rule out the genuine possibility of the hypothesis being true and so to make the hypothesis irrelevant. If it were literally the case that absence of supporting evidence produced irrelevance, then for someone sufficiently ignorant of an issue, every conceivable hypothesis would be irrelevant—a consequence that is absurd. Otherwise stated, from the notion that irrelevance is a direct function of the absence of supporting evidence, there results a paradox of knowledge, to wit, the smaller the body of evidence, the fewer the relevant alternatives, and hence in general, the easier it is to have knowledge; in sum, the less known, the better the chances of knowing.

The irrelevance in question must then apparently be relative to some appropriate body of evidence. There immediately arises the question as to what constitutes such a body. Clearly, the body of evidence cannot be too restricted, because if it were, a hypothesis irrelevant at a given time could later become relevant through the discovery of supporting evidence. This later discovery would falsify the earlier judgment of irrelevance. In these circumstances, the best anyone alert to the situation could claim of a rival hypothesis is that it is irrelevant provided no evidence is later found to support it—which is to say, that it is irrelevant provided that it does not turn out not to be. Skepticism can hardly be dismissed with claims of the sort.

On the other hand, if the appropriate body of evidence is too broadly construed—in the limiting case as all past and future evidence for all possible knowers—then it is put beyond the grasp of any concrete human being, and consequently placed beyond the scope of human concerns. The evidence must then be some intermediate compilation, such as some broad selection of data gained through a serious exploration of alternatives. Yet even here, the central task remains. Supposing no evidence is found to support a particular hypothesis, there remains the question of whether or not such evidence may turn up in the future. If it may, then it is unclear how the hypothesis may rightly be dismissed as irrelevant (how, for instance, if I may in the future wake up to find that at the present time I was actually dreaming, the dream hypothesis may be dismissed as irrelevant). If evidence may not turn up in the future, that is, if it is claimed that the broad selection and consequent findings rule out this possibility, then it should be shown how this is the case (how, for instance, the wealth of experience I have regarding the existence of my hand rules out any future discovery of evidence indicating that my hand was but part of a dream). In either instance, a good deal more must be said if a sound or even plausible case is to be made for dismissing skeptical theses on the ground of irrelevance.

Undoubtedly, there is some sort of basis in past experience for the characterization of skeptical hypotheses as far-fetched or implausible and hence irrelevant—and by the same token, for a distinction between actual or 'genuine' possibilities (or defeaters) and merely conceivable ones. Yet the problem posed by skepticism is precisely that of showing that the characterization or distinction is warranted by the evidence. The task cannot be avoided by easy generalizations and appeals to everyday practices.

APPEALS TO CONFIRMATIONAL AUTONOMY AND NONCLOSURE

Let us now consider the claim that knowledge is confirmationally autonomous, the claim that the evidence in virtue of which an everyday matter of fact is known need neither conclusively disconfirm nor even directly challenge the alternatives to the everyday truth. The central support for such a claim has to be the fact that evidence is selectively supportive—whence the prima facie plausible conclusion that justification is likewise selective, as is also confirmation.

Clearly, evidence is selectively supportive to some degree. For instance, in a murder case the evidence that points to the guilt of one suspect is generally not direct evidence for the innocence of the other suspects. Various cases discussed in the literature admit the drawing of an analogous moral. In Dretske's classic Zebra Case,[16] one might well have no hesitation in claiming to know that the animals seen on a visit to the zoo were zebras, and yet, on reflection one might judge that the evidence on which the claim was based (the relatively brief spectacle of the animals in their pen) was insufficient to rule out the suggestion that the animals were simply cleverly disguised mules. Likewise, in the Appointment Case discussed by Klein,[17] the evidence on the basis of which one might claim to know that Ms. Reliable will keep her appointment (one's knowledge of her past reliability) is not evidence in virtue of which one may claim to know that defeating circumstances will not arise; one cannot claim to know that prior to the appointment Ms. Reliable will not receive a phone call informing her that her apartment has just burned down.

Nevertheless it would be precipitous to conclude from considerations of the sort that knowledge is confirmationally autonomous. In knowledge claims generally, any attempt to confirm the truth of a thesis must encompass the ruling out of rival hypotheses. Since these competitors are dismissed on evidence additional to that which supports the thesis being confirmed, it must be acknowledged that more is involved in a claim to know than the mere amassing of evidence directly supportive of the thesis to be confirmed.

The point is readily substantiated. Let us take a simple case, one in which a car is known to be blue. It might appear at first sight that such knowledge could in principle be based solely on the supporting evidence gleaned from a few glimpses of the car. Yet on a moment's reflection, it becomes apparent that a wealth of assumptions must be made and are in fact implicitly involved in the perceptual process. Among these assumptions are the following: the blue color is not an illusion created by the play of nonstandard lighting on some other color; objects such as cars do not automatically change color periodically; objects such as cars do not have a different color depending upon the angle from which they are seen. Clearly, without the assistance of such assumptions the directly supportive evidence would be insufficient to warrant a claim to know the color of the car. Equally clearly, the function of such assumptions is to exclude rival hypotheses regarding the color of the car.

The situation is similar in the more complex cases mentioned earlier, the Zebra Case and the Appointment Case. Here too the claim to know can be rightly made only if the plausibility of the rival hypotheses is denied and, moreover, denied on the basis of evidence independent of the evidence supporting the thesis being confirmed. The independent evidence may have to do with the general reliability of perceptual experience in zoo visit conditions or with the general unlikelihood of disruptions due to catastrophic occurrences. Where

the scenarios of a zoo hoax or apartment fire are explicitly entertained, they must be ruled out as not being serious alternative
accounts. One cannot rightly claim to know on the basis of the original supporting evidence that certain zoo animals were zebras and at
the same time admit that those same animals may well have been disguised mules. Similarly, one cannot admit that Ms. Reliable might
well learn that her apartment has burned down and nevertheless on
the basis of the original evidence alone rightly claim to know that Ms.
Reliable will keep her appointment. Exclusion is achieved through
noting the implausibility of zoos housing mules disguised as zebras
or of Ms. Reliable's apartment burning down in the hour preceding
the appointment. The judgment of implausibility must obviously be
based on past experience, that is, on evidence additional to the original confirming evidence.

The upshot of the above considerations is that knowledge is not
confirmationally autonomous in any sense clearly exploitable for present concerns. A knowledge claim is based not simply on directly supporting evidence but also in large part on evidence that excludes alternatives, often by supporting an assessment of implausibility, and
hence of irrelevance. In these circumstances, it remains to be shown
how confirmational autonomy might be validly used to accommodate
the earlier test results regarding skeptical hypotheses, the fact that they
are apparently data-unfalsified and, worse still, data-unchallenged.

An alternative strategy often encountered in the recent literature is
to attempt to deny that knowledge is closed under known logical implication. Such a denial amounts to the claim that it is possible to know
some thesis, to know that the thesis entails some other thesis, and yet
not to know the other thesis.[18] Applied to the Common Sense and No
Knowledge Arguments encountered earlier, it amounts to the claim
that it is possible to know P, to know that the truth of P entails the falsity of Q, and yet not to know that Q is false. The claim undercuts both
arguments, since it denies the second premise of each. It also allows
everyday knowledge claims to be reconciled in principle with the
apparent fact that skeptical scenarios are data-unfalsified. Yet for better
or for worse, the claim must be judged wanting on a number of counts.

To begin with, while it addresses the issue of accommodating two
of the earlier test results, it fails to account for the data-imperviousness of skeptical scenarios. Thus, it is inadequate to resolve fully the
problem posed by skepticism. More seriously still, it fails in point of
fact to advance in any way the attempt to answer skepticism on the
points it does address. On the debatable assumption that closure fails,
there immediately arises the matter of explaining why it does, that is,

of explaining how it is possible to know both P and the fact that P entails the falsity of Q, without knowing that Q is false. To be cogent, any attempted explanation would have to be in terms either of something equivalent to the confirmational autonomy of knowledge or, conversely, of the irrelevance of certain rival hypotheses. As we found above, the first path leads nowhere, and the second has yet to be cut. Thus, we find ourselves no further ahead. It should be clear that this bleak assessment extends equally to the attempt to base nonclosure on the varying discriminative capacities required for knowledge claims.[19] Such variations would be pertinent to the discussion only in the unlikely event that they could be used to establish some strong version of confirmational autonomy.

It might be added that in any case it is highly implausible that Premiss 2 fails in any sense germane to present concerns. To claim to know is among other things to ascribe certainty. This aspect of the knowledge claim is what interests us, since the ascription of certainty to commonsense claims is precisely what is called into question by the apparent failure of skeptical theses to be found absurd. The predication of such certainty should be closed under entailment. Where it is certain that P is true and also certain that the truth of P entails the falsity of its rival Q, then it should follow that the falsity of Q is certain. Conversely, if the falsity of Q is not certain, then it should follow that the truth of P is not certain. On this point, as we saw earlier, the view of unsophisticated commonsense thinking is in full agreement with that of more reflective thinkers, such as Descartes and Moore, in that both find that there exists some sort of inverse certainty relation between truth evaluations accorded commonsense beliefs and their skeptical rivals. Indeed, a failure of a relationship of the sort would be quite anomalous, since a similar one clearly holds for the attribution of other degrees of warrant: if P is likely, then any of its alternatives is unlikely; if P has a better than even chance of being true, then the alternatives to P must together have a better than even chance of being false. In this context, an attack on the principle of closure of knowledge under entailment amounts to an attack on some rather rudimentary arithmetic.

Such remarks apply, of course, not only to rival alternatives of P but to effective defeaters of P, that is, to events the occurrence of which would lead to the failure of P to occur. If it is certain that Ms. Reliable will not miss her appointment, then it is also certain that she will not receive a telephone call of such a nature as to oblige her to miss the appointment. A claim to be certain entails the claim to be no less certain that any alternative scenario is false.

The only remotely plausible case for nonclosure rests on the somewhat dubious counterexamples proposed in the literature. In the much discussed Zebra Case, apparently it is found possible to claim in good faith to know that the animals were zebras, while being hesitant to claim to know that they were not cleverly disguised mules. Likewise, it is found possible in good faith to think that Robert Audi knows the familiar tree on his lawn to be a blue spruce, but to be hesitant to claim that he knows that the tree is not dyed blue.[20] However, it must be admitted that it is equally possible in good faith to find instead that the claim to know is undermined by the claim not to know the alternative accounts to be false—that it is possible in good faith to find that each admission of ignorance or possible trickery has the immediate effect of weakening the original claim to know that the zoo animals are zebras or that the tree is a genuine blue spruce. This is because the observations on which the knowledge claim is based are quite consistent (by hypothesis) with the truth of the rival theses so that, to the extent that the latter are not ruled out on independent grounds, they call into question the original claim. The conflicting intuition on the point would seem best explained as due to the force of habit: one is reluctant to abandon the claim to know simply because in circumstances of the sort in everyday life it is usual to claim to know. Significantly enough, the alleged counterexamples fail when a claim of certainty is substituted for a claim to know. It cannot plausibly be claimed to be certain that the zoo animals are zebras but not certain that they are not disguised mules—or to be certain that the tree is a genuine blue spruce but not certain that it is not merely dyed blue. Viewed in this light, the counterexamples lose all pretention to be such.

THE HOLLOWNESS OF THE CLAIM TO KNOW

The strategy of attempting to accommodate the apparent data-imperviousness of skeptical scenarios fails then, or is at least on hold awaiting the arrival of a convincing account of irrelevance. This leaves the commonsense claim to know in the awkward position of standing beside unscathed skeptical rivals that contradict it. At this point one might be tempted to compromise somewhat and, adopting yet another of Moore's manoeuvres, to declare that one's own claim to know commonsense truths is at least as certain as the skeptical denial of that claim. Yet even this humbler stance is not a genuine option: it quite overestimates the strength of the commonsense claim, or underestimates that of the skeptical position. The point is readily made by examining any concrete everyday knowledge claim and weighing the available evidence.

Consider Austin's example in which it is an everyday matter of determining whether or not there is in fact a telephone in the next room.[21]

> I go into the next room, and certainly there's something there that looks exactly like a telephone. But is it perhaps a case of *trompe l'oeil* painting? I can soon settle that. Is it just a dummy perhaps, not really connected up and with no proper works? Well, I can take it to pieces a bit and find out, or actually use it for ringing somebody up—and perhaps get them to ring me up too, just to make sure. And of course, if I do these things, I *do* make sure; what more could possibly be required?

Entry into the room finds something that looks for all the world like a telephone; fears that perhaps it is merely a clever painting are readily alleviated by approaching the object; the possibility that it is nevertheless a dummy is countered by taking the thing apart and looking inside, as well as by using it to call someone up and having the person call back. The successful passing of these various tests would normally be considered to show conclusively that the object was a telephone. The accumulated weight of evidence is quite impressive. It includes the testimony of another observer, a wealth of visual evidence with regard to the requisite shape, size, inner components, tactual evidence of weight and solidity falling within the acceptable range of variation, and auditory evidence of the appropriate sort of ringing and voice patterns, each correctly correlated with other data, places, and times. There seems little room for doubt that the perceived object qualifies as a telephone.

Now, the question to be asked is whether the evidence on which the claim to know is based is evidence that preserves the claim from skeptical assault. For instance, does the evidence in the above verification show that the telephone continues to exist unperceived? It is difficult to avoid answering that apparently it does not in any straightforward sense. The issue of continued existence is never raised in the course of the verification. Rather, it is simply assumed that there is an object in the next room, one that continues to be there whether observed or not, and the point of the investigation is to determine what sort of thing the object is. The evidence is, of course, rich and varied, and conceivably might be used in some way to support a claim of continued unperceived existence. Yet it remains to be shown what and whether that way is.

The situation is similar with respect to skeptical scenarios in which the world is a vast hoax. Here again skeptical possibilities are not even remotely envisaged. The issue of whether or not the object is a mere painting or a dummy is irrelevant to the skeptical issue, since the object could be a painting or not, a dummy or not, and still be part of a dream or demon conjuration. Indeed, it is quite unclear how any of the evidence gained by scrutinizing, picking up, squeezing, taking apart, or dialing counts in any way against the skeptical hypothesis. The wealth of evidence might conceivably be put to this purpose in some way, but it is not at all clear what that way could be.

Finally, the situation would appear to be essentially the same with regard to the third skeptical thesis which affirms the absence of any external world corresponding to one's perceptions. The issue is never raised in everyday investigations, and it is quite unclear how the evidence gleaned from these investigations could be brought usefully to bear on it.

When viewed in this light, the commonsense claim to know has a hollow ring to it. In the above example, the claim to know that the object in question is a telephone cannot be rightly judged to counter the skeptical claim that perhaps the object does not exist when unperceived, or that perhaps it is a bit player in some vast hoax. This is because the evidence gathered counts in no apparent way against the skeptical theses. To rule out the latter on the basis of such evidence is not unlike declaring a boat seaworthy on the mere basis of a thorough inspection of the sails and rigging. It is to confer a title on the basis of certain limited tests and to overlook the fact that the title guarantees the possession of certain other features completely ignored in the tests. Everyday tests provide no warrant against Cartesian skeptical theses because they are so designed as to test for something else. Consequently, the test results are irrelevant to the issue of skepticism. As one might put the matter, it is precisely because skeptical theses are treated as irrelevant to everyday concerns that everyday confirmation and knowledge claims are irrelevant to skeptical problems.

The apparent irrelevance of the everyday evidence is one and the same as the apparent data-imperviousness of skeptical hypotheses found in the earlier test results; the situation of the telephone is not essentially different from that of the hand featured in the test. If the skeptical challenge is to be countered, something other than a mere reiteration of everyday knowledge claims is required. Such claims are relevant only to the extent that they implicitly incorporate a judgment of irrelevance, which judgment, as we saw earlier, is in dire need of explication if it is to be brought to bear on the issue.

At this juncture one might attempt to make a last stand with yet another Moorean manoeuvre, that of claiming that such things are known but cannot be shown. Says Moore, "We are all, I think, in this strange position that we do *know* many things, with regard to which we *know* further that we must have had evidence for them, and yet we do not know *how* we know them, i.e., we do not know what that evidence was!"[22] In a similar vein, on the question of whether he is dreaming Moore claims to have conclusive evidence that he is awake but to be unable to say what all that evidence is.[23] The manoeuvre is echoed in recent literature by claims to be justified in thinking one has some knowledge even if one cannot show that one has,[24] or more indirectly, by the claim that in order to know it is not necessary to know that one knows.[25]

The flaw in this approach is the same as in any view that substitutes faith for reason without good reason. If it is indeed true that one knows the rudimentary commonsense tenets called into question by the skeptic, then one should have supporting evidence or reasons. If the latter is indeed the case, then it should be possible in principle to recuperate that evidence. If after a reasonable lapse of time devoted to trawling operations, none of the alleged evidence has resurfaced in the light of day, then the claim to know becomes suspect. If one cannot retrieve the evidence, how can one claim to have it? And if one does not have it, how can one validly claim to know? It will not do to respond that one once had sufficient evidence to warrant a knowledge claim; after all, what is to say that a conviction, whether in the continued existence of unobserved objects or in the existence of avenging spirits, is not a mere matter of some deep-rooted prejudice or blind leap of faith? In the absence of evidence, there is no warrant for a claim to know. This is how matters must stand until such time as the evidence is actually retrieved from wherever it is such things get misplaced.

Pending the arrival of the promised warrant (or some manner of convincing reason) it must be held that Premiss 1 of the Common Sense Argument has not been established, and that by the same token, Premiss 1 of the No Knowledge Argument has not been countered. Since the truth of the latter premiss is borne out by the test results, it may be concluded that on the evidence gleaned to date, the everyday rivals of skeptical theses are not known. If this result is thought to be grave, its gravity pales still further in the face of the full implications of the findings. The reason why the everyday view P is not known (at least in as much as it contradicts the skeptical thesis) is not merely that the evidence for P is insufficient to warrant a knowledge claim; it is that the evidence for P is inexistent. In the absence of any such evidence, there is no reason at all to think that P is true. To claim that P is true is consequently to make a purely gratuitous claim.

There is still worse to come. One of Moore's favorite manoeuvres in defence of everyday commonsense truths is to claim that skeptical theses have nothing whatever to be said in their favor. We have found that as much may be said of commonsense views, so Moore's claim, if true, would place these commonsense views on equal footing with skeptical theses, each devoid of support. Now in point of fact, there are plausible grounds for thinking that Moore's claim is mistaken. Among the principles that help to arbitrate among competing hypotheses is the time-honored rule that explanation should not multiply entities unnecessarily or postulate what there is no need to postulate. This rule, if endorsed, would seem to give solipsism a decided advantage over its commonsense competitors. Consider Observed World Solipsism, the solipsism that denies the existence of anything not now perceived. Such solipsism neither multiplies entities unnecessarily nor makes any superfluous commitments. It makes the minimal assumption consistent with the evidence and asserts nothing beyond what is warranted by that evidence. In this regard, it would certainly seem superior to the everyday view. It has the further advantage, crucial perhaps in the present intellectual climate, that it is ideally suited to the tastes of ontologists partial to desert landscapes.

As to solipsistic theses that question the reality of what is observed or the existence of any reality at all outside one's representations, it would seem that a plausible case might be made for them as well. The point was made some years back by Pierre Bayle in the following terms:

> There are two Philosophical axioms which teach us, one that nature does nothing in vain; the other, that things are done in vain by more means which might have been as commodiously done by fewer. By these two axioms the Cartesians, whom I am speaking of, may maintain that no such thing as matter exists; for whether it doth or doth not exist, God could equally communicate to us all the thoughts we have.[26]

A closely related point is made later by George Berkeley in speaking of the possible existence of bodies outside the mind: "yet to hold they do so must needs be a very precarious opinion; since it is to suppose, without any reason at all, that God has created innumerable beings that are entirely useless, and serve to no manner of purpose."[27] From this perspective, it would seem by no means impossible to construct a plausible case of sorts in favor of each of the various forms of Cartesian solipsism. The confirmational status of everyday truths with respect to their skeptical counterparts begins to border on the lugubrious.

The skeptical challenge is a serious one. It is important to be clear as to its nature. It is a request for evidence or warrant, one which in

principle may take either of two forms: a request for evidence sufficient to warrant a claim to absolute certainty or a request for any evidence whatever sufficient to show everyday claims about the world
more likely to be true than their skeptical rivals. In more recent times,
the tendency has been to construe the skeptical challenge in terms of
certainty. In addition, the claim to certainty has been equated with a
claim to know. The result of these various moves is an impressive tes-
timonial to the vigor of the booming red herring industry in present-
day epistemology. Let us confine deboning operations to a few brief
observations.

First of all, an obvious point: the most appropriate and direct
response to a request for warrant is to provide the requested warrant.
To respond with a bald claim to know, implying that the belief must be
warranted, is to miss the point. To respond with the unelucidated alle-
gation that knowledge has certain skepticism-answering properties is
to play the skeptic for an idiot. The stance is all the more regrettable in
that the skeptic is presumably oneself in one's more rational moments.

Secondly, the concept of knowledge to which appeal is made in
claims to know is the concept operative in the context of everyday
matters of fact. This concept is in point of fact an incoherent concept.
An everyday knowledge claim is both definitive and revokable. It is
definitive in that it entails the truth of the proposition known. It is
revokable in that given the nature of the evidence, it is always possible for disconfirming evidence to turn up throwing the claim in
doubt: it could in fact turn out that the zoo animals are disguised
mules, that Ms. Reliable's apartment burns down, that the spruce is in
fact dyed blue.[28] As a result, a knowledge claim has a de facto openness to revision, which openness is in contradiction with the implications of the claim itself. Indeed, if made explicit, the openness would
have to be denied. A claim to know that admitted the possibility of
disconfirmation would enunciate a contradiction of the sort: P is certain but may turn out not to be; or worse still, P is true but may not
be. The concept of knowledge is in fact a linguistic consecration of the
habit of jumping to conclusions, of treating what is highly likely at
best as if it were conclusively established. As a result, when it is made
to figure in discussions of skepticism in place of the concept of absolute certainty, it muddies the waters with questionable implications
backed up by the powerful force of everyday usage, and so obscures
the real issue, which is whether the evidence provides sufficient warrant for a judgment of absolute certainty.

The revokability of knowledge claims through subsequent disconfirming evidence is the main reason for the chronic failure of attempt-

ed definitions of knowledge despite quite valiant efforts by highly trained specialists in the field. Epistemology generally could only benefit if the concept of knowledge was dropped from all serious discussion, and its present prominent position ceded to justification and warrant. Such a shift would bring the subject back to its proper concerns, since justification is in any event the substantive constituent in any knowledge claim. Indeed, in this perspective, the search for an adequate answer to skepticism, which is a search for warrant for everyday knowledge claims, is a prerequisite for any cogent account of warranted belief and a first necessary step toward the goal of reaching the closest possible analogue to a definition of knowledge.

One striking instance of the issue-muddying caused by the concept of knowledge is the construal of the skeptical issue of absolute certainty in Unger's fashion as a matter (ultimately undecidable) of a choice between two semantic assignments for 'to know' and related expressions. Of the two, one is seen to be the commonsense assignment with its lower standards and more limited range of relevant alternatives, the other the skeptic's brainchild with its highest possible standards and unlimited range of logically possible alternatives.[29] The question actually raised by skepticism in this context is clearly the quite different issue of whether the evidence is sufficient to warrant a judgment of absolute certainty, as distinct from some lesser degree of likelihood. Apparently Unger's reason for thinking that this latter question converts into the semantic one is that the skeptic is unable to establish relevance: the skeptic can produce no reasons in support of his or her claim that all logically possible alternatives are relevant.[30] As a result, according to Unger, the field is open to two competing systems employing quite different sets of relevant alternatives. Yet surely, the reasoning here is nothing short of perverse. There is no a priori need to establish relevance. If a hypothesis is consistent with the evidence, it qualifies as possibly true given the evidence. Consequently, it is relevant until shown to be irrelevant (whether through some rationally warranted principle of relevance or, more sensibly, through the evidence provided by past experience). In none of this is there any call to weigh the comparative merits of two competing semantic systems.

Finally, the importance accorded the question of certainty is grossly exaggerated. If it is true that an estimate of high likelihood of truth is warranted for commonsense tenets, the situation cannot reasonably be judged catastrophic on the mere grounds that the guarantee of truth falls somewhere short of absolute certainty. Furthermore, the fixation with certainty obscures the fact that the proper skeptical issue is that of warrant. Insofar as the question of certainty arises, it is also a question of warrant, the warrant there is for a claim of absolute certainty as distinct from a claim of likelihood. Consequently, the question of certainty cannot be adequately answered with regard to any particular type of statement before an answer has been given to the more general issue of what warrant there is for the statement. Otherwise stated, it is only after determining what qualifies as evidence that it can be determined whether the evidence yields absolute certainty or something less.

If the skeptical problem posed by warrant skepticism is to be resolved, it must be shown what warrant there is for the everyday assumption that things continue to exist unperceived, or for the commonsense claim that they are not participants in some vast dream. Recent philosophical activity has fostered a plethora of attempts to finesse the task by convicting skepticism on charges of meaninglessness and of epistemic and/or conceptual parasitism. We shall examine these attempts at a later point. In the absence of evidence or of valid dispensatory considerations, the assertion of the commonsense position or the denial of its skeptical rival is purely gratuitous, since on the best reading of the evidence, the two positions find themselves on equal footing, each apparently devoid of evidential support. In sum, as matters stand, there is no more reason than not to think that the furniture of the world continues to exist unperceived, no more reason than not to think that the world is other than a dream.

CHAPTER THREE

THE LACONIC RETORT

Skeptical carping on the apparent lack of warrant for everyday beliefs may provoke any of a variety of short-tempered retorts. Since some of the latter may seriously pretend to provide a satisfactory remedy to skeptical doubt, it is best to examine them before going on in future chapters to the more sophisticated and complex responses put forth in more recent philosophical thinking on the topic. The pithier rejoinders fall into three groups which respectively claim skeptical concerns to be irrelevant, unreasonable, and irrational. The rejoinders themselves appeal to considerations which are *pragmatic, reasonable* or *self-referential*. Let us consider them in this order.

PRAGMATIC REJOINDERS

Pragmatic responses to a request for warrant for everyday beliefs and practices also fall into three types. These types are exemplified by the following deflationary retorts:

1. with regard to warrant, "Who needs it?"

2. with regard to beliefs, "You cannot get by without them."

3. with regard to predictive procedures, "They work."

Restated more formally, the three responses run as follows:

1. Warrant is unnecessary in mundane matters such as survival.

2. Belief is mandatory in mundane matters such as survival.

3. Predictive success is sufficient warrant for everyday procedures.

Each of these claims has a certain plausibility that is difficult to resist. Nevertheless, each is beside the point, since the point is the warrant requested by the skeptic. Since pragmatism is a widely venerated home remedy for philosophical ills generally, it is important to understand how it is a placebo at best in the present case.

One pragmatic claim is that while there may well be no rational warrant for beliefs in terms of the evidence, no such justification is necessary: life goes on very well without it. This particular pragmatic response is to be found at numerous points throughout Ludwig Wittgenstein's multifaceted reply to skeptical doubts. In particular, it undergirds the rhetorical question given in response to a request for reasons for thinking that hot plates burn, "Have you reasons for this belief; and do you need reasons?"[1] It is still more explicit in the remark, "The squirrel does not infer by induction that it is going to need stores next winter as well. And no more do we need a law of induction to justify our actions or our predictions."[2] Apparently, skeptical inquiry into justification is to be seen as an unnecessary concern.

In one sense, the view is certainly right: a belief does not require a rational justification in order to be believed or to be acted upon—any more than an investigative procedure need be shown to yield truth in order for it to be employed. Unwarranted belief, as well as action based on that belief, are in point of fact a rather common occurrence, and not merely within the confines of the squirrel community. Hence, warranted belief is certainly not necessary for action. Furthermore, one might argue, in the average case unwarranted belief hardly seems to merit serious moral censure. Indeed, it could well be that if the holders of unwarranted beliefs were all jailed, there would be no one left outside to act as jailor. Why then should the absence of warrant be cause for concern?

The answer must be sought in the nature of unwarranted belief. A belief needs a justification or supporting reasons if it is to be a justified belief, that is, a belief so supported as to be likely to be true, or at least more likely to be true than any rival thesis. The point is in no way affected by Wittgenstein's claim that a squirrel or a person once burnt needs no reasons. Commonsense tenets bereft of supporting reasons cannot be rightly judged to be more likely to be true than their skeptical or solipsistic alternatives. In a discussion of existentialist values, Jean-Paul Sartre once remarked that the trouble with self-contradiction is simply that it is self-contradiction. Analogously, the trouble with unwarranted belief is simply that it is unwarranted belief. As such, it is no more likely to be true than any other unwarranted claims including the allegedly absurd solipsistic theses.

If Wittgenstein fails to draw the conclusion to which an absence of reasons points, it is because he is victim of an error to which pragmatists, no less than most human beings, are particularly prone, the failure to envisage skeptical hypotheses as serious alternatives to commonsense tenets. Throughout his reflections on skepticism, the truth of everyday beliefs is unquestioningly assumed. Wittgenstein's induction-deficient squirrel, for example, is a nut-stalking, pantry-stuffing, busily bustling squirrel, quite beyond any suspicion of being a permanent illusion or ephemeral entity devoid of unobserved squirrel parts. As a result, Wittgenstein's question of whether reasons are needed is the question of whether reasons are needed for believing a particular set of tenets the truth of which is already assumed by the very terms in which the question is formulated. A question that assumes there is no skeptical problem is incapable of doing justice to the possibility that the skeptic may be right. When, on the contrary, skeptical possibilities are seriously envisaged, it is clear that the absence of reasons puts commonsense tenets and skeptical hypotheses on an equal footing with regard to evidence and consequently in a position where, judged on the evidence alone, neither is any more or any less likely to be true than the other. In these circumstances, it is quite appropriate to ask whether reasons are needed; they obviously are.

A second popular pragmatic response to skepticism is to point out that everyday beliefs are assumed in all activity in the world and hence even by the skeptic who professes to deny them. One forceful statement of this line of thinking is to be found in G. E. Moore's paper, "A Defence of Common Sense." Here Moore makes the very plausible claim that "*all* philosophers without exception" hold the commonsense view of the world, and that consequently the debate is not between those who do and those who do not but between those who do and those who also hold some further view inconsistent with the first one.[3] A more notorious version of this particular response is David Hume's declaration that in ordinary life we cannot avoid believing things inconsistent with radical skeptical positions.[4]

Now for purposes such as ours, this line of reasoning has two serious flaws. The lesser flaw is that it is quite ineffective as a general answer to Cartesian solipsism. The conviction that the world is but a dream does not contradict any beliefs in the multitude of beliefs presupposed by any operation in the world, for instance, by the preparation and dispatching of a light snack. Similarly, the claim that things pass out of existence when unperceived, does not rule out causal regularities among perceived phenomena and hence does not make expectations based on such regularities contradictory of the skeptical hypothesis. Only a very radical skeptic such as the Sense Datum Solipsist faces a potential conflict of interests. If the latter solipsist's conception of a world composed of unrelated ephemeral façades is conserved, there can be no ground for expectation, not even the expectation that a hand will move as in the past or that an object will remain in existence long enough to be grasped or that food will assuage hunger pangs. A practicing Sense Data Solipsist would be less armed for survival than an infant newly arrived in the world.

Yet even in the most unfavorable case, where the solipsistic thesis can have no sincere practicing adherents (for any sizeable length of time, that is), the doctrine might nevertheless be true. The fact that some minimal set of beliefs is required for living and functioning effectively in the world is no obvious guarantee that the world does not in fact conform to some solipsistic scheme or other. More than this, it is unclear how the need for some minimal doxastic commitment considered in abstraction from any further consideration, can provide any supporting evidence. What must be shown is that there is a connection between the necessity of holding commonsense beliefs and the likelihood of the truth of those beliefs, that successful living in the world requires true beliefs rather than false ones.

A third pragmatic claim is that ordinary inductive procedures and the beliefs to which they give rise are warranted by their undeniable predictive success. What better explanation can there be, it is asked, of the success of the action based on the beliefs, than the fact that the beliefs are in some measure descriptive of the world? One energetic defence of this line of reasoning is summed up by Nicholas Rescher as follows: "The best explanation of the substantial successes the scientific method has engendered is that it leads to results which afford some at least indication of 'the way it is.'"[5]

Clearly, the appeal to success cannot provide a general answer applicable to all Cartesian skeptical problems. Solipsistic hypotheses stating the world to be radically unreal in some way are in no way inconsistent with the scientific method or with the system of generalizations to which the method gives rise, and consequent successful predictions. As one might put the matter, someone deceived by a demon or dreaming the world could well make successful predictions regarding future experiences. Similarly, Ephemerata Solipsism, which questions the existence of unperceived material things, may without contradiction endorse the scientific method in general and inductive procedures in particular—as applied, of course, to perceived phenomena to the exclusion of unperceived ones. The commonsense model of the world is not the only model consistent with predictive success.

The one form of solipsism not so consistent is, once again, Sense Data Solipsism, since it recognizes no causal regularities. The appeal to success might then be thought relevant to, if not effective against, this form of solipsism. In fact, it is neither.

First of all, the appeal to success is irrelevant to the classical problem of induction. The latter is the problem of how the accumulation of confirming instances provides justification or warrant for inductive conclusions—how, for instance, the fact that all encountered instances of smoke were accompanied by fire is warrant for the claim that all instances whatever of smoke are accompanied by fire. Now, if a confirming instance is in addition a successful prediction, this does not constitute further evidence over and above that provided by its being a confirming instance. As a result, successful prediction leaves the classical problem of induction exactly where it was.

Lest it be thought that this assessment is too short, let us examine the situation more closely. The problem of induction is roughly that of showing how the fact all observed a's are b's confers likelihood on the claim that all a's are b's (and by extension, likelihood on the claim that the next a will be a b). Now, let us suppose that a number, n, of a's, let us say, $a_1, a_2, a_3, \ldots a_n$, are observed, and that all are found to be b's. Let us suppose further that on the basis of these observations a further number, m, of successful predictions are made, each to the effect that the following a will be a b. How do these successful predictions provide support for the claim that all a's are b's? If asked to give the evidence for the claim, one would point to the $n + m$ observed instances of concomitance. The fact that m of the instances were predicted does not afford any supplementary evidence beyond the observed concomitance in the $m + n$ instances. Predictions are certainly impressive, humanly speaking, but the grounds for each prediction are simply the observed instances of concomitance. Each additional successful prediction figures in the evidence merely as a further instance of that concomitance, and the fact that it is a prediction and a successful one adds nothing further.

There is a second point. Successful prediction also turns out to be irrelevant to the very question on which it is intended to throw light, the question of the structure of the world. The systematic predictive success of inductive investigative procedures can be plausibly explained, so the argument goes, only if the resulting model of the world is a faithful reflection of the way the world is. Yet this claim is mistaken. Just as a mere appeal to success cannot answer the question of why an inductive explanation is more likely to be true than a skeptical thesis, neither can it answer the question of why any explanation at all should be needed. It is alleged that the systematic success of the scientific method rules out chance or luck as a credible account of that success. Yet how so? Why should systematic success need an explanation? And why should success be indicative of anything beyond the observed facts themselves?

To bring out the point to be made here, consider a case where balls are drawn in random fashion from a huge urn and invariably found to be black. The hypothesis that only half the balls in the urn are black becomes an increasingly more implausible hypothesis as the number of draws increases. This is because the chance of obtaining a sequence consisting solely of black balls by drawing at random from a half black population, becomes increasingly less as the number of draws increases. The observed result consequently becomes less and less attributable to chance.

Now let us change the circumstances slightly and suppose that nothing is known of how the balls are drawn. In these conditions, since the balls are not known to be drawn at random, nothing may be said of the chances of drawing a black ball from a half black population—nor may anything be said of the chances of drawing a sequence of such balls. Unless there is reason to think that the draw is random or quasi-random, the notion of chances does not apply. As a result there is no rational basis for the claim that the hypothesis of a half-black population is implausible. Judged on the evidence, the composition of the unobserved population might be anything at all.

The moral from the above is directly applicable to the pragmatic argument in which it is claimed that a certain type of world is required to explain systematic predictive success. Success alone says nothing of how the observations were made. In the absence of an account of the observational procedures employed, nothing may be concluded from the observed regularities—any more than anything may be concluded about the composition of the total population from a sequence of black balls obtained in an unknown way. On the other hand, if an account of observation procedures is provided (Rescher speaks of the "design of experiments"),[6] then the question becomes that of what may be concluded given the observational procedures. This latter question is simply part of the original question of justification and is to be settled on its own merits independently of any appeal to success. Thus, in either case, with or without an account of observational procedures, success per se is irrelevant.

THE UNREASONABLE DEMAND

The tenacious and worrisome skeptical request for justification, when accompanied by a persistent failure to unearth the solicited warrant, may engender a second type of retort: the skeptic is demanding the impossible. Herein, it may be suspected, lies both the explanation of the persistence of skeptical doubts and the means to their definitive dissolution. In demanding the impossible, the skeptic is imposing an unreasonable requirement, which as such may be rightly ignored.

This line of reasoning has had numerous advocates. It is the backbone of the antiskeptical line taken by A. J. Ayer in *The Problem of Knowledge*. According to Ayer, the skeptic's complaint with everyday standards of proof is that they are logically questionable.[7] No accumulation of evidence can ever rule out the logical possibility of error or make the evidence entail the claim it is meant to support and hence bridge the logical gap between evidence and conclusion. The problem of induction is of considerable concern to Ayer, which is to say, the problem of warranted inferences from observed instances to unobserved ones. Ayer esteems the problem to be insoluble. He finds some form of a principle of the uniformity of nature to be necessary to make what is observed a reliable guide to what is unobserved, and esteems this principle itself to be based necessarily on induction. Hence, a purely formal proof based on logic and mathematics would be insufficient, while a less than purely formal proof would beg the question at issue. However, Ayer notes, the skeptic's victory is bloodless: "his demand for justification is such that it is necessarily true that it cannot be met"—and he adds, "and if there cannot be a proof, it is not sensible to demand one."[8]

More recently, a variation on the theme is defended by Rescher, whose concern centers more on deceitful demons and sinister scientists. Once again, the source of difficulty is seen to be the evidential gap between the objective factual claim and the accessible data; since the falsity of the claim is always logically compatible with the evidence, it follows that the claim can never be theoretically guaranteed. A logically exhaustive justification that conclusively rules out all skeptical hypotheses "is not a reasonable requirement," Rescher argues, and that because it is "in principle incapable of being satisfied."[9] It is rather the case, says Rescher, that when a claim is as certain as a thing of its kind can possibly be, then the old Roman legal precept applies, *ultra posse nemo obligatur*—no one is under any obligation to do more than what is possible.[10] In sum, the requirement the skeptic seeks to impose is "unworkable" and "unmeetable," hence, "improper and unjustified," or better still, "unreasonable, nay *irrational*."[11]

The charge that the skeptic is making unreasonable demands, if taken literally, is considerably off the mark. There is no call whatever to speak of skeptics generally as demanding a justification or imposing absurdly high standards. The skeptic qua skeptic is neither an adversarial spoilsport nor a tyrannical reformer. In principle at least, the skeptic is one's rational self in one's more lucid moments. As to the skeptic's concern, it is neither scandal-mongering nor methodological purification; that concern is rather to gain a correct assessment of the evidential situation with regard to certain widespread beliefs and practices. It is neither to impose requirements nor to make demands; it is to inquire whether there is any warrant for our customary beliefs and procedures. Of course, where no demands are being made, they cannot be unreasonable ones.

The charge of imposing unreasonable demands thus dissolves readily enough. The skeptic might be inclined to push this little success and to claim that all charges of unreasonableness likewise dissolve. Where no warrant is to be found, so the reasoning might run, it cannot be unreasonable to draw the less than outrageous conclusion that to all appearances there is none. Or, as one might put the matter, while it would certainly be unreasonable to demand that people fly about like birds, it is hardly unreasonable to point out that they do not. The point seems well taken. Nevertheless, it does not do full justice to the intricacies of the unreasonableness alleged to be present in requesting or questing after the impossible. Consequently, let us take a closer look at the impossibility (alleged or genuine) and at the skeptical stance adopted with regard to it.

A first point to be taken into account is that the impossibility might have to do with either of two distinct tasks. As noted earlier, a skeptical scenario used to challenge the warrant for some accepted belief, may take either of two forms, certainty skepticism, which sees warrant as insufficient for absolute certainty, or warrant skepticism which sees warrant as inexistent. The impossibility to be discussed differs depending upon the form of skepticism being considered. Let us begin with certainty skepticism.

Now, both Rescher and Ayer maintain the impossibility of reaching absolute certainty. Rescher, who tends to construe skepticism generally as a demand for absolute certainty, contends that it is in principle impossible to provide a logically exhaustive grounding such as would satisfy a skeptic; no volume of evidence can ever suffice to bridge the evidential gap and yield absolute certainty. He sometimes seems to see the task as tantamount to that of summing an infinite series.[12] Ayer, in his discussion of phenomenalism, sees the difficulty in analogous terms: any amount of evidence is always insufficient to logically entail the objective claim it is meant to support.[13] Thus, both agree with the skeptical denial of absolute certainty and hence have no quarrel with a rational skeptic on this particular point. Where they disagree with the skeptic, or rather where they think they disagree, is on the implications of the point. Both are at pains to declare that although absolute certainty is impossible, we nevertheless have our everyday investigative procedures that yield something less than unshakable certainty, and the latter is quite sufficient for everyday concerns. To ask for more is unreasonable since it is to request the impossible.

There is much that is sound in these remarks. Certainly, the importance of the question of absolute certainty is often grossly exaggerated. If, indeed, our everyday investigative procedures do show everyday claims to be extremely likely to be true, the achievement merits being judged important and highly gratifying; it should not be judged catastrophic on the mere grounds that the guarantee of truth falls somewhere short of absolute certainty. While this is true enough, the skeptical position has been quite misconceived. Certainty skepticism is concerned solely with the issue of whether everyday matters of fact are absolutely certain. It is in no way required to cast aspersions on claims to high likelihood, warranted or not, on the grounds that they fall short of absolute certainty. The question of whether likelihood claims are warranted, is the concern of warrant skepticism, which skepticism for its part is concerned solely with warrant, not with failure to achieve absolute certainty. Thus, there is, or need be, no call for a charge of unreasonableness in this context.

It is perhaps worthwhile to open a short parenthesis on the topic of absolute certainty. The possibility of such certainty is still hotly defended at times by other epistemologists. Klein, for one, gives a definition of knowledge according to which what is known is absolutely certain. However, he does so in virtue of the crucial condition that there be no genuine initiating defeaters of the statement in question,[14] a condition that effectively rules out the possibility that the statement known should ever turn out to be false. And, since only an omniscient subject could ever know that the condition obtains, knowledge of the sort with its absolute certainty has little applicability to human concerns.

In any event, to judge from appearances, the question of absolute certainty is most likely a dead issue—dead because it is an issue on which the skeptic is quite right. Most everyday situations in which knowledge claims are made are not ones that warrant a claim of absolute certainty. Further evidence might well turn up (and sometimes does) to falsify the knowledge claim. The literature on the subject abounds in cases that illustrate the point—the Zebra Case, the Appointment Case, and the Blue Spruce Case mentioned earlier, or to vary a little, the Tom Grabit Case, in which someone seen stealing a library book may have a double in the library at the time.[15] A claim of absolute certainty can hardly be warranted if the circumstances are such that the envisaged state of affairs may not obtain, since this would make the validity of the claim depend upon luck rather than evidence. There is also the formidable objection of Bertrand Russell's point that certainty is based to a large extent on inductive argument, and it is unclear how such argument could ever yield absolute certainty.[16] No less formidable is Peter Unger's point that it is possible in principle to have future experiences tending to support the thesis that one is but a skillfully stimulated brain in a vat, and that consequently, one should be less than absolutely certain that the world really is as it appears to be.[17] High likelihood at best, not absolute certainty, must suffice for everyday purposes.

It would be a mistake to attempt to avoid this conclusion with the reflection that while the attaining of absolute certainty may be analogous to the unenviable task of summing an infinite series, infinite series are readily summed in mathematics and that consequently an operation of the sort should present no insurmountable difficulty in epistemology. The aims and techniques of mathematicians are doubly irrelevant in the present context. This is easily shown.

On one hand, a mathematical summation is the fruit of a definition. The sum of an infinite series is defined to be its limit, where that limit is a number that can be approached as closely as one likes in summing the terms, simply by summing a sufficiently large number of terms. Otherwise stated, a particular value, L, is defined to be the sum of an infinite series if and only if, for any possible choice of a small positive number, w, as small as one pleases, there is some finite number, m, such that for any number, n, greater than m, the partial sum of the series consisting of the first n terms of the series differs from L by less than w. The definition is reasonable enough. If it makes sense to say that an infinite series has a sum, then L is certainly the candidate with the best credentials for the position, since by summing enough terms it is possible to reach a partial sum as close to L as one pleases. However, as a disciple of Zeno might point out, in all of this summing, finite series alone are summed, not infinite ones, and finite series have sums that always differ from L by some small amount. Consequently, L is never actually reached by summing a finite number of terms, any more than it is reached by the actual summing of the infinite series. L is simply defined to be the sum of the series. Indeed, if L could actually be reached by an operation of successive summation, there would be no need for a definition.

On the other hand, this mathematical procedure could not, in any event, be effectively transposed to an epistemic situation. The attempt at transposition would yield a definition to the effect that if certain confirming results are obtained from a large finite number of tests, then the likelihood of the hypothesis being true after all possible tests may reasonably be defined as absolute certainty. Yet by the very nature of the case, the reasonableness of the definition may be challenged. No matter what the results from any large number of tests, it is always possible to encounter contrary instances in later tests. Indeed, if the test results could be guaranteed in advance, there would be no need to run them. In mathematics an infinite series may be shown to have a limit because the terms of the series are generated by a rule allowing the value of any term in the series to be calculated, and the future behavior of the series to be known. If a series is not generated by a rule or if the rule is not known (as is the case with the test result series), then nothing can be said as to whether or not it has a limit and hence a sum. The mathematical model is inapplicable.

In contrast with that of absolute certainty, the issue of warrant is open and unexplored. The question it raises, generally stated, is whether the data, construed as evidence, provides any justification whatever for bridging the evidential gap. The question may be asked regarding any data alleged to be evidence for some particular type of judgment. In its most radical form, it is the question of whether there is *any* evidence, or *any* degree of warrant whatever for going beyond the actual data anywhere across the evidential gap. Sense Data Solipsism in its undogmatic form answers that apparently there is not.

Now, the antiskeptical view remaining to be examined is the claim that the skeptical request (or quest) for warrant is impossible to satisfy and hence is an irrational one to make (or undertake). It agrees with the radical skeptical assessment that there is no warrant but diverges from the skeptical view with its claim that the skeptical request is irrational. Let us look briefly at the grounds offered for this claim.

One such is Ayer's earlier-noted argument based on a formal/ empirical dichotomy endorsed by many epistemologists of the time. The argument runs as follows: on one hand, an inductive conclusion cannot be derived deductively from the evidence; on the other, the introduction of empirical generalizations sufficient to entail the desired conclusion would beg the question by using inductive conclusions as premises in the putative justification of induction itself. Ayer concludes that it is necessarily true that the skeptical request for justification cannot be met. He states, "when it is understood that there logically could be no court of superior jurisdiction, it hardly seems troubling that inductive reasoning should be left, as it were, to act as judge in its own cause."[18] Ayer's reasoning seems to be that because it is logically impossible for inductive conclusions to be warranted in the skeptic's sense, the issue of warrant may be ignored. It is what he terms a "fictitious" problem.

The reasoning here is similar to that put forth by F. L. Will. Will argues that once one divides the world up into a set of privileged observed items and dubitable unobserved ones, "one has in a very simple and direct way foreclosed the possibility" of redeeming the unobserved items from dubitability by an appeal to observed ones.[19] He seems to think that the skeptical request is logically impossible to satisfy and hence may be ignored. This assessment closely echoes P. F. Strawson's protest that skeptical doubts about continued existence set standards "self-contradictorily high, viz. having *continuous* observation where we have non-continuous observation."[20] As a result, according to Strawson, the skeptical conclusion drawn is the tautology that unobserved items are not observed. The crux of the matter on each of these views is that the request for warrant, on the terms dictated by the skeptic, is a request for a logical impossibility. Consequently, there is no cause to be upset by an inability to furnish it.

Despite the admirable economy of means in this line of reasoning, it must be doubly faulted (or triply so, if the inaccurate charge of imposing demands is included in the package). First of all, since warrant is what provides likelihood of truth, the response leaves intact the problem of showing commonsense views more likely to be true than skeptical scenarios. The point is one that pops up with monotonous regularity in responses to skepticism. It is assumed in the response that everyday beliefs about the world are true and that the problem of skepticism comes down to an inability to show that the beliefs have a rational foundation. The gravity of the skeptical challenge is quite unperceived, much less taken seriously. A rational belief is simply one that is made true by the evidence. To say that a belief has no rational foundation is to say that there is no reason to think it likely to be true. Thus, if the above remarks are correct in their assessment of the impossibility of a rational justification, then our everyday beliefs are no more likely to be true than their skeptical rivals.

Of equal importance, the response misconstrues the concept of warrant. If it were true, as claimed, that the apparent absence of warrant pointed out by the skeptic reduces ultimately to a tautology, then it would be not just false but *inconceivable* that there should be any warrant of the kind requested by the various Cartesian solipsists. In particular, it would be inconceivable that there should be any good reason to think that things continue to exist unperceived, inconceivable that observed instances could in any way provide warrant for conclusions regarding unobserved ones. This hardly seems to be the case. A justification may be based on any amount of data of observation, any rational principles whatever that might be relevant. It may be a demonstration of absolute certainty, or alternatively a demonstration of likelihood, probability, or plausibility. As a result, it cannot be stated with any firm assurance that the range of possible justifications has been thoroughly surveyed. It is precisely because the question of possible rational justification is somewhat open-ended that any rational skeptic must decline to claim that there is no justification for everyday beliefs and must instead advance the more modest claim that *apparently* there is none. Thus, not only is it not logically true that there can be no warrant, but there is no obvious reason to conclude that the quest for warrant must come up empty-handed.

Admittedly, the repeated failure of foundationalist attempts to show the rationality of commonsense tenets is hardly encouraging. Nevertheless, such failure is not conclusive. It may well be that the formal/factual dichotomy assumed by Ayer in his proof of the impossibility of justification of inductive procedures is oversimplified. A formal deduction is understood by Ayer to be one in which appeal is made to formal logic alone (and possibly mathematics) over and above the evidence itself. It is assumed without question that there are no further rational principles of evidence employed in fact and/or rightly employable in addition to the ones already recognized in formal logic and mathematics. No defence whatever is offered for this assumption. It might be objected that the possibility of such further undiscovered principles seems slim: the past diligence of epistemologists leaves scant reason to think that there actually are any structural bones of the kind in question still hidden in the itinerant rubble of the epistemological dig. Nevertheless, there is a prima facie plausible reason for thinking such a negative appraisal to be overly hasty.

Most sensible human beings would contend that what is considered evidence for an everyday claim according to everyday criteria, actually does constitute support for that claim. If the sensible majority is right and the evidence actually does render the claim plausible or certain enough, surely then there should be some serious prospect of showing that the evidence favors, and perhaps favors overwhelmingly, the commonsense claim as opposed to the skeptical one and that justification is not an impossible task. Indeed, the negative assessment quite ignores the widespread and often fierce conviction that the available evidence supports commonsense claims as opposed to their rival skeptical hypotheses, a conviction which strongly suggests that rationality is operative in the procedures of everyday inquiry. Kant's "scandal to human reason" may plausibly be expected to be profoundly unreasonable. The unpalatable alternative is to attribute the habitual vehement rejection of skeptical hypotheses rather to some deeply ingrained strain of epistemological racism. By the same token, it is to construe the most elementary of the epistemological beliefs of the rational animal as having no rational foundation. The suspicion of the impartial observer must be that perhaps the last word has yet to be said on the rationality of human thinking. As long as there remains a real possibility of uncovering further hidden but implicitly used rational principles of inquiry, the quest for the requested warrant for everyday views must be declared still open for business.

THE SELF-REFERENTIAL MANOEUVRE

The ideal demonstration of the irrationality of a skeptical thesis would be one that showed the thesis to be self-contradictory. Since skeptical hypotheses rarely oblige by being conspicuously inconsistent, aspiring champions of everyday knowledge often resort to the ploy of applying the skeptical thesis to the skeptical thesis itself in the hope of deriving an inconsistency. Such a manoeuvre might be termed *the self-referential manoeuvre*. It is a less than recent innovation. It was certainly not unfamiliar to the ancient Greeks, since Plato has Socrates execute just such a manoeuvre with regard to the dictum of Protagoras that man is the measure of all things. Socrates argues that Protagoras must, in accord with his own dictum, acknowledge the truth of the opinion of those who declare the dictum to be false.[21] Thus, the dictum entails its own falsity.

In more recent times, we find Hume acknowledging the contradiction implicit in the skeptical maxim, all "refined and elaborate" reasoning is to be rejected. As Hume himself points out, the maxim itself is based on such reasoning.[22] More recently still, in arguing against solipsism, Bertrand Russell employs the manoeuvre against the claim to know that the empiricist principle is true, the principle that anything known without inference must be known solely through experience and the principles of deductive logic.[23] If such a principle were known, it would be in contradiction with itself. More recently again, Oliver A. Johnson argues in like fashion against the skeptical conclusion of Hume: "But he should have gone further to recognize that when he applies the result of the second stage of his argument to his own thesis, he must conclude that the thesis is now 'reduced to nothing.' Thus, his thesis for epistemological skepticism, as he in part realizes, is logically self-destroying."[24]

The self-referential manoeuvre promises at first glance to be productive, not only of laconic retorts but of effective ones. When applied to the skeptical claim that nothing can be known, it seems to yield the stunning retort that by the same token it cannot be known that nothing can be known. Analogously, from the skeptical generalization that everything is doubtful, it apparently generates the no less embarrassing claim that it is doubtful that everything is doubtful.

However, some caution must be injected at this point. In the above applications of the manoeuvre it is assumed that the skeptical claim itself falls within the scope of the generalization enunciated and, consequently, that the claim states something about itself. This assumption is a debatable one. If such were literally the case, the statement would be senseless rather than self-contradictory or self-defeating. Let us look at the matter more closely. If the skeptical claim did encompass itself, and so say of itself that it was doubtful or unknowable, then it would include itself as one of its own semantic constituents. Consequently, any complete explication of its meaning would be impossible; it would be in part semantically vacuous and hence not be a genuine statement. In this regard, it would resemble other semantically self-referential utterances such as the putative statement expressed with the words, "This statement is true," where reference is intended to what is said with the words. Since it is impossible to determine completely what is being said, the alleged statement can be neither verified nor falsified; hence it fails to satisfy a necessary condition for statementhood and consequently is meaningless.[25]

The very fact that semantically self-referential statements are meaningless suggests rather that skeptical statements should not be construed as self-referential. Indeed, there is something suspicious about the claim that a statement enunciating a general assessment of the results of empirical investigative procedures is meaningless because it applies to itself. If such were automatically the case, then no general assessments could ever meaningfully be made. Furthermore, anyone making such an assessment (including a skeptic) would insist that he or she did not have the assessment itself in mind when making the assessment—and the speaker, of course, is ultimately the judge of what is meant by an utterance. In any event, intractability on the point is futile, since in the last resort it would simply oblige the speaker to affix to the statement some rider excluding the statement itself from the generalization being made.

All is not lost, however. While the skeptical utterance in the above cases is not strictly self-referential, it is nevertheless not free of difficulty. The grounds upon which other knowledge claims are called into question might be grounds that apply with equal warrant to the skeptical conclusion itself. Thus, there remains ample room to effectuate a self-referential manoeuvre, albeit a less direct one. A rational skeptic (the only one of interest to us) must espouse the principles of impartiality and of evaluation on the strength of reasons and evidence alone. The skeptic who challenges the rationality of common investigative procedures should expect the methods employed in reaching the skeptical conclusions to be subjected to similar scrutiny with regard to their rationality. A self-referential manoeuvre of the sort is quite telling against the skepticism of Hume, for instance. If Hume is indeed right in his contention that experience is both insufficient to ground any inference and at the same time the only basis there is, then it is absurd for him to make inferential generalizations about the limits of human knowledge.

Unfortunately for our purposes, there is little solid hope of convicting Cartesian skepticism on a similar charge. The Cartesian solipsists need make no attempt to imitate Hume or Russell in his earlier years and put forth general claims about the limits of human knowledge. Whereas skeptics who claim to know that they know nothing may fairly be asked to justify their knowledge claim regarding their own ignorance, Cartesian solipsists need make no claims of the sort. The latter may limit themselves to pointing out the apparent lack of warrant for any of the ordinary inferential practices to which appeal might be made in an attempt to establish the truth of commonsense views. Consequently, there is no obvious way of bringing the rational requirement of equally demanding standards to bear effectively on the solipsists' own practices. As a result, the negative conclusions reached by the solipsists are not themselves vulnerable to an analogous charge of lack of warrant.

One particular variant of the self-referential manoeuvre deserves mention because of its recurrent appearances in the literature. Its focus is Descartes's dream hypothesis, although it could in principle be executed against any form of unreal solipsism. The laconic retort in this instance states in substance that if the world is a dream, the thought that it is, is itself merely being dreamt. Variations on the theme abound. John Locke remarks half in jest, "I must desire him to consider, that, if all be a dream, then he doth but dream that he makes the question, and so it is not much matter that a waking man should answer him."[26] In a less flippant vein the waking Wittgenstein declares, "The argument 'I may be dreaming' is senseless for this reason: if I am dreaming, this remark is being dreamed as well."[27] Among the variations are to be found Danto's claim that if one is really arguing, one is awake; that of Guy Robinson, that we would not be in a position to make the real suppositions Descartes asks us to make, only dream ones; and Malcolm's claims that dreaming one is predicting, testing, or concluding is not actually doing any of these things, and if one was indeed dreaming, one could not know that one was but only dream that one knew.[28]

The difficulty in all these cases is to determine the exact import of the derogatory retort. Certainly, it is fair enough to argue that if the world is a dream, as the dream skeptic claims it to be, then doubts regarding the reality of the world and denials of that reality are also part of the dream and hence are not really being entertained or made. As Malcolm rightly points out, it does not follow from one's having climbed a mountain in a dream that one climbed the mountain while asleep, or that one actually climbed a mountain at all.[29] Yet, while this much is clear enough, it is nevertheless unclear exactly what interesting conclusion follows. Dreamt suppositions, doubts, understandings and assertions certainly differ from real ones in that they take place within a dream rather than in real life. Yet something other than mere environmental context is necessary here to give substance to the claim that the dreamt activity is substandard activity or a substandard version of the real thing.

Dreams are often dismissed as merely dreamt on the grounds that they are of no consequence or import. This fairly widespread assessment of dreams is a direct reflection of the essential irrelevance of dreamt events to the actual course of events in the waking world, which is generally esteemed to be the one that matters. Such causal inefficacy cannot in itself, however, make the dreamt activities be anything less than what they are. Certainly, a dreamt terror, fascination, or joy is no less the emotion it is. Hence the causal inefficacy cannot itself be the source of a judgment of inferior quality.

One reason sometimes proposed as grounds for the demotion of dreamt activities is that they are unconscious. The rationale is roughly that when dreaming one is asleep; consequently, one is unaware, and in no position to make cogent judgments about anything. Wittgenstein adopts such a line in response to the skeptical thesis that one might now be drugged: if the drug has taken away consciousness, then one is "not now really talking and thinking." Since Wittgenstein goes on to speak of dreaming and to claim that one cannot be right when in such a state, presumably he holds that sleep similarly takes away the consciousness necessary to make cogent judgments.[30] Malcolm reaches an analogous conclusion on the grounds that to judge oneself to be dreaming, one must be able to judge that one is asleep, and the latter is impossible since it is impossible to be both asleep and aware that one is asleep. The reasoning in both cases is unconvincing. It is convincing if applied to the judgment that one is unconscious—one cannot be both unconscious and aware that one is—but in both dreams and drugged states one is conscious in some mode and degree. What needs to be shown is that the state of consciousness in a dream state is such as to preclude activities that qualify as full-fledged judgments.

It does not seem possible to establish such a point from general considerations about dreams. Dreams almost invariably house some measure of emotional and doxastic involvement. On waking up one is still reverberating with fear, anger, or joy and reverberating too with expectations and convictions integral to the dream. These emotions and correlated convictions dissipate after a brief time with the realization that one has been dreaming—but they linger sufficiently to allow some assessment of their nature. To judge from the evidence there is little call to insist that one does not really have feelings in a dream, that one merely dreams one has them—or that one does not really believe but only dreams that one believes. Apart from the fictitiousness of their objects, the emotions and beliefs seem essentially the same in nature as waking emotions and beliefs. It is, of course, futile to attempt to deny the empirical evidence with general considerations regarding what dreamt activities must be like.

In point of fact, most dreams seem to involve something characterizable as unquestioning acceptance. Events unfold, the dreamer is engrossed in them, accepts them at face value, becomes emotionally involved. One of the most peculiar features of dreams, one noticeable particularly on a sudden awakening, is how convincing and absorbing they are. The dreamer is no mere casual spectator at some private showing, proffering a hedged acceptance akin to that of a theater-goer, as William Boardman would have it.[31] He or she is an engrossed participant in a lived situation. Exceptions exist, of course. When falling back to sleep, for instance, a dreamer may purposefully pick up a dream where it was broken off and hence be aware, momentarily at least, that it is but a dream. Yet one may plausibly maintain that deep sleep, as distinct from twilight sleep, truly begins only when the dreamer becomes absorbed in the dream. In the resulting cases of immersion in the dreamt situation, there is apparently no sharp qualitative difference between believing and merely dreaming that one believes.

Now curiously enough, while dreamt feelings and convictions differ little from waking ones, there seems to be no analogous similarity between dreamt thinking and thinking while awake. If I have solved a problem in a dream, then on waking I do not automatically claim to have solved a problem. My reticence in this regard is not particularly due to the fact that the problem is a dreamt problem. Rather it is due to my past experience with dreams of the sort, with finding the alleged solution dissolve before my eyes when I attempt to reactivate and critically evaluate the line of reasoning on which it is based. Ideas that seem brilliant, penetrating, or significant when I am asleep are often quite vacuous in the clear light of day. The explanation of why such is the case seems to be that while dreaming one does not think in any very full sense of "thinking." One is never actually in full possession of one's intellectual faculties. In particular, there is no critical evaluation of events. Quite impossible sequences of happenings are accepted without critical protest, although their absurdity is flagrant to a waking person—often so strikingly so that they allow immediate characterization of the events as dreamt. Indeed, all serious reflection seems reserved exclusively for waking moments. Active reflection on any problems or practical matters inhibits falling asleep or interrupts sleep if occasioned by something in a dream. In fact, falling asleep requires a letting go of any active participation in concerns or problems. Dreams insert themselves into this passive stance. For someone falling asleep they come as an interesting spectacle requiring only that one lie back and let oneself become absorbed in the unfolding sequence of events. This requirement of nonactive participation seems to hold throughout the dream. When one attempts to take action, whether to shout, run, or work out a solution to a problem, one wakes up.

If the nonactive participation helps to explain one's reticence to identify with a dreamer's thinking, it also provides grounds for Wittgenstein's implicit assimilation of a dreaming person to a drugged one. More importantly, the fact of diminished intellectual awareness during dreaming allows a plausible case to be made for the claim that in the course of a dream there can be no true judging, no warranted assessment. Any reflective judgment would require the dreamer to begin actively to think, as well as to bring accumulated knowledge to bear. Thus, it may be plausibly maintained that a judgment to the effect that one may be dreaming cannot be sensibly made, since if one were in fact dreaming, one would be in no position to make a warranted judgment.

Although the point may be granted, nevertheless it is not fatal to the skeptical dream hypothesis. The skeptic is well aware that in many respects events in dreams differ markedly from those in waking life. The skeptical thesis is not that the everyday world may be like a dream in all respects, a thesis that would be patently false given the magical transformations frequent in dreams. It is that, contrary to popular sentiment on the matter, the world possesses a feature considered typical of dreams, that of ceasing to exist when the dreamer awakes. The claim that one may be dreaming, or that the world is perhaps a dream, is not the claim that the world may in fact exhibit magical transformations or an absence of genuine reflective judgment; it is simply the claim that this present world may turn out to be unreal just as dreams do. Thus, the putative dreamer in this putatively dreamlike world is not required in the interests of consistency to renounce the exercise of all powers of judgment in order to entertain the dream hypothesis and pass judgment on it. According to the latter, the thinking and judging excluded from usual dreams are present in this one.

When the dream hypothesis is stated in its essential terms, quite benign consequences result from the rampant unreality brought to light by the self-referential manoeuvre. This is because the unreality reduces finally to a matter of dependence on the awareness of a particular subject, the dreamer. It might be correctly argued that certain judgments of such a dreamer could not be well founded—for example, a conviction that it was raining in the waking world. Yet it seems exaggerated to claim that the dreamer could not turn out to be right about any such judgment, right even where the judgment is warranted by the evidence, as with the reflection that the world is perhaps a dream. Analogous conclusions apply whether the author of the illusory world is some wily demon or an electrode stimulating scientist.

The self-referential manoeuvre does not exhaust the possibilities of self-destruction open to a skeptical thesis. A subtler possibility much discussed in recent times is that the thesis is in contradiction not with itself but with its own presuppositions. We shall postpone briefly examination of the claim. First, let us consider the coherentist or objectivist view that the source of all our difficulties is a mistaken epistemological approach, a foundationalist one in which reasons are sought where they are not needed, and the perception described is not perception as it actually occurs.

CHAPTER FOUR

THE APPEAL TO PERCEPTION

SKEPTICISM AND FOUNDATIONALISM

Objectualism, or coherentism as it is commonly termed, is the view that any empirical inquiry presupposes the existence of at least some everyday material objects such as books and brooks, cats and cabbages, as well as the everyday relations among such objects. It rejects as ill-conceived the foundationalist view of epistemology according to which knowledge of the world is a structure of empirical truths based ultimately on experiential data, or observations of apparent colors, shapes, pressures, textures, odors, and sounds. Objectualism esteems the fundamental observations to be rather the common everyday ones about full-blown, three-dimensional, real, and relatively permanent objects. Very often it adds that none of the observations is immune to rectification and that the prime criterion for acceptance or rejection is coherence or failure to cohere with the existing body of knowledge claims. The cognitive enterprise of understanding the world is considered appropriately described through Neurath's metaphor of a ship on the open sea: the sailors may repair the ship (here the body of knowledge) only plank by plank while relying on the rest to stay afloat and may never rebuild afresh in dry dock.[1]

In objectualist circles, the somewhat widespread diagnosis of skeptical problems is that such problems are peculiar to a foundationalist epistemology. Michael Williams, for instance, articulates just such a view when he declares, "once we give in to the idea that empirical knowledge needs to be placed on a foundation, we become vulnerable to skeptical attack," or when he states alternatively, "once we abandon the foundational view, our knowledge of the physical world is secure."[2] J. L. Austin is equally accusatory of the foundational approach in his estimation that one of its tenets, the tenet of the general vulnerability of statements about objects, is "one of the major devices by which skeptical theses have commonly been insinuated."[3] F. L. Will succinctly sums up his rejection of the traditional problem of the justification of inductive procedures with an analogous imputation: "It is that the justification problem is a problem within Cartesian philosophy, one which cannot properly be dealt with in isolation from the theses and preconceptions about knowledge which are at work in that philosophy."[4] Richard Rorty levels a quite distinct but no less serious charge against Cartesian philosophy: "the seventeenth century gave skepticism a new lease on life because of its epistemology, not its philosophy of mind. Any theory which views knowledge as accuracy of representation, and holds that certainty can only be had about representations, will make skepticism inevitable."[5]

If these allegations were well founded, and skepticism was in fact the peculiar creation of a misguided epistemology, then the three skeptical problems of interest to us would arise only in the context of that epistemology and could be expected to fall with it. However, as we shall see, the case against foundationalism is quite overstated, and preservation from skeptical misgivings requires more serious action than a mere renunciation of the charms of foundationalist activities.

Let us begin with the Problem of Reality with its associated solipsistic and related scenarios involving deceitful demons and vat-dwelling brains. The claim to be evaluated is the contention that hypotheses such as the dream hypothesis arise only within a foundationalist context, that is, only in a context where an attempt is being made to trace the derivation of all knowledge from more rudimentary statements than ones about material objects. The claim is eminently implausible when more closely examined. In the dream hypothesis itself, no allusion is made to mere present fragments of the world as opposed to mature, replete objects. The ephemeral profiles with which the foundationalist attempts to construct a world are no more and no less imputed to be the characters in a vast dream than are the structured and stable objects with which a coherentist works. The dream hypothesis could in fact arise in either epistemological context. Plato's earlier-mentioned characterization of it as a familiar question implies as much. The context in which Descartes introduces the hypothesis is an everyday one where he is sitting by the fire, and the rebuttal Descartes finally proposes in the last paragraph of the *Meditations* is, apart from an allusion to divine veracity, a strictly coherentist appeal to the connectedness and consistency of perceptions. None of this implies that the dream hypothesis is peculiar to a foundationalist context.

This said, it must be admitted that Unreal World Solipsism can only plausibly arise in an egocentric view of the world, i.e., in a first-person rather than a third-person epistemological account. If one adopts the point of view of science, the view of the objective eye in which one figures along with all other human beings as a third person, then there is little question of asking whether the world is one's own dream. Solipsism generally is quite incongruous in a third-person point of view.

While the point is well taken, it should be noted first of all that the first-person/third-person dichotomy is far from identical with the foundationalist/objectualist one. It is possible in principle to adopt any of four distinct epistemological approaches: first-person foundationalist, first-person objectualist, third-person foundationalist, third-person objectualist. Austin and Gurwitsch are instances of epistemologists who have adopted the second, while Quine's naturalized epistemology might be considered an instance of the third.

More importantly, any third-person account not founded on a first-person one is in a tenuous position with regard to skeptical doubts. One's epistemological position in the world, however much one may prefer it to be otherwise, is in point of fact a first-person point of view, not a third-person one. For each of us, things ultimately make sense, are understandable, and are reasonable only at the first-person level. A third-person point of view can only be secure if built on first-person foundations. If it is adopted in a blind leap of faith, it is ipso facto irrational and hence vulnerable to skeptical challenge. It is true that a first-person point of view opens the door to solipsistic theses. This state of affairs, regrettable or not, provides solipsism with a standing invitation, one that can be definitively revoked only by answering the solipsistic challenge on the first-person epistemological level where it arises.

Analogous remarks are in order in the case of the Problem of the External World. The problem may arise in any account in which perception is seen to involve representations of objects rather than the objects themselves—in person, as it were. The potential for the problem goes back at least as far as Empedocles, while the problem itself is clearly present as a necessary condition in the debate between Stoics and Academicians. It might arise in a coherentist context as well as in a foundationalist one, since a representational account of perception can be grafted on either approach as a supplementary complication occasioned by the need to explain certain perceptual phenomena. The epistemological accounts of Quine and Sellars are two instances among many of coherentist positions complicated with a representational theory of perception—hence, of coherentist positions in which the External World Problem is susceptible of being raised. In this regard, it is significant that Descartes's own solution to the problem (an appeal to divine disinclination to create a deceptive world) qualifies neither as foundationalist nor coherentist.

It is a somewhat curious historical accident that the Representational Theory of Perception was given its first elaborate philosophical formulation in modern times by the father (or grandfather) of foundationalist epistemology. When Rorty fuses foundationalism with representationalism, as he does throughout *Philosophy and the Mirror of Nature*, he is following a long tradition of fusion and confusion initiated with Descartes, institutionalized by the British empiricists, and swallowed whole by a long line of more recent thinkers from Russell and the early Wittgenstein to present-day lab-coated epistemologists. Despite the heavy weight of tradition, the problem of the justification of everyday tenets in terms of the data of actual perception, and the problem of the nature of the reality beyond the 'veil of ideas' are two distinct problems, either of which conceivably might arise quite independently of the other, or conceivably be resolved in like isolation.

While foundationalism is clearly unconnected to the above two forms of solipsism, it is equally clearly linked closely to a third. This third form questions the existence of objects, properties, and relations that are unperceived. The things actually perceived with their perceived relations and characteristics, together provide the hard-core empirical data admitted by foundationalism. These entities and characteristics are precisely the ones to which Sense Data Solipsism restricts the world in its denial of the existence of anything unobserved. Thus there is obviously a close relationship between foundationalism and radical skepticism. It is less obvious what it is.

A first observation that might be thought relevant is the following: skeptical doubts of the kind leading to radical skepticism arise naturally enough in a foundationalist epistemology, particularly if difficulties are encountered in the pursuit of the foundationalist goal; in sharp contrast, such doubts are quite incongruous within an objectualist or coherentist epistemology. Yet the observation is less potent than it seems. Doubts regarding the existence of material objects are inconsonant with a coherentist account simply because they are ruled out by the assumptions of that account. In particular, it is assumed at the outset that at least some material objects exist. Consequently, the claim that in an objectualist account there is no skeptical problem of material objects is at bottom a thinly disguised tautology. It is analogous to a eulogist observation on the part of a be-feathered medicine man that his ontology is not plagued by skepticism with regard to the existence of evil spirits. Clearly, any skeptical doubts, including doubts about the existence of full-fledged material objects, must be an affliction specific to a belief system that admits of their being entertained.

Doubts about the existence of objects are, then, peculiar to foundationalism in the sense that they are not in contradiction with foundationalist assumptions, whereas they are ruled out at the outset by coherentist ones. Yet, it by no means follows from the above that skeptical doubts or skeptical theses are the product of a foundationalist enterprise. Indeed, a like imputation of responsibility would be clearly at variance with historical fact. In Descartes's reflections, the dialectical movement is not from a foundationalist epistemology to skeptical doubts but quite the reverse. Skeptical doubts regarding the existence of material objects lead Descartes to a protofoundationalist position, one in which the empirical ingredients are something less than everyday objects, and the task is one of demonstrating the existence of full-blown objects from such ingredients in conjunction with an undefined set of rational principles. Descartes does not initiate his inquiry with sense datum statements of the kind, "it is certain I seem to see light," but rather is driven to such statements by skeptical qualms.[6] When he leaves the comfortable position of everyday belief, it is not because he finds a deviant epistemology irresistibly attractive, but because he finds the everyday position vulnerable to skeptical doubt.

Furthermore, unless objectualism can produce sound reasons to justify its approach, the latter comes down simply to an arbitrary and hence questionable ruling. The point warrants considerable stressing. It is neither a necessary truth nor an unchallengeable one that everyday objects exist, any more than it is necessary or self-evident that their existence should be presupposed in any proper epistemology. As is the case for any existence claim, sound reasons must be given for adopting the objectualist claim that everyday objects exist (or must be assumed to exist). It is a fact of life, and not a dictate of a misconceived epistemology, that one does not actually perceive fully fleshed out material objects. In visual perception, far sides and interiors are in most cases hidden from view, while in tactual perception the outside is rarely, if ever, fully embraced, and the interior is perceived as mere resistance. It is also a fact of life that at any given time incalculable numbers of things are assumed to exist out in the world in the continuation of the space in which reside the things actually perceived. The assumptions made regarding the existence of things in the world ostensibly go quite far beyond what is actually perceived. These facts of life are what make objectualism ultimately vulnerable to a request for warrant in the form of a justification for the assumptions made. The answer to the request may take and has taken a wide variety of forms. This answer, which amounts to a defence of objectualism, also coincides in the last analysis with an objectualist answer to Sense Data Solipsism. In the circumstances it cannot be cogently claimed that skepticism is the exclusive product of an aberrant foundationalist epistemology.

NORMAL PERCEPTUAL EXPERIENCE AND SENSE DATA

We are left, then, with the objectualist or coherentist dismissal of foundationalism as a misconceived enterprise. The dismissal might be thought extraneous to present concerns in that it makes no mention of skepticism. Nevertheless, it does relate indirectly to Ephemerata and Sense Data Solipsism in at least two ways. If foundationalism is rightly dismissed as a nonviable epistemological approach, then the only possible approach remaining is objectualism, a doctrine of which the central tenets are in contradiction with these two forms of solipsism. Furthermore, since both foundationalism and Sense Data Solipsism deal in entities termed 'sense data,' many points presented in the criticism of foundationalism are bound to apply equally well (or badly) to the radical form of solipsism. Thus, it cannot be too far beside the point at this juncture to examine the more salient criticisms brought against foundationalism.

An important and frequently made coherentist criticism of a sense datum epistemology is that it totally misrepresents the nature of normal perceptual experience. Such experience is always of objects and of relations among objects, so the criticism runs; it is never an awareness of those rather odd ephemeral sensuous entities the existence of which the sense datum theorist feels compelled to posit. The sense data of foundationalism and radical skepticism are not to be found as constituents in normal experience; they are, on the contrary, quite fictitious entities conjured up to satisfy extraneous exigencies. Indeed, so it is claimed, an impartial inspection of ordinary perceptual experience comes up with several negative findings, each with awkward implications for foundationalist enterprises and related skeptical scenarios. These findings are that within ordinary perceptual experience:

1. There is no awareness of a peculiar sort ('direct' or 'immediate' awareness) having sense data alone as its object.

2. There is no awareness of sense data.

3. There are no sense data.

Let us peer briefly at each.

The concept of 'direct awareness' or 'immediate awareness' is traditionally made to play an important role in sense datum theory. It purportedly explicates the nature of the awareness involved in an awareness of sense data and incidentally allows that awareness to be distinguished from the one involved in the perception of material objects. The awareness of sense data is defined by H. H. Price, it would seem aptly enough, as an awareness "not reached by inference nor by any other intellectual process (such as abstraction or intuitive induction), nor by any passage from sign to significate."[7] The criticism of sense datum theory on this point is that direct awareness so defined cannot be rightly claimed to be peculiar to sense data. Sensuous qualities, the actual presence of which in the experience is denied by a sense datum theorist, are nevertheless, so the objection runs, present in the same way as those of which the presence is undisputed. In a well-known article Roderick Firth puts the point as follows: "The experience of a man looking at a distant mountain from a warm room might comprise both whiteness and coldness, each in precisely the same manner and neither in any other manner."[8] Firth goes on to argue the equally important point that "the direct and immediate experience of anyone who looks at the world about him...always consists of a number of full-bodied *physical objects*."[9] Direct awareness is not an awareness peculiar to sense data and exclusive of objects, and consequently, Firth concludes, a distinction essential to sense datum theory collapses.

These observations are sound enough with regard to the particular point that much perception involves no reasoned inference and hence qualifies as direct awareness. An awareness of the coldness of snow on a distant mountain may well be direct in this sense. Nevertheless, what the criticism manages to do primarily is to dispose of an infelicitous characterization of the awareness peculiar to sense data. Significantly enough, when Moore introduces the concept of 'direct apprehension,' he repeatedly explains the distinction he wishes to draw in terms of what he actually perceives. In particular, he explicitly states, "I shall express this relation, which I certainly do have to a sensible when I actually see or hear it...by saying that there is in my mind a *direct apprehension* of it."[10] Considerable misunderstanding and unnecessary controversy might easily have been avoided with the coining of a more appropriate expression, 'actual perception.' The notion of 'actually seeing' or 'actually hearing' is certainly current enough in everyday commerce. In particular it figures in the evaluation of testimony at criminal trials, where it may be of crucial importance to distinguish what the witness actually saw or heard from what he or she is inclined to claim to have seen or heard. Hence, it provides sense datum theory with a familiar concept requiring only supplementary sharpening to suit its purposes. Even this rough distinction between what is perceived and what is actually perceived suffices to class the whiteness of distant snow among present sense data (it is actually seen), and to exclude the coldness of the snow (the coldness is not actually felt). Similarly, it classes the visible side of a page and the felt mass between fingers and thumb among present sense data, and excludes the hidden far side and the roughness of the edge of the cover.

The second of the negative findings is the claim that any awareness of sense data is absent from normal perceptual experience. The focus of attention in ordinary perception is some object, or aspect of an object or relationship among objects, so the claim runs, never a sense datum. Even in the case of the perception of an unknown object, investigation begins with what might be termed "an ostensible material object" (to borrow from Firth's terminology), a relatively undetermined object to be fleshed out through further experience. An awareness of sense data arises only with a radical change of attitude toward what is perceived, or more specifically, with the abandonment of usual pursuits and the raising of the question of what is actually perceived. The awareness specific to this changed attitude is hardly current, since, as Pollock points out, much hard work is necessary to achieve it[11] (an observation corroborated by von Helmholtz in his keen introspective studies of visual phenomena[12]). Furthermore, it is not uncommon for initiates in the operation of reducing an experience to what is actually perceived, to be quite surprised by what is found actually present. Such surprise is difficult to reconcile with the thesis that the awareness of sense data is an ingredient in the original unreduced experience.

Yet neither Sense Data Solipsism nor rational foundationalism need object to any of the above observations. In ordinary perception there is seldom awareness of sense data in the usual sense where "to be aware" means "to have as the focus of attention." This fact does not exclude the possibility of marginal awareness. All ordinary perception involves a marginal awareness of a wealth of further items beyond the one on which interest in centered. Let us say I look up at a thin book on a shelf of books, then look away. Let us say there is a second book, a blue one, sitting among the numerous books on the shelf. In some sense it is true that I see the blue book; it is not hidden, and so is undoubtedly present in some form along with its lettering, size and color, all of which help to constitute the background against which I see the thin book. As is commonly said after the event in such cases, I must have seen it. Yet in another sense I must say that I did not: I may be disinclined to mention it in a report of what I saw and perhaps incapable of doing so in the allotted time before the memory of it fades. In the limiting case, it is quite possible for me to look directly at something and fail to see it—to see without noticing—because my attention is divided or elsewhere. Awareness comes in a variety of modes, so it is an error to demand that all awareness be full awareness.

One mode of awareness is the actual awareness of sense data. In an everyday situation it is quite possible to claim to have been aware of some fact, P, and after consideration to revise one's estimate and to say that while one thought at the time one was aware that P, one was actually aware only that P_0. Of such a nature is the Cartesian reevaluation of the perceiving of men in the street as an actual perceiving only of hats and coats. Reevaluations of the sort presuppose an actual awareness distinct from the awareness central to the experience. A refusal to countenance such an awareness is by the same token a refusal to countenance court testimony in which a distinction is drawn between what a witness actually perceived and what that witness is disposed to claim to have perceived. There is apparently nothing to be cogently argued in favor of such a refusal.

The third finding enumerated earlier, the claim that in ordinary experience there are no sense data, would seem more the fruit of abstract reasoning than of observation. Given the fact that an experience may contain much more than the particular item to which the experiencer is attentive, sense data cannot be divorced from the experience on the mere ground that they are not the focus of attention. There is, it should be noted, no other plausible ground.

Firth attempts to find such a ground in charging incompatibility. He argues that in view of the difference in sensuous qualities and spatial characteristics between a sense datum and an ostensible material object, "it is difficult to see how there could be *room,* so to speak, for such conflicting sets of sensuous qualities in one and the same state of perceptual consciousness."[13] The conflict in qualities is used to suggest that the sense datum qualities cannot possibly be present. Yet it may be as readily concluded that the object qualities cannot possibly be present. Furthermore, the latter is the more plausible conclusion.

Consider the implications of excluding the sense datum qualities. Let us suppose that the adoption of a critical attitude toward the experience of seeing a white piece of paper reveals the color actually seen to be a yellowish grey. Now if the sense datum color was not present in the original experience, it would follow that the operation of 'reducing' the experience, that is, the mere activity of inquiring as to what is actually seen, had the power to change the white of the original experience into the yellowish gray of the reduced one. Such a transformation is not credible. Reducing must have rather a quite different effect, that of bringing about a change in judgment rather than a change in sensuous properties. The perceiver is made aware of what is actually there in the original experience, the actual shapes and colors, instead of merely reacting to them on cue through the exercise of acquired labeling habits. The discounting of actual appearances in favor of the thing's presumed real color and shape is perhaps as much a self-imposed discipline for managing the pragmatically superfluous complexity of things, as a practice inculcated by training in some crude and expedient linguistic classificatory scheme or other. The result is not "conflicting sets of sensuous qualities in one experience" but a conflict between what is actually there and the classificatory label imposed upon it—or more precisely, between what is actually there and the expectations aroused by a simplistic interpretation of the crude label. One of the more extreme consequences of the training is that a rose in the dark gets labeled 'crimson,' despite the fact that it is ostensibly black. Such is the power of indoctrination. Worth noting, of course, is the fact that no sensuous quality of crimson disputes the occupancy of the visual field with the black actually present—and that the black cannot plausibly be excluded from the experience on the grounds that the crimson leaves no room for it.

Finally, there is the finding that the careful scrutiny of ordinary experience fails to support the claim of a sharp dichotomy in perception between what is given and the interpretation of that given. Aaron Gurwitsch is one among many to point out that in seeing a geometrical configuration or listening to a melody, one has no awareness of two components, a sensuous given and its interpretation, and in particular no awareness of any nonsensory process; rather, Gurwitsch claims, the figure and the melody have "the same immediacy and intuitive freshness" as a color or a tone.[14] Gurwitsch is also one of many to point out that in most perception the sensuous items involved are not related by mere conjunction; they form a structure organized into privileged constituents that carry the interest and others that serve as a background. A change of interest causes a transformation of the total field, together with a transformation of certain of the material elements themselves. Says Gurwitsch, the boundary line in Ruben's well-known vase/profile figure is no longer the same line after a change in the meaning of the figure.[15] The implication is that interpretation permeates the given. Firth argues an analogous point with the claim that "simplicity, regularity, harmoniousness, clumsiness, gracefulness" all have the same status phenomenologically as color and shape, and that the same is true of the qualities describable as "feline," "reptilian," "ethereal," or "substantial."[16]

These various observations regarding aesthetic and physiognomic characteristics and the findings of Gestalt psychology should, however, create no difficulties for the rational foundationalist. It is easily determined that most of the characteristics in question may be claimed to be actually perceived and hence to be on a par with color and shape. The quasi depth of a figure/ground configuration is actually perceived, as are the grace and simplicity of a movement, its felinity, or ethereality. In each case it is a matter of geometric and rhythmic characteristics plainly visible in the present phenomena, characteristics the presence of which is no less actually perceived than the presence of color and shape. Phenomena of the kind undoubtedly create difficulties for a foundationalist bent on construing sense fields as tidy x-dimensional arrays of sense qualities but not for one more toughened to the vagaries of the world. More importantly for our concerns, they leave intact the foundationalist distinction between what is actually perceived and what clearly is not, to wit, the hidden portions of things, causal connections, the reality of the everyday world. Consequently, they have no bearing on the skeptical problems of concern to us, the issue of the continued existence of what is not actually perceived or the issue of the permanent possibility of illusions. Their introduction into the present context would be an exercise in irrelevancy.

NORMAL PERCEPTUAL INQUIRY AND RATIONAL FOUNDATIONALISM

Yet another common criticism of foundationalism is that it presents a quite erroneous account of perception in that it totally misrepresents normal perceptual practices and procedures. According to the proposed foundationalist model of perceptual inquiry, all everyday empirical statements of fact are inferred by rules of inference and logical transformation from a foundation of incorrigible statements regarding the data of sense. The point that ordinary perception does not in fact conform to such a model has been variously and vigorously and frequently argued, but never more succinctly and incisively than by Austin in *Sense and Sensibilia*.[17] The main points of Austin's criticism are that incorrigibility is the prerogative of no particular type of statement as such, since sense datum statements may be misdescriptions while material object statements may be in fact incorrigible given the circumstances of utterance; that the providing of evidence is the exclusive function of no particular kind of statement; and that conclusive verification is often a quite feasible operation involving a limited number of appropriate checks and is not, as foundationalism would have it, the interminable and nebulous task of checking all statements entailed by the statement to be verified. The moral drawn by Austin is that the central foundationalist question, that of how object statements relate to sense datum statements, is not a genuine question. Says Austin, it is "a quite unreal question. The main thing is not to be bamboozled into asking it at all."[18]

Foundationalism is often criticized also on a more general level. The account assumes two distinct sources of empirical knowledge, one a sensuous given that yields independent nuggets of pure empirical data, and the other, a set of self-evident rational truths or principles that allow the data to be used as evidence in support of statements about the more complex everyday objects. This second criticism denies that building materials of either type are available for the proposed construction. It is claimed, on one hand, that there is no pure uninterpreted and independent sensuous given of the sort envisaged and, on the other, that there is no sharp analytic/synthetic or necessary/contingent dichotomy separating truths of reason (or language) from factual truths. All truths are alike, it is claimed, in that they presuppose the truth of other factual truths and are susceptible of revision with a view to the accommodation of empirical findings.

While a number of these points are cogent enough, some are false and most are irrelevant to our present concerns. A first point needing to be made is that there are in fact two quite distinct foundationalist enterprises. One is the enterprise of justification initiated by Descartes, a task that differs markedly in aim pursued from the foundationalist enterprise traceable to Locke and Hume. The first undertaking has for its aim an answer to skeptical questions of warrant. The second has as its goal an adequate account of perception and human understanding. H. H. Price's classic, *Perception*, might be considered a paradigm case of this second type of foundationalist enterprise. Certain sense datum theorists, Russell for instance, pursue the two enterprises simultaneously. The two types are clearly distinct nevertheless. To mark the distinction, the Cartesian enterprise might be termed *rational foundationalism*, the Lockean, *descriptive foundationalism*.

Clearly, it would be considerably off the mark to criticize rational foundationalism for not giving an accurate account of perception. The self-appointed task of rational foundationalism is to answer skepticism, to work out in detail a rational derivation of commonsense beliefs showing how these beliefs are more certain, more reasonable, better justified, or more likely to be true than rival skeptical theses. To be successful it must produce a rational reconstruction, but it need not produce one that faithfully reflects perceptual procedures usual in twentieth-century Western adults. It need not even give an accurate description of how infants rationally acquire the fundamental beliefs that adults take for granted in their thinking—although the possibility that it might do so is certainly not to be excluded. Consequently, it would be quite unwarranted to fault rational foundationalism for not giving an adequate descriptive account, i.e., for not doing properly something it has, and indeed need have, no intention of doing.

Let us pass on to the issue of incorrigibility. It is true enough that two forms of skepticism, Ephemerata and Sense Data Solipsism and, by the same token, their faithful nemesis rational foundationalism do indeed accord sense datum statements preferential treatment as evidence. Yet they do so only in as much as such statements are statements of what is actually perceived. Any alleged empirical evidence other than sense datum reports, so the skeptic would maintain, consists apparently of quite gratuitous claims. The fact that sense datum reports are accorded preferential status does not entail that they are always successful or accurate reports. On this matter the skeptical position need presumably differ little from the one taken by Austin on the incorrigibility of such reports. Austin rightly remarks that such statements may well require qualification or retraction because of verbal slips, linguistic ignorance or inattention on the part of the speaker.[19] There is no reason to think that a Sense Data Solipsist or a rational foundationalist would be unwilling to envisage corrections of the kind. Indeed, the dangers listed by Austin threaten any attempt to give an account of the world, or more generally, they threaten any attempt at the verbalization of any view on any subject. For someone obsessed with incorrigibility, the thought must be a devastating one, but the solipsist and, by the same token, the foundationalist have been assumed to be eminently reasonable thinkers and thus surely ones who know when to make the necessary concessions to the human predicament.

This is perhaps an appropriate point at which to attempt to debone a pertinacious red herring. It is commonly alleged that to the fond eye of the foundationalist, any sense datum report is indubitable or absolutely certain or incorrigible. The myth has been fostered undoubtedly in part by Descartes's quest for what he explicitly states to be firm foundations. Yet on a moment's reflection, it is quite obviously the case that it is neither necessary nor even possible that sense datum reports in general should be indubitable or incorrigible. One of the main reasons for this fallibility is, simply stated, that there is too much going on during perception. Any perceptual judgments about events beyond the immediate focus of attention tend to become somewhat tenuous. Indeed no report whatever can be given of much of what is perceived, since it is part of a wealth of data of which there is but marginal and fleeting awareness. There can be little indubitability in reports regarding such data. Indubitability is best predicated of judgments about matters that are at the focus of one's attention, and when one is in possession of one's faculties, which is to say minimally centered, rested, and sober. Even here the judgment is certain only for the fleeting period prior to the fading of the experience and judgment into memory swiftly followed by oblivion. Any reasonable rational foundationalist will realistically recognize the tenuousness of sense datum information. As a result, it is difficult to see how instances of the dubitability or corrigibility of sense datum judgments could constitute a relevant objection to the sensibly conducted enterprise of a rational foundationalist epistemology.

In addition, it is not necessary that judgments regarding phenomena in the focus of attention should be indubitable. The proper concern of rational foundationalism is the answering of certain specific skeptical doubts, and not the acquisition of indubitable foundations. The issue of whether these doubts may be dispelled, and if so how, has little relation to any uncertainty attendant upon actual perception, whether focused or marginal. For instance, the uncertainty of the reports I might make about the visible side of a coffee mug is largely irrelevant to the question of whether or not the far side of the mug still exists when unperceived. Similarly, the uncertainty is irrelevant to the question of whether or not the mug is part of a vast dream.

Austin is quite right to claim that sense datum statements do not have a monopoly on the function of providing evidence. In fact, one may reasonably go further and endorse John Pollock's assessment that "in perception, the beliefs we form are almost invariably beliefs about the objective properties of physical objects—not about how things appear to us,"[20] or Anthony Quinton's accurate observation that descriptions of immediate experience are rarely offered as reasons for perceptual claims about material objects and ordinarily play no role at all as evidence.[21] Yet none of this bears on the issue. Where the skeptical request is for warrant for thinking that objects continue to exist unperceived, it is question-begging to appeal to instances of everyday evidence which simply assume continued existence. As noted earlier in the discussion of common sense, an appeal to everyday confirmation is irrelevant, since the confirmation fails to hold to the extent that it fails to address the skeptical request. For instance, to identify an object as a telephone is in part to recognize certain shapes, feels, and noises as being of the requisite sort. However, in as much as sortal identification also contains a predictive component, hence expectation of properties and relations not actually perceived, the identification can be at best a qualified success. As a skeptic might point out, Austin's telephone could be in fact a kangaroo at all times other than the ones at which the various observations were made—in which case its identification as a telephone becomes debatable.

We arrive now at the more general criticism, that the two building blocks alleged to provide the foundation of all empirical knowledge are items that do not in fact exist. Grossly stated, the case against the first of the two building materials is that there is not, nor can there be, any such thing as a perceived but uninterpreted datum; all perception involves conceptualization. Thus we find Quine characterizing the foundationalist's envisaged language of sense datum reports as "a fancifully fanciless medium of unvarnished news," Sellars condemning as a "radical mistake" the notion that epistemic facts are analyzable in terms of nonepistemic ones, and Williams proclaiming the incoherence of the notion that justification consists in a confrontation with "raw chunks of reality."[22] Each is defending in his own terms the dictum: no perception without conception.

The implications attributed the point lead in three distinct directions. One line pursued is that conceptualization involves quite complex structures with objectualist assumptions fatal to foundationalism. This particular claim is part of a much broader topic that will be considered only when we come to conceptual and linguistic parasitism arguments.

Another line pursued is that conceptualization introduces the possibility of error and so precludes the absolute certainty sought by the foundationalist. As Williams states the matter, "describing is not an activity which brings with it a logical guarantee of success."[23] Laurence BonJour argues somewhat similarly that any cognitive awareness, however rudimentary or primitive, has to involve something akin to a representation of an object or state of affairs, with the result that the question of justification may always be raised; reasons are required for thinking that the representation is "accurate or correct," and so the putative independent foundation cannot stand on its own.[24] Both Williams and BonJour are quite right, but since even a skeptic must recognize analogous possibilities of error in any statement made, the issue is of no relevance to present concerns.

The third line taken is the currently popular claim that there can be no independent basic empirical beliefs of the sort posited by foundationalism, i.e., basic beliefs that owe their justification to no other empirical beliefs. BonJour, for one, puts the point as follows: a basic fact would have to have some feature that confers likelihood of truth; to be aware that the fact was basic, the perceiver would have to be aware of the fact that the feature does indeed confer likelihood of truth, and hence be aware of some further general empirical fact; as a result, the belief would cease to be a basic belief for the perceiver.[25]

Yet the reasoning is off the mark. In the matter of awareness of sense data, it is inappropriate to speak of a likelihood-conferring feature. Consider the basic judgment that a possibly illusory color expanse of a certain shape is apparently located in a certain way with respect to another color expanse. The judgment counts as basic simply because of the absence of conceivable ways in which it could be false given the evidence (with the exception of incorrect conceptualization, whatever that may mean). The property in virtue of which it is basic is the inconceivability of its falsity within the context of what is actually perceived. It cannot properly be claimed that this property confers likelihood of truth, since it confers something closer to certainty. Nor can the fact that the property does confer truth be properly characterized as an empirical fact; it is closer to a logical truth.

The second type of building material, rational, necessary, or analytic truths broadly construed form a disparate lot. They comprise logical truths, definitions or statements of synonymy, mathematical truths, and a medley of independent candidates (so-called 'synthetic a priori truths' regarding the transitivity of temporal precedence, the spatiality of color, and so on.). The objectualist claim is that there is no sharp division between the four groups of necessary truths and empirical truths generally. Quine gives the view quite forceful formulation in a well-known paper, "Two Dogmas of Empiricism," in which he argues that the distinction cannot be cogently drawn.[26] The necessary/contingent distinction is of course independently undermined by twentieth-century physics. A variety of physical phenomena—the constant speed of light, the dual wave/corpuscular behavior of energy/matter, the inverse variation in accuracy of measurement of the position and momentum of subatomic particles, the peculiar behavior of polarized light, the non-Euclidian properties of space—all concur to make questionable the claim that possible states of affairs must conform to felt conceptual necessities. In this regard, Quine points out that there have been serious proposals to change logic so as to make logic reflect more closely Heisenberg's Principle of Indeterminacy and argues, not implausibly, that such proposals show logic to be "in principle no less open to revision" than are theories in physics.[27] Hilary Putnam makes a somewhat similar claim with regard to the unqualified assertion of the Law of Noncontradiction, when he argues for the conceivability of a scenario where it would be judged rational to attribute both truth and falsity to self-referential statements.[28]

Whatever the ultimate implications of considerations of the sort, their relevance to present concerns should not be overestimated. Even if they did establish that there was no hard distinction between necessary and contingent truths, it is obviously the case that the truth of objectualism and the existence of everyday objects would not follow. At best, they would provide highly suggestive support for the properly coherentist doctrine that no truth is immune to revision, a doctrine logically independent of objectualism and one that might conceivably hold in a foundationalist epistemology.

In any event, the drawing of a distinction between necessary and contingent statements is not an impossible task, for informal purposes, that is. A necessary truth on its broadest construal is one the falsity of which is inconceivable. For instance, it is inconceivable that in certain cases an aggregate of three items together with two other items should be less than five items, or more than five. Similarly, it is inconceivable that a particular state of affairs should both obtain and at the same time fail to obtain. For this reason, the denial of an analytic truth provokes, as Quine remarks, bewilderment as to what could be meant by the person making the denial; it is quite unclear what state of affairs is being envisaged.[29] The reason for the unclarity is not difficult to fathom: it is that no state of affairs is being envisaged; none can be since none is conceivable.

For the purposes of debating the skeptic, this distinction is quite sufficient. The issues raised by the skeptic have to do with the everyday world, with whether the things in that world continue to exist unobserved, with whether they are part of some general illusion. It is quite unclear how these issues could be in any way affected by the interesting but anemic possibility of the failure of logical truths in certain domains of physics. Furthermore, the distinction between truths that are not conceivably false and those that are is one that in fact the skeptic endorses, since it is operative in but slightly modified form within the skeptical dialectic itself. When the skeptic points out that everyday knowledge claims are conceivably false, the conclusion is based on the experiential fact that skeptical scenarios are conceivable given the evidence. The criterion to be satisfied in order to pass the skeptic's inspection is that no scenario other than the asserted state of affairs should be conceivable on the evidence. The criterion to be satisfied to qualify as an analytic truth is that no scenario other than the asserted state of affairs should be conceivable. The difference between the two is merely that in one case it is a matter of what is conceivable given certain evidence, in the other of what is conceivable regarding certain general structures of the world. Significantly enough, the groups of statements that pass the two tests are the groups that are admitted by the Sense Data Solipsist and consequently constitute the two types of building materials with which the rational foundationalist sets out to answer the skeptic.

EXPLANATORY COHERENCE AND RATIONALITY

Objectualism is commonly termed 'coherentism' because of the central role it accords to the criterion of coherence in the evaluation of competing hypotheses and explanations. If the criterion of coherence is a rational one, then the more coherent hypothesis, the one that best makes the evidence cohere or best coheres with it will be the hypothesis most likely to be true. To the extent that the criterion is in fact rational, it may well have a role to play in the rational foundationalist enterprise—as a criterion of likelihood of truth, of course, and not as a wet blanket to be thrown indiscriminately over any burning skeptical issue. Coherence is not the exclusive property of coherentism, and insofar as it is a putative criterion of likelihood, it may in principle participate in either a foundationalist or objectualist enterprise.

Confusion on the point might be forestalled to some extent by use of the term, *rationalized epistemology* rather than *rational foundationalism.*

It was noted at the outset that objectualism, and not coherentism proper, is the position opposed to foundationalism. The usual identification of objectualism with coherentism is in point of fact a rich source of confusion. Since 'coherence' suggests a truth-conferring property, the identification carries the suggestion that objectualism is an alternative way of doing epistemology, one with rival procedures and standards, or methods of evaluation, or an alternative way of conceptualizing the issues. The unadorned truth is that objectualism is an existence claim; it is first and foremost the thesis that everyday objects exist. When an epistemology is based on this claim (or the claim that such existence must be presupposed), then as a matter of course, coherence becomes its main criterion. On the everyday level, coherence is indeed the prime criterion for the arbitration of disputes between plausible, conflicting explanations and hypotheses. Because of the central role accorded it by objectualism, one might easily gain the impression that it has perhaps a valuable contribution to make toward settling the dispute between common sense and skepticism, and presumably settling it in favor of the former. A short excursus into an analysis of the concept is thus necessary if for no other reason than to remove the impression that coherence contains perhaps powerful and untapped resources with which to counter skepticism.

The criterion of coherence certainly plays a role of considerable importance in cognition, whether in the evaluation of rival accounts of chronological sequences of events in the everyday world, in murder mysteries, in historical reconstructions, and the like or in the evaluation of rival explanations in the various sciences. For instance, it might be argued with regard to a murder that the hypothesis of the culpability of the elderly aunt fails to fit the facts very well or fails to yield a very coherent account of what happened. In particular, perhaps, the hypothesis accords badly with the aunt's apparent lack of motive and requisite agility and gives no account whatever of the incongruous cigar-butt found beside the victim and the odd scratch on the butler's hand. In situations of the sort, the problem is to find the account that coheres best in view of the factual data and an assumed body of generalizations from a variety of domains (that people act from motives, cigars from gravity, and so on). In the evaluation of causal explanations, the task is similar in that it involves evaluating rival hypotheses according to how well they cohere or fit with a body of well-substantiated but revisable generalizations. In both types of case, there is a good deal of empirical material for the rival hypotheses to make cohere or to cohere with.

The situation with regard to skeptical theses is quite different. Consider the case of solipsistic theses questioning the reality of the world. If appeal was made to the criterion of coherence, the matter to be determined would be that of which one of two theses yields the most coherent account, the dream hypothesis, for instance, or its commonsense rival. It is far from obvious how to settle the issue. There seems little reason to claim that the commonsense view that the world is not a dream provides a more coherent account (or brings the data into a better fit) than the solipsistic thesis that the world is a dream. Indeed, the issue hardly seems an appropriate one to raise. Both theses are consistent with the data, but neither makes the data cohere or coheres with the data with a degree of success perceptibly superior to that of the other.

On reflection it is also soon clear that any attempt to use coherence against radical skepticism must also fail. Since the only data admitted are the bare instances of things actually perceived, there are no empirical generalizations or laws with which to cohere. Also it would seem to make no clear sense to claim that the thesis of continued unobserved existence coheres or fits better with the observed data than does the rival thesis of no observation, no existence. It is true that the items postulated by the commonsense thesis are more similar in nature to the observed items than are the instances of empty space postulated by the skeptical thesis, but such similarity hardly provides grounds for a claim of greater coherence or fit. In the present context, fit is not an aesthetic matter but an evidential one. Nor is there any clearer sense to the claim that the thesis of continued existence brings the data into a better fit, that is, not if the only evidence admitted consists of the mere instances of actually observed items. How is it a better fit for items to remain constant rather than to alternate with empty space?

The testimony of others might seem a promising evidential source. Other observers frequently make reports that imply the continued existence of objects hidden from one's own view and touch. Since assurances of the sort cannot be reconciled with a thesis of discontinued existence, adherence to the thesis requires espousal of the further claim that what others say in these cases is false. This claim in turn entails the further proposition that the psychology of others differs considerably in some way or other from one's own. In view of these implications, it might appear that the thesis of discontinuous existence is less plausible than its rival commonsense belief.

Yet such is not the case. The matter may be summed up as follows. The proponent of common sense espouses three theses denied by the proponent of discontinuous existence:

1. Objects continue to exist unobserved.

2. Testimony regarding places unobserved by oneself is on the whole likely to be made in good faith.

3. The psychology of others does not differ radically from one's own.

The claim being made is that the set of these three statements coheres better with the actual data than does the set of their three negations. Some support is needed for this claim. Certainly, the three statements support each other in the sense that each, if true, could be used as evidence in support of the other two. Yet as matters stand, each is unsupported by the actual data; it is simply consistent with that data. As much may be said of the three denials of the statements. Nor is there much promise in arguing that the skeptical denial of No. 1 leads to a denial of No. 3, thus insinuating that the skeptical position leads to a denial of a plausible truth. There is no independent support for that truth. Certainly, if there were any independent support for any of the three statements, support making it more likely to be true than its negation, then an argument for greater coherence could be made; either of the two remaining statements would cohere better with the data (enlarged) than would either of their respective negations. Yet likewise, if any of the three negations enjoyed independent support that made it more likely to be true than not, then an argument could be made to the effect that the two other negations better fit the data. What is needed is some measure of prior support, but as matters stand, there is none. If the practice of the evaluation of relative fit or coherence is to be applicable, it requires some measure of theoretical evidence in the form of independently supported generalizations of some form or other. For this reason, the prospects of success appear singularly slim for a coherence argument directed against a radical skeptical thesis.

The criterion of coherence is afflicted with a second and equally grave weakness making it singularly unfit for effective use against skepticism: the rationality of the criterion is not clear. Rationality in this context is a matter of relationship to truth. Even if it could be shown that a particular skeptical account is less coherent than its commonsense rival or fits the data less well, it would remain to be shown that this circumstance makes the skeptical account less likely to be true. It is not obvious that the world must resemble the more coherent model rather than the less coherent one. In the absence of a satisfactory account of the alleged connection, no case has been made against skepticism.

Part of the difficulty here is the nebulousness of the concept of coherence or fit. The concept must be clarified, a task not promising to be easy, and one that carries no guarantee of a successful demonstration of rationality. Coherence is clearly not a matter of mere consistency, since presumably one of two consistent hypothesis may be judged more coherent than the other. Keith Lehrer has proposed as a partial analysis of the concept the three criteria of consistency, closure (acceptability of deductive consequences), and nonarbitrariness.[30] The latter criterion, the only nonlogical criterion of the three, stands in need not only of further analysis but of rational justification. An arbitrary thesis is not necessarily a false one; hence the preferability of a nonarbitrary one must be spelled out and shown to be rationally warranted.

An analogous task awaits alternative analyses. Coherence is perhaps some combination of what Paul Thagard finds to be the three main criteria for evaluating explanations or explanatory theories in science: consilience, simplicity, and analogy. For Thagard, consilience is roughly a matter of the number of classes of facts explained; the more consilient the theory, the greater the number of classes of facts it explains.[31] Simplicity is a matter of the number of auxiliary hypotheses required, the simpler theory being the one that requires the fewer ad hoc hypotheses. Analogy comes down to this, that the likeness of a hypothesis to an accepted theory may be considered to be support either for the hypothesis itself or for some particular feature of it through analogical argument.[32] As Thagard points out, these three criteria do not provide necessary and sufficient conditions but rather standards that to some extent place constraints on each other.

On the somewhat plausible assumption that Thagard's three criteria are also to some degree criteria of coherence or fit, it remains to demonstrate that they are linked to truth in some interesting way. Otherwise stated, it must be shown that consilience, simplicity, and analogy provide warrant for truth. The need for such a demonstration should be clear. What reason is there to think, for instance, that the more consilient theory, the one which encompasses the greater number of classes of facts, is more likely to be true? How is comprehensiveness connected to truth? The answer is far from obvious, and yet, in the absence of an answer, there is no reason to consider consilience a rational criterion for evaluating competing hypotheses. Likewise, why should the simpler hypothesis, the one with the lesser number of ad hoc hypotheses, be more likely to be true? Why should not the world be one in which certain features are ad hoc, as it were? Alternatively, in virtue of what reason may it be claimed that the world is less likely to have ad hoc features? The answer is not immediately forthcoming.

The central point of the metaphor of the cognitive ship on the open sea is the claim that in cognition there is no getting back to a stage of world-building prior to the presence of material objects on the scene. Yet, in our above examination of criticisms of foundationalism, we have found no reason to accept such a claim. It is not self-evident that material objects and relations continue to exist when unobserved, that the tenet of continued existence is a plank so firmly fixed in the ship that it cannot be safely jettisoned. Indeed, it may be asked, what reason is there to think that the removal of the plank would jeopardize the ability of the ship to stay afloat? What grounds are there to preclude a general selective elimination and agile readjustment of planks or, alternatively, a whittling down of the complex structure into the sleeker craft championed by the Sense Data Solipsist? Analogously, what prevents a building up of the ship (as opposed to a trimming down) by the addition of some further embellishment to the hull in accordance with the taste for more fanciful and picturesque vessels of Oneirata or Demoniac Solipsism? If answers to these questions are to be found, appeal must be made to something more object-oriented than the criterion of coherence. One promising prospect is the claim that factual presuppositions involving full-fledged objects are an indispensable constituent in any empirical inquiry. The issue of presuppositions of the sort is the topic of the following chapter.

CHAPTER FIVE

EPISTEMIC PARASITISM

PARASITISM ARGUMENTS

The term, 'parasitical', makes what is apparently its first appearance in the literature in Wilfrid Sellars's well-known article, "Phenomenalism," where Sellars argues that "the frameworks of qualitative and existential appearings and of sense impressions are parasitical upon discourse concerning physical things."[1] The expression is an apt one. Natural parasites not only draw their sustenance from a host body but may survive only so long as they refrain from destroying the host. A philosophical position that is parasitic on some more general philosophical view can likewise be a viable position only so long as it does not advocate the destruction of its host. A currently widespread estimate of skepticism among professional philosophers is precisely that it undermines its own viability; it is suicidally parasitic in that it attacks the very everyday views, conceptual framework, and procedures that it presupposes for its own enunciation.

The notion of the parasitic nature of skepticism is itself much older. Its acknowledged progenitor is Immanual Kant's *Critique of Pure Reason* with its attempted answer to Hume and, more particularly, attempted refutation of Berkeley's idealism[2]—the Sensa Solipsism of the multitude, as it were. The recent proliferation of parasitism arguments directed against skeptical theses extends Kant's approach to terrain far beyond that trodden by Kant. It is worth noting that the view that skepticism is parasitic is not tied to a coherentist or objectualist epistemology with its claim that all inquiry, including that of the skeptic, presupposes the existence of objects. No less a foundationalist than Edmund Husserl is responsible for the following sanguine estimate:

"All genuine skepticism of whatever kind and persuasion is indicated by the essentially necessary countersense that, in its argumentations, it implicitly presupposes as conditions of the possibility of its validity precisely what it denies in its theses."[3] Parasitism arguments are perhaps best considered to be a natural development of the bipartisan self-referential manoeuvre encountered in chapter 3. They purport to show that the negative import of the skeptical thesis applies to the presuppositions on which the skeptical thesis itself is based.

To facilitate discussion, parasitism should be divided into two sorts, epistemic or factual, and, conceptual or linguistic. Since linguistic meaning and conceptual schemes evolve with accrued information, the distinction between the two must of course be somewhat artificial. *Epistemic parasitism* has to do with factual presuppositions; a form of skepticism that is epistemically parasitic has factual presuppositions the truth of which is denied by its own thesis. *Conceptual parasitism* or *linguistic parasitism* has to do with the presuppositions of a conceptual scheme and of language. We shall be concerned with epistemic parasitism in this chapter and take up conceptual parasitism only in chapter 8 after discussing linguistic arguments generally.

The self-referential manoeuvre effectuated in an epistemic parasitism argument can be executed only against those forms of skepticism that enunciate some factual thesis, whether an ontological thesis regarding the nature of the world or an epistemological one regarding the limits of human knowledge. The reason is the elementary one that in order for the skeptical attack to be turned against the skeptic's own thesis, there must be a skeptical thesis. If the skeptic's thesis is a purely logical one, for instance, the thesis that certain (or all) everyday beliefs are self-contradictory, then no parasitism argument against the skeptic's own view is possible. This fact allows Barry Stroud to point out rightly enough in his criticism of Quine's dismissal of skepticism that in principle a skeptical argument could be a mere *reductio ad absurdum* of the position of science.[4] The possibility does not concern the Cartesian solipsists, of course, since they put forth a particular account of the nature of the world.

Each of the two sorts of parasitism arguments (epistemic and conceptual) may be further divided into two types, *transcendental parasitism* and *parochial parasitism,* although once again the division is not always as clean-cut a one as a zealous taxonomist might wish. Parasitism of the first sort has to do with the presuppositions of any empirical inquiry whatever. The term 'transcendental' derives from Kant who used it to mean roughly 'pertaining to the possibility of necessary and universal (a priori) knowledge'.[5] The present-day use differs from

Kant's primarily in that the presuppositions considered need not be necessary truths. Parochial parasitism has to do with presuppositions peculiar to some particular concept or set of concepts and hence to some particular local, rather than cosmopolitan, skeptical thesis. In the present chapter, we shall examine three powerful attempts—by Wittgenstein, Heidegger, and Quine, respectively—to show skepticism guilty of transcendental epistemic parasitism. Then we shall turn to a parochial epistemic parasitism argument that Quine might have successfully made, one related to the External World Problem.

WITTGENSTEIN AND THE BACKGROUND OF INQUIRY

The reflections compiled in the book *On Certainty* contain the most extensive exposition of Wittgenstein's case for the inevitability of factual assumptions in everyday perceptual experience and linguistic commerce. In the latter activities, according to Wittgenstein, a special role is played by banal commonplace truths of the sort to which Moore appeals in his defence of common sense, truths such as one's having two hands, being dressed and present in a vast world that has existed for thousands of years, and so on. These truths are not truths to be discovered or enunciated. Their role is that of a necessary background, an indispensable condition for any inquiry. The world picture they constitute is variously characterized by Wittgenstein as the "matter-of-course foundation," the "inherited background," the "frame of reference," the "scaffolding," the "unmoving foundation" for all thinking and action, the "element" in which any inquiry has its life.[6] Their role is likened by Wittgenstein to that of logical truths, or to that of definitions.[7] Such truths are incontrovertible, and cannot be touched: they are anchored in all questions and answers; they do not admit of possible mistakes—or more precisely, the supposition of a mistake is impossible in the normal case, just as it is nonsensical to suppose one in the majority of cases.[8] The appropriate metaphor for the cognitive enterprise is once again Neurath's ship on the open sea, but a ship with bolted-down planks, and equipped, as it were, with mere caulking knife and paint scraper for repair kit.

In favor of his analysis Wittgenstein presents a variety of considerations susceptible of condensation into three main ones. The first of these has to do with the dictates of what might be termed 'usage grammar,' the rules of which dictate the appropriateness of statements (or lack of same). It is inappropriate to state of background truths that one knows them, that one learns them or believes them. Wittgenstein finds an illustration of this fact in the curious effect produced by Moore's attempted proof of the existence of objects. Moore's claim to know that his hand exists has an effect quite the opposite of the one intended; what was previously a straightforward matter becomes "unclear and blurred" so that, instead of agreeing with Moore, one feels inclined to deny that Moore knows anything of the sort. Wittgenstein finds the explanation of this curious state of affairs to be that one cannot correctly speak of knowing in contexts such as those chosen by Moore. One may speak of knowing only where it is possible to check, to satisfy oneself, to make sure, whereas no checking is possible in the present instance.[9] Wittgenstein's point is that where the verb "to know" may be used, it is possible to give grounds, to say how one knows, or to imagine how a thing of the kind may be known. Yet in the case of one's having two hands, there are apparently no grounds to be given and no checks to be run to see if one is right. Looking to see is hardly a check, for as Wittgenstein points out, one's having two hands is not less certain before looking than afterwards.[10] It is equally unclear, of course, what would count *against* one's having two hands. Indeed, Wittgenstein asks, how should we imagine the mistake being discovered?[11] In cases of the sort involving commonsense claims, we have no clearer idea of what would disprove the claim than we have of what would verify it. For this reason, Wittgenstein questions the soundness of an argument sometimes given in support of everyday truths, that everything speaks for and nothing against them. The argument incorrectly assumes that there are criteria for and against, says Wittgenstein; what, for instance, speaks in favor of the notion that a table is still there when no one sees it?[12] As the reader has perhaps noticed, Wittgenstein's remarks touch upon and possibly explain the awkward fact encountered in chapter 2, that skeptical scenarios are apparently data-unchallenged.

One consequence of the peculiar function performed by background truths is, according to Wittgenstein, that the very use of the expression, "true or false," with regard to statements of such truths is slightly misleading; it is unclear what tallying with the facts or agreement with reality amount to in such contexts.[13] The very statement Moore sets out to prove, the statement that there are physical objects, can no more be correctly stated than the claim to know such things; both are forms of nonsense. They are senseless not in the manner of meaningless combinations of words but in the manner of "Good morning" said to someone in the course of a conversation; their assertion is contextually inappropriate. In the same way, says Wittgenstein, when sitting at the bedside of a sick person, it makes no sense to declare that one knows that the person is sick.[14]

The second key point in Wittgenstein's observations is that language games are possible only through trust or through the unquestioning acceptance of everyday truths. Wittgenstein abundantly illustrates the point. In the game of chess, the attempt to checkmate precludes having certain doubts, scenarios involving autonomous moves on the part of the pieces and concomitant memory lapses. Similarly, for an order to be obeyed, there must be some empirical facts beyond doubt. In a game in which one is to open a door on call, a doubt regarding the existence of the door is excluded. Testing of any kind likewise presupposes something that is not tested. Doing an experiment assumes the existence of the apparatus used; doing a calculation assumes that the figures stay put, and that one's memory is trustworthy. Moore's claim to knowledge regarding his hand, is rather a claim to be able to speak of the hand in various language games with no doubt about its existence.[15] Any questioning, even the very activity of doubting, must make analogous assumptions, says Wittgenstein: "the *questions* that we raise and our *doubts* depend upon the fact that some propositions are exempt from doubt, as it were like hinges on which those turn."[16] Implied is the charge that the skeptic attacks the presuppositions of his own inquiry.

A third and not unrelated point stressed by Wittgenstein is that skeptical questioning of everyday truths amounts to the annihilation of all yardsticks and the toppling of all judgment. The practical necessity of having presuppositions is not a matter of insufficient time for investigation, with a resulting hasty but excusable decision to get on with the job. What is at stake here is the very matter of making sense. Says Wittgenstein, we could not confidently claim to understand a man who could not remember if he always had two hands. Or again, if I should mistakenly claim to be a woman, and then explain the mistake as a failure to check, it would become questionable whether I understood the words I was using. Yet again, if one doubted the existence of one's body, or denied Moore's commonsense truths, one would be taken for a half-wit or regarded as demented.[17] Such matters are presuppositions of intelligibility. To doubt the existence of one's hand, Wittgenstein argues, is tantamount to doubting whether the word 'hand' has any meaning. Says Wittgenstein, I should "stand before the abyss" with such a doubt, a fact he takes to show that "absence of doubt belongs to the essence of the language game."[18]

None of these points manages in fact to establish Wittgenstein's claim that a background of factual presuppositions is necessary to any empirical inquiry. It is true enough that as a matter of usage grammar, knowledge claims are not made with respect to everyday banalities. Assurances are tendered only about points on which the interlocutor is thought to be in some doubt. One may rightly speak of an assumed background made up of those statements about which it would be inappropriate to make knowledge claims. Yet this background varies considerably with context and speakers. No lucid chemist would ever assure another such chemist that the atomic number of gold is 79, whereas a beginning chemistry student might so assure another. Similarly, in the case of a hospital bedside conversation, the example chosen by Wittgenstein, one child ignorant of the function of hospitals might well assure another that the patient is indeed ill. It would seem safe to conclude that any common background of necessary presuppositions would have to be delimited by some criterion other than a general one of linguistic propriety.

Wittgenstein might argue that the needed criterion is the absence of criteria—that the common background is constituted by those statements for which no support may be given. Yet other difficulties then arise. A skeptic would readily agree that there are apparently no criteria for the banal perceptual judgments at issue in skeptical theses. The skeptic may reasonably go on to argue that this merely leaves quite open the question of whether or not commonsense assumptions are true, since the absence of criteria leaves commonsense claims and skeptical ones on equal evidential footing. It must be shown not just that the banal truths are in fact assumed but that they must be assumed and that they cannot cogently be replaced by their skeptical rivals.

On the other hand, the rational foundationalist may reasonably object that Wittgenstein has not shown that there are no criteria appropriate to settling banal matters of fact; he has only shown that the criteria are not made explicit in everyday circumstances. The fact that the adult interlocutor is at a loss to meet a request for criteria is admittedly suggestive but hardly conclusive. As noted earlier, Moore's opinion on the matter is that in the past we did indeed have evidence for such commonsense truths but that at present we no longer remember what that evidence was. Moore's view is hardly so implausible as to warrant the claim that any future operations in cognitive excavation are doomed to failure.

Stated more fully, Wittgenstein's view is that one learns the commonsense world picture as a child, swallowing it down unquestioningly, prior to any knowing and presumably prior to any intelligent thinking.[19] He holds apparently that the view is passed on from generation to generation, for he states, "Perhaps it was once disputed.

But perhaps, for unthinkable ages, it has belonged to the *scaffolding* of our thoughts. (Every human being has parents.)"[20] Children are not taught that books and armchairs exist, Wittgenstein rightly observes, but to fetch books and to sit in armchairs. In the process of learning and observing these various activities, they acquire pieces of a picture of the world, part of a 'mythology' that remains largely implicit but functions as the background on which true is distinguished from false.[21] Reflections of the sort belong, of course, to the domain of armchair child psychology. As such, they are certainly not more compelling prima facie than the views of Moore. Wittgenstein does not seem to have entertained the possibility that the unperceived continued existence of books may well be something infants figure out for themselves prior to, and hence independently of, the cultural inculcation of facts about the world.

The second main point in Wittgenstein's account of factual presuppositions is the claim that all language games presuppose trust and that consequently even skeptical theorizing must rest in some measure on trust. Now, it is true enough that trust plays an indispensable role in much everyday inquiry, whether it is a matter of trust in experimental apparatus, door hinges, or pencil marks on paper. Nevertheless there seems little prospect of exploiting the situation in an effective way against any of the various forms of skepticism with which we are concerned. For one thing, trust is clearly not required in the particular language game of doubting. The activity itself is a mere suspension of judgment and search for justification, an activity in which trust plays no obvious role.

Even in the language game of empirical inquiry proper, it may be questioned whether all moves necessitate trust and, in particular, trust inconsistent with skeptical theses. Trust obviously plays a very important role in everyday investigation, the more so the more reliance there is on tools or apparatus of some sort. Conversely, however, with the elimination of reliance on apparatus and the resorting to more rudimentary subjects of investigation, the role of trust reduces drastically to become quite minimal. Consider the case of groping in the dark with a hand to see if any obstacle is encountered. The trust required for such activity comprises at the most the assumptions that one's hand (the tactual mass) will continue to exist in the immediate future, that it will go where one expects it to go, that one need not push it along to make sure that it gets there according to plan, but instead one may focus one's attention ahead of it on the spot to be explored. The assumptions made are almost nonexistent. The existence of no material thing need be assumed, not even that of one's hand as a complex material body of muscles attached to bones. One's hand figures in the exploration merely as a mobile tactual volume of complex shape, the continued presence of which with regard to the rest of one's body is monitored marginally and constantly throughout the investigation. No assumptions need be made of more complex commonsense truths or of the elaborate world view claimed by Wittgenstein to be the background of any inquiry. Since the above explorative activity qualifies as genuine inquiry, it is consequently incorrect to argue in sweeping fashion that trust is presupposed in all inquiry, skeptical inquiry included. If a convincing case is to be made, it must be spelled out concretely how trust is involved in skeptical inquiry. The task would appear to be aptly described as not unlike taking the pulse of a tree fossil.

Finally, it should be noted that the trust requisite for the successful execution of everyday activities is quite consistent with all Cartesian solipsistic theses except the most radical one. In a calculation with pencil and paper, for instance, it is assumed that the figures written down do not change of their own accord. Yet, must it be assumed that the figures are neither permanent illusions nor part of a dream? It would seem not. Trust in the reality of the world is not a prerequisite for correct addition, nor is it one for any of the multiple activities that constitute everyday living. Likewise, correct addition does not seem to require trust in the continued unobserved existence of objects. It suffices that the figures jotted on paper not differ from one time of observation to the next. Continued unobserved existence is necessary neither for successful prediction of what is observed nor for successful activity.

Sense Data Solipsism alone is faced with a serious problem of presuppositions inconsistent with professed beliefs. Purposeful and effective activity in the world requires for its execution the assumption that a given sequence of coordinated events (including efforts) will yield a certain sequence of consequences. Since Sense Data Solipsism denies that past regularities provide any warrant whatever for future expectations, the doctrine is incompatible with the presuppositions of any purposeful activity. This awkward situation is the one encountered earlier in chapter 3 in the form of the pragmatic necessity of belief. As noted there, despite the gravity of the predicament in which a Sense Data Solipsist is placed by strict adherence to doctrinal dictates, it may be plausibly argued that this regrettable consequence is itself irrelevant to the issue of the truth or falsity of the doctrine. A true believer may well be reduced to ineffective activity and immanent extinction (although the latter could not be known by the solipsist), but inevitable martyrdom is no sure indication of falsity of belief.

The third of the three Wittgensteinian points noted earlier is the claim that skeptical doubts must have the effect of toppling all judgement and annihilating all yardsticks. It ceases to be known what counts as evidence and verification, and as a result, the proponent of the skeptical doubts becomes incomprehensible, akin in this respect to a half-wit or madman. Quite clearly, however, these claims overstate considerably the confusion and incomprehension attendant upon skeptical questioning. The doubts entertained by the various forms of Cartesian solipsism may hardly be fairly characterized as incomprehensible. If they could, it would be incomprehensible that they should be so widely discussed, among other places, in the present book. Any initial ignorance regarding skeptical judgment and yardsticks may be removed readily enough by probing into the object and nature of the skeptical doubts. Most of them—those entertained by Ephemerata, Oneirata, or Phantasmata Solipsism, for instance—are specific doubts of quite circumscribed import. The correlated quest for reasons is not only quite comprehensible but sane to boot. What, after all, is more understandable or more reasonable than an inquiry into reasons and relative likelihood?

Wittgenstein seems to think that if one should doubt the existence of one's hand, one might with equal right doubt that one knows what the word 'hand' means or whether it has any meaning at all. When he declares that with a doubt of the sort one would "stand before the abyss," he seems to mean that, unless one trusts in one's knowledge of the meaning of words and hence arbitrarily exempts certain empirical matters from doubt, one's doubt should be impartially extended to the very words one is using and ipso facto silence themselves. The line of argument is vigorous enough looking at first prance and seems both promising and fair, yet it contains two serious mistakes.

On one hand, it is built on a serious ambiguity. Like the rest of us, any skeptic has through childhood training acquired the rudiments of a language; certain sound-sequences and written or printed squiggles have taken on specific meanings, meanings that could not be readily dissociated from the sounds and marks despite the help of considerable effort. As a result, the skeptic finds himself or herself in possession of a system of symbols which to all appearances might be used for personal purposes in spite of doubts as to whether the correlations made are the official ones of the language. Certainly, doubts may be entertained with regard to public meanings, and perhaps the only consistent course for a rational skeptic is silence. Yet doubts cannot be entertained with regard to the meanings that meaningful words have for oneself. The fact that the words have meaning for oneself is a datum on a par with an emotional response. It is not an empirical datum of the kind that may be conceived to be false in the face of the actual evidence and hence doubted. The point is easily made by taking a word such as 'cow' and attempting to doubt its meaning for oneself, by asking perhaps whether its meaning for oneself is not the same as that of the word 'horse'. Thus, although perhaps any clear-headed radical skeptic must in good faith renounce communication with others, he or she need not renounce self-adressed professions of faith.

Furthermore, while trust in official meaning (or, at least, meaning for others) is needed for communication, nevertheless, it does not follow from this fact that trust in the commonsense tenets questioned by our various solipsists is also needed. The mere fact that meaning must be presupposed does not show that unobserved existence, for instance, must be presupposed. More generally, a need to presuppose any particular commonsense tenet, P_j, is insufficient in itself to establish a need to presuppose the further particular tenet, P_k. A successful demonstration that P_j is a necessary presupposition in any language game could be relevant to the issue of P_k only if it is supplemented by a further demonstration of a relevant connection of some sort between the two tenets. In the absence of a demonstrated connection, no connection may be assumed. Otherwise one might with equal warrant argue that the need for trust in official meaning establishes the need for trust in any common belief one pleases, the existence of God, the Holy Trinity, good luck charms, or horoscopes.

It might be insisted that nevertheless Wittgenstein does have a point where radical forms of skepticism are concerned. A radical skepticism, such as Sense Data Solipsism, manages to doubt its way into a world devoid of causal regularities and into a methodological position approaching "an annihilation of all judgment." The resulting world is one where, as Stanley Cavell puts it, "the concept of evidence has no application; anything can be followed by anything."[22] While Cavell's observation is obviously accurate, it should not be construed as grounds for the acceptance of the ordinary concept of evidence. If that concept of evidence is not rational, then it is certainly not made rational by the claim that without it there would be no concept of evidence. What is required in the present context is some effective demonstration of the rationality of the ordinary concept, for without such a demonstration there is no sound reason to think that the commonsense world view it yields is more likely to be true than a skeptical scenario in which "anything may be followed by anything." For this reason, the *reductio ad absurdum* argument implicit in the above remarks is unsound. Radical skeptical doubt is allegedly to be ruled out on the ground that the world to which it leads is an *absurdum*, a world too chaotic to be seriously envisaged. Yet an account of the world that excludes causal laws cannot rightly be reproached that exclusion if the account is correct and the world is in fact devoid of causal regularities. Indeed, accounts of the world would do better to conform to the way the world is, rather than to some concept of evidence that excludes lawless sequences on the sole ground that they collectively constitute a chaotic world. If the skeptical view faithfully mirrors the world (and the contrary has not been shown), then a *reductio ad absurdum* argument against skeptical doubt is itself somewhat of an *absurdum*.

HEIDEGGER AND EXISTENTIAL COMMITMENT

Martin Heidegger's existentialist version of the cognitive situation is in many respects remarkably similar to that of Wittgenstein, despite the otherwise pronounced differences in the views and interests of the two philosophers. In contrast to Wittgenstein's preoccupation with the challenge of skepticism, Heidegger manifests little serious concern with the issue. At one point in *Being and Time,* however, he skirmishes briefly with the Cartesian External World Problem, and in the process discloses a multifaceted line of argument which may plausibly be considered a general response to Cartesian solipsism.

The object of Heidegger's remarks is Kant's attempted 'refutation of idealism,' or proof that things other than one's own representations exist. Whereas the lack of such a proof is esteemed by Kant to be a "scandal to philosophy," Heidegger declares the scandal to be rather the fact that proofs of the kind are found necessary and are continually attempted. The nature of the existing subject, *Dasein*, makes proofs both superfluous and impossible, says Heidegger: "If Dasein is understood correctly, it defies such proofs, because, in its being, it already *is* what subsequent proofs deem necessary to demonstrate for it."[23]

What, then, in the nature of the existing subject precludes a cogent posing of the skeptical problem? Several answers may be attributed to Heidegger. The shortest one is that the subject is engaged affectively in the world by its very existence—its being is *care*, says Heidegger—so that it is and must be already in the very world for which proofs of existence are requested. To Heidegger's way of thinking, Descartes and Kant wrongly view the subject as "*worldless* or unsure of its world," a subject one may encounter in isolation.[24] To ask for a proof of the world's existence, or even to declare (in Kantian fashion) that the subject must presuppose a world, is to assume an isolated subject at the very outset. The problem can only arise, Heidegger seems to be saying, if one becomes forgetful of one's own situation of involvement in the world.

A more elaborate answer is readily derived from Heidegger's analysis of engagement in the world. Any such involvement is structured with teleological relations with regard to the end sought, relations in which things are viewed as means or as elements in a situation to be transformed. Things are consequently interpreted—viewed, for instance, as tables, hills, or food. Yet no interpretation is ever a mere presuppositionless apprehending, Heidegger argues. It requires and operates under the structures and guidance of certain fore-structures (structures Heidegger terms "fore-having," "fore-sight" and "fore-conception").[25] These structures might be loosely described as the implicit conceptual and factual presuppositions that together constitute a framework or view of the world. They are integral to any understanding, any experienced meaning. Since a world view is presupposed in any engagement in the world, a proof of the existence of the world is redundant.

A still more elaborate answer is to be found in the interpretation Charles B. Guignon gives of Heidegger's response to skepticism. Guignon sees Heidegger to be drawing a sharp contrast between two attitudes towards the world, the practical and the contemplative. Guignon has this dichotomy in mind in the following assessment: "Heidegger leads us to see that our most primordial encounter with the world is not through the mediation of mere seeing, but is rather through handling, manipulating, producing, and operating."[26] Furthermore, the practical is a necessary condition of the contemplative, according to Guignon, for he says: "In the picture that emerges in *Being and Time*, we come to see that the background of intelligibility that permeates our everyday practices is prior to, and a condition for there being anything like, scientific or rationalist forms of grounding."[27] Guignon draws the conclusion that since the world of "the contemplative attitude is *derivative from* a prior discovery of the ready-to-hand in practical affairs," any contemplative attempt at a rational reconstruction comes too late.[28] It presupposes a world, the one integral to the practical attitude, and hence it presupposes what it attempts to provide.

A further complicating factor in Heidegger's position is the role he attributes to culture in the shaping of the fore-structures of comprehension. The following passage succinctly states what Heidegger holds that role to be: "This everyday way in which things have been interpreted is one into which Dasein has grown in the first instance, with never a possibility of extrication. In it, out of it, and against it, all genuine understanding, interpreting, and communicating, all re-discovery and appropriating anew, are performed. In no case is a Dasein, untouched and unseduced by the way in which things have been interpreted, set before the open country of a 'world-in-itself' so that it just beholds what it encounters."[29] Whatever else these remarks might be intended to show, they clearly entail the claim that, since the view of the world inculcated by a culture is presupposed in all cognitive dealings, the question of the existence of the world cannot cogently arise.

Let us consider these various points in reverse order. The remarks regarding cultural shaping suggest the inculcation of an indelible and culturally relative view of the world, one that is not solipsistic and consequently is inconsistent with the theses proposed by Cartesian solipsists. On any moderately strong construal of Heidegger's remarks, a Cartesian solipsist will hold views in contradiction with his skeptical thesis. Fortunately for our solipsists, Heidegger's claim regarding cultural inextricability is highly questionable in any form in which it is relevant to skeptical issues. To begin with, there would seem to be no such thing as a belief that cannot be thrown off—provided, of course, that the belief is brought to one's awareness. Furthermore, there seems no serious obstacle to bringing the common-sense rivals of Cartesian skeptical theses to one's awareness. Cartesian solipsists do as much at their first awakening to the skeptical calling. Nor does there seem to be any serious obstacle to rejecting the relevant commonsense tenets, no obstacle in the form of an indelible imprint, that is. Thus, there is apparently no basis whatever in fact to the claim that cultural upbringing excludes the possibility of espousing skeptical theses.

The point may be put more abstractly. While the effectiveness, pervasiveness, and depth of cultural conditioning are incontestable enough, they are insufficient to ground a valid conclusion that some particular tenet, P_k, cannot be rejected. The claim of the indelibility of cultural conditioning is defendable only in a loose sense, one whereby no complete or even sizeable eradication of the effect of cultural conditioning is possible despite the firmest of intentions. What this means is that, despite valiant efforts to the contrary, there will always remain some set of unrejected culturally inculcated tenets, let us say, $P_1, P_2, ..., P_x$. Such a claim is clearly insufficient in itself to show that the particular tenet, P_k, is not and cannot be rejected. A general appeal to cultural conditioning can be no more successful than a general appeal to trust as an answer to skepticism. What must be shown is that some specific tenet, one questioned by the skeptic, is an unde-tachable plank in the cognitive ship. It must be demonstrated that P_k cannot be removed from the set of tenets constituting the world view, and replaced by the rival skeptical thesis, Q_k. While fore-structures are clearly present in everyday inquiry, understanding, and meaning, it cannot be concluded from this fact alone that it is impossible to question some particular tenet that figures prominently in those fore-structures.

It might be noted in passing that the general topic of cultural rela-tivity and culturally inculcated world views has no clear bearing on skeptical problems. Consider, for instance, the problem of the contin-ued existence of unobserved material items. How does the fact of one's being raised in a highly competitive technological society addicted to cleanliness, youth, self-assertion, and optimism have any bearing at all on the problem? It might be argued that the technologi-cal world view has necessary presuppositions in contradiction with the solipsistic denial of continued existence, but surely the same might be said of any culturally inculcated world view. There are no intercultural disputes as to whether unobserved tables become kanga-roos rather than sheep. Likewise, there are no culturally inculcated world views in which the world is held to be the dream of some par-ticular person, nor are there any intercultural disputes as to whose dream it is. The rejection of solipsistic theses is pancultural. The chal-lenge of solipsism is also pancultural in the sense that solipsism ques-tions beliefs so rudimentary that they are common to all cultures.

In addition, there is no reason to think that the pancultural ele-ments of a world view are necessarily culturally inculcated. They could well be in part built up over time by the individual from less complex views, beginning with an infantile world view akin to that of Sense Data Solipsism—in which case, one of the tasks of epistemolo-gy is to uncover the rationality of the successive moves involved. As we saw, Wittgenstein too hastily extrapolates from the obvious need for trust in everyday investigation to the claim that trust is always necessary. In like fashion, Heidegger extrapolates from the persistent and obvious presence of factual and conceptual presuppositions in everyday inquiry to an analogous claim about world views. A world view, like a corpus of trustworthy beliefs, is quite open to accretion over time. If radical skepticism is to be successfully charged with par-asitism, it must be shown that the world view presupposed at every stage is something more than the meager world of the Sense Data Solipsist. While a demonstration of the kind is clearly possible in cases of goal-directed activity of some sophistication, it is just as clearly impossible in the cases of aimless and expectationless activity to which a consistent Sense Data Solipsist is reduced.

Just as the notions of indelible imprints and cultural relativity are unhelpful to the resolution of skeptical issues, so is the pragmatic/contemplative dichotomy stressed by Guignon. The dichotomy is spurious if interpreted at all literally. There no more exists pure contemplation of the world than there does blind action in it. Indeed, it may be plausibly argued that any serious thinking requires bodily activity and, at the least, dynamic imagic and verbal operations which have more in common with action than with contemplation. While some philosophers may misconceive themselves to be occupied in a bodiless seeing, there is no apparent reason to think that skeptics must do likewise in order to give themselves over to the passion of doubting. To claim that doubt is tied to contemplation, or is only possible in a contemplative attitude, is to imply that doubt is impossible in a practical attitude. This latter claim is clearly mistaken. Doubt often does arise, and hence can arise, in situations of practical involvement. Moreover, to claim that the skeptic's request for grounds can arise only with the scientific or rationalist attitude is to propose a disparaging and debatable view of practical thinking as subrational. It is also to presuppose an exalted view of the sophistication of skeptical issues. Surely the notion that the world is perhaps dreamlike might occur to a child of a tender age and tenderer rational skills. Likewise, the question of what tables do when no one is looking would not be out of place in a fairy tale or in the musings of an imaginative three-year-old child. Guignon's pragmatic/contemplative dichotomy has no application in the present context.

Heidegger's minimal antiskeptical response, his pointing out the fact of our existential involvement in the world, is no more successful than the ones just considered. Heidegger is quite right to repudiate the conception of the subject as a pure thinking being, and to speak of the caring involvement and the spatiality of the subject—although a considerably more rigorous demonstration would be required to establish the latter point firmly. Yet even if it is granted that the subject is always existentially engaged in the world, there remains to be settled the question of the nature of the world in which the subject is engaged. Heidegger takes for granted that a world more fleshed out than any solipsistic one is required. Yet, what reason is there to think that for a world to be the object of an involvement, it must be one where things have unobserved far sides? Surely involvement is possible in a world of things that cease to exist when unperceived. Surely too, involvement is possible in a dream world. Indeed, as noted in chapter 3, in most dreams the dreamer is as a matter of fact affectively involved. Nor is the skeptical problem that Heidegger specifically addresses, the problem of an external world, brought any closer to resolution by his insistence upon an engaged subject. If a dream may provoke engagement, then it is difficult to see why a world of sensations or representations may not. The requirements of an engaged subject are apparently quite insufficient to show that the terrain of engagement must be the full complex everyday world it is commonly held to be.

QUINE AND NATURALIZED EPISTEMOLOGY

The charge of epistemic parasitism has at various times been brought parochially against one form or other of skepticism by a variety of philosophers in the analytic tradition. G. E. Moore, in his attempt to answer the dream hypothesis, reasons that a proponent of the hypothesis would premiss his case on the discernible similarity between present experiences and dream experiences.[30] Such a premiss implies that it is known that dreams have occurred. Anthony Quinton reasons that two central skeptical arguments of Descartes rest on factual considerations, the two claims that the senses are sometimes deceptive, and that what is dreamt to be the case is not so.[31] When Descartes infers the untrustworthiness of the senses from the fact that he has sometimes been deceived by them, this latter claim is itself based on the assumption of very general factual truths about the world, among which the truth that perception is sometimes reliable. Descartes's deprecation of dreams likewise presupposes, according to Quinton, the ability to distinguish between dreams and waking life, and hence acquaintance with and factual knowledge of both.

Perhaps the most interesting of recent attempts along these lines is a more general variant made popular by W. V. O. Quine. In Quine's view, any skeptical challenge is based on the findings of science and is consequently rightly seen as a challenge to science from within science itself. Since the challenge presupposes the findings of science, science not only may but must be used in answering it. In support of his analysis, Quine points out that even the ancient skeptics relied on the findings of science to challenge science. Says Quine, "the skeptics cited familiar illusions to show the fallibility of the senses; but this concept of illusion itself rested on natural science, since the quality of illusion consisted simply in deviation from external scientific reality."[32] A similar charge is brought against the skeptical problem which is the source of so much modern epistemology, the problem of bridging the evidential gap between sense data and material bodies. This problem is wrongly viewed, says Quine, as a challenge to our knowledge, one to be removed by providing a justification; its context is that of natural science. Argues Quine,

> The challenge runs as follows. Science itself teaches that there is no clairvoyance; that the only information that can reach our sensory surfaces from external objects must be limited to two-dimensional optical projections and various impacts of air-waves on the ear-drums and some gaseous reactions in the nasal passages and a few kindred odds and ends. How, the challenge proceeds, could one hope to find out about the external world from such meager traces? In short, if our science were true, how could we know it. Clearly, in confronting this challenge, the epistemologist may make free use of all scientific theory.[33]

To Quine's lights the question raised by the skeptic is a question within science to be answered by science. It ceases ipso facto to be a request for justification and becomes a request for explanation. Enlightened epistemology may consequently abandon the futile, age-old quest for a first philosophy in which to ground science and commonsense rationally and become instead a part of natural science, *naturalized epistemology*. The task of the latter is to explain a particular natural phenomenon, to wit, how the "meager input" of sensory stimulation gives rise to the "torrential output" of knowledge of "a three-dimensional external world and its history."[34] Quine does not accuse the skeptic of being parasitically self-contradictory. He takes rather the gentler tack of assuming that the enlightened skeptic will see the skeptical doubts to be the scientific doubts they are and consequently will join in the elaboration of an answer to these doubts within the confines of the scientific enterprise.

How solid is Quine's approach? The answer varies with the skeptical problem being considered. Let us first weigh its applicability to the two types of Cartesian solipsism directly threatened by Quine's observations, Unreal World and Observed World Solipsism. Then we shall examine how it might be brought usefully to bear against Internal World Solipsism.

Quine is certainly right to point out that much of the reasoning of the ancient skeptics regarding the fallibility of the senses and the prevalence of illusion rests on a base of natural science. The ten tropes of Aenesidemus, for instance, treat of various sources of differences in how things appear (a difference in constitution among animals or among human beings, a difference between sense organs, conditions affecting the subject, the location of the object, and so on).[35] A discussion of the kind draws on the findings of natural science, and presupposes the existence of perceiving animals, sense organs, cultural conditions, and so on. In addition, the numerous and varied instances of perceptual illusion cited by Descartes and other philosophers of more modern times fall equally within the purview of natural science, and their use by the solipsist might well lay his thesis open to a charge of epistemic parasitism.

Nevertheless, these considerations do not take us down to the hard core of the skeptical challenge. When careless presentations are tidied or revised after self-examination, the various forms of Unreal World Solipsism may each be judged to have no embarassing factual presuppositions. Consider, for instance, the type of illusion envisaged by Phantasmata Solipsism. That illusion is considerably more complex in nature than any illusion ever experienced: it must be a conjunction of concomitant visual, tactual, and auditory phenomena, and if tested with the usual criteria for illusions, it would be judged to be real rather than illusory. In these circumstances, the occurrence of usual run-of-the-mill illusions can hardly be considered evidence in favor of the existence of more complex ones of the sort envisaged by the solipsist. If the solipsistic illusions may rightly be termed 'illusions' at all, it is in virtue of their purported possession of the essential defining characteristic of illusions or illusory objects, that of not really being there where they appear to be.

The situation is similar for Oneirata Solipsism. The dreams envisaged by the solipsist resemble natural dreams through their possession of the defining characteristic of dreams, that of being experiences from which the dreamer may subsequently awake. If the solipsistic dreams shared any other of the features peculiar to natural dreams, features that allow dreams to be distinguished from waking states, then the solipsistic thesis could immediately be declared to be false. For instance, if the solipsistic dreams were like natural dreams in that they allow sudden physiological transformations (one's neighbor may suddenly grow fangs), then it could be argued that the world is not a solipsistic dream since no such transformations take place in it. With Oneirata Solipsism as with Phantasmata Solipsism, the skeptic must be merely putting forth a possible hypothesis and not one supported by actual occurrences.

Admittedly, actual occurrences may and sometimes do make their appearance in skeptical arguments of the Cartesian type. They need not, however, be essential to the argument. In the case of Descartes himself, any such occurrences are clearly inessential. In *The Search after*

Truth Descartes suggests that the experience of transparently deceptive appearances naturally gives rise to the fear that other experiences are illusory but cannot be recognized as such. Here the empirical data functions not as evidence but simply as a trigger to the realization that certain skeptical scenarios are logically possible—and on reflection, apparently also theoretically possible. The data suggests a possibility that is then free to stand (or fall) on its own merits. A similar interpretation would seem correct for Descartes's dream argument. Descartes declares that he is amazed to realize that there are no sure signs to guarantee that he is not dreaming. The remark implies that any characteristics of natural dreams allowing them to be distinguished from waking experience are insufficient to provide a guarantee—which in turn implies that in his dream hypothesis Descartes has in mind a dream indistinguishable from waking life (except, of course, for the fact that it comes to an end with the awakening of the dreamer).

Concrete occurrences of illusions and dreams do nevertheless serve an important function in the Cartesian arguments. A judgment characterizing something as an illusion always involves a denial of the obvious, i.e., a denial of the presence of something ostensibly there. It is made under duress as the only means of resolving an apparent contradiction. In a world in which illusions were never encountered, the very notion of an illusion might plausibly be considered an absurdity. Concrete instances of illusions are consequently useful in getting the very logical possibility of illusions to be recognized. The same is true of dreams. Imagine a world in which there were neither dreams nor illusions, so that everything was what it appeared to be. It is difficult to see how Descartes's scenarios could manage to gain the status of logical possibilities. Thus the Cartesian skeptical hypotheses do have factual presuppositions of a sort—but not ones that in any clear way might be used to substantiate a charge of parasitism.

Parasitism arguments fare no better against those forms of solipsism that question the existence of what is unobserved. Quine claims that accounts of sense data are suffused with the findings of the natural sciences. In particular, he argues, the tenet of the bi-dimensionality of visual sense data is not the fruit of introspection but rather of experimental psychology and physiology which teaches the bi-dimensionality of the retina; analogously, the tenet that auditory phenomena are a function of pitch and loudness depends on findings regarding frequency and amplitude in a vibrating string.[36] Yet while there is a good deal of truth to these claims, they do not and cannot serve as the basis for a warranted indictment of solipsism dealing in sense data and the like. Such solipsism is in no way obliged to be unfaithful to the spirit of official solipsistic doctrine and to make "sidelong glances into natural science." Solipsistic accounts of sense data may well restrict themselves to descriptions of the introspective evidence and make no use whatever of the findings of science. There is no reason to think that the observance of constraints of the sort would preclude the formulation of fairly accurate accounts of what is actually perceived—certainly accounts accurate enough for the purposes of skepticism and rational foundationalism.

It is true that in the past epistemologists as different in their approaches as Berkeley, Husserl, and Carnap all seem to have been influenced by scientific considerations, particularly in assuming the visual field to be bi-dimensional. Nevertheless, their lead in this regard need not be found compelling. Solipsistic pronouncements on the precise geometrical structure of a sense field may be confined to those items substantiated by introspection. A passably good introspectionist need be no more fixated on the bi-dimensionality of the retina than oblivious to gestalt disruptions in the geometrical tidiness of the data. On the issue of pitch and volume, it is likewise true that the conceptualization of the components of auditory phenomena is greatly enhanced by the study of the vibrating string. Nevertheless, it seems equally true that awareness of pitch and volume is not necessarily dependent on such study and that two particular features of auditory phenomena, pitch and volume, are detectable readily enough in a rudimentary way through comparison of phenomenal sounds. What is true of pitch and volume is also true of the color constituents of hue, saturation, and brightness. There is no obvious justification to the claim that the insight required to draw rough-hewn distinctions is available to scientific inquiry but not to introspection.

From time to time attempts are undertaken to ferret out factual presuppositions more deeply buried than those considered by Quine, but their prime achievement is to suggest strongly that the vein is exhausted. A good illustration of the point is Michael Woods's recent endorsement of the naturalization of epistemology. Woods makes the focus of his criticism the "bare logical possibility" proposed by the skeptic and contends that "the skeptic cannot appeal to these possibilities without making assumptions about what we can know that are inconsistent with the position of a skeptic."[37] He attempts to make two distinct points. On one hand, he claims that a skeptic can only introduce the notion of experience in terms of an alleged unrevisible certainty peculiar to experiential reports, thereby prejudging an issue that can only be settled by a general theory of human knowledge. On the other hand he argues that the skeptic has no right to assume it logically possible for immediate experience to occur independently of the external world, since such a logical possibility is excluded if experiences should turn out to be necessarily identical with brain states.[38] The first of these two claims has no relevance to Cartesian solipsism as defined earlier, since neither unrevisable certainty nor a theory of human knowledge are essential ingredients in it. The second claim invokes a logical possibility that is certainly not considered to be such in current English. Indeed, if experiences were identical with brain states, the correlated expressions would be inter-substitutable *salva veritate*, whereas any such substitution produces nonsense. Thus, instead of creating difficulties for the skeptic, efforts of the sort bring out rather the unlikelihood of successfully unearthing any deeply buried factual presuppositions shared by skeptical theses generally.

As to the enterprise of naturalized epistemology itself, it is certainly a legitimate scientific discipline in its own right. Nevertheless, it cannot pretend to supplant rationalized epistemology, and could only do so if objectualism could be shown to be true. In point of fact, it may well turn out that the rationalized inquiry has some important contributions to make to the naturalized one. Indeed, this is only to be expected. If the natural animal is a rational animal, then any elucidation of the functioning of the latter should help explain the functioning of the former.

THE REFUTATION OF SENSA SOLIPSISM

The apparent futility of attempts at a blanket conviction of skepticism on the charge of epistemic parasitism does not preclude the possibility of some more restricted and individually tailored success. If a particular skeptical thesis is such that it assumes certain specific factual truths of which the thesis denies the truth, then the thesis is irredeemably vitiated: if true, it would have to be false. Sensa Solipsism is just such a thesis.

The skeptical problem from which Sensa Solipsism arises, the External World Problem, may be roughly stated as follows: one can be aware only of one's own sensations or private representations of the world, never of the world itself; consequently, for all one can know, the external world may be in fact quite dissimilar to the world as it appears to be; indeed, there may be no external world at all. In view of this awkward situation, any number of skeptical theses might be entertained, the most drastic one being Sensa Solipsism which states that nothing exists except the solipsist's own sensations or representations. All such skeptical theses are, however, parochially parasitic in that they presuppose a particular account of perception.

The account presupposed is a familiar one, popular in scientific circles, endorsed by Descartes and Locke, and designated commonly as the *Representational Theory of Perception.* The theory maintains that all perceived colors, sounds, feelings, and so on are the end events in a long chain of causally connected events. These events include the emission of light rays or sound waves, their transmission through space, the stimulation of sensory organs, the traveling of impulses along nerve fibers to the brain, resulting brain activity of which the end products are the mental copies of the things out in the world. The copies or private representations include everything one perceives in the way of colors, shapes, sounds, odors, tastes, and tactual expanses. Thus, the theory postulates two distinct types of world: on one hand, a private world of sensations in which sensations are aspects of objects present to perception, and on the other hand, a real public world that gives rise to the sensations but is itself never actually present in one's perceptual fields. To avoid confusion we might term the first *the material world* with its sensuous material objects and the second *the physical world* with its physical objects of the sort treated in physics.

It is only within the context of the Representational Theory that run-of-the-mill visual and auditory phenomena may be considered to be sensations. In an everyday context one might speak of having a tingling sensation in one's foot or perhaps a buzzing sensation in one's ear, yet one would not, on looking at the sky, speak of having a sensation of a blue expanse. Nor would one on hearing a noise behind oneself, speak of having a sensation of noise or of having a sensation of chirping or barking. In general, to qualify as a sensation, a candidate must be located in or on the body, a condition that both the blue of the sky and the nearby noise fail to satisfy. The latter phenomena are items out in the world, not something on or within one's own body. In the context of the Representational Theory of Perception, this situation changes. It is no longer nonsensical to speak of the experienced noise and of the blue of the sky as sensations. Rather, it is quite appropriate to do so. They are sensations in as much as they are tied to events taking place in the body subsequent to the stimulation of one's sense organs. The body of which it is a question here is one's physical body, not one's material body. The portions one actually perceives of one's material body are to be counted among one's sensations; hence, they cannot be constituents in the body that has the sensations. The body that has the sensations is part of the physical world of which the sensations are representations.

Likewise, the Representational Theory is the source of the construal of the perceived world as private. Considered in abstraction from the role accorded it in the theory, the perceived world gives no indication whatever of being private. Its constituents look public enough, are handled, scrutinized, and commented upon by the public at large; considered on their own merits they give no indication whatever of being private. In one bold stroke, the Representational Theory transforms all this by declaring the rich assembly of sensuously present phenomena to be characters in a private world. With that stroke it provides the context in which it is possible to ask the question of how one can be sure there is any external world at all, given that one can never get past the veil of one's own private sensations to perceive the physical world in person.

The Representational Theory is not a gratuitous complication in an otherwise guileless world. It is introduced to account for a wealth of troubling perceptual phenomena: perceptual illusions of various sorts whether plump red suns, mirages, seeing double, comet's tails on moving objects, distorted spoons in glasses, lags in distant noises, and a wealth of other familiar phenomena, not to mention less familiar ones such as phantom limbs, color blindness, or hallucinations. Without the theory, the real world would be a world containing objects with mutually exclusive characteristics (hot and cold, sweet and bitter, shrill and grave). Alternatively, it would be a world where one of the competing characteristics is declared illusory, a world containing phantom or illusory characteristics—the pastel shades of distant mountains, shimmers on heated roads, bent oars in water, bloated objects through lenses—characteristics that are ostensibly present in the world but at the same time excluded from it in some obscure way as being merely the way things look. The world would be peopled with paradoxes. The Representational Theory resolves the ontological puzzles of conflicting characteristics or of unreal presences by placing all perceived characteristics in private worlds.

Simultaneously, the theory provides an explanation of how the paradoxes arise. It allows talk of the diffraction, scattering, and filtering of light rays, of physiological dysfunction, and so on. These explanations involve a physical world distinct from the one actually perceived. To take an example, the phenomenon of a plump, red sun hovering over the horizon is explained in terms of the diffraction, partial absorbsion, and gravitational bending of light rays, which then produce a distorted image on a retina (or photographic plate). Such is, in its essentials, the explanation of the illusion. Now the actors in this little drama cannot be inhabitants of the material world alone. The sun in that world is ostensibly a plump, red, hovering one. A non-plump, nonred, nonhovering sun is posited in a physical world, sending out light rays that are distorted by various factors in the physical world and producing a distorted image on a physical retina, which eventually gets translated into what is actually seen. For various reasons that need not concern us here, it might be argued that the posited physical world is devoid of sensuous qualities, colors, tones, smells, or so-called secondary properties generally, but it cannot be completely devoid of any form of spatiotemporal structure whatsoever, since structures of the sort figure in the explanation of the illusion. The model of a spatiotemporal physical world studded with microcosmic, sensuous, private copies of itself thus gives an explanation of the troubling phenomena present in the perceived world.

Now, it would be quite inconsistent to both accept the explanation with its complex cosmological scheme and subsequently claim that there is no reason to posit a physical world. There is a reason to posit the world, precisely the reason there was to do so in the first instance: the fact that it is part of an account which provides an explanation of certain observed phenomena. The situation is analogous with regard to Dalton's Atomic Theory. The explanation the theory affords, for instance, of the chemical combination of substances in fixed proportion by weight, is evidence for the existence of the postulated unobservable atoms. It would be inconsistent to posit atoms on the basis of the evidence and then claim that, since atoms cannot be observed, we have no evidence at all for their existence.

It would likewise be inconsistent to reject the posit of a physical world and nevertheless, as Sensa Solipsism attempts to do, keep the posit of a private world of sensations. The latter is but one element in a larger explanatory scheme. If it is considered in isolation of the other elements, it is incapable of providing any explanation of the phenomena to be explained. If it is taken in abstraction of the explanation, it has no claim to be considered private, or a representation or made up of sensations. Hence, in attacking part of the explanatory scheme (the existence of an unobservable physical world), the solipsist is destroying the explanation of the phenomena and restoring to the perceived world the unadulterated publicity that it enjoyed prior to the advent of the Representational Theory. In truly parasitic fashion, the solipsist who questions the existence of a physical world is assiduously working toward the destruction of his own thesis.

Otherwise stated, the solipsist's refusal to admit the existence of a physical world on the ground that it is an unverifiable posit, is a refusal to admit the explanatory model of a physical world studded with assorted private worlds. What remains after the rejection of the explanation is simply the everyday world with its unexplained wide variety of paradoxical phenomena. This world is not a solipsistic one. In rejecting the external physical world, the solipsist also rejects the world featured in the solipsistic account. The Sensa Solipsist self-destructs.

While these considerations are decisive enough against Sensa Solipsism, they do not altogether resolve the External World Problem. The reason is that the latter, as commonly stated, contains an ambiguity. Indeed, the ambiguity was present at its conception. Let us backtrack a little to Descartes's discussion of the reasons he formerly had for thinking there exist external objects similar to the ones he actually perceives. In his assessment of his second reason, Descartes muddies matters at a crucial point. He abruptly introduces the reflection that his sense perceptions might arise through the operation of some unknown faculty within himself. This reflection is in fact quite independent of the rest of his discussion in the sense that it might easily be converted into an autonomous argument in its own right. The discussion up to this point is the reasoning of a convinced adherent to the Representational Theory, one who forgets the origin of the theory and asks what reasons there are to think observed material phenomena resemble their unobserved physical originals. This line of reasoning is a mistake due to forgetfulness. Yet the reasoning that begins with the notion of an independent inner faculty is not a mistake; it provides the starting point for a new and sound argument. It is as if the Representational Theory established a logical possibility, the logical possibility that what is perceived may be but a mere copy. This possibility in turn suggests the logical possibility of a bad copy and, by extension, of a noncopy consisting of unreal entities having their origin in some quite dissimilar cause, perhaps even some faculty in oneself. The role of the Representational Theory in this scenario is analogous to that of everyday illusions in the Phantasmata Solipsist's scenario, or that of everyday dreams in the skeptical dream scenario: it suggests a logical possibility which is then free to stand (or fall) on its own merits.

This new line of argument is succinctly formulated by Berkeley when he says, "suppose—what no one can deny possible—an intelligence *without the help of external bodies,* to be affected with the same train of sensations or ideas that you are, imprinted in the same order and with like vividness in his mind."[39] It cannot be answered by pointing out the relationship between evidence and posits in the Representational Theory of Perception. The form of solipsism to which it may lead cannot be rightly termed a form of Sensa Solipsism, since the constituents of the solipsist's private world are neither sensations nor representations; they are quite unlike what gives rise to them and in this regard are rather more like dreams or a demon's conjurations. The resulting solipsism is, as it were, Sensa Solipsism devoid of sensa and might aptly be termed *Non-Sensa Solipsism*. This new form of solipsism bears a striking resemblance to forms of Unreal World Solipsism. Its only connection with Internal World Solipsism is its relationship to the Representational Theory, a theory it does not endorse, but uses merely to suggest the logical possibility of something like a dream. Consequently, Non-Sensa Solipsism is best classed as a form of Unreal World Solipsism, and the External World Problem may be considered solved. Insofar as the latter does survive, it fuses with the Problem of Reality.

Benson Mates, who discusses at length the problem posed by Berkeley, terms the latter problem, "the External World problem," probably in view of Berkeley's concern with "external bodies."[40] Berkeley's problem is in fact a very complex one, perhaps best seen as a number of distinct epistemological problems rolled into one. It might be considered in part the Problem of Unobserved Existence, since Berkeley argues frequently against the notion of things existing unperceived. It is in part the Problem of Reality, since in presenting his case Berkeley appeals to the fact that there are dreams and sensory illusions. It is also in part the External World Problem, since Berkeley does argue against the independent physical world of the Representational Theory. It is also in part a fourth problem raised by Berkeley's idealist claim, to be is to be perceived, with its backing of arguments to the effect that both primary and secondary properties are mental. The fourth problem, that of whether everyday objects may exist outside the mind of a perceiver, may best be considered to give rise to another form of solipsism, one that could be termed *Mental World Solipsism*. It would take us quite far afield to evaluate all the various arguments or suggestions of same that Berkeley presents in favor of this further form of solipsism. It might be noted, however, that Mental World Solipsism is in serious trouble to the extent that it is based on Berkeley's claim that "those arguments which are thought manifestly to prove that colours and tastes exist *only* within the mind…may with equal force be brought to prove the same thing of extension, figure, and motion."[41] The experienced relativity of appearances shows the appearances to be 'mental' only insofar as a physical world is posited. Hence any attempt to reach solipsism with such an argument is open to a charge of epistemic parasitism of the sort successfully brought against Sensa Solipsism.

It is also worth noting that Berkeley's most striking argument against the cosmology of the Representational Theory bears up poorly under examination. The much-quoted argument runs as follow: "In short, if there were external bodies, it is impossible we should ever come to know it; and if there were not, we might have the very same reasons to think there were that we have now."[42] Otherwise stated, if the Representational Theory is true, then it is impossible to have direct acquaintance with physical objects and hence ever be certain of their existence; if the Representational Theory is false and there are in fact no physical bodies, then we have the same reasons for thinking mistakenly that there are. The argument has often been found disturbing, at times compelling. Recently, it has been defended by Mates, who claims it has yet to be answered, and esteemed by Stroud to constitute a powerful *reductio ad absurdum* argument that a skeptic might direct against science.[43]

Now the weakness of this line of reasoning is that analogous remarks apply to any explanatory hypothesis whatever. If we suppose the hypothesis true, it is always conceivable that it is false. If we suppose the hypothesis false, we still have the same reasons we had before to conclude that it is true. It is nevertheless true that if the reasons are good reasons and consequently make the hypothesis likely to be true, then the hypothesis remains likely to be true on the evidence presented whether it is actually true or not. Berkeley's remarks amount to the mere recognition that any hypothesis may be false despite the data, and that its truth is only as certain as the evidence makes it. The situation should be unsettling only to someone addicted to absolute certainty.

CHAPTER SIX

THE CHARGE OF MEANINGLESSNESS

In the initial wave of euphoria of the linguistic turn some years back, philosophical problems in general were diagnosed as linguistic misunderstandings, problems arising when language bewitches the intelligence or goes on a holiday (Wittgenstein's metaphors).[1] Consonant with this analysis, problems were considered resolvable through a proper elucidation of the workings of language, a treatment aptly characterized by one prominent proponent as "the very full description of the symptoms."[2] While the linguistic approach has subsided in popularity to something less than a tidal bore, it is still widely deemed to have beached more than a few of the odder philosophical fish. Among the latter are often counted solipsism, Cartesianism, and sense datum epistemology, respectively pursued with Ahabian tenacity by the three linguistic philosophers, Wittgenstein, Ryle, and Austin. In this perspective the pretentions of the linguistic approach can hardly be ignored—even if in the present instance the beached fish should turn out to be primarily red herring.

While precursors may be found in the writings of Russell and perhaps of the British empiricists, the first serious attempt to resolve philosophical problems linguistically must be judged to be Wittgenstein's treatment of solipsism. The treatment spread rapidly to most other varieties of skepticism. The diagnosis was invariably that skeptical utterances suffer from meaninglessness, although the putative cause often varied considerably from one physician to the next. A charge of meaninglessness is one that at an earlier time Logical Positivism hurled at metaphysical statements generally on the grounds such statements were unverifiable. In the case of the linguistic movement, the possible sources of meaninglessness are seen to be more numerous. In what follows we shall examine briefly five of these putative sources insofar as they pertain to skeptical utterances—specifically, that the skeptic utters disguised tautologies, uses terms stripped of their meaning-giving criteria, coins terms incorrectly, ignores the verification requirement, or uses terms with no reference.

THE DISGUISED TAUTOLOGY

A particular form of solipsism arises naturally enough from the conception of the egocentric predicament predominant in the foundationalism of the 1930s. W. T. Stace gives a particularly forceful presentation of that egocentric predicament in a passage that begins:

> I cannot experience anything except *my own* experience. I can see my red but I can never see yours. I can feel a pain in my leg. But I can never feel the pain in your leg. I can feel my emotion but not yours.… I can never be you nor you me. I can never see through your eyes, nor you through mine.[3]

Since knowledge is based upon experience, Stace reasons, all one's knowledge has its origin in a solipsistic world of self-enclosed personal experience.

Wittgenstein may be found wrestling with this particular predicament and its solipsistic implications for close to twenty years. From the denial that one person can have the experiences of another, it seems to follow straightforwardly enough that one can only know one's own experiences and that one can never know those of another person. Indeed, since one can have no experiences outside one's own, it seems to follow that one can have no possible evidence that others have experiences at all. To this solipsistic line of reasoning Wittgenstein adds a further twist: the distressing egocentric situation entails a further and equally distressing semantic one. Classical logical positivist doctrine holds that a statement is meaningful only if verifiable in principle. If one subscribes to this doctrine, as Wittgenstein apparently does, then one must conclude, as A. J. Ayer does, that in as much as the experiences of others are unobservable in principle, the unverifiable statements about such experiences can have no more significance than any unverifiable metaphysical statement.[4] The converse conclusion also follows. In speaking of oneself, one's experiences and activities, one is speaking of things that are unknowable by others. Consequently, not only is it the case that statements about the experiences of others can have no meaning, but others cannot understand one's own meaning in the statements one makes about one's own experiences.[5] Wittgenstein thus has his solipsist take the implications of the egocentric predicament a step further into semantics, and so enunciate a semantic solipsism conjoined with the usual epistemological and metaphysical one. As we shall see, the resulting form of solipsism is a more complex version of Sensa Solipsism, one that we shall term *Lingua-Sensa Solipsism* to distinguish it from its classical ancestor.

Wittgenstein's efforts to answer solipsism focus almost exclusively on the semantic repercussions of the position. It is very likely that the challenge posed by solipsism served as one of the main incentives to Wittgenstein's tenacious and detailed investigations into the workings of language. Undoubtedly too, Wittgenstein's impression that the problem of solipsism yields to linguistic dissolution was found by him to be persuasive confirmation of the view that philosophical problems generally are misunderstandings about the workings of language. Significantly enough, Wittgenstein's well-known remark that the aim of philosophy is to show the fly the way out of the fly-bottle is an echo of an earlier metaphor that has the solipsist fluttering about in the fly-glass.[6]

Wittgenstein's case against his particular variation of solipsism is a complicated one made up of a wealth of independent linguistic strands. It invokes among other doctrines those of the publicity of everyday language, the impossibility of a private language, and the insignificance of nonlinguistic thinking, topics that will be treated in chapters 8 and 9. What interests us in the present section is Wittgenstein's claim that the statements enunciated by the solipsist are disguised nonsense or, more precisely, tautologies masquerading as factual truths.

The claim puts in several appearances. One of these is provoked by a peculiar complication in the thinking of Wittgenstein's solipsist. The absence of possible confirming evidence of the experiences of others is taken to entail that it is *inconceivable* that there should be experiences other than one's own.[7] Likewise the impossibility of another person having one's own experiences is taken to imply that it is not only impossible but inconceivable that one should be understood by another person.[8] The notion of inconceivability surfaces in the solipsist's claim that sensations necessarily are private. Such a claim is clearly not an empirical one, a conclusion reached perhaps from examining a selection of sensations from various people and finding them all to be private. If it were empirical, Wittgenstein points out, then it could conceivably be refuted. For instance, the claim that pains are private could conceivably be refuted by two people having a part of their bodies in common, and each feeling the sting of a wasp in that part.[9] Wittgenstein's solipsist is presumably inclined to deny such a possibility. The solipsist's claim that one cannot have another person's sensations is consequently akin to a grammatical statement, such as the statement that one plays patience by oneself.[10] It is a mere tautology, not a factual statement and, as such, has no place in factual discourse. As Wittgenstein puts the matter, if it is inconceivable that others should have one's sensations, then "it loses its sense" to say one has them oneself.[11] Similarly, if it is inconceivable that one should know another person's feelings and hence makes no sense to say that one knows, then it makes no sense to say one does not know.[12] The claim of inconceivability deprives solipsistic theses of any factual import and must be abandoned if solipsism is to enunciate anything other than tautologies. In its place the solipsist can at best make the weaker claim that knowledge of another's experiences is impossible but conceivable.

Wittgenstein has his solipsist give a number of alternative formulations of the solipsistic theses, of which two are of particular interest. One such formulation is the phrase, "Whenever anything is seen, it is always I who see." Wittgenstein points out that the solipsist is not using the words 'see' and 'I' in their everyday sense. For the solipsist, seeing what a person sees amounts to being in that person's mind and having the same immediate object of vision. The I who is subject of the seeing turns out on persistent questioning not to be a particular individual with a particular bodily appearance, personality, character, and stock of memories. The solipsist means no particular constant entity lasting over time but rather something more akin to consciousness or the experience of seeing or the point of view of the visual field. Thus, in saying 'I see', the solipsist is saying something tautological like 'seeing sees'.[13]

A second formulation of solipsism the solipsist is tempted to give is the claim, "Only this is really seen," where 'this' is meant to refer to the visual field. Yet the pointing involved is not genuine pointing, Wittgenstein argues, but instead a visual pointing that one is supposed somehow to manage with one's attention, a pointing that cannot be directed sideways or behind to what is not seen since the visual field has no neighbor. Yet it makes sense to point to what is seen only if it makes sense to point to what is not seen, says Wittgenstein; the solipsist's pointing is a tautologous version of pointing, one that makes no sense.[14]

A rather puzzling point in the above remarks is the solipsist's characterization of himself or herself as a mere gaze or consciousness. The notion of the perceiver as a pure impersonal consciousness identical with seeing is hardly one any sane person would employ with regard to everyday perception. Why then does Wittgenstein have his solipsist do so? There would seem to be several possible answers. The truth might well be that in fact Wittgenstein would endorse all of them.

Since subsequent discussion in *The Blue Book* concerns the difference between sense data and everyday objects, there is some reason to conclude that the impersonal perceiver, or pure gaze, is simply the equivalent, on the plane of sense data, of the everyday perceiver on the plane of everyday objects. Yet if such is Wittgenstein's construal of the matter, then Wittgenstein must be in error. The doubts regarding unobserved existence, causal regularities, and reality cannot possibly reduce the full-blown, everyday perceiver to something akin to a mere gaze. A reduced person, no less than a reduced pumpkin, retains all the actually perceived characteristics of the unreduced one, which characteristics in the present instance clearly go well beyond that of being a mere consciousness.

Since in both *The Blue Book* and *Philosophical Investigations* Wittgenstein immediately goes on to discuss the topic of the referent of 'I' in first-person reports,[15] there is good reason to think that the solipsist's perceiver is the first person subject. The pronoun 'I' in its first-person use is said by Wittgenstein not to be the name of a person and not to operate with the usual criteria of personal identity—whence arises the illusion that it refers to something bodiless. This bodiless subject might reasonably be considered the subject intended in the declarations of the solipsist. Yet if such were the case, the illusion is one open to everyone, and it is difficult to see why the solipsist should be signaled out for making it or why the solipsist in particular should make the mistake at all. Since it is a mistake neither peculiar nor necessary to solipsism, it cannot rightly be used to show that solipsistic declarations are tautologous.

A third and quite plausible explanation of the solipsist's view of the perceiving subject is that it results from a confused interpretation of the Representational Theory of Perception. A first point about which to be quite clear is that Wittgenstein's solipsist is a Sensa Solipsist. Various concepts integral to the solipsist's point of view are explicable only as concepts arising from the Representational Theory of Perception. One such is the notion of seeing as having something private before one's mind's eye. The notion of privacy has no place in an account of everyday perceptual activity, since in the latter, neither the seeing nor the thing seen are private. They become private only through the Representational Theory that makes what is seen the end product of retinal and cerebral stimulation in one's physical brain.

The notion that the visual field has no neighbor is also an incongruous notion within an everyday account of perceptual activities. One's visual field is simply a certain region of the world and hence something well provided with neighbors. Only in the Representational Theory where the visual field becomes something akin to a photograph somehow closely related to a cerebral negative does the assertion of a dearth of neighbors become warranted. Equally incongruous in an everyday account is the notion of perception, visual perception in particular, as a matter of having sensations.

Now, let us take a closer look at this account of perception with its notion of private sensations a perceiver has, and let us ask who is the perceiver or subject who has the sensations. It cannot be the perceiver in the material world, since the material subject and surrounding material environment figure among the sensations the subject is supposed to have. An actually perceived patch of blue sky, for instance, cannot be a sensation had by the material perceiver whose blurred nose and nebulous felt body figure marginally in the experience. Such a claim would be nonsensical since it would group both the sky and the perceiver among the perceiver's sensations. The perceiver who has the sensations must then be the physical perceiver in the physical world. This claim does make sense. The sense organs that are stimulated sending nerve impulses to the brain are sense organs in the physical world, and the perceiver who has the stimulated sense organs is the physical perceiver. Consequently, the physical subject should be the one who has the sensations.

The physical subject is, of course, nowhere to be found in the material world of which the solipsist (or anyone else) is aware. If Wittgenstein's solipsist expected to find the sensation-having subject within the confines of the material world, he would have little success, and it would not be surprising if he subsequently described the perceiving subject as a pure consciousness or pure gaze identical with the act of seeing. The latter characterization is not very far removed from one given by David Hume. In the light of his findings from an assiduous search among the contents of his mind, Hume describes the self as "a perfect non-entity," and likens the mind to a theatre devoid of location and structural materials.[16] Suspiciously enough, the mind as characterized by Hume resembles the neighborless assembly of sensations of Wittgenstein's solipsist. No less suspicious is the fact that both Hume and Wittgenstein's solipsist introduce notions and terminology peculiar to the Representational Theory into their accounts of everyday perception. Thus, it is not only possible but indeed quite plausible that when they fail to find anything more substantial than a gaze to act as subject or self, it is because they are looking for the wrong subject; they are mistakenly trying to find the perceiver who has the sensations, in fact the physical perceiver, within the flux of sensations. If such is the case, then both are conceptually confused with respect to the implications of the Representational Theory. In this regard it is an interesting footnote that Wittgenstein makes the claim that a solipsist's 'visual room' is something that has no owner; its owner is not to be found in it, and it has no outside.[17] Wittgenstein seems to have been quite unaware of the connection of 'visual rooms' of the sort with the Representational Theory. Be this as it may, if Wittgenstein is identifying the self with a being in an outside inaccessible world, then it is hardly surprising to find his solipsist reduced to uttering what appear to be tautologies.

It should be clear, however, that a more enlightened Sensa Solipsist need do nothing of the sort. In speaking of the perceiving self, the solipsist may quite sensibly mean the perceiver in the material world, and there is no clear reason to speak of that particular perceiver as a pure gaze or consciousness. Furthermore, the Sensa Solipsist has no need to characterize the actually perceived world as one with no outside; the outside of that world is simply the continuation of space in any specifiable direction. The absurdities Wittgenstein quite nicely brings to light are not those of the Sensa Solipsist. The operation of elucidation helps to empty the fly-bottle only of those solipsists similarly confused.

As we saw earlier, Sensa Solipsism is an epistemological problem resolvable within epistemology. Indeed, insofar as it is an epistemological problem, it *must* be resolved epistemologically if it is to be put definitively to rest. The move Wittgenstein makes into semantics in his attempt to answer the problem is a misguided changing of the subject. If it holds out an illusion of promise, it is only because semantics reflects epistemological acquisitions. In our subsequent inquiries we shall find this negative assessment of the move into semantics repeatedly corroborated.

CRITERIA REJECTION AND ILLICIT COINAGE

By far the simplest of antiskeptical linguistic arguments is one that might be termed the *Paradigm Case Argument*. It consists simply of a lexical reminder that such-and-such is what is ordinarily meant by a given expression. When the skeptic expresses doubt as to whether an observed phenomenon such as *f* actually is an *F*, the answer to come back is that an *f* is precisely what is called "an *F.*" Wittgenstein often makes use of this line of reasoning. To the question of whether experiential criteria justify belief, he responds with the further questions, "What is *called* a justification here?—How is the word 'justification' used?"[18] In like fashion, to the question of whether it is right to be guided by the propositions of physics, he retorts that this is what is called "being rightly convinced," or again, what is called "an empirical foundation" or "a good ground."[19] Similarly, skeptical doubts regarding knowledge provoke the observation, "if we are using the verb 'to know' as it is normally used,...then we very often do know things of the kind."[20] An analogous line of reasoning lies behind Austin's retort, "Well, if that's not seeing a real chair then *I don't know what is.*"[21]

As it stands, the answer is insufficient to provide anything close to a dismissal of skeptical doubts. The latter arise only in cases where to characterize a phenomenon is to go beyond a mere description of what is ostensibly there in the phenomenon and to attribute to it certain characteristics the presence of which is susceptible to doubt. In asking whether an *f* is an *F*, the skeptic is asking whether an *f* has these further characteristics. To reply that the expression, "an *F*," is by the norms of the language rightly applied to phenomena such as *f*, is simply not to address the skeptic's question. The latter could be answered only by showing that the norms of the language do provide good reason to think the characteristics are present. Indeed, if linguistic practice alone were sufficient for epistemic justification, the beliefs of any linguistic community whatever would find themselves justified. As Don Locke puts the matter, "a similar argument could, at appropriate times, have been used to prove anything from the flatness of the earth to the existence of the gods in the trees."[22]

Nevertheless, the resources of the paradigm case argument are not exhausted with the rebuttal of the above claim. It may be plausibly maintained that the criteria operative in the use of an expression are what give the expression the meaning it has and that consequently the rejection of the criteria deprives the expression of its meaning. Unless new criteria are provided, the expression is meaningless. This point may be turned against the skeptic if, as is often the case, the latter needs the expression in order to draw a distinction essential to the statement of the skeptical thesis. Where the skeptic makes essential use of an expression, yet questions its criteria and endows it with no new criteria to give it meaning, a promising case might be made for the claim that the skeptic is talking nonsense.

Attempts of the sort abound. This particular line of reasoning is implicit in the following dismissal by Quine of skeptical qualms and attendant proposals of rational reconstruction: "For surely the key words, 'understood', 'real', and 'evidence' here are too ill-defined to stand up to such punishment. We should only be depriving them of the very denotations to which they mainly owe such sense as they make to us."[23] It is also the backbone of Wittgenstein's quip that if, as the skeptic claims, all behavior might be pretense, the concept of pretense would be unusable since it would have no criteria in behavior.[24] It is quite explicit in Bouwsma's assessment of the Cartesian question, "Am I awake or asleep?" Descartes cannot be using the constituent expressions as they are ordinarily used, Bouwsma points out, since if he were, the question would have a ready answer—whence Bouwsma concludes that Descartes must be using language "which is significant only in terms of the distinctions which he has abandoned."[25]

Austin gives the line of argument one of its clearest and most elaborate articulations when he reasons as follows with regard to skeptical doubts:

> These doubts are all to be allayed by means of recognized procedures (more or less roughly recognized of course), appropriate to the particular type of case. There are recognized ways of distinguishing between dreaming and waking (how otherwise should we know how to use and to contrast the words?) and of deciding whether a thing is stuffed or live, and so forth.[26]

The procedures give the words their meaning, and without the procedures there would no longer be a contrast to be drawn. The distinction is normally drawn, Austin rightly points out, not by the detection of some positive characteristic, reality, but in terms of some specific way in which a thing might be *not* real. Consequently, Austin argues, the question of whether a thing is real must suggest or presuppose some specific way or ways of being sham: to ask the question, for instance, of a rabbit or of an oasis is to suggest that the first may be stuffed and the second a mirage[27] (and not the contrary).

The threat posed by many of these claims is dissipated by the point noted in the preceding chapter that Unreal World Solipsism is raising an issue quite distinct from that raised in everyday issues of unreality. The scenario envisaged by the Oneirata Solipsist is not an everyday one, which as Bouwsma rightly points out, would be readily dismissed. It is one whereby the everyday world including both waking life and natural dreams is but a vast dream. Such a scenario certainly does not appear to be meaningless. It is quite conceivable that one should awake one day to make the envisaged discovery. Likewise, it is conceivable that one should in some roughly analogous fashion discover one day that the everyday world is the conjuration of a deceitful demon, or some all-pervasive and systematic illusion. The relevant experiences, that of waking up in some other world, or of being informed by some demon of the unreality of the world, information backed perhaps by an explanation of how the illusion was realized, would consequently play the role of criteria in virtue of which the skeptical thesis was judged to be true. Thus, it can hardly be rightly claimed that the reality/sham distinctions drawn are devoid of criteria and hence meaningless.

Cartesian skepticism regarding unobserved existence voices concern with the alleged rationality of the everyday criteria, and the warrant the criteria provide for commonsense views on the relevant issues. This form of solipsism consequently finds itself in a quite different dialectical situation from that of skepticism about reality. It rejects the standard criteria for determining what objects do during periods of time when they are unobserved. The accusation against such skepticism should be, on the line of thinking being examined, that the relevant expressions, "unobserved object," "hidden far side," have been thereby rendered meaningless. Yet surely this accusation overdramatizes the consequences of the solipsistic rejection. Certainly spatial expressions such as "hidden place" or "unobserved region," seem meaningful enough. In the simplest case the places to which reference is made are merely the prolongation of some expanse of visually, auditorially, and/or tactually perceived space. One's own body as felt is clearly spatial, just as is anything visually perceived; the unperceived place is the spatial prolongation of a line between two perceived places. Consequently, it is meaningful to speak of a hidden place or region. Yet if such is the case, surely it is also meaningful to speak of the possible occupants of the hidden place or of its possible emptiness. If the hidden place can be conceived to be occupied or unoccupied, then to say that the corresponding expressions are meaningless is to fly in the face of the obvious.

It would be futile to object that the solipsist rejects the ordinary criteria, leaving no criteria with which to determine whether the unobserved place is occupied or not, and that in these circumstances the solipsist cannot meaningfully use the correlated expressions. To do so would be to overlook an obvious rejoinder. If the problem is simply that there are no criteria, the solipsist may easily propose that the following criterion be used to remedy the deficit: if a thing is observed, it exists; if it is not, it does not. If the further objection arises that such a criterion is arbitrary or irrational, then the solipsist might propose one based on the Principle of Parsimony: an unobserved place is occupied or not depending on which thesis involves the lesser ontological commitment. Simple arithmetic analysis clearly yields a decision in favor of solipsistic frugality. It should not be overlooked that any fears of meaninglessness due to an absence of criteria are simultaneously allayed.

There is, to be sure, some danger of dissatisfaction with the solipsist's proposed criteria. It could be argued that the Principle of Parsimony has not been shown to be rational. Yet the solipsist could point out that in the absence of a demonstration of warrant, the everyday criteria are no more rational or truth-assuring than any other consistent set of criteria that might be advocated. As matters stand, there is no sound reason to accord ordinary criteria either preferential status or preferential treatment. If the arbitrariness and irrationality of criteria produce meaninglessness, then they do so for the everyday criteria no less than for the solipsistic ones; arguments of the sort yield equal meaninglessness for all. It must be admitted that there seems little to reply cogently on this latter point.

The key expression, 'sense data', cannot fall under the preceding criticisms. The term has been coined for epistemological purposes, and hence, it cannot involve a distortion of normal usage. Any criticism of its meaningfulness must rather question whether it has been correctly coined, so its use involves a misuse of language, perhaps serious enough to produce nonsense.

One version of such a claim concerns the skeptical request for justification of commonsense beliefs in terms of reports about sense data. The request involves what Gilbert Ryle stigmatizes as a "logical howler" on the grounds that it confuses sense data with objects, or sensations with observation. Observing entails having sensations while the contrary is not true, Ryle argues; sensations are not things one observes but things one has.[28]

The short answer to Ryle is that it is also a logical howler to equate sense data with sensations. The sense data integrated into a Representational Theory of Perception (the sensa of Sensa Solipsism) may rightly be so characterized, but not the sense data reached by stripping everyday objects of all characteristics other than ostensible ones. The items so reached would seem more aptly characterized as stripped objects. Indeed, there is no apparent reason whatever to characterize property-shorn stretches of sensuous material, whether visual, tactual, or auditory, as sensations. A mottled brown surface, a feline cry, a hard expanse under circling palm, not one of these sense data, when considered simply on its own merits, cries out to be labeled a sensation. It is not private—or at least not ostensibly so. It is not had—as sensations are—but perceived. A patch of brown, a whine, and a firm resistance are seen, heard, and felt, a fact that on Ryle's linguistic criterion classifies them as objects and not as sensations.

Another form of the claim of improper coinage aims at the verb that takes expressions for sense data as its direct object, the expression 'directly perceive'. The sense datum theorist's use of the expression is esteemed, for instance, by Austin to be "obscurely metaphorical" and then "ultimately meaningless." Austin's chief complaint is that it is given no definition and little explanation; as a result, it is quite unclear what constitutes perceiving indirectly for senses other than vision—what constitutes hearing indirectly, touching or feeling indirectly, smelling indirectly.[29]

Austin's complaint is indicative primarily of a certain degree of pedagogical ineptitude on the part of classical sense datum theorists. The intended sense of the expressions 'directly perceive' and 'immediately perceive', when used by sense datum epistemologists, is clear enough. As noted earlier, it is a straightforward extension of the expressions 'actually perceive', 'really see', and so on, as used in everyday contexts. A witness at an inquest or trial, for instance, may be enjoined to relate what she (he) actually saw as opposed to what she thinks that she saw, or what she actually heard a person say as opposed to what she assumed the person meant. The distinction being drawn in such cases may be readily expanded into a broader distinction between what is actually perceived of a thing (a visible side, a tactual façade, an aroma, a warmth) and what is not (a far side, the inside, and so on). The resulting distinction is sufficiently clear to avoid the problems Austin finds regarding indirect perception as opposed to the direct sort. One may significantly ask and easily answer the question of what is actually perceived and what is not with regard to senses other than sight. Let us borrow momentarily some of the cases judged by Austin to create difficulty. Touching a person with a barge pole fails to qualify as actually feeling the person; at best, there is actual feeling of the gripped part of the barge pole, of tension in one's arms, and of variable downward pulls, upward pressures, and backward thrusts; there is no reason to claim one actually feels the person. Feeling a pig in a poke is actually feeling a resistance to pressure over a volume that is roughly pig-shaped; it is not actually feeling a pig. In smelling an apple pie, the actual smelling is a mere awareness of a specific qualitative presence in the nasal region of one's tactual face; there is no actual smelling the apple pie since presumably the latter is an independent object situated elsewhere in the world.

There is nevertheless one sense in which complaints about the definitions of 'actually perceive' and 'sense data' do have some basis in fact. Ultimately, one of the two terms must be defined ostensibly through examples, since any other type of definition turns out to be circular. For instance, let us define 'sense data' in terms of 'actually perceive,' and then attempt to give a noncircular definition of the latter. We might attempt to define 'actual perception' roughly to be 'perception taking as its object what remains after the deletion of anything the denial of which is consistent with the perceptual evidence'. This yields a working definition of sorts, but any attempt at explication reveals its circularity. The possibility of doubting a thing's presence is determined by confronting the data with the hypothesis of the thing's absence. Spelling this out involves saying what is meant by 'the data' or 'the perceptual evidence', and clearly in the present context the expressions means 'sense data' or 'what is actually perceived'. Thus, the definition states the tautology that actual perception is perception taking as its object what is actually perceived.

Benson Mates's explication of the concept of direct perception, while satisfying on many counts, likewise cannot be erected into a definition without circularity. As a first step, Mates introduces the notion of 'relative direct perception', and then defines 'direct perception' as perception directly relative to nothing else. On Mates's analysis, a thing is said to be directly perceived relative to another if it could continue to be perceived even if the other did not exist, whereas the other could not be perceived if the first did not exist.[30] One merit among many of this approach to the analysis of the concept is that it avoids mention of indubitability or incorrigibility and thus allows for the possibility of erroneous sense datum reports. It should be recognized, however, that it does not yield a noncircular definition. The joker in the works is the word "could." The possibility being entertained cannot be a matter of mere conceivability: the object could conceivably be perceived even if the sense datum did not exist since a different face of the object could be perceived. Thus, the possibility being entertained is one of conceivability given a particular experience; hence, it is one of compatibility with the given perceptual evidence. Now, the evidence in question must be the actual evidence. If it were the evidence in the everyday sense of evidence where what is perceived is a full material object, the supposition of the nonexistence of the object would not be consistent with the evidence. The possibility involved is thus one of consistency with the actual data. Since the actual data is what is actually perceived, the account is circular if construed as a definition. This result must not be taken to show that either the concept or the definition is defective. Definitional circularity does not necessarily indicate conceptual confusion. Indeed, 'perception' itself as used in everyday discourse, has ultimately no non-circular definition except an ostensible one.

It is interesting that of the two concepts of 'perception' and 'actual perception', the latter is a more plausible candidate for the role of primitive concept in a formal system. Consider the following some-what rough-hewn equivalence:

I perceive a mug if and only if:

1. I actually perceive a mug-shaped surface;

2. I know that what I actually perceive is not illusory in any way;

3. I know that behind what I actually perceive, a hidden surface continues forming a moderate-sized container with a handle and capable of holding liquids.

Generalized and formalized this equivalence could be made to yield something approaching a definition of 'perception' in terms of 'actual perception.' The converse operation appears to be impossible.

THE VERIFICATION REQUIREMENT

The term, *verification requirement*, might be used to characterize any requirement similar to the logical positivist verification principle, itself an often-revised principle of which the import was roughly that for a sentence to be cognitively meaningful it must express a state-ment that can be verified or falsified by the evidence of empirical observation. The term, *instantiation requirement*, might be used for an analogous meaning requirement formulated with regard to terms and expressions rather than full sentences. A requirement of the latter sort is to be found in the claim voiced at times by linguistic philosophy that for a term or expression to be meaningful there must exist cases in which the use of an expression is appropriate. Otherwise stated, the requirement is that if the expression "an F" is to be meaningful, then there must be or have been instances of F's. If such a condition does in fact hold for expressions generally, then the fact of the mean-ingfulness of such expressions would suffice to establish the central doctrine of objectualist epistemology, the doctrine that any cognitive enterprise presupposes the existence of objects.

The claim that there is such a requirement is implied in the follow-ing remark by Wittgenstein: "When one says: 'Perhaps this planet doesn't exist and the light phenomenon arises in some other way', then after all one does need an example of an object which does exist. This doesn't exist,—as *for example* does...."[31] A closely related line of reasoning, one which enjoyed its five minutes of celebrity some years back, construes skeptical scenarios as abnormal occurrences possible only on a background of normal ones. This line is to be found in Ryle's succinct remark that in a country with no coinage there could be no counterfeiters,[32] and in Austin's claim that "talk about deception only *makes sense* against a background of general non-deception."[33]

In general form, the reasoning is quite obviously unsound. Expressions such as 'unicorn', 'goblin', or 'evil spirits' are meaningful enough. If instances were a prerequisite for meaningfulness, the existence of creatures instantiating these expressions would find itself guaranteed. Thus, the most that may be maintained is that in the case of at least some of the words in our language, there must be actual instances to which these words truly apply. The problem then arises of how to determine which expressions are the favored ones graced with actual instances.

It is a plausible enough suggestion that there must be some instances of such sensuous things as colored patches and sounds. How indeed could names of colors be meaningful if no speaker had ever experienced any concrete instances of colors in the world? An analogous case might be made for acquaintance with instances of shapes and spatial characteristics. To be able to converse about spatial relations and configurations, one cannot be totally unacquainted with such things or with structurally similar items. Although this conclusion gets us moving in the desired direction, it is difficult to see how it may take us far enough to be useful in countering solipsism. While there may well have to be instances of colors and shapes, for example, instances of red and others of oval shapes, it would in no way be precluded that the instances may cease to exist when unobserved, or that they are mirages or constituents of a dream. The semantics of words for sensuous qualities and geometrical characteristics is consequently not a very promising source of refutations of skeptical claims.

The situation is similar with regard to the existence of instances of the things named by object words. Even when it is granted that at least some object words must have instances, these instances could well be solipsistic ones of a kind quite unthreatening to a solipsistic ontology. The instance of a cat necessary to make the word 'cat' meaningful might still be found in a world in which all cats were complex illusions (or alternatively, dreamt cats or demon conjurations). Likewise, the fleeting, partial cats of the Ephemerata Solipsist's world would suffice to provide the required cat instances. There is no obvious reason to think that any of the required instances of cats must be fully fleshed out solids, or that to qualify as a cat, a candidate must be endowed with unperceived cat parts—or, as one might put the matter, that it must be substantive cat rather than merely physiognomic one. Wittgenstein quite rightly insists that ordinary language does not function with very rigid criteria, a point Austin illustrates with the comment that no refund is warranted on the protest that a five-legged pig is not a pig.[34] Indeed, physiognomic or ephemeral cats do not seem to fall outside the range of unrigid criteria governing the possible application of the word 'cat'. It would certainly be unwise to use the word 'cat' without warning in ordinary conversation to refer to some such physiognomic entity, chiefly if one wishes to avoid serious misunderstandings and unflattering personal appraisals, but that is another matter.

A verification requirement proper, one having to do with sentences rather than mere expressions, may appear initially to show more promise. The requirement cannot reasonably be too severe, however. As the logical positivists noted, it cannot be required of a sentence that to be meaningful the statement it purports to make must be in principle capable of being conclusively verified. The sticking point here is that such a requirement would call for knowledge or absolute certainty to be possible. If certainty of the sort were a prerequisite for meaningfulness, a vast number of everyday claims could well turn out to be meaningless, for as argued earlier in chapter 3, conclusive verification in many cases appears to involve something akin to the summing of an infinite series. Any condition for meaningfulness should require at most high likelihood, warrant, or good reason, rather than knowledge. Good reason should replace knowledge even where the verification requirement is diluted as by A. C. Danto to a mere possibility of knowledge.[35] The summing of an infinite series is not a possibility for a human observer.

In addition the requirement must make allowances for cases in which it is possible to have evidence supporting the statement but not subverting evidence, or alternatively, where it is possible to have evidence against the statement but not in favor of it. There are criteria for determining whether an item is a part of a dream or an illusion and that whether the envisaged hoax is of the everyday sort or of the kind envisaged by a skeptic. On the other hand, as Austin points out so nicely, there are no criteria for determining that something is real. Nevertheless, one would not wish to claim that judgments attributing reality are meaningless. A similar situation is encountered at times in mathematics, for instance in the matter of determining whether the sequence 0 1 2 3 4 5 6 7 8 9 is to be encountered anywhere in the decimal expansion of some particular irrational number. While an examination of the expansion to some finite number of digits may resolve the question if the sequence is encountered, there is no test (or rather, there may be no known test) that shows that the sequence cannot be encountered in any possible continuation of the expansion however far. Nevertheless, it hardly follows that the issue of whether there is such a sequence is made meaningless by this fact. Criterial peculiarities of the sort appear to have no adverse effect on the meaningfulness of the pertinent statements.

These considerations leave us with a somewhat weakened form of the verification requirement. Our present version states that for a sentence to be meaningful, it must be possible in principle to have good reason for judging the statement it purports to make very likely to be true or very likely to be false. The question to be examined now is whether solipsistic statements may be shown incapable of satisfying this requirement.

The solipsistic scenarios that call into question the reality of the world do appear to envisage a situation in which the verification requirement is satisfied. Generally, the scenario has it that at some future time one comes upon weighty accumulation of evidence in favor of the existence of the world described in the skeptical scenario. One wakes up in strange surrounds containing strong evidence that the past one remembers was but a long dream, or alternatively, one begins receiving messages from a self-described demon seized with remorse for his or her past deceptions and bent on revealing the sham of the world. Since such events are conceivable, it is possible in principle for the skeptical thesis to be made likely by the evidence. There is no significant difference on this point between skeptical hoaxes and everyday ones.

Where the two differ somewhat is in the fact that when the question arises as to whether some everyday item is a hoax, it is possible to settle the issue one way or another with a limited number of tests. Such tests are impossible in the case of the familiar Cartesian scenarios. There are no tests that may be run to determine whether the perceived world is part of a solipsistic dream or demon's conjuration. On the solipsistic hypothesis the sham can be revealed only by some unpredictable future experience. Likewise, it would be useless to embark upon a trip to Alpha Centauri with a view to rummaging about for brains in the relevant receptacles, since the postulated brain inhabits a different spatiotemporal system (also postulated); one can only stand and wait for some future revelation indicating the illusory nature of the everyday world. The skeptical hypotheses are verifiable but not testable. Unfortunately, there is no clear way in which this peculiarity of the skeptical theses might be used to show that they fail to satisfy the verification requirement for meaning.

One mention-worthy and valiant attempt in this direction is due to Thompson Clarke. The target is the skeptical dream scenario, and the claim made is that the scenario excludes the possibility of a warranted judgment about one's dreaming, and so is senseless.[36] Clarke argues that the notion of being asleep implies that of real surroundings, which in turn implies that the surrounds could in principle be known to be real by outside observers. Yet such a possibility is, according to Clarke, ruled out in principle by Descartes's concept of a dream as an experience indistinguishable by any marks or features from that of a waking world; the outside observer could not know the surrounds to be real since his own experiences might be part of a dream. This circumstance leads Clarke to reason as follows:

> It is inconceivable that I could now be asleep, dreaming, *if* no outsider could know my real environs because in the same boat, for the same reason, because he, too, could not know he was not asleep, dreaming. Does Descartes's possibility even *seem* to make sense, if we ask ourselves how the Evil Demon, or God, could know that he, too, wasn't dreaming—and allow that neither could?[37]

Clarke's claim is that Descartes's dream hypothesis is ultimately senseless; it contravenes the minimal verification requirement that it should be possible in principle for some observer to verify a distinction (real/sham) drawn in the hypothesis.

Yet the reasoning is clearly unsound. Certainly, any reality/sham distinction conceptually implies something real, a state of affairs or world with respect to which something else is unreal. Certainly too, it is not extravagant to claim that it should be possible in principle for some outside observer (an observer who is a constituent of the real world as opposed to a constituent of the unreal one) to have good reason to think that the cosmos contains a reality/sham dichotomy of the kind. However, the concept of a reality/sham dichotomy does not imply that the real section of the cosmic dichotomy must be real *simpliciter*, i.e., that it cannot itself be unreal with respect to some further reality. The Cartesian dream scenario already involves the notion of a dream within a dream, since this is what everyday dreams become on the solipsistic hypothesis. The notion is not absurd. Nor is it absurd to hypothesize that the postulated world with respect to which the present world is but a dream is itself in turn only a dream with respect to some further reality. The wily demon who conjures up a world solely in order to deceive Descartes might similarly be himself the artifact of some further wily demon. Such a state of affairs is certainly conceivable enough. Indeed, there is nothing incoherent in the notion of a cosmos ordered like a series of Chinese boxes with each world an appearance or sham with regard to some further world. In any of the numerous dichotomies, let us say the nth level dichotomy, the real world in that dichotomy would be the unreal world at level $(n + 1)$ of reality/sham dichotomies. It would be possible in principle for a real observer at any level to have reason to think there is a reality/sham distinction to be drawn at that level. This circumstance should suffice to assure the meaningfulness of the expressions 'real' and 'sham' at that level. Surely these expressions could not be rendered meaningless by the mere fact that there are no marks or features of the real world to which the real observer may appeal to determine whether or not the real world is not a sham at a higher level; for the meaningfulness of the distinction it suffices that it is possible in principle for *some* observer to make a warranted claim, and that condition is satisfied. The condition may be satisfied at any level: a succession of demons does the trick. In Clarke's argument it is quite incorrectly assumed that the observer (God or Demon) capable of attesting to the dichotomy of one level must also be in a position to say whether or not there is any higher level of dichotomy.

In a eulogistic account of Clarke's reflections on the issue, Barry Stroud construes the essential point of Clarke's reasoning in a way that makes it a variant on the self-referential manoeuvre encountered in chapter 3. Stroud reasons that if there really is no way of telling at any given time whether or not one is dreaming, then any knowledge gained later could itself also be but an element in a dream. Says Stroud: "My later claim to knowledge would then be as vulnerable to criticism as my present claim is. So that if I do not know now that I am not dreaming, I would not know then that I had been dreaming earlier either."[38] Dream skepticism calls itself into question, according to Stroud, in that it calls into question the very possibility it proposes.

Stroud's interpretation is no less unsound than the version that features demons or gods. In the second version, there are two discontinuous stretches of waking experience. The second stretch presumably contains certain experiences that suggest the first was a dream: perhaps an awakening to find oneself sleepy-eyed in the presence of an ebullient and pedagogically disposed demon. The discontinuity in conjunction with the explanatory experience give reason to think that the prior stretch of experience was a dream. The conclusion is well founded given the evidence. It is in no way threatened by the possibility that the second stretch of experience is a dream with respect to some third stretch of experience due to begin at some later time. Such a possibility leaves the evidence exactly as it is. If that evidence provides firm support for the conclusion prior to the introduction of the envisaged possibility, it should continue to do so afterward. To think otherwise can only be to take too seriously the derogatory connotations of the word 'dream', and to assume incorrectly that genuine reasoning and knowledge are impossible in any experience that may aptly be termed a dream. As noted in chapter 3, if 'a dream' is taken to mean merely 'an experience that comes to an end with an awakening', then there is no reason to exclude genuine thinking and reasoning from a dream. There is no apparent obstacle to my experiencing a series of awakenings in which each prior awakening is part of a dream relative to the next, and the awakening prior to that an awakening which is part of a dream within a dream, and so on.

It seems safe to conclude, then, that the skeptical hypotheses that question reality cannot be rejected as senseless on the ground that they fail to meet the verification requirement. Not only do they seem to make sense, but they are verifiable in principle—albeit by an occurrence aptly described as an unprovokable, unforeseeable revelation: an awakening to another world, or a spectacular message from a brain-probing scientist. The theses are verifiable but not testable.

The situation is slightly different with regard to skeptical theses denying unobserved existence. Skeptics dubious of everyday claims about unobserved phenomena reject, by the same token, certain widely accepted empirical generalizations and investigative procedures. Despite this rejection, it is unclear how to turn the verification requirement to effective use against the skeptic denying unobserved existence or unobserved regularities. Consider the situation. The requirement for meaning is that it should be possible for some observer to have good reason one way or the other on the issue being raised. That issue concerns the occupants of the unobserved regions of present and past space that continue the present and past space of actually observed phenomena. Now, it is apparently meaningful enough to speak of regions in a space that is the extension of the space actually observed, even though the regions themselves are not actually under observation at present. By the same token, it is meaningful to speak of places in a past or a future that are an extension of the space and time flow of actually perceived events, even though the places are not now actually observed. Furthermore, since it is meaningful to speak of such regions of space and time, it must be meaningful to speak of them as occupied or unoccupied with sensuous entities of various kinds. Finally, it is conceivable enough that the unobserved regions of space should be now observed by some perceiver. That perceiver might even be the solipsist, since it is certainly conceivable that the solipsist should now have been observing these places instead of the ones he or she is actually observing. Hence, such talk is meaningful under the verification requirement, the requirement that for an utterance to constitute a meaningful statement it must be possible for some observer to have good evidence for or against it.

Thus, although the skeptic admits no criteria that might now be employed to determine whether the space is occupied, the skeptical claim that it is occupied by nothing remains meaningful. A plausible case for meaninglessness might be made if it could be shown that on the skeptical thesis no conceivable observer can have any good grounds for determining one way or the other whether anything occupies the unobserved spatial and temporal regions. Since the solipsistic claim is compatible with the required conceivable support, there is little prospect of establishing a case of the sort.

THE REFERENCE REQUIREMENT

One of the more recent semantic hurdles to the skeptical dash toward solipsism is one erected by Hilary Putnam, and which centers on the issue of the conditions for successful reference. The object of Putnam's attentions is the skeptical thesis that one might be a mere brain stimulated and sustained in a vat by some playful scientist, but it should be added that with minimal change the argument could be made equally effective against Oneirata, Demoniac, or Phantasmata Solipsism. The case, briefly stated, is that the thesis is self-refuting: a vat-dwelling brain would be unable to think of such real objects as trees, or brains and vats, because reference to real objects would be impossible for the brain. Reference, Putnam argues, requires that there should be some connection between a word and its referent, a particular sort of causal relation in virtue of which the former can refer to the latter. Words do not refer magically on their own, Putnam reasons, nor do they refer via occult noetic rays; the conclusion drawn is that they can only refer through a causal connection of the appropriate sort.[39] In the scenario of a brain in a vat, the plight of the brain rules out the appropriate causal connection between the brain's thoughts and objects in the world. Hence, if true, the skeptical thesis could not be thought by the brain.

The argument admits of some variation. It may be claimed either that the common nouns 'brain' and 'vat' thought by a brain in a vat would fail to refer or, alternatively, that they would refer to the phenomenal brains and vats produced by the scientist's stimulation. In an assessment of Putnam's argument, Anthony Bruechner alludes to yet a third variant born of what he terms "the Burge-style strategy" and according to which such expressions uttered in the context of a solipsistic world would have no determinable meaning.[40] Whether the diagnosis is failure of reference, displacement of reference, or indeterminacy of reference, the skeptical utterances are being found dysfunctional. If warranted, the pronouncement would be fatal to solipsistic theses that question reality.

The flaw in the argument in all three of its versions is that it presupposes an erroneous account of reference. On that erroneous account, sortal nouns may successfully refer and consequently be meaningful only if they have a causal connection of a specific sort with their referents. This claim has some plausibility when it is a matter of a recognizable species and substance—insofar as it amounts to a requirement of acquaintance with the species or substance either on the part of the speaker or of other members of the speech community. In this regard, the requirement might be seen as a revamped edition of the paradigm case argument. Yet there are far more serious objections involved.

It is quite inaccurate to allege a need for a referential causal relation for terms applying to more speculative or problematic natural kinds. Natural kinds of the sort make their appearance quite regularly in history and in science. Two distinct questions may arise regarding them. One is simply the very basic question of whether a natural kind of the sort is conceivable. The second is the more interesting one of whether instances of the kind exist, thus allowing meaningful factual assertions about the kind. The first question receives an affirmative answer when it is a matter of species terms such as 'goddess', 'centaur', 'Yeti', 'extra-terrestrial visitor', 'dinosaur', 'quark', 'blackhole', 'superplasma'. The second question is answered affirmatively for certain of them, negatively for others, while for still others the issue is undecided, since it is undecided whether the term refers to anything. Now, Putnam's claim is that for the term to be meaningful an appropriate causal connection is needed, a condition that can be fulfilled only if the second question is answered affirmatively. Such a claim implies that many of the above-listed terms are meaningless. This result is clearly wrong-headed. In speculation about possible situations and explanations of observed phenomena, there is no need of an appropriate causal connection to assure the meaningfulness of the natural-kind terms of which the function is to designate the envisaged referents.

In point of fact, in establishing or denying meaning to natural kind terms, considerations of causal connections often play no role. Fictional species are often ruled to be fictional because of a failure to satisfy known natural or physical laws, rather than from any lack of testimony as to their existence. Unobservable kinds, such as electrons or quarks, are postulated to explain a variety of phenomena, hardly a situation aptly described as providing a requisite causal relation between name and referent. Similar situations are not uncommon for natural-kind terms in anthropology and evolutionary biology. For instance, the fate of the two distinct species of *Australopithecus robustus* postulated by Dr. D. C. Johanson hangs on considerations of plausibility given other evidence on evolutionary propensities rather than on an appropriate causal connection between name and referent.[41] Such is the case for any species postulated as an element in an explanatory account. There is no hands-on causal baptism of the natural kind either at conception or at birth.

The situation is identical for natural kinds posited in speculative hypotheses. Certainly, no causal connection would seem needed for meaningful speculation. The expression, 'intelligent life in other solar systems', is a meaningful expression whether it has a referent or not. It has not been made meaningful through being in a causal relationship of a requisite kind to a referent. Nor is such a relationship necessary for the meaningfulness of sortal nouns used to designate states of matter subsequent to the Big Bang in speculation on the creation of the universe. If such speculation can be meaningful, there is little cause to declare meaningless all skeptical speculation about natural kinds, such as the vat-dwelling brain, the deceitful demon, or waking dreamers. The allegedly necessary causal relationships are no less lacking in one case than in the other.

In fairness to Putnam, due attention should be accorded the arguments he gives in favor of his thesis of the need for a causal connection for reference and hence for meaning. Central among these is the claim that signs do not refer of themselves, and consequently, reference must be achieved through some sort of connection between sign and referent; since it is implausible there should be a magical connection, Putnam concludes there can only be a causal one.[42] A second claim is that a 'mental state' or 'what goes on inside people's heads' (Putnam's terminology) is insufficient to fix reference, a point Putnam argues from a number of examples both actual and fictional. He concludes that consequently something more, a causal connection, is needed to achieve reference.[43] It should be noted that both of these lines of reasoning make the assumption that reference is a necessary part of meaning. This assumption plays a key role in Putnam's reasoning in the brain-in-vat scenario, for his claim is precisely that since the brain could not refer, it could not even think the vat scenario.

Putnam is quite mistaken with regard to the function of reference in meaning. Strictly speaking, reference as understood by Putnam is not a part of meaning at all; in the vast majority of cases, the referent figures in meaning only as a posit on the part of the speaker. Furthermore, contrary to what Putnam claims, when there is reference, it is always and only determined by the concept of the referent operative for the speaker. Putnam could hardly be further from the truth when he claims that "meanings just aren't in the head."[44] Whether it is a matter of natural-kind terms, those indecisive classifiers much discussed in the literature, or of proper names, those allegedly pure designators, meaning is always and solely conceptual—except, of course, to the extent that it contains an indexical component or reference to the actual perceptual situation of the speaker.

A somewhat extensive semantic investigation will be required to establish these points. We shall undertake this exploration in the following chapter, first into meaning generally, then into the place of reference in meaning and the issue of how reference is determined, then into the topics of the meaning of natural-kind terms and of proper names. As the investigation will show, any proper account of meaning must be Cartesian, which is to say, it must be a first-person account of the phenomenon for the individual for whom the phenomenon exists, as well as an account that is sensitive to the epistemological limitations of the individual perceiver. The undertaking is worthwhile for more than one reason. It will obviously be useful for the immediate purposes of exposing the falsity of the views on which Putnam's argument is based. It has far more than such local import. It will also be of considerable help in showing the falsity of other claims presupposed in linguistic parasitism arguments generally and having to do with linguistic meaning. Perhaps most importantly, it will provide a more accurate account of meaning than those in current commerce, an account of meaning involving merely associations, concepts, and indexical elements in perception and consequently one that may be willingly and warmly endorsed by the various Cartesian solipsists (and their nemesis, the rational foundationalist).

CHAPTER SEVEN

CARTESIAN SEMANTICS

MEANING AS PERSONALIZED ASSOCIATE

Linguistic meaning is but one species of a somewhat prolific genus. A brisk perusal of the senses of the verb 'to mean' readily turns up a wealth of cases similar to the linguistic ones in having a structure of the sort:

c means C for s,

where c is an occurrence, C is what is meant, and s is some conscious organism. For the cognizant observer, smoke means fire (which is not to say that 'smoke' means fire), the reddening of leaves means that winter is on its way, and a tinny clatter means that the mail has arrived. In a more fortuitous vein, for some people the smell of pea soup means the Canadian winter, while for others that of roasting chestnuts means a French provincial town in autumn. A work of art such as a theatre dance has meaning for those who observe it, although that meaning may vary considerably and be one thing for its choreographer and performers, another for the average spectator, yet another for a dance critic, and undoubtedly a quite different meaning still for the average Yanomami tribesman. Signals and gestures also mean for the appropriate observer; for the coconspirator, one lantern means intruders by land, two lanterns intruders by sea; for Westerners generally, a beckoning gesture means that one is to move toward the beckoner; for the French, the pivoting of an index finger means an imputation of mental disorder.

One might be inclined to insist that nevertheless linguistic meaning

141

differs in kind from the meaning present in other kinds of occurrences and that to think otherwise is to be misled by the idiosyncracies of the verb 'to mean.' Yet to do so would be a mistake. Linguistic and non-linguistic meaning may be indistinguishable. The smoke seen billowing out of a bedroom doorway and the succinct commentary 'Fire!' carry the same information, give rise to the same conviction, elicit the same response. Likewise, the clatter from a mailbox may be equivalent in import to the utterance, 'there's the mail.' Indeed, for this reason the imitation or accentuation of natural occurrences may be used for communication. Heavy steps on a porch and the slamming of a door may be used to inform of an arrival, while a deliberate scowl and harsh tone of voice may be used to convey displeasure more effectively than do words. Where language is superior to other forms of communication is in its immeasurably greater flexibility and scope, and not in the nature of the meaning in which it deals.

The signifiers, or the occurrences that mean, fall into two groups: natural occurrences (smoke, the smell of chestnuts) and artificial occurrences (art works, gestures, linguistic utterances). The latter are not simply man-made, since as much may be said of such occurrences as the clatter made by the postman, the smoke made by a nicotine addict, and manufactured tools; they are in addition made precisely *because* they mean or have meaning. The producer of the signifier is aware that the signifier has meaning and assumes, safely enough generally, that it has the same meaning for others. This characteristic of the signifier makes it a fitting instrument for some larger purpose such as communication, entertainment, affective manipulation, and so on. The artificial signifier differs, then, from the natural signifier in that its meaning is its *raison d'être*; it is made to mean. In virtue of this fact, artificial signifiers admit of two constructions with the verb 'to mean':

For s, c means C; by c, s means C.

The distinction between natural and artificial signifiers is a tricky one to draw at times. A flurry of activity, for example, may be either a constituent in a natural process, or the vehicle of an intended communication of intent or of prior commitment.

Whereas the signifier is a sensuous entity perceptually present, such is not the case for the signified, or what is meant. The fire meant by smoke is not actually perceived, nor is the newly arrived mail meant by the remark, 'There's the mail.' The same is true of the elderly grandmother meant by the odor of rosewater, the approaching intruder signalled by a lantern, the displeasure meant by a deliberate scowl. Indeed, if the signified is actually present perceptually, then there is no need for a signifier in its capacity to bring the signified to mind.

The signifier may on occasion give rise to some visual image, or even to an auditory, olfactory, or tactile-kinesthetic one, but such images are not equatable with what is meant. One reason for this is that they represent but one among many possible illustrations and so are not exhaustive of the meaning. A second is that their presence would seem optional. Indeed, much of the time it might be said, borrowing an image from Wittgenstein, that if God himself were to look into one's mind, from its sensuous contents alone he could not tell what is meant.[1] Nevertheless, one knows what is meant. An image, a replica, a description may illustrate that meaning, just as an actual occurrence may concretize or fulfill it, as when it elicits the avowal, 'That is exactly what I meant,' or 'That is the sort of thing I meant.' The meaning itself, however, cannot rightly be equated with either.

Meaning is mind-dependent not only in the sense that it is always meaning for someone but also in the sense that the someone in question must be to some degree aware of that meaning. If something has a particular meaning for oneself, then one must be aware of it, however dimly. An investigation into the meaning a thing has for oneself (perhaps through an explication by some other person of the meaning the thing sometimes or often has for other people and hence perhaps for oneself) may be quite revelatory and bring out aspects and connections of which one was hitherto aware only obscurely. Yet any such revelations can never come as a total surprise. There must be some awareness of the meaning prior to the revelation, since otherwise the revelation would not be revelatory of a meaning the thing had for oneself prior to the revelation. The mind-dependancy of meaning entails that there can be no such thing as meaning by proxy. In answer to the question of what something means for oneself, it would be nonsensical to reply, "it means for me what it means for Sally, whatever that is." Meaning is a personal possession like hunger, or belief, or a sense of humor; it is not something a second person may have in one's stead. By the same token, it is personalized; it is a function of one's particular past experience and training. At the limit it may be highly individualized, as in the case of the wealth of past events conjured up for Proust by the aroma of madeleines, or the religous significance of horses for the stable boy in Peter Shaffer's *Equus*.

It would make for a tidier account if a meaning were equatable with possible states of affairs. Such is indeed the case for factual meaning, that is, meaning geared into the world as a projection from perceived to unperceived fact. When perceived smoke means fire, the fire meant is a state of affairs situated in the world in the neighborhood of the observed smoke. The remark, 'There's the mail,' voices a conviction regarding an unperceived state of affairs in an assumed appendage to one's immediate environment. The situation is quite different for meanings simply brought to mind by occurrences: a French provincial town associated with an odor, the entertaining figments playfully conjured up by word combinations or by the movement juxtapositions in a Merce Cunningham dance, or the meaning of the single word 'Mama' uttered in play outside any context which could convert it into a greeting, proposition or supplication. In cases of the sort, meaning is a mere associate lacking the anchors that would make it into a possible state of affairs.

A construal of meaning in terms of belief or propositional attitudes, as by Brian Loar,[2] has the great merit of tying meaning more explicitly to a conscious organism, even if such a construal is inadequate for an exhaustive account of the phenomenon. The associate of an occurrence, whether the occurrence is linguistic, imagic, or perceptual, is an associate for a subject, person, or animal; it is what the observed occurrence leads the subject to expect, or brings to mind. A lexicon of associates is as personal as belief is personal. Where social conventions govern an association, as with language, that association functions only to the extent that learning and training have made it an association for the individuals in a particular group. Wittgenstein's declaration that "the meaning is not a mental accompaniment to the expression,"[3] must be understood within the constraints of a few serious qualifications. Meaning is a far broader phenomenon than linguistic meaning, and to all appearances, occurs independently of and prior to language. In all cases of its occurrence, meaning is an associate for a conscious being. Hence, the denial that linguistic meaning is a mental accompaniment to an expression cannot sensibly be taken literally and must be seen rather as a dramatic way of pointing out that linguistic expressions have their meanings determined by social practices. It is precisely because an expression may have a similar mental accompaniment for each individual in the social group that it can play a role in a particular social activity.

Our concern in what follows is to give an account of linguistic meaning to the limited extent of determining the semantic contribution of proper names and natural-kind terms to the factual statements in which they occur. In any attempt to communicate through language, an utterance may in principle be attributed a number of different meanings. Among the possible interpretations of an utterance are to be counted: (a) what the utterance means for the speaker, (b) what it means for the hearer, (c) what it means for the experts, (d) what the speaker assumes it to mean for the hearer, and (e) what the hearer believes it to mean for the speaker. It is fairly obvious that in view of the person-dependency of meaning, we must be concerned with *a*. Yet, since the speaker utters the words in view of communication, the interpretation that interests us most must be the fuller one, *d*. It would clearly be a mistake to construe a speaker's statement as *c*. To do so would be to make something that is person-dependent into something of which the persons involved might be quite ignorant. By the same token, the repetition of certain sound patterns by two West Indian parrots would qualify as a conversation in Creole.

REFERENT AS POSIT

With this brief survey of the terrain, let us turn to the topic of proper names and their semantic contribution to factual statements in English. It is best to begin with what that semantic contribution is not. Current mythology sees reference as essential to, if not constitutive of that contribution. On one of the more extreme but less obscure views of the role of reference, one sometimes termed 'objectualism,'[4] the referent or the concrete individual to whom the noun refers, figures as an actual constituent in the statement being made. The notion that the semantic contribution of the proper name directly involves the referent has a certain prima facie plausibility to it. For instance, if I use the name 'George' and am asked whom I mean, I might explain that I am referring to my next-door neighbor, George, certainly a concrete enough individual. Furthermore, if circumstances are favorable, I might actually point out the man in person as the man to whom I am referring. Nevertheless, there are a number of serious reasons for concluding that the view is mistaken and that reference plays merely an indirect role in meaning. We shall briefly consider a few of these. In each case the argument will be restricted to proper names, but its extension to natural-kind terms is obvious.

First of all, it is a grammatical illusion that in cases where the verb 'refer' is rightly used there is such a thing as an activity of referring which involves a concrete individual. The grammar of the verb 'refer' gives rise to the misconception (see Wittgenstein for further details on this type of thing) that referring is a three-term relation involving a speaker, a proper name, and a concrete individual (the referent). However, when concrete cases of referring are examined, no such relation is to be found, a three-term relation now effectuated by a speaker with regard to a concrete referent through the uttering of a word. To concretize matters (seldom bad policy in philosophical discussion), let us suppose that my neighbor George is on vacation in Tahiti and that I remark that George must be enjoying himself. Clearly, I am now referring to George with the proper name 'George'. Yet, when I examine what I am now doing, or introspect the experience, search as I may, I find nothing that might be taken to be a relation of referring to George. George is clearly not present. What is present is merely myself uttering the word 'George'—a word with an aura of familiarity and ready retinue of cognitive associations of all sorts, mnemonic, typical and predictive images, verbalized information, affective resonance. No amount of ferreting about among these materials turns up the concrete individual George. Nor does it turn up any perceivable activity having the concrete George as its object. When I refer to George, there is no pointing at George, no nodding, no glancing in his direction. (Indeed, I am quite unaware of what that direction is.) None of the sound waves, light waves, or heat waves, none of the gravitational or magnetic waves emitted either by me or by the word 'George' may reasonably be taken to constitute a referential relation to George, an individual now situated on an island half way round the world. If I am sending out mental probes or noetic rays in George's direction, nothing I find in my experience warrants my claiming as much. To judge from the available evidence (and how else is one to judge?), the alleged relation of referring simply does not exist.

It would be futile at this point to appeal to a causal theory of reference, and attempt to establish a referential relation with George via a causal information chain initiated with George's baptism. The question is how I can set up, through a sound I utter, a present relation of referring to an individual in Tahiti. How can the fact that the sound I now utter is similar to a sound uttered at the climax of a gathering about an infant George many years ago allow me or the sound to refer now, and thus enter into a present relation with the concrete George, now situated across the Pacific? If the answer is that the sound I now utter involves the vacationing George in virtue of a chain of repetitions of similar sounds going back to a long-past solemn ceremony, then the account being proposed features incantation rather than causality. It endows the word with some magical power in virtue of a past rite. An unbroken causal chain with links of the proper sort may indeed guarantee that I am using George's official name, and furthermore, it may explain how I came to know what that name is. Yet whatever the usefulness of causal chains for other explanatory purposes, they do not have (and were not intended to have) anything to do with the question of how a speaker can actually involve an absent individual in a present act of referring simply by uttering a sound of a certain type. To introduce causal chains into the present context is to change the subject.

My referring to George consists essentially of my uttering a meaningful sound and doing so in most cases in the presence of another person for whom the sound is likewise meaningful. If the other person were not present, my referring to George in Tahiti would be essentially the same as my thinking of George, an activity that might well consist primarily of the flashing before my mind of a schematic image of George's familiar face or silhouette in a tropical setting. In either case the concrete individual George does not enter the picture at all, or rather, does so only hypothetically as the person who, if present, would be recognized as the individual meant. Thus, there is no three-term actual relation of referring of the sort:

For s, 'c' refers to c.

It would be closer to the truth to say that there are two relations conjoined, a factual relation and a hypothetical one, each involving a hypostatized meaning. Where 'C' represents the latter, these may be expressed as follows:

For s, 'c' has C.
For s, C would be concretized by c.

The notion that there exists such a thing as a real relation of reference involving a concrete referent is an illusion created by the grammar of the verb 'to refer'. As a result, such alleged reference can have no direct connection with the semantic contribution of the proper name.

Referring is, if possible, even less a real presently effectuated relation when it is a matter of referring to some individual situated in the past. In such cases, the articulated sound and/or its articulator would have to manage to set up a relation both over a spatial expanse and back across time to some individual now long deceased. Allegedly, this concrete individual, for instance, the poet Homer dead now for almost three millennia, would become involved in a statement now being made in some quiet corner of the twentieth century. How could this long-dead Homer enter into a present relationship with an utterance and some present speaker?—or worse, still be, as the objectualist would have it, an actual constituent in the statement the speaker makes? The metaphysical implications of such claims are staggering. Less exciting but more plausible is the humdrum account whereby a historical character, whether Pericles, Vercingetorix, or Queen Victoria, is a posit in a historical scenario that provides the best explanation for the present existence of certain writings, records, remembrances, and relics of the past.

A similar conclusion follows from cases of failure of reference. To make matters concrete, let us suppose that I hear a noise at the door, and that it is the time when the postman, Cliff, usually drops off the mail, so that consequently I remark to myself, "There's Cliff." Let us suppose further that the postman is not at the door—worse still, that he was vaporized earlier by a parcel bomb. One result of this regrettable event is that the concrete individual to whom the name 'Cliff' purportedly refers is no longer to be found anywhere in the world. Nevertheless, my remark, "There's Cliff," provoked by the noise at the door, is not thereby made meaningless. Indeed, when I make the remark, I know very well what it means, what would verify it or falsify it, what I would expect to find at the door. Since the remark is meaningful for me, the word 'Cliff' must be meaningful for me, and meaningful despite the fact that unknown to me its purported referent does not exist. It appears then that a proper name figuring in a factual statement may very well be meaningful whether or not there exists in fact an individual to serve as its referent. From this it follows in turn that in such cases the concrete referent can have no direct role to play in the semantic contribution of the proper name to the statement made.

This conclusion should not be thought precipitous. Admittedly, the destruction of the referent of a name ultimately deprives the name of its meaning. Once I learn of the postman's demise, I can no longer use the proper name 'Cliff' in factual present-tense statements to refer to the postman. Yet, while this is true enough, it nevertheless remains true that my prior remark, "There's Cliff," made in ignorance of the postman's death, was meaningful at the time it was made. Indeed, it was as meaningful for me as any remark I have ever made or could hope to make. Furthermore, it might even have been meaningful in the English of the experts, if no member of that illustrious body was as yet aware of the tragedy. True enough, it would not be meaningful in God's English, as it were, but our concern is only with the natural language, English, as it is used by its less than omniscient speakers. This English must be admitted to be an unavoidably imperfect tool in all its idiolects, those of the less than omniscient experts no less than the substandard ones of everyday currency. The obvious moral to be drawn in the case of the dissipated postman is that the semantic contribution of a proper name cannot be a direct function of reference. One might attempt to avoid the moral by proposing the hypothesis, admittedly conceivable enough, that reference is nevertheless directly involved in those cases where there actually exists a referent, and not in cases where there does not. Yet such a hypothesis is not simply gratuitous (a serious enough defect in itself), but it is implausible to boot. No inspection of meaningful nouns, however thorough, will allow a language-user to say which ones refer to existing individuals and which ones do not. Since the meaning is an associate *for* the language-user, surely if the existing referent were essential to the meaning, the language-user would in some way be aware of the referent, at least to the point of being aware of whether there was one.

Apparently then, what we find is that nouns may be meaningful whether they actually have a referent or not and that the existence of a referent is neither a necessary nor a sufficient condition for the meaningfulness of a proper name. Existence is not a necessary condition since a proper name may be meaningfully used even when the name has no referent; it is not a sufficient condition since the language-user must also be convinced the name has a referent. The important factor is rather the language-user's belief in the existence of a referent. Belief is a necessary condition for meaningfulness, since otherwise from the point of view of the language-user the name has no referent and hence cannot be meaningfully used in factual discourse; belief is a sufficient condition, since with belief the proper name is meaningful for the language-user and continues to be so until the belief is shaken.

A final case which is particularly instructive for present concerns is that of the failure of substitutivity *salva veritate* of co-referring terms. The now classical illustration of such failure is Quine's Ortcutt Affair,[5] in which a certain Ralph sees a mysterious brown-hatted prowler but fails to recognize the man as the highly-regarded Ortcutt. To make the case apply squarely to proper names, we may suppose Ralph convinced that the prowler is the notorious Ortie, an agent for the French Ministère de l'Horticulture. The substitution of 'Ortcutt' for the co-referring name 'Ortie' in the doxastic ascription, "Ralph believes that Ortie is a spy," converts a true statement into a false one. The obvious moral, the one generally drawn from the Affair, is that in belief contexts semantic contribution cannot always be simply equated with reference.

However, the ramifications of the Ortcutt Affair cannot be so neatly contained. Indeed, the proffered moral is more than somewhat dubious, since it would have semantic contribution vary with grammatical context and be one thing in belief ascriptions and another in simpler statements. When one's suspicions on this curious claim are seriously pursued, it soon becomes apparent that the Ortcutt Affair is not the fruit of a mere local aberration; failure of substitutivity is not confined to belief contexts, but is on the contrary a quite general linguistic phenomenon. To make the point, consider the simple assertions which Ralph might make regarding the prowler, Ortie. A substitution of 'Ortcutt' for 'Ortie' in any of these assertions would be resisted by Ralph. The reason is that for Ralph there would be failure of substitutivity *salva veritate* (since from his point of view the substitution would convert a true statement into a false one), as well as failure of substitutivity *salva oratione* (since the substitution would yield a different statement, one about a different person). Here we have a speaker-deemed failure of substitutivity (or two such failures) in a simple assertion. Such failures of substitutivity are not peculiar to Ralph but may occur anywhere. They may occur even in the English of the experts, for surely experts, like all human beings, are capable of committing the error of positing two individuals where there is in fact one. The latter possibility could be excluded only through the unwarranted attribution of omniscience of the experts. The conclusion to be drawn apparently is that in any idiolect of English (with the exception of God's English) a failure of substitutivity may occur in any context.

Now, if the semantic contribution of a proper name were in some way directly related to its concrete referent, these failures would be inexplicable. One and the same referent would figure in the meaning of both statements. How then could they differ in truth value and meaning for the speaker? In Ralph's case, for example, the two proper names 'Ortie' and 'Ortcutt' would refer to one individual, let us say, an elderly gentleman now asleep in his bed. How is it possible for Ralph to fail to be aware that the referent is identical in the two cases? It is not a matter of Ralph's referring to two past acquaintances whom he failed to recognize as one and the same man; he is allegedly referring to one and the same individual in the present. Surely Ralph would have to be aware of the fact. Otherwise, he would be using words, the meaning of which must be the meaning they have for him, but he would be unaware of that meaning. Conversely, if Ralph is aware of the meaning of his words (which he must be since otherwise they would be meaningless for him), it is incomprehensible that Ralph should insist that their referent, the one individual, is two distinct men.

To explain failures of substitutivity, it must be recognized that the semantic contribution of a proper name is a posited individual rather than a concrete one. On the basis of past experience, the speaker posits or assumes the existence of two distinct individuals now out in the world, each related through a unique spatiotemporal sequence to a past acquaintance. Since the posited individuals are not posited as identical, the substitution of the name of one for that of the other is a logical mistake in the speaker's eyes.

When it is mistakenly assumed that failure of substitutivity is restricted to doxastic contexts, it is also being assumed that the English in question is that of a semantically omniscient speaker. There is, of course, nothing wrong with constructing a canonical notation or formalized version of English which is that of an omniscient speaker, although it might be noted parenthetically that if one is going to assume that the speaker is omniscient, one might with equal warrant assume the omniscience of all subjects of doxastic ascriptions and so obtain a version of English in which there are no failures of substitutivity at all. Such a formalized version of English could well be more useful than natural English for many purposes since it would obviously have the great advantage of being simpler than the untidy language of less than omniscient speakers. However, it would be wrong (a mistake) to claim that the resulting system formalized natural English and to conclude that belief contexts have the peculiar property of sometimes making aberrant a reference that is otherwise direct and unproblematic. To do so would be to commit the error of misconstruing as a phenomenon of the natural language what is in fact a mere consequence of the simplificatory measures adopted. A similar error underlies the claim of the undecidability of arithmetic, the error of imputing the existence of undecidable statements to the nature of arithmetic when such existence follows in fact from the simplificatory measure of admitting as well-formed, sentences that are self-referential in the interpreted system.[6]

THE DETERMINATION OF REFERENCE

Clearly the above conclusion that a referent is directly involved in meaning as a posit only, and not as a concrete individual, applies *mutatis mutandis* to sortal nouns for natural kinds, that is, to terms for species (lemons, tigers) and terms for substances (water, gold). It has far-reaching implications in that it implies that all meaning, referring included, is conceptual, except to the modest extent that meaning is indexically tied to the actual perceptual situation of the speaker. The conclusion establishes the falsity of Putnam's earlier-noted assumption that reference involving a concrete referent is essential to meaning. It does the same with Putnam's claim that meanings are not in the head, since on the above conclusion meanings are never anywhere else. It is in direct conflict with many tenets of the so-called New Theory put forth notably by Putnam, Saul Kripke, and Keith Donnellan, and which esteems reference to play a central role not only in the meaning of proper names but also in that of natural-kind terms.

Our concern in the present section will be with one of the central tenets of the New Theory, the claim that conceptual content is insufficient to determine reference. This tenet is part of a theory of reference, and not of a theory of meaning, so consideration of it may seem to take us somewhat off course. However, the tenet is generally taken to provide strong support for the New Theory view that meaning must involve more than conceptual content. Hence, investigation of the issue amounts to more than a frivolous outing.

The tenet that conceptual content is insufficient to determine reference is true enough to the extent that it is the claim that reference determination includes an indexical component, a relationship to the speaker and the speaker's present perceived surrounds. It is mistaken, however, to the extent that it is the claim that such determination must involve something more, some causal relation to a referent or the concrete referent itself. To help avoid confusion we might borrow John Searle's term *intentional content*[7] to encompass both conceptual content and the indexical component. The claim which concerns us is the stronger claim that determination of reference involves more than intentional content. However, since the tenet generally advanced and defended is stated in terms of conceptual content, we shall be concerned with this latter claim until such time as the indexical component becomes crucial to the discussion.

Support for the tenet is provided by appeal to a variety of cases both actual and conceivable, cases in which reference is allegedly underdetermined by conceptual content. In some of these cases it is indeed true that intentional content—conceptual content supplemented with indexical components—is insufficient to determine reference but only in the sense that the intentional content is insufficient to do so unambiguously. If the claim being made is that the expression in question has a referent, and that the intentional content is insufficient to pick out that referent, then the claim is false; there is no referent apart from one indicated by intentional content, and if the latter is insufficient to determine a unique referent, then there is no such unique referent.

The contrary is in fact assumed to be true by the argument which purports to show that meaning is not wholly a matter of conceptual content. The argument runs as follows:

Conceptual content may sometimes underdetermine reference.

Therefore, meaning cannot be wholly a matter of conceptual content.

Clearly the argument implicitly assumes the truth of the premiss that reference is necessary to meaning and would not be a valid argument without it. The assumption is equivalent in the present context to the claim that any meaningful noun has a referent. We found good reason in the preceding section to declare this assumption false. Consequently, the conclusion, that meaning is not wholly a matter of conceptual content, does not follow. As a result, even if the various cases of alleged underdetermined reference were actually cases of underdetermined reference (which often they are not), the argument they are intended to support would be unsound. In point of fact, the only sound argument to be made from the cases (on the supposition that they are good cases) is one that runs in the opposite direction. From the premisses that conceptual content may sometimes underdetermine reference and that meaning is wholly conceptual, it follows that sometimes reference may not be part of meaning. What the conclusion amounts to concretely is that when conceptual content underdetermines reference, no referring takes place.

Let us turn now to the cases of alleged underdetermined reference. A well-known argument by Putnam features a person unable to distinguish elms from beeches. Putnam's claim is that in the person's idiolect the two terms 'elm' and 'beech' would be alike in conceptual meaning but vastly different in their reference—an inexplicable situation, he concludes, unless there is more to meaning than conceptual meaning.[8] Yet surely this assessment is far too hasty. If I talk about elms and beeches without being able to distinguish the two, then the fair assessment is rather that I do not know what I am talking about. And since apparently I do not know what I am allegedly referring to, it becomes questionable whether I may properly be said to be doing any genuine referring at all. If asked to point out a sample of the sort of thing to which I am supposedly referring, at best I could narrow down the field somewhat and rule out certain types of trees—let us say, oaks, or cedars, or maples—as not being types to which I am referring. When put in the presence of an elm, I could not affirm that the given type of tree, as distinct from a beech type, is the type of tree to which I am referring when I use the word 'elm'. In these circumstances, it would seem incorrect to claim that I am actually referring to elms as distinct from beeches—and hence, incorrect to claim that the case shows that there may be reference despite penury of conceptual content.

A different tack might be attempted at this point, and the claim made that in using the two terms 'elm' and 'beech', I am referring to the two different species of trees to which other people refer with the terms. It should be borne in mind, however, that the notion of referring by proxy is to be handled with considerable caution. In the strict sense it is no more possible to have another person refer in one's stead than it is to have someone mean in one's stead. Another person is no more capable of actually referring for me than of believing for me, or of being hungry for me. When I claim to be referring to what other people refer to, what I am doing is taking the fact that a word is meaningful to other people and using that fact as a way of identifying something in the world, to which thing I may then refer. In these circumstances, the meaning of the term 'elm', as I use it, turns out to be roughly equivalent to 'the species of tree called "elm" by other people'. Of course, since the reference of the term so used is determined by conceptual content, the case does not support the claim that there may be reference underdetermined by conceptual content.

Devitt and Sterelny esteem conceptual error to provide substantive grounds for detaching reference from conceptual meaning. In particular, with regard to the use of the term 'whale' in former times, they reason as follows: "Central to what most people used to associate with 'whale' was the description 'fish'. This description is false of whales. Yet all those people referred to whales by 'whale'."[9] Apparently, the point being argued is that people managed to refer correctly despite conceptual error, hence independently of conceptual content. Yet the reasoning here is more than a little obscure. The fact that reference is determined through a set of somewhat inaccurate criteria (or allegedly inaccurate criteria) does not show that the criteria do not determine reference for the persons using them. At the very worst it makes the somewhat depressing point that a defective conceptual scheme sometimes yields the same results as one without the defects.

A more influential argument, one also due to Putnam, features a fictitious scenario involving a Twin Earth exactly like our own planet except for the molecular structure of water which on Twin Earth is a complicated structure representable as XYZ. Putnam's claim is that for the inhabitants of Twin Earth and ourselves, the word 'water' would have the same conceptual meaning although the referents would differ, theirs being the substance XYZ and ours the substance

H_2O.[10] Putnam concludes that conceptual meaning does not determine reference. Once again, the conclusion is precipitous. There is no clear reason to claim that reference varies independently of conceptual content. Prior to the espousal of Daltonian atomic theory, 'water' means a substance defined by descriptive characteristics and perhaps other physical and chemical properties; hence, it refers to substances having in fact the molecular structure either of H_2O or of XYZ. Afterward, when 'water' is taken by a speaker to refer to a substance with molecular structure H_2O or is taken to refer to a substance with XYZ, both the conceptual content and the reference have changed; 'water' refers to Earth water alone or to Twin Earth water alone, depending upon the speaker. None of this shows reference to be underdetermined, or determined independently of conceptual content.

The situation is not improved by Putnam's supplementary scenario in which Twin Earth water is a 20 percent solution of alcohol in water and Twin Earth people are constitutionally unable to detect the alcohol. The word 'water' would in fact have a different referent for the two populations, despite the fact that its conceptual meaning would be identical in the two cases.[11] Yet it is quite unclear how the example might establish the intended conclusion that reference is not determined by conceptual content. For Earth people a certain conceptual meaning determines the referent of 'water' to be water; for Twin Earth people the same conceptual meaning determines the referent of 'water' to be either water or a 20 percent solution of alcohol in water. In either case the conceptual meaning determines the referent.

Since a proper name refers to an individual, and hence to something definitively individuated only through spatiotemporal location, it may appear somewhat easier to construct cases in which the reference of the name is not determined by conceptual content. A proper name version of the Twin Earth argument presented by Devitt and Sterelny has a friend Oscar declaring his intention to vote for Reagan. The conceptual meaning of 'Reagan' for Oscar and Twin Earth Oscar is stipulated to be exactly the same. Then comes the crux of the case: "No association of descriptions or mental images will make Oscar's words refer to Reagan rather than to Twin Reagan.... We must look to some relation that language and mind have to things outside themselves to explain meaning."[12] Yet once again, the conclusion is too hastily drawn. In this particular example, while the two conceptual contents are identical, the indexical component of 'Reagan' for Oscar and for Twin Oscar is different. Oscar posits the referent of 'Reagan' to be on the planet on which Oscar is living, a resident in the very country a part of which is under Oscar's very feet. Twin Oscar does likewise with respect to Twin Earth. For each of the two Oscars, a twin found on some other planet would not qualify as the chosen candidate. This locating of the postulated individual with regard to the perceptually present world of the speaker is an indexical element in the meaning of the proper name, one that to some degree must be found as a component in the meaning of any proper name for nonfictional individuals. Thus, in the given case, there is no need to appeal to a meaning constituent beyond intentional content (conceptual content and indexical components).

The example might be made more promising by introducing interplanetary voyages on the part of the two Reagans. We might suppose the two Reagans to meet halfway between the two planets, and in the resulting confusion to lose all inkling of which planet is Earth, which Twin Earth. If the two subsequently arrive on Earth, Oscar (along with everyone else) will be unable to distinguish between the two Reagans, and to say which is Reagan, which is Twin Reagan. One might be tempted to argue that in these circumstances the conceptual content of 'Reagan' for Oscar is insufficient to determine the reference of 'Reagan', and that hence we finally have a case where meaning is more than intentional content. Yet such is not the case. It is not at all clear that when Oscar uses the word 'Reagan', he manages to refer to Reagan. If put in the presence of the two Reagans, Oscar is unable to say to which of the two he is allegedly referring. True enough, he knows that one of the two is spatiotemporally continuous with the Reagan of past years, so he knows that Reagan exists and he may wish to refer to him. Yet in a very real sense he cannot refer specifically to either of the two men as 'Reagan', since he is incapable of saying to which one he is referring. The situation would be similar if my beloved wedding ring were to get mixed up with other rings identical in appearance with it, or if I should name a grain of sand 'Harry', and then lose it on the beach. There is a sense in which it might be claimed that I am now referring to a particular individual despite the fact that there is no way of my knowing which individual that individual now is. Yet there is another sense in which I cannot properly be said to be referring to that individual at all because I have no way of determining which individual the individual is. Whatever the correct assessment of the degree of reference that obtains in the situation, it seems clear that the reference is rightly considered a direct function of intentional content, and is not a constituent of meaning necessitating appeal to some other source.

It may be concluded that for the determination of reference there is no need to appeal to anything beyond elements that may be characterized as 'internal', conceptual content and indexical elements from the perceptual context. There is no need to bring in external considerations such as causal links between name and referent or the concrete referents themselves to act as constituents in the statements made. The alleged need to determine reference is not the only reason for which an appeal to external phenomena is sometimes thought necessary in an account of meaning. Akeel Bilgrami, in his review of *Intentionality*, finds Searle's motivation for embracing internalism obscure and states that in his opinion the most convincing motivation for externalism in semantics is that it alone insures the publicness of meaning.[13] Yet, it is unclear why any need should be felt for a guarantee beyond the one there may be for the interpersonal similarity of feelings, emotions and private life generally. The providing of such a general guarantee is one of the tasks of rationalized epistemology. If motivation is required for an internalist rather than externalist account of meaning, surely it is simply that an internalist account is imposed by the nature of the phenomenon itself.

THE SEMANTIC CONTRIBUTION OF
NATURAL-KIND TERMS

While the referent of a noun figures only as a posit in the meaning or semantic contribution of that noun, it is nevertheless possible in principle that the meaning is a posited referent stripped bare of all characteristics, rather than a posited individual decked out in the conceptual content of the noun. In other words, while conceptual content may be both necessary and sufficient for the determination of reference, it may have no further role to play in semantics. Let us turn back now to the question of meaning.

On the prima facie, most plausible view of the matter, the meaning of a noun for a speaker is the speaker's concept of what it is to be a thing of the sort, which concept is indicated to a considerable extent by the answer the speaker would endorse to the question of what the noun means. Descriptive or ostensible characteristics are invariably involved in such concepts as well as in answers to the question of the meaning of a natural-kind term, whether the answer takes the form of a verbal description or of an ostensive definition with samples of the kind present or past. Hence, it is reasonable to conclude that descriptive or ostensible characteristics figure to a considerable extent in both the speaker's concept and in the meaning of the corresponding term.

Now, this view is esteemed to encounter serious difficulties with certain natural-kind terms. For many sortal nouns an explication of meaning or concept may be both succinct and adequate. Many nouns have so precise a definition that they seem designed primarily to further brevity (e.g., 'spinster', 'conifer', and 'quadruped'). Artificial-kind terms ('chair', 'hammer', and 'boat') may generally be easily explicated in terms of the function or purpose that members of the kind are designed to serve. Many natural-kind words ('pebble', 'lake', 'hill', and 'cloud') are definable readily enough in terms of agglomerations of particular substances satisfying quite simple requirements as to shape, size, and/or location. Yet in the case of the majority of natural kinds, whether species or substances, no concise encapsulations of defining characteristics are forthcoming; rather, we encounter tentative and often unrigorous descriptions that vary with the speaker and fail apparently to give rise to analytic truths. The suggested conclusion, and indeed the one drawn by New Theorists,[14] is that ostensible characteristics are incapable of filling the required function in the case of such terms and that, by default, the semantic contribution must be some referent largely stripped of descriptive characteristics.

Now, the true culprit here is not the untidy concepts, but rather the mistaken notion that concepts must be something tidy. The nature of concepts is an empirical matter, hence one to be settled by empirical investigation rather than regimenting legislation. When investigated empirically, empirical concepts of natural kinds are found in point of fact to deviate vastly from the assumed model. The difference in nature could have been predicted on a moment's reflection from the fact that natural kinds are discovered empirically, not defined *ab initio*. The resulting concepts are ways of grouping the phenomena encountered in an untidy world. They have consequently a number of features that they do not share with other more constructed concepts; in particular, they are flexible, egalitarian, accumulative, idiosyncratic, and error-prone. Let us review each of these characteristics briefly before considering objections to the account.

First of all, natural-kind concepts are disturbingly *flexible* in a variety of ways. The similarities in descriptive characteristics in virtue of which particular objects or substances are grouped in one kind are similarities that often admit of a considerable degree of variation. Cows may vary considerably in color and bulk, as well as to some extent in the shape and proportions which are peculiar to cows, and provide the everyday, drive-by criteria for cowhood. Similar remarks apply to the color and size of crystals constitutive of granite. Furthermore, a member of a kind may lack some typical characteristics altogether, provided it has enough other typical features, as is the case with a round lemon or a small-eared fox. In addition, the appearance of members of species may admissibly change with posture and activity, or yet again with age, just as substances may change their descriptive characteristics with temperature. Fortuitous events may also bring about a variety of permissible variations: a tiger may be diseased, maimed, scorched, bleached, skinned, or dead, and nevertheless continue to qualify as a tiger.

While such flexibility may be disconcerting to the nonlayman, it is not lawlessly aberrant; it follows the rough-hewn dictates of a judgment of strong similarity, dictates that permit a wide degree of variation provided strong similarities of some sort are preserved. If the degree of change is too great, a member ceases to meet membership requirements. In particular, after a certain degree of mutilation or decomposition, an individual ceases to qualify as a member of its species. For analogous reasons, a turkey-shaped mutation of a tiger would fail to qualify as a tiger in the eyes of most speakers; although sired and born of thoroughbred parents, its size, shape, and behavior would preclude its being viewed as a tiger, even by the eyes of its nearest of kin.

A further feature of natural-kind concepts is that they are more or less *egalitarian:* any characteristic of the kind has access to the content of the concept. A typical account of a species sets forth striking macroscopic characteristics—usual size and shape, structure, and dynamics; distinctive sense characteristics (visual, auditory, tactile, aural, or olfactory); and typical behavior and reactions—which are illustrated, if possible, by samples or by references to past encounters. Yet except for practical considerations of time, patience, and ignorance, there is no reason to limit the description of a kind to the more salient characteristics to the exclusion of others. In an account of what it is to be a lemon, the gloss, wrinkles, and porelike indentations of the surface, the pulpy white inner peel, the tear-drop pouches of liquid within the inner sections, and even the cellular structure of the various membranes are no less essential in fact than the general shape and color: each of these various features contributes to make a lemon the particular kind of thing it is. Any general truth about members of the kind would seem to have as much right as any other to be considered constitutive of what it is to be a member of the kind. The same holds for behaviors, whether typical behaviors or context-dependent reactions to particular stresses or conditions (some of which may provide convenient membership tests). This egalitarianism would seem a direct consequence of the lack of initial defining conditions and is not shared by concepts of artificial kinds (whether of spinsters or of chairs).

Concurrent with their egalitarianism, natural-kind concepts have the feature of being epistemologically *accumulative*, that is, of growing with increasing knowledge of the particular natural kind. Just as there is no apparent limit to the meagerness of content of a concept short of vacuity, so too there is none to its richness short of complete knowledge. A person's concept of germanium might consist of no more than a suspicion that it is an element rather than a plant, or his or her concept of elm might be so vague as not to preclude confusion with beeches. Nevertheless, such concepts may well figure in quite meaningful statements (albeit perhaps, singularly uninformative ones). Indeed, during an explication of some unfamiliar natural kind, the hearer's concept of the kind is born at some rudimentary level of general descriptive characteristics and grows with each increment of information.

As a result, sufficient conditions for membership in the kind are never definitive, but are sufficient only relative to a given degree of knowledge. Further information leads to conceptual restructurings and nomenclatural revisions. A whale was a fish as long as 'fish' meant 'sea-dwelling animal,' and the mammalian features of whales were considered curious but unimportant. Descriptive characteristics alone may well prove to be quite insufficient to determine membership, a point readily made through a brief visit to the jars of salts stored in a chemistry laboratory. Microscopic and molecular structure may come to be added to macroscopic characteristics and behavior. The Twin Earth substance with molecular formula XYX in Putnam's Twin Earth scenario would, in virtue of its phenomenal characteristics, qualify as water prior to the Daltonian revolution in chemistry, and the discovery that phenomenal water may have either of two molecular structures; after that time, the existence of two distinct substances might well be recognized.

As a result in part of the above characteristics, natural-kind concepts are *idiosyncratic* or *epistemically personalized;* they are a direct function of the speaker's knowledge and experience and hence vary from speaker to speaker. The fact was noted some years back by John Locke who, taking gold as an example, remarked that children find the shining color of gold to be its essential characteristic, whereas some adults might add weight and fusibility, others yet other characteristics, presumably malleability or chemical inertness.[15] If anything, these concepts vary somewhat more than was intimated by Locke. A goldsmith, a banker, and a chemist, for instance, each have widely differing concepts of gold. Communication is not thereby precluded since for the latter it suffices that the concepts of speaker and hearer should overlap to some extent. The element common to both (assumed to be such by the speaker) constitutes the semantic contribution of the natural-kind term, or what at an earlier time Searle termed its "descriptive presuppositions."[16]

The empirical nature of natural-kind concepts also makes them *evidentially incomplete* and *error-prone*. Generalizations are based on incomplete evidence, and it is always theoretically possible that exceptions to rulings based on past findings should turn up—that, for instance, moon rocks should contain a metal like gold in every respect except that it is blue. Furthermore, the past rulings may turn out to be based on perceptual and observational error. The proneness to error and the evidential incompleteness of empirical concepts rule out absolute certainty regarding the presence of any particular typical characteristic. The result is that even in the case of kinds with no observed instances of abnormalities (e.g., gold), there can be no analytic truths ascribing a particular characteristic, only truths stating general membership requirements according to the dictates of a 'cluster logic'.

It might be added that many natural-kind concepts are also distinctive in the sense that they often deal in distinctive characteristics, such as the peculiar shape typical of a cow, the specific hue of copper, or the aroma of coffee. Most terms commonly used in English for the description of such characteristics are quite approximate. For instance, to characterize copper simply as reddish-brown is to fail to capture the specific hue peculiar to the metal. On the other hand, terms coined with a view to capturing the envisaged characteristics (perhaps by definition as do the terms 'coffee-flavor', 'copper-color', or 'cow-shape') are only fully understood by speakers already acquainted with the characteristic. The result is that attempts to give an adequate account of membership conditions often seem redundant (witness, for instance, the quite warranted ruling that to qualify as a cow a candidate must be cow-shaped).

The information on which the concepts are based may be firsthand or secondhand, and a somewhat different type of concept results in the two cases. Firsthand knowledge of distinctive characteristics can at best be but roughly conveyed to someone with no such acquaintance. A speaker who knows through acquaintance knows there is a kind (at least one instance of it) with certain characteristics and can at best be mistaken about official nomenclature. The known sample is both a continuing source of information as well as assurance regarding the characteristics of a particular kind. For someone well acquainted with gold, the only conceivable scenario in which it could be true that no gold is yellow, is a fantastic skeptical scenario featur-

ing gratuitously selective illusions or hallucinations or equally gratuitous memory lapses. On the other hand, a speaker who has not
learned of characteristics through acquaintance has secondhand information only as reliable as his or her sources. Recognition is speculative rather than immediate. Here there is obviously greater room for
error and uncertainty and, correspondingly, less warrant for the attribution of some general characteristic to the kind.

Descriptivist accounts, such as the one just sketched, see descriptive or ostensible characteristics as essential constituents in the meaning of natural-kind terms. The main criticism addressed the descriptivist approach by its rival New Theory turns on the claim that the
possession of descriptive characteristics is neither a necessary nor a
sufficient condition for membership in a natural kind. In particular, it
is claimed that if the possession of certain descriptive characteristics
were a necessary condition, the statements predicating those descriptive characteristics of the natural kind would be analytic truths. Just
as it is analytically true that a chair has a back, so it should be analytically true, for instance, that gold is yellow or that tigers are striped.
None of this, so it is claimed, is the case.

New Theorists are, of course, quite right to point out that a list of
descriptive characteristics is often insufficient to guarantee membership. Both Kripke and Salmon argue, reasonably enough, that a creature indistinguishable from a tiger but genetically incapable of interbreeding with tigers would not be a tiger.[17] They are quite right
insofar as the speakers they have in mind are members of the scientific community, although to temper elation it should be added that for
less sophisticated speakers such a creature might well continue to
qualify as a tiger. Nevertheless, it seems clear that descriptive characteristics alone are often insufficient to allow drawing all the classificatory distinctions we make.

It is also true that no particular descriptive or ostensible characteristic is ever a necessary condition for membership in a natural kind.
Membership conditions for some particular kind may be quite flexible. In addition, the fact that natural-kind concepts are evidentially
incomplete and error-prone makes them vulnerable to skeptical scenarios such as Kripke's thought experiment in which it is supposed
that the yellow color of gold is discovered to be an illusory appearance of its real color, blue.[18] The conceivability of such scenarios
makes it a factual truth and not a necessary one that gold is yellow.
(By contrast, there is no conceivable scenario, even a wild skeptical
one, in which a spinster could be married.)

However, this fact is an insufficient ground for the much more general claim that no descriptive characteristics figure in any way in the necessary conditions for membership, that a candidate may qualify for membership and yet have none of the usual ostensible characteristics. Kripke argues for the more sweeping claim and, taking gold and tigers as examples, maintains that just as it is conceivable that gold should be found to be blue, it is also conceivable that specimens of gold and of tigers should be found to have none of the ostensible characteristics of usual gold and tigers.[19] The latter claim seems clearly exaggerated. Contrary to what Kripke states, it is simply not true that if all the usual characteristics of gold were found to be illusory the substance mistakenly thought to have these characteristics would be considered to be gold. Let us suppose that the reality behind the illusion is found to be something quite different, for instance, a dull, blue, crumbly, chemically active substance. There would no longer be any such thing as the untarnishable, lustrous, warm-colored substance now called 'gold'. The general feeling to result would undoubtedly be that gold had been found not to exist. Gold is valued precisely for its characteristics, and a substance having none of these would no longer be what people mean by 'gold'. A few chemists might disagree, but they would be overwhelmingly outnumbered in any poll taken on the meaning of 'gold' for the pollee.

It would be futile to vary the scenario and have a hitherto unknown, blue crumbly substance discovered with atomic number 79, hence an allotrope of gold. It could not be argued that the existence of the allotrope shows that phenomenal characteristics are not necessary characteristics. The original gold would merely be recognized as only one form of a broader kind (possibly given a distinct name such as *Aurum* to avoid confusion); the conditions for membership in this one form would remain unchanged; a candidate would have to be yellow, lustrous, chemically inactive, and so on to be this particular form of gold. Consider the similar case of graphite and diamond which are two allotropes, one a sheet-bonded and the other a crystal-latticed structure of carbon atoms. It would be absurd to argue that since the descriptive characteristics of graphite do not provide necessary conditions for being carbon, they do not do so for graphite either.

The situation would seem essentially the same in the case of a species such as the tiger. Let us suppose a case where tigers give birth to an animal sufficiently different from usual tigers in ostensible characteristics to no more merit classification as a tiger than as a lion. Suppose too that the animal is capable of interbreeding with usual tigers, and hence qualifies as a tiger biologically. The upshot would simply be the advent of a new breed of tiger. To be a member of the usual breed, a candidate would have to have the usual characteristics with regard to color, shape and so on. The member of the new breed would fail to qualify for membership in the usual breed, although of course it would belong to the larger species of tiger encompassing the two breeds, and that in virtue of its reproductive capabilities.

Perhaps one of the reasons behind the impression that ostensible characteristics are somewhat inessential to meaning is the mistaken view advanced in particular by Putnam and Kripke[20] according to which essential properties lie primarily in an underlying microstructure revealed by scientific investigation. This theory is clearly mistaken about the functioning of species terms. If microstructure to the exclusion of macrostructure constituted the essential properties of a species such as a lemon, then a blenderized lemon frozen into the shape of a cube would remain a lemon in virtue of its retained underlying structure. For similar reasons, the cloud of debris produced by a parcel bomb would be properly characterized as a postman. Such absurd consequences show that more than microstructure is involved: general shape, structure, and typical sensuous characteristics. Chromosomes and DNA, molecular configurations, atomic numbers and orbitals all owe their importance in science to the help they provide in understanding and explaining perceived phenomena. If no correlation existed between events at the two levels, if events at the microlevel pursued their own course independently of the perceived phenomena, microstructure would drop out of serious scientific consideration. In many cases such structure would not even constitute an interesting but irrelevant sideshow, since it is not observable; it is simply posited as an explanation of the observed phenomena. Microstructure supplements rather than replaces macrostructure in explications of what it is to be a particular thing.

Furthermore, concern with microstructure is both recent and relatively restricted. Its role in meaning was certainly minimal at the time of cave painting, or of the construction of the Gothic cathedrals, minimal too more recently at the time of the battle of Shiloh. Even today, such concern is not too prevalent beyond the scientific community, as is evident from the attitude of the average truck driver, stenographer, or artist on the matter. To concretize the latter point, let us suppose that objects indistinguishable from lemons in every aspect—appearance, taste, internal structure, and so on—are found to contain walnut DNA and to come from walnut trees. Now consider what the practical import of microstructure would be once the initial shock was past. It is highly doubtful that in supermarkets, the objects would be displayed in the nut section beside pecans and hazelnuts, or that for culinary purposes they would be treated as walnuts and not as lemons. Neither nutrition nor gastronomy deal in DNA; neither do everyday concepts. If DNA enters the picture at all for the average speaker, it is as an obscure inner structure that certain esteemed authorities consider very important, but which has no significant import on the meaning of words. Scientific findings do have ultimately some effect upon concepts and terminology, but the trickle-down effect is so slow and uncertain that it is quite unwarranted to place them center stage in the semantics of everyday discourse.

Thus, the answer to the question of whether the ostensible characteristics of natural kinds give rise to analytic truths must be both negative and affirmative. It may be true, as New Theorists point out, that no particular ostensible characteristic is an essential characteristic of the kind, but it is false that ostensible characteristics impose no constraints whatever on membership. Where variation from the norm goes beyond some ill-defined degree of compliance, a degree that varies from kind to kind, a candidate ceases to qualify. The predication of ostensible characteristics to the requisite degree is consequently an analytic truth. As a result, one might speak of a 'loose definition' of a natural-kind term, or of 'loose analyticity'.

The consequences of the various characteristics of natural-kind concepts, their flexibility, accumulativeness, and idiosyncracy, are untidiness in definition, complication in communication, and tedium in formalization. However regrettable these consequences, they afford in themselves no warrant to deny that descriptive characteristics are essential to the semantic contribution of sortal nouns. The untidy semantic system is in part a reflection of an untidy world, in part an appropriate response dictated by the practical limitations of knowledge acquisition. As one might put the matter, any complaints in this regard are best addressed not to the workers in the field but to the management.

THE SEMANTIC CONTRIBUTION OF PROPER NAMES

Let us now turn back to the more complicated issue of the semantic contribution of a proper name. The concept of the particular individual named by some proper name is clearly no less an empirical concept than is the concept of some natural kind. It is more complex than the latter in that it involves not only the characteristics of the individual qua member of the kind, but the further characteristics peculiar to that particular member. This circumstance suggests that the semantic contribution of a proper name should be similar in nature to that of a natural-kind term. The suggestion finds immediate corroboration in the type of answer proffered in everyday situations as an explanation of whom one means or to whom one is referring. Such explanations take the form of (a) accounts of descriptive characteristics and/or (b) ostensive definitions involving direct acquaintance with the individual decked out in the characteristics and/or (c) accounts featuring profession, status, notable accomplishments, and/or (d) simply whatever description suffices for the speaker's purposes. Accounts of the sort are explications of the speaker's concept of the individual named. Thus, on the most straightforward reading of the situation, the semantic contribution of a proper name is the speaker's concept of the individual named to the extent that the speaker assumes it to coincide with the concept of the hearer.

It is not surprising that individual concepts turn out on empirical examination to have the same features as natural-kind concepts—flexibility, egalitarianism, accumulativeness, idiosyncrasy, and proneness to error. A paradigm illustration of one aspect of the flexibility of individual concepts is Wittgenstein's query, "Has the name 'Moses' got a fixed and unequivocal use for me in all possible cases?—Is it not the case that I have, so to speak, a whole series of props in readiness, and am ready to lean on one if another should be taken from under me and vice versa?"[21] The essential notion is that no characteristic or action attributed an individual is in principle immune to retraction on subsequent discovery of error. Certain characteristics stand on more solid ground epistemologically: it is difficult to imagine plausible circumstances in which a woman might discover that her husband of long standing was, contrary to what she has always thought, neither white nor male. Nevertheless, there is apparently no fixed answer determining which set of characteristics and actions is essential to the individual meant by a given proper name. The operative criteria are discouragingly loose and untidy.

The egalitarianism of individual concepts is perhaps best illustrated in the limiting cases. A concept may be close to vacuous, as in the case of the concept of an unknown individual whose name is found in a phone book, carved on a tree or tombstone, or written on the inside cover of a secondhand book. It is scarcely less emaciated when its source is the vague memory of a face glimpsed at the other end of a crowded room. Nevertheless, such concepts are sufficient to allow a correlated proper name to be meaningfully used in factual discourse. On the other hand, a concept such as that of a speaker's spouse, child, or sibling may be so rich and detailed as to preclude convenient exposition. In practice, an explanation of who is meant is often limited to salient characteristics or relationships or focuses on some occurrence witnessed by both speaker and hearer. Yet any characteristic of the individual (bounding gait, sense of humor) or any relationship or activity (wife of a past acquaintance, presence in the corner seat at last Friday's performance) may in principle figure in the part of the speaker's concept assumed to overlap with that of the hearer.

An important factor in the diversity of individual concepts is their epistemic source. Direct acquaintance yields a very different concept from one built on secondhand description. When I am acquainted with my neighbor, George Porge, I am familiar with his distinctive physiognomy, his peculiar features with their relative size and location, his peculiar silhouette with its particular proportions and angles, his voice with its specific quality and flow, his personality and mannerisms, the atmosphere he exudes. My description of George for someone unacquainted with him would leave out what for me are his most distinctive features. I might mention, for instance, his short, wiry build, his shock of reddish hair, freckled cheeks, and energetic walk, all of which might with luck help to identify George at an airport exit; but I would make no serious attempt to describe the features that for me make George the individual he is—the peculiar line of his jaw, his distinctive laugh and twinkling, inquisitive eyes—features I am tempted to claim would allow me to identify him anywhere in the world. My concept of George is one that could be fully shared only by someone also well acquainted with him.

Secondhand concepts may differ considerably from firsthand ones in yet another respect. Very often, particularly in the case of individuals far removed in time (Moses, Thales, Aristotle, or Jonah), not only is there no possible acquaintance with the individual or with a photograph, portrait, or bust of the same, but there are no secondhand descriptions of personal characteristics. What we have instead are reports of deeds, activities, and works. These sometimes support likely inferences as to personality and character, but the resulting individual concept is quite different from one acquired through acquaintance. Such diversity obviously engenders no insurmountable obstacle to communication, since for the latter a modicum of agreement suffices.

Nor does diversity preclude analyticity, any more than does flexibility or proneness to error. The properties of individuals, including ostensible properties, give rise to a considerable number of analytic truths. Let us run through these briefly.

First of all, there is one general analytic truth for any individual named and that is the truth which states species membership. It is an analytic truth, for instance, that the postman Cliff is a human being. When Cliff is vaporized by a parcel bomb, the name 'Cliff' does not become the name of the cloud—which of course it would have to become if 'Cliff' named a mere spatiotemporally continuous agglomeration of matter or a pure referent in abstraction from all characteristics. In point of fact, it names a particular agglomeration of matter only so long as the latter has the structural characteristics that allow it to qualify as a human being. Similarly, it is analytically true that Excalibur is a sword. 'Excalibur' would cease to name anything if the sword so named were hammered into a ploughshare—although on a purely referential account of proper names it would have to name the ploughshare. Likewise, it is analytic that Potidaea is a city. Potidaea ceased to exist when the city was destroyed by the Huns, which is to say, when Potidaea ceased to be a city and hence a member of its kind. What now remains on the site are the ruins, not the city. Species membership is part of the semantic contribution of any proper name.

It is also analytic that an individual at a particular place and time is the same individual as one of the same natural kind materially and spatiotemporally continuous with the first. Aristotle young and Aristotle old are the same man. Something more than mere spatiotemporal continuity of a natural kind is required, since an abrupt and sizeable change in personality (or a Jekyll/Hyde physical transformation) would be taken as grounds for speaking of two different individuals.

To these must be added more locally and loosely analytic truths, i.e., truths analytic only relative to a particular concept itself somewhat flexible with regard to interpretation, correction, and supplementation. Such flexible and locally analytic truths include, among other things, some indication of spatiotemporal location for the individual named. This is necessary in order for the name to play a role in factual discourse—to be the name of a real character rather than of a fictional one. At the very minimum the individual named is posited (assumed) to be 'out there somewhere' in the unperceived extension of the spatiotemporal world actually perceived by the speaker. This positing is the grain of truth in semantic objectualism, particularly in the claim that the concrete referent is integral to the meaning of the proper name. It is also the source of Kripke's hesitation to remove spatiotemporal characteristics from among the essential properties of Aristotle, a hesitation he voices in his remark, "Maybe it's hard to imagine how he could have lived 500 years later than he in fact did."[22] The posited individual is posited by the speaker to be in some spatiotemporal location (generally loosely defined) relative to the speaker's perceived world. This location relative to the speaker introduces an indexical element into the posit. As a result the meaning of a proper name such as 'George' for a speaker on earth would be different from the meaning of 'George' for the putative twin of the speaker on Twin Earth. For each speaker 'George' would mean the particular neighbor George who lives in a house located next door to his or her own house, itself located in a known way with respect to the speaker's present immediate environment and body.

In addition, for speakers acquainted with some individual, a candidate who hopes to qualify as that individual must satisfy very rigid conditions. These conditions are so strict in the case of a close acquaintance that barring some radical change due to a serious accident, the practical possibility of thoughtful misidentification is excluded. They remain quite strict even in the case of a fleeting acquaintance, one insufficient to guarantee success in a police lineup. If, contrary to known physical laws, a corpulent, phlegmatic individual were abruptly to replace the short, wiry one on the very spot where the latter was standing the instant before, the newcomer would not qualify as the same individual for any minimally alert onlooker. To qualify as the same individual certain requirements beyond spatiotemporal continuity must be satisfied, requirements regarding ostensible characteristics of shape, size, and so on—just as for species membership a certified pedigree is insufficient to permit a turkey to qualify as a tiger.

The conditions are nevertheless flexible conditions, which is to say that the attribution of any one particular ostensible characteristic is never a necessary truth. For instance, it is not necessarily true for an acquaintance that George Porge has a hooked nose. Apart from the complicating circumstance that hooked noses are fragile elements in a turbulent world, it is conceivable (although highly implausible) that past observation of what was apparently a hooked nose was in fact a gratuitously selective hallucination. It is never inconceivable that any particular characteristic is in fact different from what it appears to be, and for this reason alone, the predication of a particular characteristic can never be a necessary truth. It is inconceivable, however, that a large number of characteristics should be in fact different—not inconceivable in the sense that such error is impossible but in the sense that, beyond some ill-defined degree of change, the individual constituted by the characteristics would no longer qualify as the same individual.

The situation with regard to nonacquaintances is somewhat analogous in its broad lines. For the speaker the proper name names a particular individual posited by the speaker on the basis of the testimony or convictions of others coupled perhaps with material evidence. In the extreme case, the accepted testimony contains no indication whatever of descriptive characteristics. The speaker assumes that the individual is or was a concrete identifiable creature of flesh and blood, and that the proper name has an ostensive definition with its retinue of quasi-analytic truths, all unknown to the speaker. In these circumstances one might expect the semantic contribution of the proper name to reduce for the speaker to something like a bare individual. Yet such is far from the case. The story told about the individual comes to outweigh in semantic importance the logical implications of the naming conventions. The proper name comes to be synonymous with the concealed definite description (including an indexical element of spatiotemporal location); it becomes the name of an individual defined loosely as the person to whom such and such occurred and who acted in such and such a way.

Consider the hypothetical situation in which it is discovered that Aristotle's works were in fact written by Aristotle's successor, Theophrastus, who attributed them to his master to enhance their chance of acceptance. Now suppose that a male scholar had previously written a study on Aristotle's views on explanation as revealed by careful analysis of his works. On recovering from his initial shock, the scholar would undoubtedly maintain that the discovery had little bearing on the conclusions of his study. He would point out that in his study for all practical purposes the name 'Aristotle' is synonymous with 'the author of these works', an assessment with which it would be difficult to disagree. The scholar in his close study of the texts is concerned exclusively with what is stated or not stated in the work; in these circumstances he is using the name 'Aristotle' simply as a means of referring to the author of the texts, i.e., as a concealed definite description. He has no intention of saying anything whatever about a nonauthor to whom the works were wrongly attributed. If one should deny the truism that speaker intent determines meaning and insist that the name 'Aristotle' must refer here to Aristotle and cannot mean the actual author, then one must be prepared to make the absurd claim that the scholar's careful study is composed largely of false assertions. The more sensible view is that the mistaken attribution of authorship is somewhat like a misprint in a legal document, awkward but essentially irrelevant, since intent is clear from context.

The point lands us in the midst of the objections raised by New Theorists against a descriptivist account of proper names. One such by Donnellan features a scenario according to which there never was an Ionian natural philosopher called 'Thales', but merely a well-digger of that name about whom myths were generated.[23] Donnellan's claim is that the descriptive account must be mistaken, since 'Thales' would refer to the well-digger and not the descriptive referent. Yet the claim hardly seems warranted. People discussing a person whom they took to be the father of Greek science would be outraged to be told that they had actually been talking about a well-digger. They would undoubtedly insist that it had never entered their minds that there was such a person as Thales, the well-digger, that their concern was with what they believed to be a philosopher-scientist, and that if indeed there was no such person then they were not talking about anyone. Surely they are the best judge of what they meant. This is, of course, not to say that there are no conceivable cases in which speakers might be unsure as to what person they meant. If 'Jonah' should turn out to name a person who had been a prophet of sorts but who had never been near the sea let alone a giant fish, the situation would be less clear; there would arise the insoluble problem of determining the precise number of specified properties a candidate must possess in order to satisfy the nebulous set of flexibly necessary conditions.

Perhaps the most persuasive objection to descriptivist accounts is one raised by Kripke. To make certain actions and characteristics analytically true of an individual is to make those properties and actions necessary properties and actions of the named individual and consequently, according to Kripke, to rule out on logical grounds the possibility of the individual's having been different and acted differently. Using the biblical figure Moses to illustrate his point, Kripke argues that if 'Moses' is defined as the man who satisfies some number of a certain cluster of descriptions, then "there couldn't be any counterfactual situation in which he didn't do any of these things."[24] Kripke makes essentially the same point by arguing that on such a definition of 'Moses', if it were discovered that no one did any of the things in question, then it would have to be concluded that Moses did not exist. This would be a mistake, according to Kripke, since Moses might well have chosen to spend his life at the Egyptian court rather than in the desert. Transposing an argument Kripke presents with regard to Aristotle, there may be added a further embarassing point: when the supposition is made that Moses did none of these things, the term 'Moses' is used to refer to the man so supposed; in these circumstances, a term allegedly defined to mean the man who did certain things, is used to designate a man who did none of them.[25]

Yet despite its plausibility, Kripke's reasoning must be mistaken at some point. Let us suppose I am fascinated by Moses and spend considerable time studying and discussing the man. Moses then becomes for me the man in the biblical account (assumed to be accurate on the whole), the man who did certain things (roughly). My very conception of Moses is that of a leader at a certain crucial time in Israelite history. My concept of Moses places no apparent restrictions whatever on Moses's freedom to have chosen a life of luxury at the Egyptian court, since I am quite willing to admit that Moses was free (at an earlier time in his life, obviously) to choose to remain in Egypt. I am also quite willing to admit that, if he had so chosen, he would not have become the leader he was, although he would have been called 'Moses', and would even be Moses according to the criteria governing the identity of individuals. Nevertheless, he would not be the man I now mean when I speak of Moses, the man I esteem to have been a great leader. If Moses had chosen to stay in Egypt, then the man I mean would indeed never have existed—contrary to Kripke's claim. To claim that the man I mean is in some way identical with a different man (the one Moses would have become if he had in fact chosen a life of luxury at the court) is akin to catching me up with some legal technicality. Surely, I would like to protest, in the meaning of a word there is no small print; a word means only what it means for the speaker. Thus, there seem to be conflicting intuitions on the matter. How is the conflict to be resolved?

The solution lies in an understanding of the nature of the identity relation. The individual who led the Israelites out of Egypt is identical with one living at an earlier time at the Egyptian court, as also with the individual found floating about in the bullrushes. This identity might be termed 'diachronic identity'. In virtue of it, the name 'Moses' refers to all three of the above individuals. Now clearly it cannot be plausibly claimed to be analytically true of the infant that he is a great Israelite leader. As a result, one could be tempted to argue that since the concepts of Moses the man and Moses the infant have nothing in common, the content of neither figures in the meaning of 'Moses'. (Indeed, Kripke might have based his argument on the aging process and not appealed to choices and counterfactuals at all.) Before leaping to such a conclusion, however, one should notice the fact that in explaining whom one means or to whom one is referring in using 'Moses' to refer to either the man or the infant, one would answer the question by explicating one's concept of the man or of the infant. On the prima facie most plausible view, the meaning is the concept. Thus, one is driven to the view that there are two different meanings correlated with the name 'Moses'. The one name may be used to refer to either the infant or the man, and its meaning is different in the two cases. The two individuals are, of course, related through a diachronic identity as different temporal stages in one event, the life of Moses, or Moses over his lifetime. As Hume pointed out with regard to the small plant that develops into an oak tree,[26] a diachronic identity does not entail an identity of characteristics or even of substance of the individuals involved. There need not be identity of concept or meaning. Hence, analytic truths that hold with regard to the name 'Moses' used to refer to one individual need not hold for 'Moses' used to refer to the other.

The hypothetical Moses who spent his life at the Egyptian court might be considered to be diachronically identical with the infant Moses, just as is Moses, the leader. The hypothetical Moses introduces yet another concept of Moses correlated with the name 'Moses' and hence yet another meaning. The analytic truths that hold also vary with meaning and the referent envisaged. Thus the various problems invoked by Kripke find an easy solution in the fact that the meaning of 'Moses' varies with the intended referent. The analytic truths that apply in the case of Moses the leader are inoperative for the hypothetical Moses who remained at the court. If Moses had stayed in Egypt, there is a sense in which Moses would not have existed (the leader would not have), and yet another in which he obviously would have existed.

The situation does not change essentially if in place of an individual in some dim past, we substitute as the subject of speculation an individual who is an acquaintance or near acquaintance. To borrow Kripke's example of Hitler,[27] we might suppose Hitler successful in gaining admission to the Vienna Academy of Fine Arts, and so enamoured of a lovely Jewish student encountered there as to become, after terrible internal conflict, disinterested in politics for life. 'Hitler' may be used to refer to the hypothetical Hitler or to the real Hitler. What is analytically true for 'Hitler' in one of its uses would differ somewhat from what is analytically true in its other use. Such a situation offers no grounds to claim that 'Hitler' must have the same meaning in both cases and consequently be largely devoid of conceptual content.

The conclusion to which the evidence points is that the semantic contribution of the proper name, like that of the natural-kind term, is its intentional content or, more precisely, the intentional content that the speaker assumes the word to have for the hearer. This conclusion is corroborated by the fact that it offers an explanation for a number of semantic phenomena, among which Frege's puzzle—the fact that identity statements involving two proper names may sometimes be informative—as also the fact that affirmations of existence ("Homer existed") and denials of existence ("Santa Claus doesn't exist") may make sense. It fleshes out the explanation of speaker-deemed failures of substitutivity and also helps to explain why historical characters are so like those in novels, differing from the latter solely through their being posited as standing in a real spatiotemporal relation to the present-day world.

As might be suspected, a similar account of natural-kind terms finds similar corroboration in the informativeness of statements of the identity of two species. It explains, for instance, how the statement that Oregon myrtle and California laurel are the same species (barring residency requirements) may be informative for someone who knows the first only for its carving wood and the second only for its fragrant leaves. It further explains how affirmations and denials of the existence of species (the existence of yetis) may make sense. Such statements simply add or subtract a spatiotemporal location to a kind meant.

In view of the irremediable untidiness of natural language, it is not surprising that in artificial formal systems meaning or semantic contribution is equated with a bare referent stripped of ostensible or descriptive characteristics. Such systems are certainly neither illegal nor immoral and may indeed be highly useful and even necessary for certain tasks. However it is a mistake of considerable disservice to philosophy generally to assume that the semantics of the natural language faithfully reflects that of the simpler systems and to make this assumption the cornerstone of an attempt to resolve outstanding philosophical problems. In particular the semantics of artificial languages has no discernable possible bearing on Cartesian skeptical problems. The semantics of natural English does. Yet as we have seen, meaning in English is resolutely conceptual, a function of the speaker's beliefs and associations, and indexically tied to the speaker's actual perceptual situation. As such, it is ideally suited to the purposes of Cartesian solipsists, any of whom would gleefully admit the existence or presence of associations, beliefs, and an actual perceptual situation.

CHAPTER EIGHT

CONCEPTUAL AND LINGUISTIC PARASITISM

ON CONCEPTUAL SCHEMES AND THE ONTOCENTRICITY OF LANGUAGE

The charge that a skeptical thesis is conceptually or linguistically parasitic is the claim that the thesis makes essential use of concepts that have presuppositions denied by the thesis itself. Conceptual parasitism is concerned with the presuppositions of a particular conceptual scheme, linguistic parasitism with those of language. If the two are distinguished, it is to encompass the possibility that a particular conceptual scheme may be integral to forms of thinking that are not linguistic. Linguistic parasitism arguments make two broad assumptions about language, both of which must be true if the argument is to be sound. The two assumptions are summed up quite succinctly in the following remark by Quine: "Conceptualization on any considerable scale is inseparable from language, and our ordinary language of physical things is about as basic as language gets."[1] One assumption, somewhat loosely stated, is that the concept of an object (as exemplified in our incessant everyday encounters) is central to language, central to its conceptual structure, to its functioning, and to its meaning. This assumption might be termed the tenet of *the ontocentricity of language.* Juxtaposed to it is the second assumption that all thinking—or more moderately, all thinking worthy of philosophical consideration—is essentially linguistic, i.e., tied to public language. This second assumption may be termed the tenet of *the linguacentricity of thought.*

Clearly both assumptions must be true if the linguistic parasitism argument is sound. The argument purports to show that a skeptical thesis is inconsistent with the presuppositions of everyday language, that is, with the presuppositions of the very vehicle in which the skeptical thesis is enunciated. The demonstration must obviously show in addition that the skeptic can neither enunciate the skeptical thesis in some region of language unfettered with presuppositions of the sort nor express it without contradiction in some revised edition of the language. Yet even if the demonstration is successful on both counts, it must furthermore show that it is impossible to express the thesis consistently in a private language, perhaps one invented for that very purpose or, yet again, in some mode of nonlinguistic thinking, whether imagic or simply perceptual thinking devoid of any symbols whatever. These various alternative formulations must be excluded before the antiskeptical demonstration can be considered effective.

A successful linguistic parasitism argument must consequently clear a number of quite substantial hurdles. We shall find good reason to think that no linguistic argument directed against Cartesian solipsism (Sensa Solipsism excepted) is able to clear *any* of them. This is not to say that there is no truth in Quine's above-quoted claim. Indeed, most ordinary language does relate to everyday material objects; furthermore, conceptualization on any considerable scale does seem to be inseparable from a non-iconic symbolic system such as ordinary language. Nevertheless, the questions raised by Cartesian Solipsism with regard to reality and existence are extremely simple in nature, and as a result, they involve neither sophisticated conceptualization nor complex systems of symbolization. For this reason, as we shall see, they escape the strictures implicit in Quine's remark.

In principle, a conceptual parasitism argument poses a potentially more serious threat to skepticism than does a linguistic one, for the reason that the particular conceptual scheme envisaged might well be integral to all languages, including private ones, as well as to nonlinguistic thinking. The view that skepticism is conceptually parasitic owes its present vogue to P. F. Strawson who succinctly states it in the following passage: "So with many skeptical problems: their statement involves the pretended acceptance of a conceptual scheme and at the same time the silent repudiation of one of the conditions of its existence."[2] The charge to be answered by the skeptic is that the skeptical thesis presupposes a certain conceptual scheme (or more modestly and parochially, a certain concept), while contesting one of the conditions of that scheme (or concept).

Any antiskeptical linguistic argument based on the instantiation requirement or on the verification requirement might be converted readily enough into a parasitism argument, provided the solipsist makes essential use of the relevant terms to enunciate a solipsistic thesis. Since we found earlier that neither requirement can be exploited effectively against solipsism, the corresponding parasitism arguments could fare no better. However, criteria of application are but one group of possible presuppositions for a term, or concept or conceptual scheme, so the field of possible parasitism arguments to explore is not as yet exhausted.

It would be a mistake to think that a Cartesian solipsist may avoid a conviction on parasitism charges by an adroit and timely change of skeptical goal. It is certainly true that a demonstration of parasitism is one of implicit contradiction, so that it is possible in principle to present the conjunction of the skeptical thesis together with the parasitism argument as a *reductio* demonstration of the incoherence in the scheme itself. Barry Stroud suggests just such a strategy for the skeptic, that of accepting the parasitism argument and drawing the conclusion that talk involving certain concepts does not make sense,[3] while Garrett L. Vander Veer envisages that of questioning "the validity of the framework as a whole."[4] Yet the adoption of such a strategy is not a serious option for our solipsists. The latter are fairly viewed neither as irresponsible scoffers indulging in some more refined form of bigot-baiting nor as serious thinkers questioning whether any serious thinking at all about the world is possible. Each solipsist is a committed cosmologist proposing a thesis broadly outlining the structure of the world and consequently cannot look kindly on a *reductio* demonstration of the absurdity of a presupposed conceptual scheme. Thus, the solipsist's vulnerability to a successful conceptual parasitism argument cannot be remedied by a manoeuvre of the sort. As a respectable family man or woman, the solipsist may advocate modest conceptual reform but not violent revolution.

It should be added that it would be misleading for the solipsist to attempt to argue, as Stroud and Tlumak do, that a successful linguistic parasitism argument does not establish the truth of certain presuppositions but that it establishes at best that certain beliefs must be held.[5] There is no such distinction to be drawn by the solipsist in the present context, nor indeed by any skeptic reasonably accused of parasitism. The parasitism argument purports to show that some proposition, P, is in some way a presupposition of the skeptical thesis, Q, which itself is in contradiction with P. It is not a viable option for the solipsist to claim that P is simply a presupposed belief which may well be a fiction. Insofar as P is considered a fiction, it is not believed, and insofar as it is accepted, it is not considered a fiction. If the skeptic asserts Q, and Q presupposes P, then the skeptic has no choice but to endorse P. For committed skeptics such as our Cartesian solipsists, there is no general waiver exonerating them from linguistic or conceptual parasitism. They have no choice but to answer the charges piecemeal, each on its own merits, and to demonstrate their agility at skipping through the thicket of allegations of unwitting self-destruction.

As we shall see, the various Cartesian solipsists (the Sensa Solipsist excepted) come through the trial neither scathed nor ruffled nor winded. Since by now the reader is undoubtedly surfeited with anti-skeptical arguments that puff and strut their hour on the stage before collapsing into the wings, there could well arise the question of why it should be necessary to run through yet another string of perfor-mances of the sort. The answer is that there is no other course to take to demonstrate the failure of parasitism, of linguistic philosophy gen-erally, and indeed of the predominant fad of the day, coherentism, to make any significant contribution to the resolution of basic philo-sophical problems. Furthermore, there is certainly no compelling rea-son at the outset to deny the possibility of erecting a successful con-ceptual or linguistic parasitism argument. The point is readily demonstrated. Sensa Solipsism, for instance, could quite successfully be convicted of conceptual parasitism (and would be, if the task were not made unnecessary by the fact that the doctrine has already been shown to be epistemically parasitic). Sensa Solipsism is the claim that nothing exists beyond one's own private world of sensations or repre-sentations. This statement of the thesis makes essential use of the con-cepts of 'sensation' and 'representation'. These two concepts presup-pose an account of the world in contradiction to the thesis itself, an account featuring an independent world, the actions of which on the solipsist's body in that world give rise to the sensations or representa-tions experienced by the solipsist. Hence, Sensa Solipsism is concep-tually parasitic. Other forms of solipsism could well suffer from the same defect. Only the repeated failures of attempts to convict of para-sitism can give good grounds for thinking that further attempts are futile, and that only to the extent that the repeated failures apparently exhaust the field of conceivable presuppositions on which a para-sitism argument might be based.

With regard to the conceptual parasitism of Sensa Solipsism, it is interesting to note that both Strawson and Sellars may reasonably claim to have established just such a conclusion via an analysis of the conceptual frameworks of material bodies and sense impressions structuring our everyday experience of the world. Sellars speaks of the framework of the sense impressions as "parasitical" upon dis-course about material objects.[6] Strawson speaks of the "identifiability-dependence" of private experiences upon the identifiability of persons.[7] Both Sellars and Strawson espouse tenets that have the result of enclosing the perceiving subject in a private world like that of a Sensa Solipsist. For Sellars, perception involves the having of sense impressions, and the grammar of sense-impression talk precludes its making sense to say that two perceivers have the same impression. For Strawson, 'private experiences' may be equated with 'sense data', an equation which entails that all sensuous elements in experience are private. Insofar as Sellars and Strawson intend to direct a charge of conceptual parasitism against Sensa Solipsism, they are essentially right. If they are not totally right, it is for two reasons. One of these is that the presupposed conceptual scheme figuring in the charge of conceptual parasitism is integral to the Representational Theory of Perception. Since the latter is an empirical theory, the more appropriate charge is epistemic rather than conceptual parasitism. The other is that the accounts of both Sellars and Strawson harbor a particularly serious conceptual confusion, one with a distinguished lineage, traceable through Wittgenstein, Russell, Hume, and Descartes and obtained by introducing the concepts of the Representational Theory of Perception into an everyday account of perception. The mixing of the two accounts gives rise to manifest absurdities. For instance, within the everyday perceptual context, if all phenomena are declared to be representations or experiences, then any person visibly present to oneself becomes one's representation, and the other person's experiences become experiences of something that is one of one's own experiences. At the same time, one's own visible body, the public entity allegedly having one's experiences, becomes one of its own private representations. Any valid conceptual parasitism argument (as also any coherent account of perception) must choose either the terrain of the everyday framework or that of the Representational Theory of Perception and not confuse the two.

THE PUBLICITY OF LANGUAGE

The claim that any language is a public practice built on public criteria and public behavior owes its present widespread acceptance largely to Wittgenstein. The publicity of criteria is seen to follow from the publicity of language itself. Language is spoken to people by people and taught to people by people. As Sellars puts the matter, "language is essentially an *inter-subjective* achievement, and is learned in inter-subjective contexts."[8] It is assumed to follow from this point that any criteria governing the use of language must be criteria for everyone and any justification for a particular use must be one that everyone can understand.[9] A further conclusion drawn is that the falsity of solipsism is thereby established. The point is neatly encapsulated in David Pears's exposition of Wittgenstein's views: "Meaning is linked with intention, and intention is linked with public criteria. It follows that, though the later philosophy is anthropocentric, it could never be solipsistic. The base line to which we must always return is a shared language with public criteria."[10] Clearly, we have here the makings of a transcendental parasitism argument against solipsism. The latter advances a thesis in a language the presuppositions of which are in contradiction with the thesis itself.

This line of reasoning would make short shrift of Cartesian Solipsism were it not quite obviously fallacious. It naively assumes a clean-cut public/private dichotomy in virtue of which the publicity of criteria is judged incompatible with solipsistic privacy. The alleged dichotomy vanishes on any attempt to flesh it out concretely. On the solipsistic thesis that the experienced world is sham—the mirage, dream, or conjuration envisaged by Unreal World Solipsism—it must be nevertheless a sham of which speakers, language, and criteria are an integral part. It is a sham in which speakers use language governed by public criteria and teach that language together with its public criteria to prospective language users. The publicity of criteria in no way conflicts with solipsistic privacy. Indeed, even the private world of an Internal World Solipsist, such as the Sensa Solipsist, is a world in which other speakers figure on occasion, along with commonly perceived objects and public criteria for making correct statements about such objects. The public/private dichotomy that serves as key stone of the argument is simply an illusion generated by simplistic labeling.

A similar conclusion follows if the world in question is the truncated remnant envisaged by Observed World Solipsism. That world is nevertheless a remnant in which figure other speakers, language, and attendant public criteria. The world admitted by the solipsist is quite public in the sense that its contents are in principle observable by other speakers and on occasion may contain fragments of such speakers. Consequently, the criteria employed in successful communication with these speakers would be public criteria. One might plausibly object that the usual public criteria would no longer obtain in such a meager world. However, this would be to raise an issue other than that of the necessary publicity of criteria.

It is true enough that language is taught in a public context and that most often the criterion for determining whether a pupil has mastered a lesson is appropriate public behavior on the part of the pupil. Yet this fact should not be allowed to obscure the more basic fact stressed in the preceding chapter that any meaning, including linguistic meaning, is an associate for a particular conscious being. The function of teaching or training is to set up the desired association. Teaching—broadly construed—is not a necessary condition for there to be meaning per se; it is rather a necessary condition for there to be meaning in accord with the meaning for other members of the community. When the pupil's linguistic behavior is incorrect, often it is not that an expression has no meaning for the pupil but rather that it has taken on an idiosyncratic meaning not shared with the other members of the community at large. The solipsist has no need to endorse the broad picture of a community of unobserved language users with their practices and rules. He or she may converse in some meager corner of the world through sounds endowed with whatever associated meaning they happen to have and with whatever ephemeral speakers happen by.

One unfortunate result of the overestimation of the role played by public criteria in the functioning of language is a tendency to belittle the role of the private object in language and hence in thinking generally. The trend is threatening, not just to pains and feelings but to other private matters such as meaning, thinking, understanding, and knowing and by extension to the Cartesian subject. By his conception of meaning Wittgenstein is led, despite his assurances to the contrary, to eliminate the private object from language altogether.

The process of elimination begins with the somewhat plausible claim that behavioral criteria are necessary if private experiences are to have any working relationship with language. The point is succinctly made in the following passage: "What would it be like if human beings showed no outward signs of pain (did not groan, grimace, etc.)? Then it would be impossible to teach a child the use of the word 'tooth-ache'."[11]

The next step is to detach the private object from any direct connection with language. In Wittgenstein's beetle parable, each speaker is imagined to have a box, the private occupant of which is called 'a beetle'. The word 'beetle' could not function on the model of a word designating an object, the argument runs, since the nature of the thing in the box would be irrelevant and might differ from one box to the next, be anything or nothing at all.[12]

The final step is to dismiss private objects altogether as irrelevant to language. The step is implicit, even if unintended, in Wittgenstein's claim that if a person used the word 'pain' correctly with regard to pain behavior, it would not matter that his memory was faulty and he called different feelings by the name.[13] It is equally implicit in the remark, "Always get rid of the idea of the private object in this way: assume that it constantly changes but that you do not notice the change because your memory constantly deceives you."[14] The suggestion in both cases is that the private object is like a wheel unconnected to the mechanism of language; it does not effect use and hence is not part of meaning.[15] Andrew Oldenquist, for one, quite explicitly endorses this interpretation of Wittgenstein's meaning when he comments with regard to the teaching of color words to a child, "What sense-datum he has is irrelevant to what they are trying to teach him, and what they are trying to teach him is what 'red' means."[16]

If valid, the more radical line taken in the third step would eliminate all private experiences from possible discourse. Coupled with the thesis of the logocentricity of thought, it would lead to the conclusion that the private objects open to introspection cannot even be thought. Since a plausible criterion of existence is that a candidate be at least thinkable, the nonexistence of mind, for instance, could thereby be established. This exciting result, however, is based on a line of reasoning that is far from impeccable. The supposition is made that private objects change and that corresponding memory lapses prevent the changes from being noticed—whence it is concluded that private objects are irrelevant to language. If indeed the reasoning were valid, then anything could be shown to be irrelevant to language simply by making an analogous supposition of changes coupled with appropriate memory deficiencies. It might even be supposed that behavior constantly changes and that no one notices the changes while correctly correlating language with the private object. It could then be concluded that behavior is irrelevant and the private object essential. It is true that on a supposition of behavioral changes, it becomes incomprehensible how people manage to identify the feelings of other people. Yet on Wittgenstein's supposition that private objects change, it becomes incomprehensible how people manage to identify their own feelings. In both cases something akin to divine intervention is required if language is to function as it now does. The argument suggests rather the indispensability of both private objects and behavior for the normal functioning of language.

The beetle parable is equally incapable of establishing the irrelevancy of private objects to language. Even if the beetle is actually different from box to box, each could nevertheless play the role of a paradigm for the meaning of the word 'beetle' for each particular beetle owner. Furthermore, if beetle owners are allowed to make reports on the characteristics of their private beetles, then the contents of the box would begin to matter in determining the common meaning (if any) of the word 'beetle'. It is certainly not outrageous to suppose that beetle owners could give descriptive reports based on analogies with public phenomena. In illustration of the point, consider a possible extraterrestrial visitor, a metal sphere endowed with sensory apparatus, perceptual ability, and the intelligence and faculties requisite for the learning and exercise of language. Let us suppose that in its behavior the sphere gives no apparent sign of ever feeling emotion of any kind. However, oddly enough, after assimilating a good amount of English, including certain uses of the words 'inside', 'this', and 'body', the sphere is sometimes heard to say 'inside this body' and to add some descriptive phrase such as 'calm', 'swirling', 'clear', 'pulsating', troubled', 'dense', 'effervescent', 'evanescent'. Barring lies and pranks, the most plausible explanation of the phenomenon is that the creature is attempting to describe some sensuous stuff perceived as located within it and that it is doing so in virtue of analogies between certain features of its sensuous interior world and other features of its sensuous exterior one, exterior features it has learned to describe with the relevant descriptive phrases. Despite a total absence of behavioral criteria, the creature would be talking of private objects.

It is true, as Wittgenstein claims, that an inner process needs outward criteria of some sort,[17] but the outward criteria need be neither behavior nor indeed anything causally related to the inner process nor anything contemporaneous with it. If behavioral manifestations were a necessary condition for the communication of inner processes, one could never relate one's dreams and visual images. What is required for communication is simply some measure of a common world, which measure may in principle be quite meager. If the visiting extraterrestrial sphere was sightless and, like a bat, explored the world with sonar, it might nevertheless manage to convey some notion of both its outer and inner worlds in virtue of the structural and dynamic resemblances of those worlds to the visual-tactual world we know—provided of course a common language exploiting those structural resemblances was devised. Thus, in the end, the claim of public criteria reduces to the prosaic requirement that two speakers must to some degree share a common world for communication to be possible. As noted earlier, this requirement is one that Cartesian Solipsism easily meets.

A more plausible case may be made for the quite different point stressed by Coval among others,[18] that the use of language to inform other people of one's feelings—pains, itches, fevers—has certain implications inconsistent with the professed views of a skeptic who denies the existence of other minds. Informing or telling of one's feelings has a purpose and is not simply a gratuitous act. It would certainly be an interesting task to determine exactly the necessary presuppositions of speech acts of the sort, but it is also one of which we shall forego the pleasure. In the worst of scenarios, the solipsist would have to be silent with regard to private experiences. There is no obvious way in which such a state of affairs might have seriously embarassing results for solipsism, for instance, entail that the solipsist must decline all use of language with regard to private phenomena or renounce the use of language altogether. Hence, we shall do best to bypass the issue.

THE PRESUPPOSITIONS OF TEMPORALITY AND IDENTITY

Parochial parasitism arguments are based on the presuppositions of the concepts or of the language peculiar to some skeptical thesis. In the nature of the case, there is no clear way in which a sham/reality distinction may be argued to have presuppositions incompatible with solipsistic theses. On the other hand, opportunities of the sort abound with regard to solipsism questioning unobserved existence. Such solipsism reduces the world to the flux of sensuous data of which the solipsist is aware. Hence, it acknowledges the existence of at least three distinct items: (a) a temporal flux, (b) a perceiving subject, and (c) sensuous data. In this and the following sections, we shall consider these three items in turn together with their correlated charges of parasitism.

The temporal flux plays the central role in that patriarch among conceptual parasitism arguments, Kant's self-styled "refutation of idealism."[19] In skeletal form, the argument runs as follows: the skeptical viewpoint that doubts the existence of independent objects does grant there is inner experience, or a flux of evanescent sense data; yet a necessary condition for any temporal succession is that there be something permanent; hence, the flux of sensations requires the existence of something permanent outside the flux. It follows that what the skeptic denies, viz., the existence of something permanent, is a necessary presupposition of that thesis.

Kant's argument is directed against a position akin to Sensa Solipsism in that it contains expressions such as "representations," "an intuition in me," "things outside me," and states somewhat dubiously that the required permanence cannot itself be a representation, since representations "as representations themselves require a permanent distinct from them."[20] However, the crux of Kant's reasoning is simply the claim that succession requires permanence. This contention is not compelling. There is nothing conceptually impossible in the notion of a world in which objects materialize and dissipate like clouds in a turbulent sky or like notes in an unfamiliar symphony. In order for there to be succession, all that is required are two terms, one temporally prior to the other. For permanence more is needed: succession together with a relation of identity between the two successive terms. In these circumstances, it is difficult to see how permanence might plausibly be argued to be a necessary condition of succession.

In his attempted reconstruction of Kant's Transcendental Deduction, Strawson suggests that the necessary permanence that concerns Kant should rather be seen as "the spatiotemporal frame of things at large."[21] In support of the proposal Strawson contends that the seeing of objects and events as located in such a framework requires some object be perceived as the same at different times and hence as permanent. The claim is defended by Strawson earlier in *Individuals* in the course of a parasitism argument directed against a slightly different type of skeptic, one who wonders how we can ever be sure of judgments of identity in cases of noncontinuous observation. Strawson's answer is that the doubt only makes sense if the two items or terms of the putative identity relation belong together in one spatiotemporal system. A unique spatiotemporal system is possible in its turn, Strawson argues, only if there are "satisfiable and commonly satisfied criteria for the identity of at least some items in one sub-system with some items in the other."[22] Strawson supports this latter claim with a *reductio* argument. Without such "unquestioning acceptance of particular identity," Strawson reasons, "we should, as it were, have the idea of a new, a different, spatial system for each new continuous stretch of observation.... Each new system would be wholly independent of every other."[23]

Strawson's phrasing of the argument suggests a conclusion in terms of prerequisite beliefs (the kind discussed by Stroud), but Strawson clearly intends to establish a more straightforward thesis, similar in this regard to the Kantian conclusion based on an alleged inconceivability. Strawson's reasoning is that the concept of 'the same individual' implies a permanence of the individual across periods of noncontinuous observation. It follows that skeptics who deny unobserved existence (the Ephemerata and Sense Data Solipsists) could not have this concept. For them, for instance, a cat that was hidden momentarily would have ceased to exist, and hence, a reappearing cat could not be considered continuous with a hidden cat that was itself continuous with the original cat. More dramatically, Strawson reasons that after a period of total nonobservation, as during sleep, none of the things observed would be considered identical with things observed previously—and since position is defined by objects as much as objects by position, the spatial system itself would not be identical with the previous one. As A. C. Grayling states the matter in his forceful defense of Strawson, "unless we can indeed reidentify particulars we should have no grounds for thinking of the world as a SINGLE spatio-temporal system."[24]

Strawson's argument here is very similar to the one given by Kant, and it fails in analogous fashion. Just as permanence turns out not to be a necessary condition for a relation of succession between two terms, so permanence turns out not to be a necessary condition for a relation of identity either. Spatiotemporal continuity is assumed to be required for identity given the prevalent belief that things do continue to exist unobserved, but there is nothing in the concept of 'the same individual' that actually necessitates such existence. Everyday reidentifications are not effectuated on the basis of continued unobserved existence. The prime criteria are location and ostensible characteristics. For example, two shoes are recognized in the morning as being one's own in virtue of their characteristics of shape, size, color, deformations, and so on, coupled with their location. This recognition of the shoes as being the same shoes as the ones that one took off the evening before would be in no way jeopardized if the shoes had in fact passed out of existence that night for eight hours or so. A skeptic who denies continued unobserved existence would be using the criteria we use most of the time in any event for reidentification.

Strawson claims that if no continuous unobserved existence were posited, there would be no grounds for positing a single spatiotemporal system and that consequently each new stretch of observation would constitute a new independent spatiotemporal system. This line of reasoning quite misrepresents the actual situation. The important point to note is that there are no grounds for positing distinct systems. Without such grounds, to claim that the two stretches constitute distinct systems is to draw a distinction without a difference. It follows that there is no need to come up with grounds for positing a single system; the absence of grounds for positing distinct ones provides all the grounds needed.

To make the point concretely, consider the situation found by an Ephemerata Solipsist on waking up in the morning. The question to be determined is whether for the solipsist the new waking world must be, or is, a new spatiotemporal system distinct from the one constituted by the waking world of the night before. To be noted first is the fact that there can be no question of a new *temporal* system. The two waking periods are already temporally related, one prior, the other posterior in time, and hence, they are part of one temporal system. Events or phenomena in the two periods are obviously temporally distinct and continue so whether the two spatial systems are related or not. The issue is whether the two observed *spatial* systems are distinct or not, or more precisely, whether or not the solipsist must, as Strawson claims, consider each reappearing waking world as a new spatial system different from a former one. An affirmative answer has absurd implications. It would imply, for instance, that a solipsistic prisoner after ninety days of solitary confinement would be obliged to speak of ninety new and distinct worlds. More generally, Strawson's claim would have to hold even when there was no observable difference in the constituents of two successive waking worlds. That is to say, it would have to hold even when on the basis of our ordinary criteria of similarity and location, each individual in the 'old' world would be judged identical with its counterpart in the 'new' one. Yet in such a situation, on what basis could the old and new worlds be distinguished? A distinction between the two would amount at most to a mere matter of priority or posteriority to a particular temporal gap. It would otherwise be a distinction without a difference. The only reason there would be to claim that the two apparently identical individuals are not identical is the absence of temporal continuity, i.e., the existence of a temporal gap between the two. In these circumstances, to insist that the individuals must be different individuals by reason of a temporal gap is simply to claim that the individuals are different in the sense that they are separated by a temporal gap. Thus, even if Strawson's claim were granted and it was declared that the skeptical hypothesis leads to a segmentation of the world into different systems, these systems would be different systems only in the sense of being separated by temporal gaps. To accuse the skeptic of dividing the world up into many different worlds would amount to accusing him of asserting gaps in the world—a charge to which the skeptic would readily accede.

THE PRESUPPOSITIONS OF THE CONCEPT OF SELF

The second item recognized by the radical solipsist to be present in the flux of experience, is a perceiving subject, or self. In his book, *Individuals*,[25] Strawson presents a very powerful and influential argument to the effect that this self must be a person, i.e., a being to which both corporeal characteristics and states of consciousness are properly ascribed. The focus of Strawson's discussion is the neo-Kantian issue of the necessary conditions for the self-ascription of states of consciousness or experiences, or more specifically, what the nature of the self must be for such self-ascription to be possible. Habitually one ascribes one's various experiences of thinking, seeing, feeling, imagining, and so on, to oneself, i.e., to a self and to a single self. The question raised by Strawson is what justification one has for doing so; why ascribe one's experiences to one self rather than to many selves or to nothing at all? The answer Strawson proposes and defends is that the concept of the self as a subject of experiences is not a primitive concept capable of standing on its own; the primitive concept is that of a person.

The crux of Strawson's argument for his claim is a point he characterizes as a "purely logical one"; the ascription of experiences to oneself only makes sense if it is possible in principle to ascribe experiences to others. Explains Strawson, "The idea of a predicate is correlative with that of a range of distinguishable individuals of which the predicates can be significantly, though not necessarily truly affirmed."[26] What this point implies, according to Strawson, is that there should be a possible set of individuals, the subjects of experiences, who are both identifiable and of the same logical type. Strawson reasons that the subject of one's own experiences cannot be a Cartesian private subject. If it were, then other subjects would also have to be Cartesian subjects. Yet if such other subjects were private Cartesian entities, they could not be identified or picked out by oneself as other subjects of experiences. Hence, a necessary condition for the ascription of experiences to others could not be fulfilled. As a result, one could not even ascribe experiences to oneself. The conditions for the ascription of experiences are fulfilled, Strawson argues, only if the subjects of experiences are persons and hence entities with identifiable bodies.

Strawson's claim that other private selves are not immediately identifiable provokes the retort that such selves are readily identified indirectly via bodies. Any encounter with another person involves an immediate awareness—visual or tactual—of a body. The person's private self may be identified indirectly as the self standing to the perceived body in the same relationship in which the Cartesian self in one's own case stands to one's own body.

Strawson's answer to the objection is that such an account of identification presupposes what it attempts to establish. It assumes that one may already identify one's own experiences as one's own when precisely the point at issue is one's right to do so. Argues Strawson, one cannot reason from the case of one's own experiences to the experiences of others, or from one's own self to that of other selves because, unless one already has the concept of other selves, one has no conception of one's own self. One is oneself but one individual in the range of individuals to which experiential predicates apply; prior to the setting up of that range with its other possible selves, one has "not even the syntax" of one's premisses.[27]

Strawson finds his conclusion to have a number of important implications. For one thing, it provides the backbone of a conceptual parasitism argument against solipsists such as the Monopsyche Solipsist who question the existence of other minds and skeptics who consider any reasoning from another person's behavior to that person's private feelings to be at best a shaky inference. Skeptics (and solipsists) of the sort make essential use of the notion of personal experiences in speaking of their own experiences, and yet deny one of the conditions for the possibility of the notion of personal experiences by denying that others have experiences. Consequently, they undermine the very presuppositions that would allow the skeptical thesis to make sense.

A second implication Strawson draws is that Descartes's notion of a nonspatial private thinking self is incoherent. If subjects of experiences were private beings of the sort, then the very concept of a self would collapse; there would be no concept of one's own self because no concept of other possible selves, and no concept of others because no concept of oneself. The moral drawn by Strawson is that the subject of experiences must be a person, which is to say, a corporeal being as well as a conscious one. Although Strawson does not explicitly characterize it as such, the argument might be considered a parasitism argument against the Cartesian view of the self.

Now, Strawson makes repeated use of possessive adjectives and pronouns in his formulation of the argument as well as in his rejection of indirect identification. Possessive expressions such as 'my' or 'one's own' immediately call up expressions such as 'your' or 'his' and indeed seem to make sense only in opposition to other possessors. To avoid such connotations it is advisable to restate the argument using personal pronouns such as 'I' and 'me', an operation that should in principle not effect the validity of the argument. The revised argument would run somewhat as follows: One may have the concept of this Cartesian subject, the self to which perceptual, intellectual, and affective predicates are ascribed only if one may ascribe such predicates to other Cartesian subjects, something one cannot do since one cannot identify them.

In its restated form the argument is quite unconvincing. It is unconvincing because it assumes that having the concept, 'this Cartesian subject', is dependent upon the possibility of identifying other Cartesian subjects. The assumption has a distinct air of gratuitousness. It is certainly possible to have the concept of a particular kind through an encounter with simply one member of the kind. It is possible too to have the concept of a particular member of a kind, even when the individual is the unique member of the kind. Surely then, it would seem, it is also possible in principle to have both these concepts even in the absence of the least notion as to how to go about encountering other members of the kind. A total absence of knowledge of other possible members can hardly have the effect that there can be no concept of the kind even in the presence of the one known member of the kind. To be aware of a pain, for instance, and subsequently have the concept of pain, is it necessary to be able to identify other pains, in particular those of other people? On the face of things, it would seem not—unless, of course, it is being surreptitiously assumed that the only possible concepts are those already in place in everyday public language.

The point is often missed. In his defense of Strawson against criticisms by Stroud, A. C. Grayling elaborates on Strawson's semantic point that for the ascription of mental states and mental activities, one must have "criteria of a logically adequate kind."[28] As Grayling forcefully states the matter, to understand the meaning of a term is to be able to use it, which at the very least means knowing its "assertability-conditions," or being able to recognize empirical situations in which the term is properly applied and hence can be applied.[29] Grayling criticizes the skeptic (and later, Stroud) as someone who thinks incorrectly that there is an understanding/applying dichotomy, that it is possible to understand the meaning of a term and yet not concede that there are situations in which it may be applied. There is no such dichotomy, says Grayling; to use the term is to accept the presuppositions of the family of concepts of which it is a part—at which point it is "wholly fruitless and idle" to raise skeptical doubts.[30]

Grayling's discussion fails to do justice to the skeptic's concerns. The skeptic has no serious doubts about the existence of his or her own self and the ascription of feelings, states of mind, and the like to that self. What is doubtful for the skeptic is that warranted assertions of existence and ascriptions of the sort may be made for other selves. The claim in Strawson's argument to which the skeptic would take exception is the claim that one needs the concept of others in order to have a concept of self. That claim is obviously false to the skeptic's way of thinking since there is a self continually present in the skeptic's own experience. The fact that the skeptic's present concept of self is integral to a larger scheme of concepts should not constitute an insoluble problem for a profession of solipsism. Any conceptual scheme, until proof of the contrary, should in principle be open to revision. Since in the present scheme the criteria employed for ascriptions to oneself are quite different from those operative in ascriptions to others, it should in principle be possible to reject the second part of the scheme and keep the first. Alternatively, it should be possible for the skeptic to follow Stroud's suggestion of rejecting the whole scheme,[31] at least temporarily, in order to construct a new scheme that allows the skeptic's own self to be identified in the skeptic's actual awareness of it; subsequently, when the skeptic asks whether there are other such selves with like experiences related in like fashion to other visible or tactually perceived bodies, he or she finds no warrant for assertions of the sort. Thus, it is clear there are sufficient grounds for divorce. The details may be left for the lawyers to work out.

THE NATURE OF THE CARTESIAN SELF

In the above answer to Strawson's argument it has been assumed that the Cartesian self or subject is something that may be encountered in one's experience and so give rise to the general concept of a Cartesian self. It is doubtful Strawson would heartily endorse the assumption. In fact, it would seem rather to be Strawson's peculiar conception of the nature of the Cartesian subject that prods him to ask what reasons one has for ascribing one's experiences to one self rather than to many selves or to none. Since this question functions as a preamble to Strawson's argument, his conception of the Cartesian self could well play the role of a premiss in a subterranean argument running unavowed beneath the official one with its "purely logical" point. Let us bring this peculiar conception to the surface.

For Strawson, an incorporeal subject of experiences is apparently a nonentity. In *Individuals* he characterizes the Cartesian subject as a "pure individual consciousness," or "pure ego," identifies it with the entity vainly sought by Hume in the flux of perceptions, as also with the Kantian "I think," a pure formal unity, and muses that it is perhaps what Wittgenstein had in mind in saying that the subject is not part of the world but its limit.[32] He also endorses Lichtenberg's dictum that Descartes ought to say "there is thought" rather than "I think."[33] The implication is that a search for the thinking subject among the materials in the flux of experience finds merely something akin to a pure gaze indistinguishable from what is seen. In an earlier passage Strawson suggests a similar view in the course of a thought experiment involving a world composed purely of sound. In such a world, Strawson argues, the perceiver would not have sufficient grounds for a concept of self. Strawson considers the act of initiating sound as a possible source of selfhood, but dismisses the phenomenon as insufficient to yield the concept of a self, on the grounds that the mere making of sound might be adequately described through a distinction between what is done and what is found to happen.[34] This absence for Strawson of any identifiable subject in the flux of experience may well be the unformulated ground for his conclusions regarding the self and, by extension, the explanation of how he can sensibly ask for grounds for attributing experiences to one self (at least one and at most one).

Strawson's query is a popular topic discussed extensively in the literature of the period. We find Ayer, for instance, wrestling repeatedly with the issue of the relation among experiences that makes them experiences of one and the same self.[35] In his logical positivist days, his solution is to rely on the fact that the experiences all contain elements of the same body. In subsequent works he admits certain alternative psychological criteria, then finds it necessary to posit an unanalyzable relation among experiences. Later still, he settles on the fact that the experiences stand in a causal relationship to a particular body. Ayer's view of the self, apparently identical with that of Strawson, creates the problem of the ascription of states to a single self. In this perspective, the conclusion drawn by Strawson is plausible enough. The anemic subject constituted by a pure transparent consciousness has no characteristics allowing it to be identified as one self rather than many or none. It would be quite unable to identify itself, let alone identify other subjects. Its resulting identity crisis would leave it little choice but to endorse Strawson's precept: no identification without materialization.

The key issue then is whether some more substantial subject may be uncovered among the materials in the flux of sensuous data, a subject that may justifiably be claimed to extend over time and to warrant the introduction of a noun for its designation. It must be remembered that the subject to be sought is not the subject that has representations or sensations (private visual ones of the everyday surrounds). As concluded earlier, the conceptual baggage of the Representational Theory has no place in the present discussion. Now, when this point is kept firmly in mind, it is found that Strawson, like Hume before him, is clearly mistaken. A tenacious rummaging about in the Humean flux of experiences turns up, in point of fact, two subjects of the required kind. Each of the two may lay claim to be temporally extended. Each may be characterized as Cartesian in view of its essential privacy. Let us make their acquaintance.

One of these subjects is neither invisible nor intangible. On an unskeptical and unsophisticated everyday view of perception, there is little doubt as to what (or who) is the perceiving subject. The perceiver is the quite visible organism that stares, approaches, circles and handles, pokes and sniffs, perhaps manifests excitement or disgust, ponders, wonders, on occasion emits articulated sounds, and so forth. This thinking, feeling, visible person is the subject to whom experiences are attributed. Now when a skeptic, such as the Ephemerata Solipsist, denies the existence of anything unobserved, he or she truncates in fact not only the perceived object but the perceiving subject. The bodily aspect of the perceiving subject reduces to that part of the everyday perceiving subject that is actually seen, felt, or heard. The skeptic, as a perceiving subject, reduces bodily to what the skeptic actually sees and feels of himself or herself. The visible part is often very little: the top side of a hand and forearm repeatedly intruding from the periphery, an occasional knee or foot, the permanent blur of a nose. The felt part is a rather complex configuration of pressures, feelings, pulls, tingles, and throbs, most often present as a mere dull tactual permanence of which the salient features vary somewhat with each movement made but, at times, with a shift of attention, transformed into a clearly outlined mobile and sensous solid. So much for the bodily aspects of the perceiving subject. The mental aspects, the thinking, imagining, reasoning, and remembering remain, of course, the fugitive and somewhat insubstantial events they always were.

The more radical doubts of a skeptic such as the Sense Data Solipsist reduce the perceiving subject still more since they question the coordination of the visual and tactile-kinesthetic aspects. These doubts also call into question the reality of what is actually felt and seen. Nevertheless, there remains a being of sorts to fill the position of perceiving subject for the radical Solipsist, a reduced but complex person, a tactile-kinesthetic body endowed with feeling and movement. This tactual entity is clearly one of the constituents in the skeptic's flux of sensuous data, present in some form or other in any perceptual experience. It is unquestionably a most significant aspect of that subject, and where a choice must be made between it and a now unrelated visible remnant of a visual body, it has an overwhelmingly stronger claim to be the viable heir to the perceiving subject of ordinary experience. Consequently, it must be considered the subject of perception, the subject that feels, sees, and hears and that, by extension, is the subject of experiences or the subject to which experiences are attributed. This subject corresponds roughly to the Husserlian lived body, to the analysis of which the second book of *Ideas* is largely devoted.[36]

A strong case may be made for the presence of a second, and considerably less substantial, experiencing subject in the flux of experience. This is the Cartesian ego or thinking subject. The possible presence of this subject in the skeptic's flux of experiences is already suggested by Strawson himself with his claim that in any experience, "even in the most fleeting and purely subjective of impressions," there may be distinguished "a component of recognition, or judgment."[37] Descartes would certainly agree. In the *Sixth Meditation* Descartes declares that sensing in its very concept involves some sort of intellection and hence is not conceivable without a thinking substance to which it is attached.[38] This remark regarding the presence of intellection in any sensing is echoed repeatedly throughout Descartes's writings. In his *Replies to the Second Objections* he makes immediate awareness or knowing (*connaissance*) one of the defining characteristics of modes of thinking, the operations of which include those of the senses; a similar definition in a passage in the *Principles* makes immediate perception the defining characteristic, and in the same passage sensing is classed as a knowing (*connaissance*).[39] Again, in his replies to Hobbes, Descartes speaks of intellectual acts among which he includes sensing, and he states their common characteristic to be thought or perception or consciousness *and* knowing (*conscience et connaissance*).[40] Thus, it would seem that the concept of sensing as the mere presence of something sensuous, the "raw feel" of which Rorty speaks,[41] has no place in Descartes's analysis of experience. There is no experience devoid of intellection, and consequently, no sensing unaccompanied by thinking. Further corroboration is to be found in Descartes's claim in a letter to Gibieuf that the thinking subject always thinks, even during sleep.[42]

Thinking is, properly speaking, nonsensuous. In this regard, it resembles meaning, the phenomenon considered earlier in chapter 7, which phenomenon is an integral part of thinking in Descartes's sense. Sensuous items may well play a crucial role in thinking, but they cannot pretend to be the sole constituents in the thinking to be found in an experience. The nonsensuous constituent must be included in any description of experience that aspires to be an adequate description. The sensuous aspect in two experiences could be the same while the thoughts were different. Descriptions in which the nonsensuous constituent was ignored on the grounds that it is nonsensuous would then be identical even though the experiences being described were different—which shows that something must be wrong with the description proscriptions that exclude the nonsensuous aspect of thinking. In any event, to leave out the nonsensuous constituent of thinking is to leave out what is for the experiencing subject not simply an essential constituent but often the most important one. It is what fleshes out what is perceived from the meager base of what is actually perceived; it is the meaning had by scenes and events, sounds and squiggles, as well as the goal or purpose of actions.

Admittedly, the admission that thinking must be included in any adequate description of the temporal flux does not take us very far. It amounts merely to admitting Lichtenberg's account, "there is thinking," while leaving in abeyance Descartes's "I think." The point to be noted for present purposes, however, is that there is no clear obstacle to one's having a concept of thinking as opposed to other kinds of phenomena—and furthermore, no clear obstacle to one's distinguishing thinking from other kinds of phenomena through some device of one's semantic system. This is an important first step in the direction of a concept of a Cartesian thinking being.

A second step is the incorporation of an identity of thinking over time. Thoughts persevere, as do lines of reasoning, investigations, envisaged goals, memories, the weight of past experience. This too could be noticed. An adequate notational representation of the thinking would require some device filling the function of a process name, albeit a device less sophisticated than a personal subject pronoun. The pronoun is a device admitting of other persons, and would be required only for a third step. For example, if one should associate the experience of thinking with a particular body (one's own), one might very well be led to conceive of the possibility that similar phenomena are associated with other bodies. The accommodation of such possibilities in the symbolic system would necessitate the introduction of a device allowing a distinction to be drawn between the thinking processes associated with one body and the thinking processes associated with another body. The device adopted need not be a system of proper names or personal pronouns—indeed, it could not be if the symbolic system was imagic and hence iconic—yet for the purposes of interest to us, it would be functionally equivalent to such a system since it would distinguish among distinct thinking processes, each associated with a certain body. The correlated concept of a distinct thinking process, possibly contemporaneous with others, would capture much of the notion of a Cartesian ego.

The most important step in the genesis of the concept of a thinking self is the second, the one that expands thinking from a perhaps instantaneous and ephemeral item in the flux of experiences into a process lasting over time. The step is clearly justified by the phenomena. In the contemplation or examination of something, for instance, or in a focused pondering of possibilities or in the tracing out of ramifications, there is identity over time. To Strawson's question of why such experiences are ascribed to one subject rather than to several or to none at all, the answer is that there is a unity of intention in them. To say merely, "there is thinking," is to give a woefully incomplete account and moreover a misleading one, in that it suggests an absence of any proper unity of the process as one process. On the other hand, to maintain that there are several temporally discrete selves is to introduce gratuitous divisions and, as in the earlier-noted case of object identity over time, to institute a distinction without a difference.

Grounds for identity over time are to be found in a variety of other phenomena. An espoused aim, for example, may lead to an array of cognitive undertakings all united through their contributing to a common goal. Moreover, thinking at any given time is colored and enriched with the cognitive acquisitions of past experience, with an ever-growing accumulation of a wealth of familiarities, discoveries, and techniques arising from passive exposure to phenomena, and from active investigation of them. Memories of past activities, spectacles witnessed, reflections, and feelings tie experiences to a present awareness in some form of unity. The memory of an event is also a memory of a past participation, of standing in relation to the event in the position one presently stands to present events. Not only the perceptual involvement but the kinesthetic and emotional involvement as well may be relived in the reexperiencing of the past, sometimes in the case of the latter with astonishing intensity. A long-buried grief, or terror or shame or disgust, may come back with quite overwhelming force on the occasion of some idle musing or probing. Each of these phenomena in somewhat different fashion provides grounds for speaking of a cross-temporal relationship and of claiming that there is one self rather than many or none. The identity over time is obviously not a matter of permanent characteristics enduring through the years. Identity is seldom substantive in any event, as Hume aptly points out with regard to an oak that grows from a small seedling into a huge tree, or with regard to plants and animals generally.[43] Nevertheless insofar as the various instances of one's thinking have close relationships to other instances at other times, it is plausible to claim that, in the case of a self, the existence of these relationships is precisely what makes for one self rather than for many or none.

The Cartesian thinking subject cannot plausibly be dismissed as a nonentity in the manner of the transparent consciousness or gaze envisaged by Strawson. Both the Cartesian subject and its fleshed out tactile-kinesthetic peer—the subject of the Sense Data Solipsist—may be found in the materials of the solipsistic flux and consequently identified, just as they may lay claim to be the subject of experiences, i.e., the subject that sees, hears, and feels. To claim of either subject that it can be identified only if other subjects are identifiable is on the face of things to make a quite gratuitous claim. The subject is clearly present in the flux and consequently would seem susceptible of being noticed, picked out, and recognized independently of the identification of any other subject. The existence of one subject implies a range of possible subjects but only in the very loose sense that when there is one instance, there could be others.

THE PRESUPPOSITIONS OF THE
CONCEPT OF SENSE DATA

The concept of sense data is a particularly easy target for a charge of linguistic parasitism. Everyday discourse deals primarily in full-fledged material objects and has been molded to that end. Hence, it is only to be expected that any attempt to use language to speak of sense data should be characterized as a form of parasitism. Let us begin exploration of such possible parasitism arguments with a third and interesting conceptual parasitism argument presented by Strawson, this time directed explicitly against the radical skeptic's notion of a pure sense datum experience. The argument is a part of Strawson's heroic attempt to reconstruct Kant's Transcendental Deduction. Strawson's aim is to show that any experience, including that of such a meager world as the one admitted by a Sense Data Solipsist, must presuppose the possibility of a subjective/objective distinction inconsistent with solipsism.

Strawson's point of departure is the conceptualizability of the data of experience. As Strawson puts the matter, "there can be no experience at all which does not involve the recognition of particular items as being of such and such a general kind."[44] Wittingly or not, Strawson is endorsing Descartes's view that all awareness involves intellection. Strawson goes on to argue that recognition is possible "only because of the possibility of referring different experiences to one identical subject of them all."[45] He asks what the experiential basis of this notion is, or in other terms, what elements in the skeptic's flux of experiences allow him or her to ascribe experiences not only to a sub-ject but to a single subject (and hence to distinguish between the awareness and its accusative). Strawson rightly points out that the question is not answered by merely stipulating that the experiences belong to one consciousness, or by declaring the consciousness to be that which is aware of them all.[46] The skeptic must find a ground for a self-ascription of experiences within the materials of his meager world. The necessary ground, Strawson goes on to argue, can only reside in the distinction of a subjective experiential component within individual judgments of experience, a distinction equivalent to that between 'seems to me as if' and 'is'. On the general level, says Straw-son, this distinction makes for a dichotomy between a "subjective order and arrangement" of experiences, and an "objective order and arrangement" of the things of which the experiences are experiences, an objective order independent of any particular experiential route through it. This distinction is what allows the history of a person to be characterized in part as "an embodiment of a temporally extended *point of view* on the world."[47] Without this distinction, Strawson rea-sons, the skeptic would have no grounds for the ascription of experi-ences to a subject. And yet, says Strawson, any such subjective/objec-tive dichotomy is excluded for the skeptic by the very terms of the skeptical thesis. The conclusion drawn is that the skeptic implicitly denies a necessary presupposition of the skeptical hypothesis.

Strawson's line of reasoning is very odd at several points. He argues that conceptualization requires some form of recognition which in turn requires reference of the experiences to one subject. He claims that the latter can only be provided by a possible subjective/objective distinction within experience. Yet surely the con-ceptualization and recognition themselves provide any grounds they may require for a reference to one subject. Any experience of recogni-tion, for example, is itself evidence for a subject identical across time. There is no need to appeal to a subjective/objective dichotomy to do the job for it. The very notion that all experiences involve the concep-tualization of data is a generalization from experience. It could not even be made unless there was in each particular experience some ground for distinguishing, however roughly, between the datum and its recognition, the datum and its conceptualization. Since the distinc-tions are to be found in the experience, there is no problem of ground-ing them.

It is true that such instances of conceptualization and recognition cannot provide what Strawson claims to be necessary for them to be conceptualization and recognition, namely, a reference to one identical subject, the same in all one's experiences. It is true too, as Strawson claims, that a subjective/objective distinction implicit in each experience might plausibly provide the desired relation to a single subject. Yet apart from the dubiousness of the claim that a single subject of all experiences is required for there to be conceptualization, that subject is to be found in any event rather in one's projects, memories, and cognitional accretions. Once again Strawson fails to take the Cartesian thinking subject seriously, and once again he equates the thinking subject with a bare consciousness. Indeed, this mistaken conception of the self could well be what leads him in the first place to claim that there is a serious danger of the act of awareness being indistinguishable from the item of which that act is an awareness.

Finally, the objective side in the subjective/objective dichotomy sketched by Strawson contains two distinct elements of objectivity: a reality opposed to a seeming, and an objective order admitting of alternative routes encompassing more than what is actually perceived of it. These two notions of objectivity correspond in a curious but ultimately uninteresting fashion to the two distinct sets of concerns that occupy our two groups of Cartesian solipsists: concerns about the reality of what is observed and about the existence of what is unobserved. It is difficult to hold that the first element is a necessary condition for the very possibility of the ascription of experiences to a single self. If such were the case, there would follow the dubious ontological doctrine that self-consciousness is fully possible only because the world contains illusions. The doctrine would solve Descartes's problem of why a benevolent creator would allow sense deception but is otherwise quite gratuitous. The second element in Strawson's subjective/objective dichotomy has no such awkward consequences, but it is useless as a weapon against solipsism. The reason is that Sense Data Solipsism does not exclude other possible points of view on the world. It denies only that such points of view could contain phenomena the solipsist does not now perceive. Indeed, the very formulation of the solipsistic thesis implies that there are other possible points of view. The claim that phenomena unobserved by the solipsist cease to exist can only mean that these phenomena cease to exist where they were perceived before, thus implying a possible point of view that would find empty space. Furthermore, the visual, auditory, and tactual phenomena admitted by the solipsist are all spatially structured hence contain a space beyond what is observed and, consequently, a world through which there are alternative routes. Thus, the second element of Strawson's subjective/objective dichotomy contains nothing denied by the solipsistic thesis.

The concept of 'sense data' would seem on the face of things an easier target for a charge of linguistic parasitism. Everyday discourse deals primarily in full-fledged objects. Its concepts are for the most part those objective constituents, relations, and operations in an abiding fleshed out world. If recourse is had to so specialized an apparatus in order to speak of sense data, the resulting discourse may reasonably be expected to be parasitic on discourse about everyday objects. One of the earliest successes of parasitism arguments in this direction is H. H. Price's repudiation of the sense datum epistemology he developed at considerable length in his book, *Perception*. Price's later disavowal, which appears in a second preface, is based on the consideration that any explanation of the sense datum terminology must involve giving suitable instructions, which necessarily make use of words for material objects. Price reasons as follows: "If these instructions, and others like them are to be understood, the material-object language of common sense must be understood already. And how can we have learned to understand it, unless some material-object words have ostensive definitions?"[48] In these circumstances, skeptical doubts are logically incoherent, Price argues, since the very terminology in which they are expressed could never have been understood if the doubts were warranted.

Richard Rorty, in his reconstruction of Strawson's reconstruction of Kant,[49] makes a not too distant point. Experience requires conceptualization, Rorty points out, which in turn requires the subsumption of particulars under universals. The latter is only possible through the notion of an object, Rorty goes on to argue, his claim being that without such a notion, words for particulars would not have a sense or role different from that of words for universals. The requirement of the notion of an object can apparently be filled, Rorty claims, only by the concepts of 'physical object' and 'experience of a person', neither of which have any possible place in a solipsistic conception of the world. Once again, the keystone of the argument is the question of the presuppositions of the concepts actually embodied in the language being used. While Rorty grants that the case against the skeptic is not airtight, he esteems nevertheless that it is as tight as the nature of the case will allow, and tight enough to exclude skepticism. To formulate the solipsistic thesis, the skeptic would have to devise another language, Rorty claims, and specifically, "spell out the rules of a language game which would either dispense with the classifying of particulars under universals or would involve the particular-universal distinction without including names for either physical objects or experiences."[50]

An alternative tactic for Rorty's line of attack would be to focus on universals rather than particulars. Factual information is readily enough found to be incorporated in kind concepts and property concepts and hence in the very meaning of linguistic predicate expressions. This incorporation of facts within concepts is what Wittgenstein has in mind in his remark, "What we call 'measuring' is partly determined by a certain constancy in results of measurement."[51] The phenomenon is more fully explored by Sellars who speaks of the role played by "material moves" in constituting concepts as well as in providing for inferences and explanations. A person learning the language of simple observation predicates, color words, for instance, must not only be put in standard conditions by his teacher, Sellars argues, but must recognize the conditions as standard, i.e., he must learn general facts of the form, A is a reliable symptom of B.[52] This in turn, Sellars argues plausibly enough, involves the location of objects in space and time and, consequently, the material moves incorporated in expressions for spatial relations, situations, and transformations. Sellars finds these circumstances to point to the conclusion that the notion of a language containing no material moves is "chimerical," and that consequently the classical skeptical problem is "an absurdity." Stated otherwise, "the skeptic's notion that any move beyond a language which provides only for the tautologous transformation of observation statements is a 'venture of faith' is sheer nonsense."[53]

While impressive enough, particularly when united, these various considerations are not decisive against skeptical theses. Certainly, it would be difficult to quarrel with the claim that the common subject-expressions and observation-predicates of everyday language involve conceptual presuppositions inconsistent with radical skepticism. Yet it does not follow that the concepts of any possible language must do so, nor does it follow more modestly that the concepts integral to any version of English must do so. Let us first consider the matter of predicates.

As Sellars sees the situation, there cannot be a language devoid of "material moves," and the only question that might be raised is the question of which set of material moves it is more reasonable to incorporate. Yet surely, such a generalization is far too sweeping to be adequately justified by a few observations—for instance, on the way in which color predicates are generally used in English. Common practice in English might be suggestive but has of itself no authority to preclude the possibility of alternative practices. More importantly, even in English itself, prevailing practice does not exclude marginal practices. In attempts to give an appropriate characterization of the color of an afterimage, for instance, considerations of lighting and other conditions of observation play no role whatever. An analogous situation obtains in the case of rainbows and mirages. What, one may ask, is standard lighting for a rainbow? Standard conditions play little role in judgments about sounds and feeling, or in the application of predicates such as "shrill" or "painful." Here again, one may ask what material moves inconsistent with skepticism are indispensable to reports of the sort. Apparently none.

Natural-kind terms—those old favorites such as 'lemon', 'tiger', 'gold', or 'water'—would appear at first sight to present less easily dismissed difficulties. The criteria for the correct application of such terms are certainly quite complex. Nevertheless, as noted in chapter 7, the meaning for a particular speaker of a sortal noun such as 'gold' evolves with increasing knowledge. Surely what evolves may also regress to a simpler, more rudimentary level. There seems no obstacle in principle to substance terms regressing to some simpler phenomenal level. To avoid incompatibility with more sweeping skeptical disclaimers of knowledge, substance terms would require deep supplementary revision—a separation of visual appearances from tactile ones, for instance, but the resources of English are certainly not unequal to the task.

Species terms such as 'lemon' or 'rabbit' would require similar revision. Yet here too, while the task is hardly an engaging one, it cannot be judged unrealizable. There is no clear obstacle to the skeptic's applying the revised terms to any of a wealth of physiognomically recognizable figures. The terms 'moon' and 'sun' have been and sometimes still are used in this physiognomic way, and the practice surely could be extended to 'rabbit' or 'lemon'. It is true that in everyday circumstances, when the expression 'rabbit' occurs in conversation, it is automatically assumed by the interlocutor that the intended referent is a thing endowed with many if not most of the general characteristics of the average furry, timid and ear-bedecked solid labeled 'rabbit'. It is also true that it would be found outrageous should a speaker without prior warning use 'rabbit' to mean some ephemeral rabbit-façade of the sort that pops up from time to time in the world of the radical solipsist. Nevertheless, the assumption that the referent of the expression is the fully fleshed-out animal rather than the radical solipsist's truncated survivor is not an assumption unsusceptible of revision. It is not a necessary truth that rabbits are not hollow and have unperceived rabbit parts. The assumption that rabbits are more than façades is part of the background of knowledge assumed in everyday communication, a background that might be (and sometimes is) questioned or altered through appropriate discussion and explanation. The meaning of natural-kind terms is accumulative, and surely what may be pasted on may also in principle be peeled off. The solipsist's proposed revision would thus not seem to face intractable semantic difficulties.

By the same token, there is little that is compelling in Rorty's claim that in a language the role of a particular can be filled only by a physical object or by the experience of a person. If ephemeral events such as battles, fires, and earthquakes may be viewed as particulars, it is unclear what valid grounds there might be for excluding ephemeral rabbit façades. In point of fact, there is no danger whatever of universals being left to lie about in "mere collations"[54] in the absence of physical objects to particularize them. Rorty's fear that they would is due to his mistaken view of a sense datum experience as "an experience such that no concepts are used in it save those of sensory qualities."[55] Sensuous qualities invariably arrive packaged in expanses of some shape, relative location, and duration. They are already particularized. The only question to arise is which particular is the most convenient one to adopt as one's referent.

The above considerations point to the conclusion that ontocentricity is not a necessary feature of language. This conclusion in turn raises considerable doubt about the soundness of Price's conclusion that sense datum discourse is parasitic on object discourse. If one should use object terms in explaining what is meant by 'sense data', the appeal to objects is due to the constraints of convenience of exposition rather than to any ineluctable dependency. Imagine for a moment how a sense data solipsist might explain to himself or herself what is meant by 'a sense datum', for instance, that of a lemon visually present. The explanation need not involve reference to physical eyes and full-bodied lemons. It would refer to a present shape, color, texture, and sheen and need involve no objects whatever.

The failure of the various linguistic parasitism arguments based on the ontocentricity of language should not be found surprising. On one hand, the world of the radical skeptic is reached through skeptical scrutiny of the everyday objective world and consequently might be expected to retain some measure of the publicity, criteria, and structure of the latter. It is itself a rudimentarily objective world, the limit in a series of progressively less objective worlds reached by progressive questioning of the everyday one. On the other hand, the English language is a quite malleable instrument and surely has sufficient resources to tolerate a simplificatory reform adapting it to a more rudimentary objective world such as that of the solipsist. Indeed, as observed earlier, one of the characteristics of empirical concepts and hence of the correlated linguistic expressions is accumulativeness. Clearly, if the meaning of an expression may be expanded and enriched with the acquisition of further information, that meaning must admit in principle of the reverse operation, that is, of being contracted and impoverished with the questioning and rejecting of the alleged information.

THE PRESUPPOSITIONS OF WARRANT ESTIMATION

To liven up matters for the more mathematically minded, a few words should be said about one further possible point of attack for an antiskeptical conceptual parasitism argument. The radical skeptic maintains with regard to induction that observed phenomena fail to provide any support whatever for empirical generalizations encompassing unobserved phenomena. Now, this skeptical thesis might seem to be in contradiction with theorems of the probability calculus. If it could be argued that the calculus is a formalized version of the notions of probability employed by the skeptic in making his claim, then it might be possible to show the skeptical claim to be in contradiction with its own presuppositions.

Just such a line of reasoning is adopted by D. C. Stove in an attempted response to Hume (attributed by Stove to Van Thun[56]), which if successful, would be acutely embarrassing to both Sense Data and Ephemerata Solipsism. Humean skepticism regarding induction, Stove argues, makes the claim that observed confirming instances of a generalization do not increase the probability that the next instance will be a confirming one. According to Stove, this claim is easily translated into the notation of the probability calculus. Let "$P[Ba/E]$" mean "the probability that the individual, a, has the property B given the evidence E." Let us suppose that a_i has been observed to have B, and that a_j is the next a to be observed. In Stove's estimation, the skeptical claim is plausibly construed to imply that the probability that both a_i and a_j have B given the evidence E is unchanged when the observation that a_i has B is added to the evidence. Expressed in the above notation, the skeptical claim so construed is that $P[(Ba_i \& Ba_j)/E]$ should be equal to $P[(Ba_i \& Ba_j)/(Ba_i \& E)]$. Now, through the judicious manipulation of various plausible-looking axioms of the probability calculus, it may be established that $P[(Ba_i \& Ba_j)/(Ba_i \& E)]$ is greater than $P[(Ba_i \& Ba_j)/E]$. The conclusion drawn by Stove is that the Humean skeptical thesis is in contradiction with a tautology of the probability calculus, the truth of which it presupposes.

There are a number of serious mistakes committed in Stove's argument. One is that it misconstrues the skeptical claim of evidential irrelevance as the claim that probability remains constant no matter what the evidence. The skeptic's position is rather that the irrelevance of the evidence makes it nonsensical to speak of probabilities at all. On this point surely the skeptic is right; where the evidence is irrelevant, there is no probability given the evidence. What, for instance, is the probability (expressed as a number between zero and one) that the next bird to fly by will be white, given the fact that George over in London had orange juice at breakfast? Does the question make any sense? The essential irrelevance of the evidence would lead the skeptic to dispute the claim that the various axioms and theorems of the probability calculus qualify as tautologies. The Negation Axiom in particular, an axiom that incidentally plays a crucial role in Stove's proof, would be rejected by the skeptic. In a simple case, the axiom states that the sum of the two probabilities, the probability that the next a has B and the probability that the next a does not have B, must be equal to 1. The skeptical claim is that past evidence is irrelevant. Hence, even if the skeptic were to agree to attach a numerical value to the probability that the next a has B, the only value consistent with his judgment of the irrelevance of evidence would be the number 0. The skeptic would attach the same number to the probability that the next a does not have B given the evidence and, for the same reason, that the evidence is irrelevant. Thus, for the skeptic the sum of the two probabilities could not be 1. From the skeptic's point of view, the axiom is obviously invalid, as is any effective antiskeptical proof based upon it.

Stove is, of course, quite right that if the skeptic's claim were rightly translated as the claim that $P[(Ba_i \ \& \ Ba_j)/(Ba_i \ \& \ E)]$ is equal to $P[(Ba_i \ \& \ Ba_j)/E]$, then it would be clearly false, as is shown by the earlier-mentioned theorem proved by Stove. This result gives little cause for excitement. Stove's theorem states that the probability of finding that both of two a's have B is improved if one of the a's is found to have B. Clearly $P[Ba_i/Ba_i]$ i.e., the probability that a_i has B given that a_i has B, must have the value of 1. Hence Stove's theorem states essentially that $P[Ba_j/E]$ is greater than $P[(Ba_i \ \& \ Ba_j)/E]$, a truism which holds in virtue of the mere fact that any proper fraction is greater than the product of itself and some other proper fraction. It is difficult to think that a skeptic concerned with induction would be inclined to deny such an elementary arithmetical truth.

In point of fact, however, if the skeptical claim were translatable into probability theory, it would not be so translated. It would have to be construed as the claim that whatever the value of $P[Ba_j/E]$, that value is not increased by the addition of Ba_i to the evidence. This is the claim that $P[Ba_j/(Ba_i \& E)]$ is not greater than $P[Ba_j/E]$. If Stove is to present a relevant proof, he must establish that $P[Ba_j/(Ba_i \& E)]$ is greater than $P[Ba_j/E]$, that is, he must establish that the probability of Ba_j is increased by the addition of Ba_i to the evidence. Now, this proposition cannot be derived in a probability calculus based essentially on ratios of class membership. The reason is simple enough: the proposition is always false.

The point may be made with a simple illustration, the case of drawing cards at random from a shuffled deck of any composition and calculating the probability of drawing a spade. The probability that the next card drawn will be a spade may be expected to decrease with each spade drawn. This is because the removal of a spade decreases the number of spades remaining in the deck and hence decreases the proportion of spades. The one exception is the case where all the cards are spades and, consequently, where the probability remains constant (at 1). In no case does the probability increase.

This circumstance may be stated more generally in the probability calculus as the proposition that $P[Ba_j/(Ba_i \& E)]$ is greater than $P[Ba_j/E]$. Where N is the number of a's, and n the number of a's which have B, then on a random drawing of a_j, $P[Ba_j/E]$ is equal to n/N. If prior to the drawing of a_j, a_i is drawn and found to have B, then $P[Ba_j/(Ba_i \& E)]$ is equal to n - 1/N - 1. Since N must be greater than or equal to n, it follows arithmetically that n/N is greater than or equal to n - 1/N - 1. In the case where not all a's have B, and so N is greater than n, the probability that the next observed instance will be favorable decreases with each favorable instance observed. Where all a's have B, and consequently n is equal to N, the probability that the next instance will be favorable remains the same with each favorable instance observed. In no case does the probability increase, no matter how many favorable instances are observed. The skeptical claim that favorable instances do not increase the probability that the next observed instance will be favorable not only does not contradict the theorems of the calculus but ironically enough, it is borne out by them. Consequently, there can be little hope of disproving the skeptical thesis by showing it to be parasitical on the probability calculus and hence to presuppose the truths it denies.

CHAPTER NINE

THINKING OUTSIDE PUBLIC LANGUAGE

PRIVATE LANGUAGE AND CRITERIA

Any aspiring linguistic parasitism argument has three main hurdles to clear if it is to succeed in showing the skeptical position to be self-refuting. It must not only establish that any variant of a public language presupposes a conceptual scheme of public objects in contradiction with the skeptical thesis, but it must also show the impossibility of entertaining the thesis either in a private language or in any other mode of thinking outside language. In view of the conclusions just reached—that public language is not incorrigibly ontocentric and that the various Cartesian solipsistic theses may be safely stated in a revised form of English—an examination of the remaining hurdles might appear somewhat superfluous. We shall proceed with one nevertheless. If it can be shown that fundamental philosophical problems such as those posed by solipsism are susceptible of being formulated in a private language and in nonlinguistic modes of thinking, then the temptation to search for yet further linguistic and conceptual refutations will be quelled, as will perhaps also unduly enthustiastic estimates of the import of the linguistic turn to philosophy generally.

In the literature the possibility of private languages is rejected usually on the basis of either of two grounds, both taking their inspiration from remarks by Wittgenstein. One is the notion that language is a practice or custom, the other that concepts and conceptual schemes are integral to the public language with which they are acquired. The inspiration in both cases seems to have been Wittgenstein's determination to show the impossibility of solipsism, or more precisely, of his particular version of the doctrine. Both are introduced in the *Investi-*

gations with a discussion of a language describing inner experiences and understandable in principle by one person alone.[1] The close genealogical relationship of the two arguments does not, however, preclude their relevance to other forms of skepticism and to private languages generally, and so they may in principle aspire to take linguistic parasitism arguments generally over their second hurdle. Each requires some discussion.

Central to Wittgenstein's account of language is the view that linguistic behavior involves reacting to signs in accordance with rules, and that obeying a rule is a custom, institution, or practice.[2] Wittgenstein apparently finds this latter fact sufficient to support the conclusion that a private language is impossible, for he reasons as follows: "I could not apply any rules to a *private* transition from what is seen to words. Here the rules would really hang in the air; for the institution of their use is lacking."[3]

The obstacle Wittgenstein sees here cannot be simply that the practice is a private one, since a private practice certainly would seem possible in principle; people do manage to train themselves to do things, to give themselves habits, and they could in principle at least inculcate in themselves certain associations of symbols and events. Nor can the mere fact of getting the associations started be the envisaged obstacle here. A similar difficulty must be and is overcome in the case of a public language each time a new word is coined—as it would be, for instance, in getting the word 'phorange' adopted as the name of the phosphorescent orange color used to warn motorists. The budding private language inventor would have to set up the association despite a total lack of reinforcement from others, but the task could not be deemed unfeasible.

Nor can the objection be that the private language would be unworkable due to the blurring or collapse of the distinction between what seems right and what is right. Any personally devised system of symbols could be quite useful to the extent that its semantic correlations are remembered, and remembered correctly, and that extent could be considerable. A failure to remember would cause inconvenience rather than serious trouble since such failure would require only that a new correlation be instituted. Remembering incorrectly would pose a greater threat since errors of the sort could in principle defeat any purpose the system might have. This is the point made by John Kekes when he argues that a solipsist could not correct the mistakes inevitably made, could not know whether the invented rules were being followed, and hence could not achieve the purpose for which the language was designed.[4] Yet surely such an assessment is far too pessimistic. A like menace stalks any solitary activity, in that success is limited by the reliability of one's faculties. A solipsist aware of the risks involved, and of the reliance placed on memory for the successful achievement of the purposes pursued, might reasonably take his or her chances with a fallible instrument rather than none at all.

The difficulty Wittgenstein has in mind has to do rather with standards of correctness. On the practice of rule-following, he declares: "Hence it is not possible to obey a rule 'privately': Otherwise thinking one was obeying a rule would be the same thing as obeying it."[5] He makes a similar objection to a proposal to impress upon oneself a symbol-connection, and so remember it correctly: "But in the present case I have no criterion of correctness. One would like to say: whatever is going to seem right to me is right. And that only means that we can't talk about 'right'."[6]

Curiously enough, Wittgenstein's attitude with regard to private rule-following does not have the empirical, open ring found elsewhere in the *Investigations*, but it echoes rather the formal jurisdictive tone of the earlier *Tractatus*. Wittgenstein states flatly that a justification must produce something "actually *correct*," and he characterizes private language as sounds one may "*appear to understand*."[7] When he argues that the distinction between what is and what seems right would collapse, or that there would be no such thing as following the rule correctly or incorrectly, he seems to be implying that there would be no such thing as following a rule at all, hence no such thing as a correlation of symbol with symbolized, and hence, no such thing as meaning.

In a discussion of Wittgenstein, Anthony Kenny interprets Wittgenstein's remarks in terms of a failure of the private statements to meet the requirements of statementhood. Kenny takes Wittgenstein to be arguing that in a private language where 'S' is the name given to a particular private sensation, the statement, this is S, cannot be true or false. Says Kenny, "Even to think *falsely* that something is S I must know the meaning of 'S'; and this is what Wittgenstein argues is impossible in the private language."[8] The crux of the matter, according to Kenny, is the absence of criteria.

Essentially, such is also the crux of the difficulty on Kripke's construal of the matter. Kripke proposes that the central problem of *Philosophical Investigations* be seen as a paradox about meaning.[9] The paradox is that any interpretation of a rule may be made to accord with the rule; nothing in the contents of one's past or present experience suffices to exclude alternative interpretations or versions of what is meant, nor is sufficient to guarantee that some particular correlation of symbol to symbolized is the standard one. There results a general skeptical problem about meaning according to Kripke, a problem to which Wittgenstein's answer is provided by a description of the activities of teaching and of concept-ascription, both of which provide the criteria for rule-following. A corollary of this answer, Kripke goes on to say, is that there can be no private language: a putative private language user would operate in isolation and hence fail to satisfy the assertability conditions for it to be said that the individual possesses a concept or is following a rule.[10] It is, of course, somewhat inaccurate to characterize the failure as a corollary of the conclusion, since any argument from assertability conditions is valid only if a private language has no criteria of its own. The difficulty with a private language would be more correctly stated as the inability of the speaker to satisfy criteria in virtue of which utterances may qualify as statements.

The issue on all these various construals is whether symbols in a private language may have meaning. It is important to be clear first of all that the issue of whether or what a symbol means is not the question of whether or what the symbol now means for oneself. If, in thinking of George, one should represent him through an image, it would be nonsensical to wonder whether one means George or someone else with the image. One's confidence that one means George is not, of course, based on any unambiguously interpretable marks contained in one's image. The image itself, considered as a mere configuration of sensuous material, is susceptible of a variety of interpretations. Nevertheless, one knows both that one means with it and what one means with it. In like fashion, there are no marks and none are needed in order for one to know what one's present interpretation of a rule is. The situation for semantic meaning is analogous to that of perceptual assumptions. At the sight of a book cover, the assumption is automatically made that there are pages beneath the cover—as evidenced by the surprise a discovery of seaweed would provoke. The assumption is not revealed through introspection and the finding of sure marks. It is either already known in the sense that one may immediately state what it is, or if not, it can be uncovered by trying out various candidates until one encounters one that one esteems to be right. The same is true of one's present interpretation of a rule or the meaning a sign has for oneself. The question of the meaning of the sign for oneself is readily answered, if only by the realization that the meaning is unclear.

The issue of meaning raised by Wittgenstein is then not the issue of present meaning for oneself but rather the issue of whether the known present meaning of a symbol for oneself is in accord with past meanings for oneself. Thus when Wittgenstein argues on the issue of private meaning that there is no distinction between what is right and what seems right, and hence that one cannot speak of 'right', he must be claiming that such is the case with regard to the past meaning of the symbol for oneself. Yet when stated in these terms, the claim is clearly unwarranted. Certainly, if one must rely solely on some past memory to discover what the correlation at that past time was, then what seems right is the only testimony one has. Nevertheless, what seems right does not thereby become identical with what is right. What is right is determined by what the correlation actually was; what seems right is determined by what one remembers the correlation to have been. There is no need to equate the two. True enough, it is beyond one's present capacity to compare the two or to determine whether and how they differ. Nevertheless, even if one cannot say what is right, one may speak of 'right'.

The retort at this point could well be that precisely it makes no sense to speak of 'right' if one cannot say what right is. Kenny has Wittgenstein make just such a claim through the denial that a statement qualifies as a statement when made by a speaker of a private language who purports to give the meaning of a term. In the absence of criteria, he says, such utterances are meaningless. Yet this line of reasoning presupposes an overly strong verification requirement for meaning. Here once again, one would do better to follow Wittgenstein's injunction to look and see rather than legislate.[11] Statements about past meanings qualify as meaningful by virtue of the fact that there was a past with oneself, symbols, and meanings in it. The statements remain meaningful whether or not one now has adequate criteria for determining what the past meanings were. The verification requirement of a possible observer is satisfied since one was oneself that possible observer in the past times in question. No stronger requirement need be satisfied.

It is worth noting that the private language inventor would not be alone in basing a judgment about the past on a single past memory. Let us say, for example, that this morning when I awoke, I was dreaming of an encounter with an ambling, invasive troop of well-meaning but clumsy African elephants. My sole evidence for this claim at present is my memory of the event. If the language inventor's judgments are esteemed to be meaningless, then so must my judgment that I was dreaming of elephants. So must also a long list of similar judgments devoid of supplementary support.

Kripke puts forth an interpretation that has Wittgenstein base skepticism about meaning on the absence of any mental state that distinguishes meaning some particular thing from meaning another; since no answer to the skeptical challenge is found, the conclusion is drawn that there is no fact about oneself that constitutes one's meaning.[12] The answer to this line of reasoning is that the same might be said of any intention, knowledge, or meaning; none of these are sensuous states, and not even God, by looking at the sensuous contents of one's mind, could perceive what they are. Nevertheless, there is a fact of the matter that constitutes one's intention, knowing, or meaning. One is aware of what one intends, knows, or means, as is shown by the fact that if asked, generally one may say readily enough what it is. Consequently, in its past use any symbol had a meaning that one could have specified at the time. The only skeptical problem that may arise in the context concerns the reliability of memory.

In the light of the above considerations Wittgenstein's depiction of private language becomes more than somewhat cavalier. Private language is characterized as language in which what seems right is right, where there can be no appeal to "something independent" and "actually *correct*,"[13] the implication being that in this regard it contrasts sharply with public or genuine language. Yet a fish-eyed stare at public and private language finds the difference between the two in standards of rightness to be more aptly described as quantitative rather than qualitative. A private language would not be totally devoid of checks and evidence with regard to past meanings and rule interpretations. Any hypothesis as to a particular past meaning would be susceptible of being supported or countered by the vividness or tenuousness of past memories, by its accord or disaccord with remembered activities and events, and by its accord or disaccord with present observed states of affairs, possibly including records kept in a private notation. Such checks simply mirror on a lesser scale what takes place in a public language. The most notable difference in the two cases is simply in the number of speakers of the language. The point gets obscured by the wealth of printed material cluttering daily life. Yet suppose for a moment all this written material removed. A question as to the meaning of some verbal expression in the public language could be settled only by majority opinion or by appeal to the acknowledged authorities in such matters. This is to say that the question could be settled only by appeal to what seems right to certain speakers of the language. What seems right to certain speakers, their best judgment, is not different in kind from what seems right to one speaker alone.

It is true that the pooled mnemonic abilities of the members of a community certainly provide more reliable support than the mnemonic ability of a single speaker. But this is only because of the empirical fact that people generally misremember independently of each other, and a collective mistake is more unlikely than an individual one. For the same reasons a language spoken by two persons is in a superior position on the whole with regard to conformity with past use than is a language used by one person alone. The reason is simply that on the whole two heads are better than one. It hardly follows, however, that the language invented and used by one person alone is so different that its utterances fail to qualify as statements. In this perspective a language invented for private purposes would seem more aptly characterized simply as the least reliable member in a long series of possible languages that have increasingly more reliable means of checking for past usage.

PSYCHOLOGICAL NOMINALISM AND THE MYTH OF THE GIVEN

A second serious objection to the possibility of a private language has more general import in that with minimal modification it may be converted into an argument against the possibility of nonlinguistic thinking, or thinking outside language altogether. This second objection stems from the very plausible view that the various concepts making up the conceptual scheme in which we think are language dependent; they were acquired when we learned the language, and without such learning, we would not now have them. Of course, if it is true that our concepts are inculcated in us only with language, there can hardly be such a thing as thinking outside language.

The doctrine of the linguacentricity of our concepts constitutes one of the main currents running through Wittgenstein's *Philosophical Investigations*. There Wittgenstein states, for instance, that the concept 'pain' is learned when language is learned, implying that without language we would have no such concept or, more generally, that we would have none of the concepts we actually have. The grounds for the claim are to be found in the views on sameness he expresses in the immediately preceding passage.[14] In a discussion of how images are compared, Wittgenstein declares that the images may be recognized as the same only if the conventions of the language make 'same' the correct word to be used. The conventions of the language according to which two particular pains are to be classed as the same feeling, are likewise learnt with the learning of the language. The words 'same' and 'rule' are related as are 'proposition' and 'true', Wittgenstein remarks at another point,[15] an analogy which implies, of course, that, since rules are social practices, conceptual classifications must likewise be a social phenomenon. Presumably, as much might be said of logical concepts, since in a discussion on the nature of negation Wittgenstein declares, "There cannot be a question whether these or other rules are the correct ones for the use of 'not'. (I mean whether they accord with its meaning.) For without these rules the word has as yet no meaning."[16] The point is neatly turned against the would-be private language inventor by Wittgenstein, who counters the inventor's proposed account of language creation with the claim that the words employed in the explanation—'sensation', 'have', and 'something'—are all words in a common language.[17] The very concepts employed by a would-be private language inventor come from our public language. The implication is that any private language invented would be conceptually parasitic on the public one.

Wittgenstein's view coincides more or less with the view espoused by Sellars under the name of "psychological nominalism," and which Sellars glosses as the doctrine that *"all* awareness of *sorts, resemblances, facts,* etc., in short, all awareness of abstract entities—indeed all awareness even of particulars—is a linguistic affair."[18] According to this view, there is no cognitive awareness prior to language. On the more general level, the claim is that the conceptual structure of language, or what Sellars terms the "logical space" of particulars, universals, facts, and physical objects existing in space and time, is tied to language. As Sellars sums up the matter, "The primary connotation of 'psychological nominalism' is the denial that there is any awareness of logical space prior to, or independent of, the acquisition of a language."[19] Wittgenstein himself nowhere explicitly makes such a sweeping claim, but it is strongly suggested both by his diagnosis of philosophical mistakes as the result of a linguistic confusion and by his rather abrupt dismissal of the possibility of wordless thought.[20]

In his presentation of the doctrine, Sellars opposes it to what he calls "the Myth of the Given," a misconception to be found in accounts of perception offered by the British empiricists and classical sense datum theorists. The myth amounts essentially to the assumption that the awareness of simple sorts or sensuous qualities, "determinate sense repeatables," is an unacquired ability exercised in immediate experience.[21] Sellars argues that the notion of an unacquired awareness of simple sorts forms an inconsistent triad when conjoined with two other very plausible truths, the claim that the immediately given as such does not present itself already packaged and classified (a particular red datum, for instance, is not as such already classified as red), and the claim that the system of classification is conventional and hence acquired.

Sellars's point is sometimes succinctly stated as the claim that there is no perception without conception. The point has a long history. Nelson Goodman is able to remark not unreasonably, "the overwhelming case against perception without conception, the pure given, absolute immediacy, the innocent eye, substance without substratum, has been so fully and frequently set forth—by Berkeley, Kant, Cassirer, Gombrich, Bruner, and many others—as to need no restatement here."[22] The point is often esteemed to have a promising future. Williams sees in it a decisive defence of the coherence theory of justification as opposed to a foundationalist one. On the former, justification is a matter of accommodating a belief to a body of accepted beliefs rather than of confronting 'raw chunks of reality'. The latter notion is incoherent, Williams argues, and is impaled on the following dilemma: "either our confrontation with the given is just one more variety of perceptual judgment, in which case we no longer have a point of pure contact between the mind and the world, or else the content of the given is ineffable, in which case it cannot provide a rational check on anything, cannot favor one hypothesis over another."[23]

Now, how much bearing does all of this have on solipsism and the possibility either of retreating to a privately invented language or of thinking outside language altogether? Let us trudge back to the topic of the pure given and its conceptualization.

Sellars's claim is that there is no unacquired awareness of determinate sense repeatables. Sellars is quite obviously right insofar as the claim is that the awareness one has of the determinate repeatables correlated to the classifications of one's own English idiolect is an acquired awareness. However, this fact is insufficient to rule out all possibility of an awareness of repeatables that is unacquired. The lines of demarcation drawn by the system of classification one has acquired, are unquestionably arbitrary in the particular sense that they might, with as much apparent right or necessity, have been drawn quite differently. For instance, colors might with relative ease be divided into a far greater number of distinguishable hues than the mere dozen or so which English-speaking children are taught. Instead of being grouped by hue, colors might conceivably be classed according to brightness or saturation or even according to the reflectivity or the texture of the colored surface. Yet the recognition that there are alternative systems of classification perhaps as good as the present one does not entail the conclusion that none is any better than a system of classification established in some random fashion. In point of fact, all the ones suggested above would have considerable advantage over a random classification.

The reason for this advantage is that while data do not classify themselves, nevertheless they stand in relations of similarity to other data. The degree of similarity varies. Certain patches of color are more alike than others, certain sizes and shapes more alike. In some cases, there is no distinguishable difference other than one of spatiotemporal location. The closer similarities might be termed *ostensible similarities* to distinguish them from other more distant similarities, although there is obviously no sharp division between the two. These relations of ostensible similarity, however rough-hewn, suffice to provide a natural basis for rudimentary classifications. A classification according to hue or saturation, or brightness or texture is a classification based on ostensible similarity in some respect and consequently does not yield a purely arbitrary collection of items. In principle, any such classification could be suggested by the similarities noticed in the data and adopted as an essential part of the basis of a private language or nonlinguistic mode of thinking.

The standard nominalist response at this juncture is to claim, as does Nelson Goodman at a similar juncture,[24] that any two items stand in some relation of similarity to each other, so that any set of items, however chosen, stand in some relation of similarity to each other. While the claims are indisputably true, they are insufficient to entail the intended conclusion that there are no ostensible similarities and that all similarities are on equal footing. The fact that any two objects, an apple and a key, for instance, are physically similar in some respects, does not alter the fact that the first, the apple, is in some ill-defined but obvious sense more similar in its physical characteristics to certain other objects, other apples, than it is to the second, the key. The fact that anything is in some degree and in some respect similar to anything, cannot obviate the additional fact that some things are more closely similar than others. A set based on ostensible similarity will be superior in certain important respects to a set of which the members are chosen at random, despite the accurate nominalist observation that the members of the latter will stand in some relation of similarity to one another. This is quite clearly true if the similarities in question concern physical and sensuous characteristics to the exclusion of relations based on spatiotemporal position. The relation of similarity holding among the members of the fortuitously formed set will differ from the one provided by an ostensible similarity (unless it is by chance itself an ostensible similarity) in that it will not be a relation that holds both for *all* members of the set, including as yet unencountered ones, and *only* for members of the set. The relation of similarity holding between a particular apple and a particular key is unlikely to be one that also holds for unencountered, randomly chosen members and, at the same time, only for those particular individuals. The standard nominalist observations on similarity simply ignore the phenomenon of ostensible similarity.

Inasmuch as psychological nominalism states that all similarities, including ostensible physical ones, are "a linguistic affair," the doctrine is mistaken. There are a variety of ostensible similarities among perceived items available to serve as a basis for classification. Indeed, if such were not the case, the behavior of creatures devoid of language—animals, prelinguistic children, and certain deaf, deaf-mute, and mentally retarded people—would be inexplicable. They all apparently make distinctions and effectuate recognitions that could only be based on ostensible similarities.

Equally inexplicable would be the coining of metaphors. By definition, a new metaphor has no basis in the official classifications of the language. If there were no natural similarities to serve as its basis, it would have no basis whatever. Equally inexplicable too would be the quite obvious fact that some metaphors are much better than others, some are deeper, some quite striking, some so obvious as to leave one wondering why it went previously unnoticed. Metaphors call attention to ostensible similarities ignored by the official system of classification.

Most importantly, perhaps, without similarities independent of language, the acquisition of language itself would become inexplicable. For an infant to repeat a sound in its appropriate context, it must recognize a second context as being similar to the previous context and, furthermore, attempt to reproduce a sound similar to the previous sound. Indeed, any training presupposes, among other things, an ability on the part of the creature being trained to recognize such ostensible similarities. In the particular case of language training, the complexity and arbitrariness in the choice and grouping of ostensible similarities complicate the task—among other things, certain similarities must be learned to be discounted, such as that of mortar to porridge, or of sheep to dogs—but the task would be prohibitively difficult if the sortal classification in the language were based primarily on random groupings.

Thus, although it is clearly a mistake to assume that perceptual phenomena present themselves prelinguistically sorted according to the mode of classification of some particular language, it is no less a mistake to claim that there is no natural basis whatever for any system of classification. To do so would be to replace the Myth of the

Given by a Myth of Conceptual Creationism. Ostensible similarities structuring the given need to be elucidated rather than argued away. The numerous and differing classificatory schemes to which they may give rise are not purely arbitrary. Of each it may be said that it is in some measure a reflection of relations which hold in the world, and not some arbitrary grid imposed on amorphous material.

In light of the above considerations, the claim that there is no perception without conception is of somewhat dubious import. It echoes on the terrain of perception the truism that any useful symbolic system must be one in which repeatables represent repeatables. Conception is the noting of similarities. These similarities bring the items in the passing show into some relationship with each other. An awareness of the given devoid of any awareness of similarities (supposing such a state to be psychologically possible) would be useless for purposes of cognition (albeit not perhaps for purposes of entertainment). However, it would be misleading on these grounds to dismiss the given as an ineffable something and to declare cognition to be a matter always involving beliefs alone. The similarity between two items grounds the awareness of the similarity, which awareness verifies a belief in the similarity. There is no crucial distinction to be drawn here, one so significant that it may serve to establish the erroneousness of a foundationalist account of perception and the inevitability of a coherentist one. Coherentism cannot sensibly deny there is a similarity between two similar items, a similarity that grounds the awareness of the similarity. Hence there can be no sensible quarrel with foundationalism on this point.

PUBLIC LANGUAGE AND RATIONALITY

Despite the implausibility of psychological nominalism, as originally stated by Sellars, we have not finished our wrestle with the doctrine. With a few concessions to natural fact, the heart of the doctrine may be preserved within what is certainly a more modest reformulation but also one with more widespread appeal. Animals demonstrate an undeniable ability to recognize kinds and individuals and to make appropriate discriminations. They are much less readily accorded reasoning ability and much less still any semblance of rationality. The absence of rationality is often seen to form a pair with the absence of language. The immediate suggestion is that rationality is language-dependent in the sense that a creature can be rational only if it has acquired a public language. The revised version of psychological nominalism to which this suggestion gives rise might be termed *rational nominalism*. It clearly poses a serious threat to the claim that it is possible to think (in particular, to think solipsism) outside a public language.

The more restricted version of psychological nominalism is defended by Rorty when he draws a distinction between awareness as discriminative behavior and awareness as the ability to justify what one says.[25] Awareness of the first sort is denigrated by Rorty as mere "reliable signaling." Insofar as it is manifested by children (as differentiated from computers and rats), and hence by potential makers of reports, Rorty concedes that it might be termed a knowing of sorts, i.e., a knowing of what something (pain, red) is like. Nevertheless, Rorty maintains, only awareness of the second sort is true knowing. It involves, at the very least, the placing of an item in a class, a knowing of what sort of thing some kind of thing is, a relating of classes to other classes, a giving of reasons. Rationality is to be found only with such awareness. Thus, the apparently troublesome unacquired awareness of similarities considered earlier becomes, on Rorty's view, dismissible as an aptitude on a par with that of amoebae and photoelectric cells.[26]

We have seen that psychological nominalism overstresses the element of convention or arbitrariness in the choice of similarities serving as the basis of the classificatory scheme of a language. Rational nominalism must place a similar emphasis on convention if it is to be nominalism. Insofar as it does so, it may analogously be accused of seriously overstressing the element of convention in logical and mathematical concepts. The topic is a vast one, but to illustrate the general point, let us take the concept of negation operative in English. The nominalist claim is that the concept is determined by the rules governing the relevant linguistic expressions, which rules are the rules of a particular language, and furthermore, conventional in that other rules might have been adopted. Wittgenstein's remarks on the topic of the Law of Double Negation (the principle whereby two negations are equivalent to an affirmation) are presumably intended to go far toward establishing the conventionality thesis. Yet, they fail to do so. It is true, as Wittgenstein points out, that in a language in which negation was expressed by pitch, there could be no double negation.[27] However, this point establishes nothing, since one might analogously argue that in a language that had no notational device whatever for negation, there would be no negation, double or otherwise. Likewise, it is also true enough that a double negation could in principle be given the meaning of a reinforced negative in a notational system.

Indeed, in some cases it has precisely this meaning in English. For instance, if someone shouts, "No! No! No!," one is not required to count the negatives in order to determine what the person means (odd number for negation, even for affirmation). Nevertheless, there are several weighty reasons to deny the implied conclusion that the grammar of a double negation is purely conventional or the product of arbitrary decision. Let us look at these.

First of all, there are certain natural constraints on logical and linguistic possibilities to be respected. Any language in which the Law of Noncontradiction holds cannot both allow negative statements to be substitution instances of logical laws and also treat a double negative as a reinforced negative. The reason is that the Law of Noncontradiction for a negative statement would yield a negative statement conjoined to a reinforced negative statement, with the rather awkward result that all negative statements in the language would be logical impossibilities. An example readily makes the point. In virtue of Noncontradiction it is logically true that it cannot be both raining and not raining. It is also logically true that it cannot be both not raining and not not raining. If 'not not' was equivalent to 'not', this second logical truth would be the claim that it cannot be both not raining and not raining—a claim to the effect that the absence of rain is a logical impossibility. It is obviously not obligatory that negative statements should be possible substitution instances in Noncontradiction, but the consideration could well be of appreciable weight in determining the course taken by the evolution of the concept of 'negation' in a language.

There are in addition strong experiential grounds in favor of a decision to make a double negation an affirmation rather than a reinforced negation. It does not seem extravagant to claim that an anticipation is the rudimentary analogue of an affirmation and to find (as Husserl does in *Experience and Judgment*) that the disappointment of an anticipation is a rudimentary analogue of negation.[28] If the correlation is pursued, the rudimentary form of double negation becomes, naturally enough, the nonfulfillment of an anticipated disappointment—a state of affairs equivalent to the fulfillment of an original hope or expectation. The equating of double negation with affirmation thus has a natural experiential base. It is certainly the case that if one were attempting to devise a notation in which failures of anticipated disappointments might be symbolized, then there would be a good reason to have a Law of Double Negation. This is not to say, of course, that one might not choose to have a double negative symbolize a strong disappointment on the model of emphatic negation. The option is there, but the price to be paid is that there would be no simple way of symbolizing the disappointment of an expected disappointment.

It is important to point out, as Wittgenstein does, that the concept of negation operative in English could have been different and is to some extent conventional. It is nevertheless an unwarranted oversimplification of the situation to claim that the concept is conventional *simpliciter*. It is an even greater distortion of the facts to conclude that the concept arises only with natural language—or that it could only so arise. Any private language inventor, taking his cue from disappointed expectation, might have a concept of 'negation' similar to the one operative in English. Since the case of negation may be taken to be representative of the more rudimentary logical and mathematical concepts, then the latter, no less than classifications based on similarity, cannot rightly be characterized as a "purely linguistic affair."

A more modest form of the doctrine of rational nominalism would abandon the nominalist tenets, and claim simply that the learning of a public language is a necessary condition for the possession of rationality. This seems to be Rorty's position. Despite the modification, the doctrine suffers nevertheless from serious defects, chief among which is the fact that it does not accord with the findings from an impartial observation of the facts. True enough, it grants an ability to recognize to infants and animals on the grounds that they exhibit discriminative behavior. Yet it fails to note that both often exhibit intelligent behavior as well, behavior that seems on occasion explorative, thoughtful, insightful, and even deductive. The behavior of a nine-month-old child presented with some novel object it grasps, studies, sucks, shakes, and passes from hand to hand would seem aptly characterized as 'rudimentary investigation'. The same may be said of the behavior of an eleven-month-old child throwing things out of its playpen one after another and observing intently what becomes of them, or the behavior of a fifteen-month-old child absorbed in putting pebbles and shells into a pail and taking them out again. Such activity, however banal, cannot be plausibly assimilated to mere stimulus/response behavior on par with salivation.

The incongruity of such an explanatory model is particularly striking in certain cases of the sort termed 'anecdotal'. One such is Jean Piaget's report of a sixteen-month-old girl resolving the problem of getting a chain out of an insufficiently opened match box. After a moment of inactivity in the course of which the child looks at the slot, slowly opens and closes her mouth several times, at first a little then more and more widely, she suddenly puts her finger in the slot and pulls open the box.[29] The only plausible construal of such behavior is that it involves analogical thinking in which the opening of the mouth is associated with the slot in the box and an inference from past experience of what a finger can do with a mouth. Surely such behavior qualifies as intelligent. Surely too, when faced with intelligent behavior of the sort, one should be prepared to accept its theoretical implications. If infants and animals are accorded the capacity to recognize on the basis of their behavior, it hardly seems methodologically consistent to deny them some measure of thought, inventiveness, and rationality when they behave in an appropriately thoughtful, inventive, and rational manner.

Equally embarassing is the failure of rational nominalism to accommodate the findings of studies in child psychology. Consider the case of one such aspect of logical space particularly relevant to solipsism, that of the acquisition by the infant of the notion of the continued existence of unperceived objects. Piaget's observations distinguish a number of stages in such acquisition.[30] At the age of six months, an infant may look for a dropped object if his or her cheek or hand is in contact with it. By eight months, the infant will have progressed to the point of a genuine groping for objects that have fallen outside the field of vision (behavior that suggests belief in the continued existence of at least some tactual objects). At the same age, however, the infant does not accord an analogous permanence to visual objects: he or she may cry with impatience on seeing some object, perhaps a bottle, then stop abruptly each time the object is completely hidden, as if the object ceased to exist when unperceived. Between eight and ten months the infant may look for an object seen to have disappeared nearby, yet curiously enough, at a location where it previously found the disappeared object. Only at about twelve months of age does the infant look for the object invariably and exclusively at the location at which it disappears. These observations suggest a long apprenticeship in learning of the permanence of objects that cease to be observed—and significantly enough, an apprenticeship that takes place prior to the acquisition of language. If one wishes to claim that only with the acquisition of language does the child acquire the general structures of logical space including the particular concept of continued unobserved existence, then one must face the seemingly insuperable difficulty of explaining what is going on in the behavioral changes of the infant prior to that time.

In addition to its flying in the face of the empirical evidence, rational nominalism can give no plausible account of the acquisition of language itself. The very rational intelligence required for the comprehension and learning of something as complex as language, is available, according to the doctrine, only after the language has been learnt. Rorty in particular seems quite unaware of the catch-22 nature of the difficulty, for he presents a version of the acquisition of rationality made still more implausible by its suddenness. Here is what he says: "We may balk at the claim that knowledge, awareness, concepts, language, inference, justification and the logical space of reasons all descend on the shoulders of a bright child somewhere around the age of four, without having existed in even the most primitive form hitherto."[31] The account would have it that creatures devoid of language are capable only of knee-jerk response to stimuli and that such "protoplasmic counterparts of record-changers"[32] become transformed into rational cognizant beings merely through exposure to certain forms of auditory stimuli; furthermore, this marvelous transformation is not a gradual matter but is the brusque precipitate of the requisite degree of verbal saturation. Such an account is its own *reductio ad absurdum*.

Rational nominalism yields a phylogenetic account of the acquisition of language no less implausible than the ontogenetic one. If logical space can only be acquired through learning a language, then any account of the historical origin of language by *Homo sapiens* becomes impossible—except, of course, through something equivalent to divine intervention. At some moment in the history of mankind, God would have made the gift of speech to a hitherto nonrational and mute humanity—presumably, by summoning some earlier-day Moses to Mount Sinai to undergo a crash training course in language and language games. At the very least, it would seem, one must concede both to mankind and to individual humans prior to the acquisition of language a degree of rational intelligence sufficient for the invention of language and its subsequent transmission to others.

CONCEPTUAL SCHEMES AND CULTURAL RELATIVITY

The doctrine of psychological nominalism (or rational nominalism) receives strong circumstantial support from the empirical evidence of the diversity of cultures and conceptual schemes uncovered in anthropology and ethnolinguistics. The evidence might well be thought strong enough to support a version of the doctrine that embarrasses solipsism by precluding the entertaining of solipsistic theses outside public language. Indeed, cultural relativity is so widely pervasive a phenomenon that it is sometimes esteemed to be the central support for a coherentist view of what constitutes justification and rationality, as opposed to a foundationalist one. This latter estimation is mistaken, for, as noted above, the contradictory of foundationalism is objectualism, not coherentism; coherentism does not entail objectualism, and we have found no rational grounds whatever to endorse the truth of the latter. Lest it be thought nevertheless that cultural relativity supports psychological nominalism to the point of undermining solipsism, let us take a brief but closer look into the matter.

In what does the evidence consist? Linguistic studies lead Sapir, for instance, to claim that the language of a particular group of human beings plays a crucial role in the formation of the world view of the group, that it leads its speakers to impose meanings rather than discover them in experience, to define possible experience through unconscious projection of its formal limitations.[33] From his study of American Indian languages Whorf draws a more radical conventionalist conclusion as in the following passage: "We cut nature up, organize it into concepts, and ascribe significances as we do, largely because we are parties to an agreement to organize it in this way—an agreement that holds throughout our speech community and is codified in the patterns of our language."[34] The ways of organizing may differ strikingly, as in the case noted by Whorf of the replacement of verb tenses in Hopi by a relation of temporal precedence, from which there results a very different metaphysics of time.

Mention must also be made of the indisputable fact of the historical relativity of conceptual schemes. Kuhn's study of changes in scientific viewpoints leads him to speak of "the incommensurability of competing paradigms" the proponents of which "practice their trades in different worlds."[35] The hermeneutical studies initiated by Heidegger and Gadamer bring out the historical relativity of ontologies and world views, a relativity seen as enmeshed in language. Gadamer is particularly strong on this latter point; he speaks of "the fundamental linguistic quality of man's being-in-the-world" and does not hesitate to declare that "language is not just one of man's possessions in the world, but on it depends the fact that man has a world at all."[36] The notion of the relativity of world views receives no less impressive evidence in its favor from the findings of Foucault's extensive investigations into historically changing viewpoints and attitudes.

Now let us ask what import these various findings have on the issue of solipsism. It was readily found above that the variety of possible classifications based on rudimentary perceptual similarities is irrelevant to the possibility of a private language or of thinking outside language. Conceptual schemes contain a wealth of other structures that vary considerably from one historically situated scheme to another. The basis of these other structures in the perceptually given (if any) is seemingly much more complex and difficult to decipher than that of the rudimentary classifications. Yet when an attempt is made to trace out concretely the possible effects of the variety, the relativity of these other structures is soon found to be no less irrelevant.

Consider Whorf's example of the absence of tenses from Hopi, and of their functional replacement by a relation of temporal precedence. What possible bearing does this structural difference have on the skeptical issue of whether things continue to exist unperceived or on the skeptical issue of whether the world is not some vast illusion? Apparently none whatever, since both schemes concern the organization of what is perceived and its organization independently of the issue of whether or not it is illusory. Or again, consider a language where instead of saying "Here comes George, and he looks angry," one states something more aptly translated as "It is about to be Georging angrily." In the second language George is seen more as a manifestation of some greater whole, an event on a par with the weather, rather than the autonomous source of activity suggested by the structure of the first language. However, for present concerns it is of no importance which conceptual scheme is being used. The difference in viewpoint on George's place in the grand scheme of things has no bearing whatever on the skeptical issue of the continued unperceived existence of George, any more than it has on the possible illusory nature of the world.

Similar observations are in order for the differences in paradigms discussed by Kuhn, or the differences in ontologies, prejudices, and attitudes uncovered by Heidegger, Gadamer, and Foucault. In point of fact, each no less than the others would undoubtedly be astounded at the idea that their findings regarding variations in world views could have anything to do with the skeptical question of whether tables become kangaroos when no one is looking. These various world views are all irrelevant to skeptical issues. The skeptical questions may consequently be posed with equal acuity within each of them. In these circumstances, it is difficult to see how the solipsist's adoption of one rather than another could matter. Thus, even if the solipsist should be unable ever to be completely rid of the cultural bias peculiar to a particular historical period, that fact cannot preclude the formulation of solipsism in a private language or mode of nonlinguistic thinking and hence a formulation invulnerable to a charge of linguistic parasitism.

Oversimplifying matters somewhat, one might say that cultural relativity is ontological and axiological relativity and that it is epistemic relativity only to the extent that a given conceptual system discourages or makes difficult the raising of certain questions within the course of empirical investigations. The roots of the ontological and axiological differences are difficult to locate. It is a highly intriguing question whether one conceptual scheme is more rational than another or more justified in that it is a better reflection of the way things are. Answering the question, or even determining whether the question makes sense, is a matter that can be settled only be tracing out concretely what possible warrant may be provided by the experiential evidence for the various competing views. Such might be a further task for rational foundationalism or rationalized epistemology beyond its self-assigned one of answering Cartesian solipsism. It is quite unclear how such a task could ever be carried to completion if, following Donald Davidson's lead, one were to proclaim the absurdity of the scheme and content dualism, that is, of the notion that there is, on one hand, an organizing system or conceptual scheme, and on the other, something given by the senses and waiting to be organized.[37] One can hardly evaluate which scheme is best warranted by the evidence if one denies the existence of the evidence. In addition, if all languages embody a conceptual scheme, and there is no thinking outside language, one would appear to be badly positioned to evaluate warrant. For such evaluation to be possible, either the conceptual embodiment must be rejectable or it must be possible to take up a point of view outside language in some other form of thinking devoid of ontological assumptions. Fortunately or unfortunately, none of these issues are our present concern, however.

NONLINGUISTIC THINKING

The third presupposition of linguistic parasitism arguments is the notion that any serious thinking requires language and that, consequently, skepticism in its various forms can be thought only through language. At issue here is not the superiority of linguistic thinking for the purposes of doing philosophy. There undoubtedly are numerous operations open to linguistic thinking and which cannot be duplicated nonlinguistically, although on this point as elsewhere, a convincing case would best be made by trotting out the alleged operations and introducing them to all concerned. Our present interest is in the much more modest issue of whether nonlinguistic thinking is sufficiently sophisticated to entertain basic philosophical problems of the sort posed by Cartesian Solipsism. The topic of nonlinguistic thinking is obviously far too vast to receive adequate treatment here. We shall confine ourselves, therefore, to a few cursory runs over the terrain with a view to gleaning a few relevant insights into the matter.

Let us begin with the fact that there is such a thing as nonlinguistic thinking. The question of existence is an empirical one, and as such, its accuracy should be determined by appeal to empirical data. Now, the empirical data in the matter of everyday thinking abounds in instances of thinking which is to all appearances nonlinguistic. Consider the following banal cases, typical of a wealth of cases easily gleaned from everyday experience, of which none apparently involve language. I hear a faint noise, listen a moment, then turn toward the window expecting to see a small bird on a branch; I start across a street, notice an approaching car and judge it will not give me time to cross unjostled; I walk across the parking lot toward what looks like my car, then as I get closer, begin to have doubts that are then confirmed on my seeing an undented back left fender.

It is undeniable that some form of thinking is involved in each of these cases. Each involves the evaluation of a situation, a reliance on relevant data and background knowledge, and a judgment or expectation. In each case, if a mistake was made, it would be appropriate to remark that it was incorrectly thought (reasoned, concluded) that such and such was the case. Furthermore, not only is language apparently not involved in these examples, but it need not be involved in any of the three cases—not even in the guise of a redundant, silent chronicle. Noticings, identifications, and conclusions may all be nonverbal. Any accompanying chatter or internalized verbalization is inessential in the sense that one may quite easily imagine it to be absent in each case with no serious detriment to the thinking process and the conclusions reached.

The tempting linguacentric rejoinder is to claim that despite the apparently nonlinguistic nature of the thinking in such instances, nevertheless they presuppose a conceptual scheme and view of the world that is acquired through language alone; they are structured by it and bear its indelible stamp. This answer does not bear up too well under scrutiny. Consider each of the three above examples in turn. In the first example, what indispensable role does language play in the acquisition of the ability to evaluate the direction of a noise, of the ability to recognize a certain type of noise as one produced by small birds, or of a disposition to expect trees to contain birds rather than horses. Yet the acquisition and exercise of such abilities qualifies as thinking. In the second example, what need is there for language in the acquisition of the ability to evaluate the relative immanence of approaching cars or the future trajectories of moving bodies and to adopt certain appropriate courses of action? Yet such activity involves some degree of calculation and conclusion drawing, hence thinking. As Sheets-Johnstone points out regarding similar cases of nonhuman animal behavior, it would be absurd to claim that no thinking is involved in the tandem strategic pursuit of a zebra by two female lions.[38]

Of the third example it may be asked how verbal thinking is essential to the discovery of a parking lot misidentification. Recognition itself is nonverbal. In the case of my car, its peculiar shape, the shape in virtue of which I would confuse it with no other make of car, is something for which there are no terms in the language. Nor can language do other than grossly approximate the car's specific shade of white, somewhere between cream and chalk, its dull shine, dirt stains, and intermittent rusty spots, all of which play a key role in the recognition of the car as my car. The richness of detail, texture, and organizational complexity—the pith of the given—is far more amenable to recognition than to verbal description. Indeed, it might be argued that such features are not only not describable adequately in language, but for the most part, they are not even noticed in the strict sense. Their absence may give rise to a suspicion that a particular object is not the one expected, without one's being able to pinpoint let alone verbalize the grounds for the suspicion. A familiar dent in a fender, for instance, is far more easily recognized than described, and the awareness of its absence may not only be nonverbal but nonthematic and subliminal. In these circumstances it is difficult to see how a remotely plausible case might be made for the claim that language is essential to a realization that one has made a mistake in identification.

In this context it is useful to recall that meaning is not a phenomenon exclusive to words and language. Any item of a certain type may mean, suggest, or bring to mind another type. Smoke means fire, which is to say that perceived smoke gives rise to an expectation of fire somewhere in the immediate neighborhood of the smoke. As a result, there may be rudimentary thinking, or association and expectation, anchored in the actual perceptual situation itself independently of language. The recognized item may be quite specific and give rise to an expectation of some further quite specific item. Knowing one's way to a particular location is often a matter of a sequence of recognitions of such items, each with its expectation of a next stage on the way located in a certain direction with respect to the preceding one. For instance, on finding the narrow, winding street one is following open onto a crooked square, one is suddenly aware that the little street over on the left beside the shoe display is what must now be taken. Essentially the same process is involved in finding one's way from the front porch to the kitchen refrigerator. Nothing in the performance of the feat requires the services of language. Indeed, one might well be hard put to give adequate directions to a person unfamiliar with the route and, in attempting to do so, find it necessary to run through the various stages of the journey visually in one's memory so as to be able to give a more adequate linguistic translation.

In countless cases where thinking is the solving of some practical problem, the role of language is once again minimal. Many times known techniques are simply considered, tried out, the results observed, and further manoeuvres effectuated. The practical skills involved are themselves best acquired by watching and imitating, and adeptness at them is quite independent of any ability to give a comprehensible account of the steps of the operation. The weighing of alternatives is often a matter of simply 'seeing' which is more promising. Putting some mechanical device together, like putting a jigsaw puzzle back together, is essentially a matter of spotting the correct spatial fit. The spotting and evaluating of candidates for the occupancy of a peculiarly shaped gap is in turn very like recognition in its attunement to fine detail. It does not require the intervention of language. Indeed, language in its present form is inadequate to the variety and complexity of shapes and sizes involved in tasks of the sort. The point is not that there could not in principle be a language with a distinct term for each perceptively distinguishable shape since of course, there could; it is that distinctions can be and are made independently of language.

In an off-site consideration of a problem, there is a greater opportunity for language to play a significant role since the problem must be represented (re-presented) in symbolic form. The role of language in this case is one it shares with visual imagination, schematic drawings, models, and the like. The relative value of each mode of representation varies with the circumstances, with scale models the clear winner were their construction not so unfeasible. Here as elsewhere in the resolution of practical tasks, the thinking involved is thinking that does not require the services of language. When language is actually used in such tasks, it would appear to have two main functions; one is communication in view of coordination of collective efforts, the other retention, the keeping in mind of some present task to be pursued, or the recording of the essential steps from past successful operations.

Diehard advocates of the linguacentricity of thinking could well be unimpressed with the marvels of practical thought. However, there is a nonlinguistic activity prestigious enough not to invite immediate disparaging remarks on the nature of the thinking involved, and that is the game of chess. Here language plays an analogously subsidiary role. Language may provide convenient shortcuts in teaching and learning techniques and may make available an accumulated wealth of information from the prior experiences of others. In actual play, however, language plays no significant role. Thinking consists primarily of envisaging possible moves and possible consequences and of evaluating comparatively the resulting positions. It is difficult to imagine anything more than a redundant role for language in the first of these operations. The envisaging of a possible move is ocular (or with beginners, manual), rather than verbal. The envisaged move is traced out kinesthetically through eye movements which shift the focal center of the visual field in accordance with the exigencies of a certain shape of piece. With an envisaged pawn move, for instance, the center of vision might advance one square forward bringing with it a phantom pawn and two choppy diagonal threats to opposing pieces, or it might advance one square forward diagonally while an opposing piece is conjured away, or transformed in imagination into the moved pawn, while subsequent moves are considered. When the possible moves envisaged are those of a bishop, the square on which the piece rests is taken as a point of departure for either of two vectorial diagonals of squares radiating out in quasi relief and that may terminate suddenly at any square on the trajectory, which then becomes in its turn the focal point of radiating vectorial diagonals. Eye movements are so necessary to the planning of moves in chess that an observant player might manage to read an opponent's thoughts by observing such movements. By contrast, lip-reading would be a singularly sterile operation.

Language might seem to play a greater role in the comparative evaluation of resulting positions. Whereas tactics are learned rather by example, chess strategy is a subject of discussion. As a result, verbal injunctions and maxims regarding strategic considerations are susceptible of popping up in the course of the game. Even here, however, language plays the role of facilitating access to the lessons learned by others rather than of providing an exclusive route to information. There seems little doubt that the desirability of particular strategic goals is discoverable nonverbally in the course of play. Good position, a prime example of a strategic goal, is neither more nor less than a position that affords relative freedom of movement to mount promising attacks easily supported by reserve resources and in comparative security from dangerous counter thrusts. Such a position is a perceptually experienceable state of affairs (provided a player is sufficiently adept at the game to give a fair estimate of possible moves). A succession of sound drubbings has considerable pedagogical potential to encourage the discovery of connections between the positioning of pieces and the movement possibilities afforded. Clearly, the seeing of these connections is no more conditional on language than is the seeing of the movement possibilities themselves. In its relationship to language, chess thinking differs little from practical thinking: for both, language is a helpful but less than indispensable auxiliary. The point is obviously of crucial importance for any adequate account of thinking. It cannot be plausibly denied that chess-playing involves thinking. Indeed, a sculpted chess board under the gaze of Rodin's *Thinker* would not be incongruous—nor could it be plausibly denied that the thinking involved was essentially nonlinguistic.

SOLIPSISM IN NONLINGUISTIC THOUGHT

Having achieved a moderate degree of success in our little exercise in public relations, let us now turn to an issue more concretely germane to the entertaining of solipsism nonlinguistically. The issue is that of whether there are nonlinguistic analogues of the basic logical operations of linguistic thinking. Let us begin with the operation of assertion.

In an example considered earlier, a chirp coming from the direction of a window gives rise to the expectation of seeing a small bird on a branch. The expectation might be concretized by the image of a small bird. The image is free-floating in that its actual orientation with respect to the perceptual context is irrelevant; there is no need for one's gaze to situate the image on the branch at the site of the expected bird like an imagined pawn on its forward square. On the other hand, the expected bird does have an intended location on the unobserved branch, itself located relative to things actually observed (the desk under one's elbows, the floor under one's feet). The image is meant to represent the located bird, but its own location is as irrelevant to the bird's location as is the location of the sound one might produce by uttering the words 'a bird!'. The image of the bird is but one part of the syntax of the assertion being made. The perceptual context is also an essential constituent in the assertion, since it provides the place of the sound and hence the location asserted to be occupied by the bird. Assertions in imagic thinking may obviously be somewhat less context-dependent. Whatever the details, they remain closely tied to perception, either in that the context is essential to the assertion being made or in that the images themselves are likenesses of things perceived. An interesting consequence of the close ties with perceptual experience is that the various syntactical structures and attendant ontologies possible in language are not to be found in imagic thinking. The latter is free of this one possible source of cultural bias.

Inasmuch as the bird image in the above example materializes a conviction or an expectation, it is a constituent in something analogous to a self-addressed statement in which figure the image, the intended location (in part perceived with the chirp), and the conviction with which the thought is entertained. It would not be difficult to vary the situation somewhat, to make the sound heard ambiguous so that the image of the bird competes with that of a cricket, and serves to enunciate a possibility rather than a certainty. The image might alternatively be accompanied by a feeling of puzzlement or unrequited curiosity. The image itself in abstraction from its context is neither a conviction nor an hypothesis nor a question. It becomes one through its affective and kinesthetic context. The same might be said of the simple expression, 'a bird', which also becomes a conviction, possibility, challenge or question through its context of utterance.

Clearly, a wide variety of convictions, expectations, and entertained possibilities may be articulated by images in imagic thinking. In such thinking logical constants have no imagic analogue. Disjunction takes the form of a choice to be made among alternative imaged possibilities. It remains essentially what it is in nonsymbolic thinking, i.e., an experienced bodily hesitation between successfully entertained alternatives. Conjunction is dual expectation. An analogue of negation may be seen in the earlier-noted experience of a disappointed expectation and, by extension, in that of an anticipation for which hope is sinking. In imagic thinking it may take the form of the expectation of a disappointment of an imagined situation, or alternatively the form of an image of a state of affairs in which the anticipated situation does not obtain. It would not be too far from the truth to say that in imagic thought the logical operations of assertion, conjunction, disjunction, and negation are the affective context; they consist essentially of some specific type of bodily dynamics and feeling vis-à-vis a state of affairs envisaged.

Some form of generalizing already exists at the level of nonsymbolic thinking. A particular event gives rise to an expectation of a further event of some type, as when a chirp arouses the expectation of seeing a small bird. Generalization from past observed concomitances is clearly involved. In imagic thinking the expected event is illustrated with an image. Since the image, although vague, is individualized, there arises Berkeley's problem of how it can be an image for some general type of occurrence.[39] Yet the difficulty is hardly a serious one.

If an individual chirp may be heard as an instance of a certain kind, then surely an individual image of a bird may be seen as an instance of a certain kind. It is a representative image, one admitting of potential replacement by alternative images of individuals of the same type, an image of the sort discussed by H. H. Price.[40]

Interestingly enough, imagic thinking qualifies as rational on the criterion for rationality proposed by Jonathan Bennett, to wit, that rational behavior is behavior in which it is possible to manifest beliefs about the past independently of beliefs of a general kind and vice versa; hence, it is behavior that manifests reasons as distinct from knowledge of particular facts.[41] In imagic thinking, knowledge of a past fact is manifested in a memory image usually containing salient peculiarities of the past situation and having a latent capacity for further precision. In contrast, knowledge of a general fact gives rise to an image in which few features are significant and of which the replacement by an image of the same general type would be a matter of indifference. The context of intentions and concerns further precludes a confusion of a belief about the past with a belief of a general kind. In reliving some past event imagically, there is no danger of one's becoming confused and wondering whether one is perhaps generalizing instead of remembering. Imagic thinking thus qualifies as rational on Bennett's criterion.

Finally, with regard to the ability of imagic thinking to encompass logical reasoning, a curious and striking phenomenon is of considerable interest. The grasping of a particular logical truth may often be found to involve an appeal to some form of spatial relation and hence to an operation that conceivably could take place outside language. Consider the matter of determining whether a particular syllogistic argument is valid. One very unsatisfying procedure that might be followed is to consult a table of valid syllogisms and valid conversions and by comparison to determine whether the argument being considered has a form reducible to one of the valid forms. The reason the procedure is unsatisfying is that it puts one in the position of an intellectual minor deferring to higher authority. Let us suppose one wishes to convince oneself of the validity of the syllogism. To concretize matters, let us suppose that the argument to be tested is the following:

Premiss 1:   All bams are cams.

Premiss 2:   No cams are dams.

Conclusion: Therefore, no dams are bams.

After a moment's reflection it becomes clear that the conclusion does indeed follow from the premises, and hence that the syllogism is valid. The interesting question is how one manages to reach this conclusion. One might make some sort of sketch in which three groups are represented, perhaps through three overlapping circles, as in a Venn diagram, and the information given by each of the two premises is represented by some feature of the diagram—perhaps by the shading of certain possibilities. The conclusion is a straightforward reading of the spatial features of the diagram according to the conventions followed. A first group (the bams) is found exclusively within a second (the cams) which is itself cut off from a third (the dams), with the result that the third must be cut off from the first. One might also simply try to 'grasp the meaning' of each premise and then realize that given the situation, the resulting conclusion has to hold. Grasping in this case amounts to the forming of scanty, schematic images of some form or other—one of inclusion, one of separation—and finding that a certain situation must hold. Grasping, whether through diagrams or schematic images, may clearly take place in the absence of language. Once again, the doctrine of the linguacentricity of thinking flies clearly in the face of empirical fact.

The above cursory and necessarily incomplete survey of nonlinguistic thought should suffice to challenge the notion that all philosophical thinking is necessarily tied to language. It should suggest also that the epistemologically rudimentary theses of solipsism may be formulated or entertained nonlinguistically. To the extent that solipsism is susceptible of being so entertained, to that extent too it is immune to refutation by linguistic parasitism arguments.

Perhaps the thesis most easily entertained nonlinguistically is that of Oneirata Solipsism. The imagic envisioning of the hypothesis amounts essentially to imagining oneself waking up and finding a world quite different from the world in which one normally finds oneself. The performance of such a feat of imaginative prowess is quite feasible, given that one has previously lived through the common experience of dreaming and waking up. A few meager images of an anticipated awakening might be conjured up, the imagic lacunae being filled in intention only, as is usual for imagined future eventualities generally.

In principle, imagic thought would allow the hypothesis to be entertained even if dreams had never been experienced, just as it allows the entertaining of a seemingly limitless variety of fantastic hypotheses (featuring demons or scientists)—but the point is of minor importance. The assumption of a prior experience of dreaming and waking clearly need involve no assumption beyond that of an experienced sequence of events. Entertaining the dream hypothesis is merely imagining the continuation of present experience to be a sequence in certain respects similar to the past sequence of dreaming then waking. Such an operation involves neither awkward factual presuppositions nor the semantic presupposition of a dream/reality dichotomy involving the ability to identify either reality or dreams, and hence no presuppositions in some regard in contradiction with the skeptical thesis. It is in fact quite possible to imagine waking states converting into dreams, each with its subsequent waking state in an indefinitely long procession, like the temporally sequenced Chinese boxes encountered earlier. Oneirata Solipsism is a thesis that could be entertained by a thinker devoid of language. In these circumstances, the attempt to refute the theory on a charge of linguistic parasitism does not promise to be a particularly fruitful pursuit.

The situation with regard to other forms of Cartesian solipsism is only slightly more complicated. In the case of Phantasmata Solipsism, for example, an experience of an optical illusion or mirage could serve as a model for the imagined occurrence of analogous sequences of events involving banal but hitherto dependable everyday objects—although it should be added that in principle the actual experience of illusions is not (any more than that of dreams) an indispensable prerequisite for the imagic formulation of such occurrences. What makes Phantasmata Solipsism seemingly more difficult to entertain than Oneirata Solipsism is the fact that illusions generally are localized (at least everyday illusions are merely oddly behaving portions of an otherwise sensible world), and consequently the hypothesis of a general illusion necessitates an operation of generalization. But the difficulty is more apparent than real. If the imagically formulated dream hypothesis may encompass the whole of the world, so might the imagic hypothesis of a mirage on a worldwide scale. Alternatively, each of a number of present items might in turn be imagined to be an illusion or a mirage, in much the same way that a particular item may be imagined to be a bird in virtue of its song. Here, the generalization equivalent to the solipsist's claim, "everything is an illusion," is implicit in each act of imagination and makes an oblique appearance in each of the iterated operations.

Ephemerata Solipsism, which denies the existence of any unobserved sensuous items, might be entertained in either one of two analogous ways. Particular items encountered might be imagined to have no further sides, no interior—nothing beyond what is visibly or tactually there. Alternatively, the whole of what is present might be encompassed as some composite sensuous entity beyond which there is nothing. For Sense Data Solipsism, a further refinement must be appended: any expectations based on regularly observed concomitance are to be suspended. Such an operation would not seem unfeasible in principle. In brief, while the nonverbal versions of the various Cartesian solipsistic theses thus lack the tidiness and conciseness of their corresponding linguistic formulations, they are nevertheless appropriately characterized as entertainable hypotheses. As a result, it would be futile to attempt to refute the nonlinguistic versions of these skeptical theses by an appeal to linguistic considerations.

The various Cartesian solipsistic theses are thus susceptible of nonverbal formulation. This fact alone suffices to show that any attempt to convict the theses on a charge of linguistic parasitism must fail. It thus drives the last nails into the coffin of any remaining hope of showing the solipsistic theses to be linguistically parasitic. It simultaneously corroborates the earlier conclusions reached regarding epistemic and conceptual parasitism. Cartesian solipsistic theses (Sensa Solipsism excepted) are quite clearly not parasitic. With the disappearance of the last clear hope of justifyinging the existential claims made by objectualism, the latter account takes on the status of a quite gratuitous hypothesis. If Cartesian solipsistic theses are to be shown to be false or unlikely to be true, the enterprise must be undertaken on the skeptic's own terrain, that of actual experience.

CHAPTER TEN

THE GIVEN

THE NEED FOR INTROSPECTION

First of all, the very warmest of welcomes is extended to all those who have stayed with the argument up to this point. The journey has been long, arduous, and tortuous. It has also been necessary, as is perhaps more apparent at this point than at the outset. In no other way is it possible to attain the first of the two earlier-stated goals, that of establishing convincingly the futility of all attempts to resolve the remaining classical Cartesian skeptical problems in any way other than through a foundationalist approach.

Two broadly construed skeptical problems still remain to be resolved, the Problem of Unobserved Existence and the Problem of Reality. As we saw earlier, in neither case is the problem to justify a judgment of absolute certainty (a chimerical pursuit akin to the summing of an infinite series), nor is it to justify a more modest claim of everyday evidentially unentailed knowledge (an equally chimerical pursuit of a conceptually confused goal). Both problems have to do with warrant, or with the rational grounds that allow the bridging of the evidential gap between the experiential data and the everyday, commonsense tenets. The driving force behind Cartesian solipsism is the disturbing circumstance that apparently the solipsistic theses are not just consistent with the evidence but also unfalsified and unchallenged by it and, hence, that there is apparently no rational warrant whatever to leap the evidential gap in the particular direction of commonsense beliefs. In the absence of warrant, there is no reason to think that the structure of the world is more accurately portrayed by commonsense tenets than by the corresponding solipsistic ones. Both are unchallenged and unsupported by the evidence—whether the data of what is actually perceived, as in the case of solipsism that denies the existence of anything unobserved, or with some possibly less restricted set of data, as in the case of solipsism that denies the reality of the world. In the absence of further rational grounds beyond mere consistency with the evidence, nothing further may be rationally claimed.

Objectualism, or coherentism, is the doctrine that any proper epistemology must begin with the fact or assumption that everyday objects exist. The coherentist approach has shown itself to be impressive in its impotence either to provide warrant for its own existence claim or what comes to the same thing, to advance a solution to skeptical problems concerning everyday existence. The appeal to perceptual procedures and corresponding perceptual experience of Western adults fails to provide any warrant for the acceptance of commonsense beliefs or, conversely, for the rejection of skeptical ones. The criterion of coherence turns out to be inapplicable. The appeal to meaning is futile: skeptical scenarios featuring widespread sham are meaningful because verifiable in principle by some subject, while those denying unobserved existence are meaningful given their concern with unobserved places to be found in spatial projections of the actually perceived world. With the exception of Sensa Solipsism, the various forms of Cartesian solipsism cannot be shown to be parasitic, i.e., to make essential use of empirical knowledge, of concepts, or of language, and yet to deny tenets the truth of which is presupposed by that use. The claim that everyday factual truths are part of the scaffolding of any possible inquiry is inaccurate, just as is the claim that the presuppositions of our everyday conceptual scheme constitute necessary assumptions for any worldview. It is equally far from true that skeptical theses are in contradiction with the presuppositions of English and hence cannot be coherently entertained. There is no insurmountable obstacle to formulating the central theses of Cartesian solipsism in a revised version of English, in a private language, or outside language altogether in imagic thought.

With the elimination of a coherentist solution, there remains but one course offering any promise of success against Cartesian solipsism, a foundationalist investigation of rationally warranted claims in terms of the evidence of what is actually perceived. The manifest failure of the pretensions of the linguistic turn leave no choice but to return to the abandoned project of Husserl, of Russell, and of Carnap. Moore's alleged evidence for commonsense tenets—the evidence that Moore claims to have once had but now not to remember—must be ferreted out and presented in such a way as to provide rational grounds or warrant for bridging the evidential gap in the direction of commonsense belief.

The enterprise of uncovering a rational justification of common sense was termed 'rational foundationalism' in chapter 4. As noted earlier, to avoid difficulties with recalcitrant layers of misleading connotations, it is more wisely termed *rationalized epistemology*. There is no reason in principle to exclude the criterion of coherence from a foundationalist toolkit, so the enterprise is incorrectly viewed as a foundationalism opposed to coherentism. There is no reason in principle to deny cultural diversity and necessary bias, or ontological and axiological relativity, so the enterprise is incorrectly viewed as a sociological foundationalism that construes the march of history as the ineluctable evolution of rationality. Nor is there any reason to deny the possible implications of the Kuhnian concept of paradigmatic revolutions. The foundationalism with which we are concerned is much more modest in scope. One of its clear aims is to uncover the warrant there may be for beliefs of a very rudimentary nature, such as the belief in the permanence of material objects. As noted in the preceding chapter, a belief of the sort would seem acquired by infants through their own efforts and prior to the acquisition of language; it is furthermore pancultural, at least to judge by the failure of anthropologists to unearth a culture where such permanence is denied. In these circumstances, the belief might be expected to be impervious to fluctuations in cultural inculcation as well as paradigmatic dynamics.

A rationalized epistemology has, then, as one of its main aims to uncover rational grounds for the epistemological construction of the everyday world of common sense from the meager scraps of the world admitted by the radical skeptic. In keeping with the project, an appropriate point at which to begin our investigation into warrant is with an inventory of the materials actually to be found in the Humean flux, or the world of Sense Data Solipsism. The point of departure is also an appropriate enough one for a treatment of the Problem of Reality. The latter problem may well arise at any epistemic level including the minimal one of the Sense Data Solipsist. As we shall see, it is closely tied to the egocentric epistemological predicament in which any knower is placed. A sketch of some of the materials constitutive of the Humean flux of experiences was begun in chapter 8 where it was asked whether the elements to be found in the flux were adequate to provide an answer to Strawson's charges of conceptual parasitism. That account should now be deepened with a number of supplementary observations, by no means definitive or exhaustive of the field.

Our interest is in the data of actual perception and the items the presence of which in experience cannot be called into question by a rational, radical skeptic. In the investigations that follow, the findings will simply be those yielded by introspection and will be presumed verifiable in their essentials by anyone who takes the trouble to introspect. Such a manner of proceeding might well be found methodologically objectionable on a number of counts. A few words should thus be said in its defense.

The introspection to be practiced here is perhaps best described as more attentive perception. Our interest is in uncovering what is actually perceived, hence what is actually present in perceptual experience. Consequently, introspection in the present instance amounts for the most part to calling into question one's preconceived notions as to what should be present, as well as one's ready-made answers prompted by years of social training. To the extent that it does this, it coincides with what Husserl termed "parenthesizing,"[1] the suspension of everyday belief operative in phenomenological analysis. To some extent, it relies on memory and the reliving of past experience, and to that extent it is properly considered to be retrospection rather than introspection. Be this as it may, it is scarcely, as William Lyons puts it, a "sort of second-level process of monitoring, inspecting, registering, or immediate retrieval of data in regard to first-level perceptual or cognitive-appetitive processes."[2] It is primarily simply more careful perception, of the sort practiced in principle by the radical skeptic or solipsist.

The crucial difference between introspection and other forms of investigation is that introspection is an investigation of experience and hence often of private objects or private phenomena. The structures, relations, and characteristics of particular private phenomena have the peculiarity that they are observable by one person only. Another observer can only observe his or her own particular, private phenomena (boxed beetle characteristics and behaviors). Nevertheless, the privacy of the phenomena observed does not preclude the possibility that the observations have universal interest and application. Two introspectors may easily compare notes, very much as easily as any two observers may of some public phenomenon. Insofar as the private phenomena (beetle characteristics) are found to be alike from one private scene to the next, they allow the introspectors to formulate generalized descriptions that apply to most and perhaps all private phenomena of the same kind. One introspector may correct another, debate findings, point out unobserved or misleading features, just as any two public world observers may do of animal behavior, a strange noise, a tennis match, or a piece of music. The privacy of the observed phenomena introduces complications but not insurmountable obstacles to arriving at generalizations.

Training and practice are clearly helpful in gaining accurate introspective reports. One is no more a good introspector at birth than one is a good swimmer, a good detective, a good molecular biologist, or a good pianist. Present-day Western society hardly encourages expertise in introspective activity. School children are taught to measure and manipulate, almost never to introspect affective reactions, thinking processes or perceptual activities. The activity is decidedly un-American and scarcely less un-British or un-European. Not only is it not practiced, but worse still, everyday concerns with objects out in the world, concerns made habitual through years of cultivation, have the result, as von Helmholtz points out, of gravely vitiating introspective reports when they are made.[3] None of this provides good reason to disparage introspection itself. Nor is it significant that a broad opinion poll coupled with a calculation of average introspective findings would probably fail to yield an accurate account of some particular sort of experience. The fact that the same would also be true of a broad opinion poll on the height of particular trees would not entail that the practice of estimating tree heights should be abandoned.

The sorry estimation in which introspection is held, especially in current scientific circles in America, is more than somewhat puzzling. For certain private phenomena, introspection is the only mode of access available; no observation of behavior allows an observer to relate the dream of another person, for example, or the person's line of thought or flux of feeling. For other private phenomena, behavior is more revealing of its nature, but nevertheless an interpretation of the behavior is only possible through one's having had a similar type of experience oneself. The need for introspective reports in science is acknowledged through the fact that they are often admitted, even if surreptitiously under the alias of 'verbal reports'. In any event, there is little cause to carry the prejudice over into philosophy and to adopt the methodological approach of treating other human beings, including oneself, like exotic interplanetary life forms to be described only in terms of behavior. It is epistemologically as well as humanly absurd to cut oneself off in this way from the only firsthand source of information one has of what it is like to be a human being. Certainly, introspection may well not be the last word on the nature of the various private 'mental' activities central to philosophical concerns, but it decidedly is the first. In some cases, it is the only word. For our purposes in particular, it is indispensable. The Sense Data Solipsist or radical skeptic is to be met on the home ground of what is actually perceived, and only introspection can provide a survey of the terrain.

STRUCTURES OF THE VISUAL FIELD

With these few sweeps of the broom across the methodological path, let us turn now to a brief examination of some of the general structures of the various sense fields. A sense field may be roughly described as the largest aggregate of what is actually perceived at any particular time in a particular sense mode. For each sense field we shall consider the following four structures: (a) the general shape of the field, (b) the uniformity of the contents of the field from one region in the field to another, (c) the spatial dimensions of the field, and (d) the nature of perspective within the field. As we shall see, these vary in significant ways from one field to the next, ways that turn out to be of some relevance to the issue of solipsism. Since the visual field is familiar enough, it is a good place to start.

Let us begin with the monocular visual field which is made up of everything seen by one eye alone at any one given time. It may be somewhat accurately characterized as being at its maximum extent roughly oval in shape. It is not uniform, which is to say that it does not make up a homogenous whole: items in the central area may be comparatively detailed and distinct in outline, whereas items removed from the center are blurred, darker, and more grossly featured, while those on the periphery are nebulous blobs of rather indistinct color. It seems fair to say that the monocular field is two-dimensional. Objects seen must have at least two dimensions since they occupy areas; whether they have more than two is less clear, although they hardly seem to have a third dimension in the way they have the first two.

To settle the issue we shall need some criterion for determining how many dimensions a sense field has. Mere impression is not the most satisfactory basis for a decision. A remark made by von Helmholtz promises to be very helpful at the present juncture. In discussing the monocular field of vision, von Helmholtz makes the following claim regarding any continuous two-dimensional surface: "Every closed line drawn upon it divides it into two portions, and we cannot pass from a point on one portion to a point on the other without crossing the line."[4] The circumstance outlined by von Helmholtz immediately suggests a criterion of two-dimensionality: a structure is two-dimensional if and only if it is divisible by a closed one-dimensional figure such that a point cannot pass from one portion to the other without cutting the figure. If desired, the criterion may easily be generalized to yield a test for any number of dimensions. So generalized, it might run as follows:

> *The von Helmholtz Dimension Criterion:* A spatial structure has n dimensions if and only if it can be divided into two portions by a closed figure of one less than n dimensions, which is to say, if it can be divided in two such that a point cannot pass from one of the two portions to the other without passing through the closed figure.

On this criterion, a line (an ideal one) turns out to be one-dimensional. The line is divisible into two portions in the required way by a second figure of zero dimensions (a point), as is shown by the fact that a second point cannot go from one of the two linear portions to the other without passing through the closed figure (the first point). A solid turns out to be three-dimensional since it is divisible in the required way by a plane.

As might be expected, when von Helmholtz's criterion is applied to the monocular visual field, the latter is found to be quite clearly two-dimensional. If the test is run with a line or loop of thread (representing the closed figure) and with a dot having a diameter the thickness of the thread (representing the point), we find that the dot cannot pass from the space on one side of the thread to that on the other without either hiding or being hidden by some part of the thread. The one-dimensional thread divides the field in two in the required way, and consequently the monocular visual field must be two-dimensional.

There remains the issue of perspective. The notion that there is such a thing as perspective in the monocular visual field would seem based on the presence of two rather curious phenomena in the field. One of these is the looming of an object (and the converse, its diminishing). The other is the fact of the disappearing of one item behind another. One might claim that these two phenomena constitute perspective. It should not be thought, however, that such perspective requires a third dimension. Neither of the two phenomena introduces depth into the field or even necessitates the postulation of depth for its explanation. When an item looms in the visual field, it has apparently simply increased in size to occupy more of the field; when it recedes, apparently it simply shrinks to occupy less area. When an object passes from sight behind another, it has apparently been swallowed up by the other. The most that may be said is that these two phenomena provide cues in estimates of depth if the visual world is assumed to be three-dimensional.

Let us now consider the binocular field. It differs from the monocular field in a number of significant ways. At its maximum extent, the binocular field is perhaps half again as long as it is wide (or half again as wide as high using normal bodily position for orientation). In addition, it fails to be uniform in two distinct ways. Not only are items outside the center less distinct in features and outline, but they are in double, or paired with a nearby duplicate. Items are single and distinctly detailed only in a very restricted central region—and that too only on the condition of being at the focal center, or center of focus. For instance, if one's hand located two feet in front of one's face happens to be the focus of one's vision, other items situated in the center but in front of or behind the hand are in duplicate. If one's eyes diverge rather than focus on some object, everything in the field is in duplicate. The binocular field has in fact a very complex structure.

As might be expected, the heterogeneity of the binocular field complicates any answer to the question of how many dimensions it has. Clearly, the visual items in the field must have at least two dimensions. Even the fuzzy and indistinct items occupy an area of sorts. On the other hand, it would seem unlikely that items seen in duplicate have more than two dimensions. The main question is whether certain items at the center of focus in the field and without a double have a third dimension. Such items certainly appear to have some sort of depth when compared to items centrally placed in a monocular field; they stand out from their background in a way the monocular item does not. To reach a more warranted decision on the issue, we must appeal once more to von Helmholtz's criterion.

Running a test on the binocular field with von Helmholtz's criterion is not the straightforward matter it was with the monocular field. Not only does the spatial structure differ at the center of focus from what it is elsewhere in the field, but the center of focus has a depth variation, as it were. For instance, if the focus is some item five feet away, then any other items in roughly the same line of vision but closer or further away will be present in duplicate. Something remotely analogous exists in the monocular field, but there the variation is merely one of distinctness. The proclivity to duplication has somewhat unwelcome effects on the testing process. If one testing device, a thread for instance, is placed far from the other, a dot, the thread may be seen double while the dot is seen single, or the contrary. The result is a state of considerable perplexity as to exactly what is being tested and with what. The sensible solution is to maintain the two testing devices in close proximity to each other in whatever place is being tested; in these circumstances, they will either both be single or both be double. Perplexities reduce to manageable proportions.

It should come as no surprise that the test results are found to vary with the region of the field being tested. The visual field appears to be two-dimensional for the most part. That part of the field outside the center of focus is clearly so, to the extent that visibility permits testing. When the center of focus is distant, items in the center are also clearly two-dimensional. When the center of focus is closer, a foot or more away, for instance, there is present something like a third dimension. The test findings in this latter case need to be traced out in some detail.

Let us assume that a thread and dot are the two testing devices. The dot is made to pass behind or in front of the thread so that it passes from one section to the other of the two sections created by the thread. If the thread and dot are too distant from each other when one passes behind the other, one will be seen double. If they are kept a small distance from each other, an eighth of an inch maximum perhaps, each is seen single. Let us suppose the thread runs vertically and that the dot is moving horizontally from one side of the thread to the other. In these particular circumstances, when the dot passes behind the thread or in front of the thread, at no moment does the thread hide the dot or the dot the thread. At the crucial moment, the dot is seen to give a short hop forward in its direction of movement. This slight quirk of behavior allows both dot and thread to be present at all times. The dot consequently passes from one portion to the other of the two portions supposedly created by the thread and does so without being hidden by the thread or without hiding it. Since the thread does not divide the field in the required way, the field cannot be declared two-dimensional—a result which suggests that the region tested has a depth or third dimension. A claim of the sort can be made only for a very small part of the field, a very thin region at the focal center, when that center is in fact about a foot or so from the eyes.

These findings do not constitute the full story. It should be added that the movement of the dot described above is a horizontal one. When the movement is vertical, there is no unbroken passing of the dot from one portion of the field to the other; at the moment of passing, either the dot is hidden by the thread or it hides the thread. The test in this case yields the conclusion that the field is two-dimensional for that particular direction. The depth attributed this particular spot in the field consequently must be seriously qualified. To avoid misconception it might be characterized as *horizontal depth*. Horizontal depth is, of course, peculiar only to items in the focal center of the field and not too distant.

Finally, some mention should be made of the peculiar phenomenon of quasi depth to be found in both the monocular and binocular fields. Some striking and widely known instances of quasi depth are the reversing Necker cube and Rubin's face-goblet figure. A very much simpler instance is provided by the following figure:

O

The above oval may be seen in four distinct ways: as a white circular mound on the page, as a white circular depression on the page, as a black hoop raised on a white page, or as a black hoop sunk into the page. Each of these figures displays quasi depth. It is quite unclear how a test for dimensions might be run on figures of the sort using von Helmholtz's criterion and even less clear how it might manage to show the figure with quasi depth to be three-dimensional. On the other hand, a figure in quasi depth cannot simply be declared to be two-dimensional. Such a ruling would ignore the phenomenon altogether.

These various findings give no clear answer to the question of the number of dimensions of the visual field. It is far from obvious that a conferral of three-dimensionality is warranted by the above-noted suggestions of a third dimension. On von Helmholtz's criterion, there is a third dimension of sorts, a very shallow depth that is 'horizontal' and found only in a very restricted region, i.e., within the focal region of the focused binocular field. The extent to which the binocular field has depth may appear insignificant, but to counterbalance the appearance somewhat, it may be noted that this curious type of depth is to be found both in the part of the field where attention is directed and at the crucial distance of arm's length. To beef up the case still more, note might also be taken of the unsettling phenomenon of quasi depth. In the circumstances it is very difficult to know how to answer the question of the number of dimensions possessed by the binocular visual field. The question is misleading, of course, in that it is so worded as to imply that there is only one answer, and that answer a whole number. If an answer were mandatory, the most reasonable estimate would be that it has 2¼ dimensions. Perhaps the absurdity of the answer says something about the question.

Perspective in the binocular field differs little from that of the monocular one. Talk of perspective amounts finally to talk of the two phenomena of looming (or shrinking) and hiding (or disappearing behind). What is generally termed 'perspective' is, strictly speaking, not a property of the visual field at all; it is rather a property of the three-dimensional model used to explain phenomena that occur in the two-dimensional visual structure. More exactly, perspective explains the phenomena on the supposition that, in fact, things generally neither change size nor are swallowed up by others, that is, on the suppositions of the size conservation and continued existence of objects. The denial of both these suppositions is quite consistent with what is actually perceived. Consequently, neither supposition would be endorsed by a Sense Data Solipsist. The objects in a world limited to what is actually seen would be essentially two-dimensional.

STRUCTURES OF THE TACTILE-KINESTHETIC FIELD

Let us move on now to examine the tactual data that figure among the contents of the world of the radical skeptic or Sense Data Solipsist. Oddly enough, it sounds odd to speak of a sense field with regard to any sense other than vision. If we define a sense field as the aggregate of everything actually perceived through a particular sense, then we should be able to speak of a tactual or tactile-kinesthetic field, an auditory field, and so on. Let us now examine the tactual field with respect to the four features of shape, uniformity, dimensions, and perspective.

The boundaries of the tactual field coincide roughly with the outer surface of one's body. Its shape, consequently, is variable and may coincide roughly with any of the shapes the felt body may take. What is actually felt at any particular time is never the complete surface of a table top (or even of an apple). It is only a section more or less immediately contiguous with some surface of the body, since the various portions of the surface can only be run over serially by fingertips and palms which fail to touch all portions and contours at any given instant.

Tactility is generally taken to include in addition to the specifically tactile feelings from a touched object, the pressure on and from an object as well as its coldness or warmth. These various types of feeling may be present simultaneously in what is apparently one and the same place. When touch is made into a generic sense in this way, there is little reason not to include feelings of pressure generally—as the floor under one's feet or the wall against one's shoulder—as well as feelings of heat and cold, and feelings of pain and pleasure and of proprioception. In point of fact, not only are there no sharp dividing lines among the regions occupied by the various types of feeling, but there is continual overlap. For this reason, the feelings are properly lumped together to make up one domain with the sense of touch, one sense field with diverse overlapping feelings. Our present aim is to map out the world of the radical skeptic or Sense Data Solipsist, and even for such a skeptic, the various feelings in any simultaneous array are perceived as fused, shading off into other composites in contiguous regions; at any particular time they form one spatial system impervious to fragmentation into separate systems through the weathering action of skeptical doubt.

That these various contiguous feelings are indeed contiguous cannot be doubted. It cannot be doubted, for instance, that the feelings present in one's throat are contiguous to those in the region of one's chest, which feelings in turn are contiguous to those in one's shoulders. No leap of faith is required to assemble the feelings into one spatial system. The pangs of hunger, for example, are directly felt as located with respect to other feelings, such as the slow pulsations of one's breathing or the ache of one's tired back. Neither training nor exploration are necessary to locate hunger pangs or to forestall mistakes—locating them in one's feet or head, for instance. Similarly the location of a thumping heart or aching tooth within the complex configuration of concomitantly felt feelings is given at the same time as the qualitative presence of the thump or ache. The spatial system formed is not correctly termed a *tactual* field, since a good deal more than touch is involved. A more appropriate appellation would be the *tactile-kinesthetic* field, although even this term abbreviates somewhat the variety of sorts of feeling that constitute the field. The body with which the field coincides more or less may in turn be termed (abbreviating somewhat) *the tactile-kinesthetic body.*

The various feelings which constitute the feelings or substance of the tactile-kinesthetic body vary considerably in consistency from one time to another. One's feet, for instance, are often present as mere amorphous lumps, never completely absent from the scene, but accorded little attention except when they protest or need to be tucked snugly into bed. Merleau-Ponty aptly describes the experience of the felt body leaning on a desk as two stressed hands behind which the remainder of the body trails like the tail of a comet.[5] Feelings or tactual presences may retreat almost to the point of disappearance in the presence of an absorbing visual or auditory spectacle. They may also, on the contrary, leap suddenly into detailed prominence with a shift in attention. The feelings in one's left knee that undoubtedly have slumbered in obscurity as background participants since one's present activities began some time back, may suddenly take on an impressive precision and intensity simply by their being made the focus of five seconds of undivided attention. To appreciate the power of attention in this regard, one need only close one's eyes and focus one's undivided attention for a few seconds on the feelings of one's brow, then shift one's attention to the sole of one's left foot, and after a few seconds, shift again to one's right wrist. Each of what were formerly scarcely perceptible masses spring suddenly into relief, detail, and intensity, to become the central feature of the body. Most of the time one's attention is elsewhere, and the body as a whole is sunk back into nebulosity and imprecision. It may, of course, also be brought into sharp relief in other ways, for instance, by an abrupt plunge into cold water, or through the tensions and pulls of vigorous movement. It may be brought out to a lesser extent by the onset of some particular feeling: a poke, a brush, a pressure, an itch, a tingling, a discomfort, an ache, a wave of joy, of anger, or of excitement.

The extreme variation in the uniformity of the tactile-kinesthetic body makes an assessment of the number of its dimensions subject to qualification. Nevertheless, when the particular feelings in some part of the body are the focus of one's attention, generally there is little doubt that the scrutinized region qualifies as three-dimensional. Perhaps the most obviously three-dimensional region is one's chest fleshed out by the muscular effort and pressures of deep-breathing. Any hesitation on the point may be dispelled by a cold shower. The latter not only creates an outraged envelope round the felt breathing, thus showing the chest to be three-dimensional (at least during the time of the shower), but it also encourages closer awareness of the fainter envelope of tactual feelings actually present at other times. Another clear instance of three dimensions is readily found in the feelings of the mouth and tongue enveloped by tension in cheeks and lips. Given the assistance of a modest degree of attentiveness and acumen, there are few if any portions of the body that fail to manifest three dimensions. For the better part of one's conscious life, the body is structured throughout with various and sundry tensions and stresses. It is rarely an inert mass pinned immobile against a floor or mattress and fleshed out three-dimensionally with varying degrees of dull heaviness. Generally, the feelings of heaviness are accompanied, and to some extent replaced, by various tensions necessary to maintaining an erect position. They are accompanied as well by the various stresses and pulls involved in any bodily movement or activity. These various kinesthetic feelings in conjunction with the incessant sense of weight flesh out the body and give it density or volume.

The von Helmholtz criterion yields a ruling of three dimensions for any observed portion of the body. A closed line traced down a finger or a thigh, or round a wrist or waist, does not divide the tactile-kinesthetic body in two. A tactual dot may be imagined to pass from one side of the line to the other, cutting the line of division by passing through the felt mass of body under the skin. Pressure, feelings of movement, or pain may help to give volume to a region being tested. But even in their absence, it is generally possible to trace out the bridge of feeling that shows the feeling not to be two-dimensional.

Feelings and tactual items generally, including the lines and points needed in tests for three dimensions, have a regrettable tendency toward nebulosity, imprecision, and evanescence, a circumstance that makes testing difficult. This is particularly so at times when one's attention is directed visually to some absorbing event in the surrounds. To complicate matters further, observation of the nature of the body when one's attention is directed elsewhere is an extremely difficult undertaking. It would be inadmissible to make claims as to what the nature of the body must be when unattended on the basis of extrapolations from observations of the attended body. Not only is such a procedure questionable in its own right, but it presupposes a notion of permanence that a Sense Data Solipsist would no more accept with regard to the tactile-kinesthetic body than for table tops and apples.

Awareness of the three-dimensionality of the tactile-kinesthetic field is enhanced in some measure by the vertical coordinate made continually present with the pull of gravity. The pull is present in the form of a heaviness which fleshes out all regions of one's body. It is ever-present and relentless, a force requiring unremittingly a complex counter-effort if one is to achieve an upright position and remain in it. In as much as this vertical coordinate is a power to be ignored at one's peril in any movement or activity, it can hardly fail to get one's attention, and so to be perceived as one of the essential structures of three-dimensional space.

Finally, there is the matter of perspective. Curiously enough, the tactile-kinesthetic field (or body) differs markedly from the visual field in that it has nothing that may be likened to perspective. No point in the field—or out of it—plays the role of a point of view such that items perceived are smaller the further away they are from the point. One's tactile-kinesthetic hand, for instance, does not feel smaller and smaller as one moves it further away from the chest and the rest of the body. In addition, there is no hiding of the feeling in one part of the body behind the feeling in another because of a change in position of the parts. One's hand does not cease to be tactually present because one has put it in one's pocket or hidden it under a leg or behind one's back.

The lack of a perspective in the tactile-kinesthetic world has the consequence that no literal sense can be made of talk of tactually perceiving the world from a certain point of view. The perspectival cues found in vision are nowhere present in tactual perception. To speak of a point of view in tactual perception can only be an incorrect way of speaking of the very limited range of any present tactile-kinesthetic awareness, the fact that it does not go beyond the limiting surface of one's own body. Indeed, if one could perceive the whole world through feeling, as one does one's body, one would perceive the world without a point of view of any sort.

The most significant difference perhaps between tactility and vision is the marked difference in the degree to which a third spatial dimension is present in each. In the case of the tactile-kinesthetic, the whole field is (or may be) three-dimensional. In the case of the visual, actually perceived depth is extremely shallow. This curious state of affairs strongly suggests that the tactile-kinesthetic body is the prime source of one's first awareness of three-dimensional structures. It is undoubtedly the prime source of one's first awareness of three-dimensional enclosure and hence of the relations of being inside of something and of being outside of something in three-dimensional space.

RELATIONS AMONG THE SENSE FIELDS

Traditional psychology recognizes five senses: sight, hearing, touch, taste, smell, to which pentarchy proprioception is sometimes appended. The mode of division is inappropriate if one's interests lie in sense fields. Impartial scrutiny of what is actually perceived in the flux of experience must recognize that rather intimate relations hold between the sensuous items of one sense and those of another—relations other than that of temporal concomitance. In view of the intimacy of these relations, proprioception and touch were classed together earlier in one sense field. For similar reasons, the sense fields of taste and smell would seem more properly included in the tactile-kinesthetic field.

Consider a moment olfactory and gustatory data. They are actually perceived as sensual modifications in the nasal cavity and on the tongue, respectively, and hence as located within the tactile-kinesthetic body. The bitterness, warmth, and aroma actually perceived with a sip of coffee are perceived as partly fused, partly contiguous to one another and to the kinesthetic feelings defining mouth, tongue, and nostrils; they are perceived as modifications or sensuous expanses situated within a single spatial system and standing in relations of close proximity to one another. The perceived intermingling is precisely what gives plausibility to Aristotle's thought experiment: "Suppose all the rest of our flesh was, like the tongue, sensitive to flavour, we should have identified the sense of taste and the sense of touch."[6] As a result of this intermingling, no Sense Data Solipsist would have cause to consider them to be conceivably distinct spatial systems related only loosely to the system of tactile-kinesthetic data.

We are left then with three sense fields—the visual, the tactile-kinesthetic, and the auditory—and the unexamined question of the relationship in which they stand to each other. Before considering the auditory field, let us attempt to answer the question for the first two sense fields.

As will be recalled, the Humean radical skeptic or Sense Data Solipsist rejects all connections that are not ostensibly present in the actual data, which is to say, all connections the existence of which is subject to doubt. Bearing this in mind, let us ask what are the ostensible relations that hold between the visual and the tactile-kinesthetic sense fields.

It is clear enough that at any given time, events taking place in the two sense fields are simultaneous. The denial that a foot twitch one now actually feels and a flutter one now actually sees are taking place at the same time would be clearly in contradiction with the evidence. But while there is no room for doubt on the matter of their perceived simultaneity, it is less clear whether and how they stand in some spatial relation to each other. The minimal spatial relation would be that the visual field is situated in some manner or other with respect to the tactile-kinesthetic body, contiguous as it were to the front side rather than to the side or back of the felt head. Yet there is some difficulty in determining whether or not the visual field is actually perceived to be so contiguous. The source of the difficulty is that an alleged awareness of such a relationship might be easily construed as an inference from past-noted correlations. Certain kinesthetic feelings of eye muscles, for example, are accompanied by certain changes in the visual field; felt movements of the eyelids accompany changes in the scope of the visual field including its complete disappearance; discomfort or pain occasioned by light is felt in a certain region of the face (and not in the feet). Reasonably enough, a Humean skeptic would question the correlations in such cases on the ground that the actual visual and tactual evidence provides no apparent warrant for any claim of the connection. The question is whether, independently of experientially noted and inferred connections, the two fields are actually perceived to be situated in some general way with respect to each other.

It would seem that the answer must be that they are. While one may be in some doubt about the matter when one's head is immobile, nevertheless, the visual field appears to have the same orientation with respect to one's tactile-kinesthetic head whenever the latter moves. It is conceivable, for instance, that the world should be of such a sort that when one turns one's tactile-kinesthetic head, the visual field remains at its previous location with respect to one's feet, for instance, but takes up a new location in the direction of one's ear or the back of one's head. Yet the visual field does not in fact do so. It moves with one's head, and remains situated in front rather than behind or beside. Consequently, we must conclude that the orientation is part of what is given. The two fields, visual and tactile-kinesthetic, are spatially related, at least to the extent of having some rudimentary orientation with regard to each other.

It is clear, however, that the two fields are not materially related, which is to say they are not so related that items in one field unite with those in another to form material objects together, objects having properties such as color, shape, weight, and odor, each of which is actually present in only one of the two sense fields. The possibility of such a relation is discouraged by the disparity in three-dimensionality between the two sense fields, but the lack of connection runs more deeply. When one is aware of a material object actually present in the two sense fields, one is not actually aware that the two actually perceived items form one object. For instance, on seeing one's left foot, one is not actually aware of the unity of the foot seen with the foot felt. The hypothesis that the two do not form one object is quite consistent with what is actually perceived. As a result, a radical skeptic may sensibly raise the question whether there are any rational grounds for thinking that any items at all in one field go together with items in the other to form unitary objects. The Sense Data Solipsist raises the question, and finding no grounds to warrant the assertion of a material connection, denies that there is any. The orientation that the visual field is actually perceived to have with regard to the tactile-kinesthetic field is a very rudimentary one. The two fields are related in the manner of two moving pictures playing side by side in one room—or to improve on the image, the visual field is related to the tactile-kinesthetic one like the picture on a television screen to the events in the rest of the room: it has a location in the room, but no apparent further connection with anything going on in the room.

The auditory field is the most difficult of the three fields to describe, however brief the projected sketch. Sounds are nebulous items that generally have a directional orientation but not a sharp or unique one. Each sound is more prominently in some one rough location but is otherwise present everywhere somewhat like an enveloping sea, as in the much-used metaphor. For instance, one might actually perceive a particular sound as located behind, above, and to the right of one's head. At the same time, however, one perceives sound similar in pitch and harmonics located all around, and perhaps one may be inclined to say, reverberating through one's body.

It is not obvious that it makes any sense to speak of the shape of the auditory field. Sounds are experienced as oriented, a feature which suggests that the auditory field should be likened to a sphere with oneself at the center. Yet, while sounds may vary in intensity, it is not obvious that they vary in depth. Certainly sounds become fainter as the source of the sound recedes, but what is actually perceived would seem most aptly construed as a phenomenon structurally analogous to looming. Similarly, it is not obvious that the notion of spatial volume is applicable to sounds or to the auditory field. The fact that sounds are experienced as located suggests that the field is a three-dimensional field, but in the absence of depth, the three dimensions collapse into something akin to the two-dimensional surface of a sphere. Attempts to apply von Helmholtz's criterion yield ambiguous results. Two sounds may be made to approach each other so that at some point, if neither sound is unduly. loud, both continue to be heard as if at the same location. Yet this fact gives no clear cause to claim that one is heard behind or in front of the other. A coincident location is not necessarily indicative of a depth, since it may as easily be claimed that sounds are interpenetratable entities that do not exclude one another.

The auditory field, like both the visual and tactile-kinesthetic fields, fades into nebulosity when attention is directed elsewhere. Unlike the two other fields, the auditory field is uniform. It has no focal center as does vision, and apparently no phenomenon of highlighting specific regions with a shift of attention as in the tactile-kinesthetic field. As for perspective, it may be said that sounds become crisper and less muffled as their source approaches the ear. This perspectival phenomenon can certainly serve as a basis for inferred judgments of distance, although, to repeat, it is not clearly the case that there is actual perception of depth.

The auditory field is for the most part not materially related to the tactile-kinesthetic field. The contrary would be surprising, given the disparity in spatial structure between the two systems. The location of a sound is a feature of the sound on par with its pitch, intensity, and harmonics, and it might serve to distinguish two otherwise indistinguishable sounds. The location of the sound remains in the absence of any second sound and hence is, as suggested earlier, a location relative to the tactile-kinesthetic body. There seems little ground for claiming any further spatial relation between the two fields. Most sounds do not stand in a relation of proximity to tactual phenomena in the manner of olfactory and gustatory data. In addition, it is not obvious that they are actually perceived as proximate to tactile-kinesthetic feelings of the head, any more than located at a distance from those feelings. An actually heard ticking, for instance, is conceivably quite unrelated materially to a simultaneously felt watch—although the two are concomitantly perceived and the location of the ticking is in the same direction as that of the tactually perceived watch. It seems fairly obvious too that the auditory field is not materially related to the visual one. Indeed, most of the time, phenomena in the two fields are not even directionally congruent—but even where items in the two fields share a direction relative to the felt body, they are otherwise conceivably unrelated.

On the basis of the evidence of actual perception, the evidence admitted by the radical skeptic, it would seem correct to say that the five senses constitute three very loosely related spatial systems. These are a tactile-kinesthetic system containing transient gustatory and olfactory sensuous expanses located in specific regions of the tactile-kinesthetic body, an auditory system suffused with directionally oriented sound enveloping the tactile-kinesthetic head like a spherical halo, and a visual system, complex, delicately detailed, and anchored like a giant television screen before the upper tactile-kinesthetic face.

The sole structure of the three able to lay serious claim to being three-dimensional is the tactile-kinesthetic body. Auditory space and visual space each possess features that facilitate their accommodation into a three-dimensional system, but neither is itself frankly three-dimensional. The implication is that the awareness of the three-dimensionality of the material world arises first and foremost through an awareness of the three-dimensionality of the tactile-kinesthetic body. In the world of the radical skeptic, the visual and auditory structures stand merely in a loose relation of position with respect to the tactile-kinesthetic one. Yet if the items within each were coordinated with items in the others to form one world of material objects, there is little doubt that the source of the three-dimensionality of the resulting world would be the three dimensions of the tactile-kinesthetic system. The suggestions of three dimensions present in the other systems are quite meager, whereas the tactile-kinesthetic structure gives firsthand awareness of what a three-dimensional world is like. This is not to say it is inconceivable that in a purely visual world a perceiving subject akin to a mobile pure gaze should conceive and construct a three-dimensional visual world. It is to say, however, that given the presence of the tactual world, any such independent construction, whether ultimately feasable or not, is unnecessary. A three-dimensional visual system results automatically from the coordination of visual items with corresponding tactual ones.

Yet another phenomenon providing an important element of structure to the tactile-kinesthetic field is gravity. The latter phenomenon is almost exclusively peculiar to the tactile-kinesthetic system. Visual objects fall on occasion, and on rarer occasions still, auditory items do likewise. In contrast, the felt tug of gravity is something ever-present. Its omnipresence makes it a constant directional coordinate for organizing tactual space, as also a constant obstacle to be overcome, an incessant weight and burden. Sounds and colored shapes are weightless, even when falling, and in this respect are ethereal. The tactile-kinesthetic is the realm of the concrete par excellence. It is there that weight is to be found, as well as pressure and resistance to effort, those properties that in our everyday world give three-dimensional solids their solidity.

In taking up the stance of a radical skeptic, Hume characterizes the self or the mind as "a bundle or collection of different perceptions, which succeed each other with an inconceivable rapidity, and are in a perpetual flux and movement."[7] While the description is perhaps not inaccurate as far as it goes, it goes no further than a short hop. The flux of experience is perhaps an ever-changing stream, but it is also a stream having relatively permanent structures and considerable organization. It consists of three semi-independent spatial systems, each with qualitatively distinctive sensuous occupants. Two of these, an essentially two-dimensional and delicately detailed visual expanse, and an ever-fluctuating sea of sound, are each anchored to a rudimentarily three-dimensional voluminous heaviness, elongated and ramified in shape, flexible and mobile. If, to borrow Hume's metaphor, the mind is a theater where perceptions repass, glide away, and mingle, then it is also one where a restless, gargantuan permanence is firmly planted midstage. There within this tactual presence, exhilaration, lassitude, irritation and affection alternate and play out their capricious antics amidst a cast of transient and insubstantial visual and auditory supernumeraries.

CHAPTER ELEVEN

THE SELF

THE CARTESIAN SELF AND THE SELF THAT FEELS

The brief outline of the world of the Sense Data Solipsist sketched in the preceding chapter is incomplete as it stands. No explicit mention is made of what must be the main character in any solipsistic drama, the solipsist himself or herself. The aim of the present chapter is to remedy the situation by identifying the self in the flux of experience. The task was initiated in chapter 8, where two Cartesian subjects were encountered, one the residue of the everyday self that survives the skeptical scrutiny of Sense Data Solipsism, the other the immaterial thinking being unveiled by Descartes's methodical doubt, the being that finds it may doubt the existence of everything bodily but not its own existence. It is time to choose between the two or, more precisely, to determine which of the two is more properly taken to be the self of the radical skeptic who surveys the sparse solipsistic terrain. On the face of things, it is perhaps a little curious that there should be any disagreement whatever between the two conceptions of the self. Both are reputedly derived from the everyday notion of the self through properly conducted skeptical scrutiny. Yet, since the two selves differ, one conception must be incorrect. As it turns out, the mistaken conception is that of Descartes. The source of error is ultimately Descartes's failure fully to appreciate and do justice to the role of the tactile-kinesthetic body in the various activities of the self, in thinking generally and in willing and in affectivity in particular. The matter is somewhat complex, so let us start at the beginning with the two skeptical enterprises and the two resulting conceptions of the self.

The Sense Data Solipsist adopts the policy of denying the existence of anything not actually perceived. One immediate casualty of the policy is the everyday conception of the self as a fleshed-out person existing among like creatures in the everyday world. This perceiving self reduces primarily to a tactile-kinesthetic body, since the visual body, when reduced to what is actually perceived, is hardly more than a few fugitive visual scraps, which furthermore are materially unconnected with any felt counterpart.

The policy adopted by Descartes is likewise that of calling into question whatever may be doubted. To this end, Descartes resolves to pretend that he may be dreaming or that everything he perceives may be the fabrication of a deceitful demon attempting to delude him. The one point he finds he cannot doubt is his own existence; this is because to doubt, one must exist. The point soon leads Descartes to part company with the Sense Data Solipsist—wrongly so, although this remains to be shown. Descartes's reasoning is that since he finds he must exist despite the supposition that nothing spatial exists, he cannot be anything spatial or corporeal. In *The Search for Truth* he has Polyander eloquently put the matter as follows: "On the contrary, these suppositions simply strengthen the certainty of my conviction that I exist and am not a body. Otherwise, if I had doubts about my body, I would also have doubts about myself, and I cannot have doubts about that. I am absolutely convinced that I exist, so convinced that it is totally impossible for me to doubt it."[1]

It is easy to object to this line of reasoning on the ground that the conception of oneself on which it is based is perhaps inadequate; from the fact that one has no awareness of being a body, it does not follow that one is not a body. From what Descartes says in his preface to the *Meditations*,[2] he apparently encountered just this criticism of his reasoning in the *Discourse* and was sufficiently impressed with it to feel obliged to give it explicit consideration. In the *Sixth Meditation* he argues that his conception of himself is an adequate one in that he has a clear and distinct idea of himself as a "thinking, nonextended thing," and a clear and distinct idea of body as something extended and nonthinking.[3] It follows that his conception of himself as possibly existing independently of a body is a correct one. It also follows, incidentally, that a prerequisite for the immortality of the soul is thereby established.

The addition yields a very powerful argument. If Descartes is right and his conception of the self is an adequate one, then his conclusion that he conceivably could exist without a body would seem to follow unassailably. The strength of Descartes's argument is rarely appreciated, and indeed, the argument itself is rarely addressed. Descartes's metaphysical dualism of two substances, extended substance and thinking substance, the mind/body dichotomy he posits within the person, and the very notion of an immaterial, unextended, thinking substance have over the centuries all attracted an impressive volume and variety of criticism. The criticism almost invariably ignores the reasoning that leads Descartes to his views in the first place and so fails to treat the issues at their source. While metaphysical speculation may be found more exciting, and may even with luck produce a *reductio* demonstration that something has to be at fault in the original premises, it does not show what that fault actually is. The crucial issue is whether the Cartesian conception of the self is tenable, i.e., whether the self is to be conceived of independently of any notion of body or extension. If it is, of course, it cannot have the tactile-kinesthetic body as an essential constituent, and the concept of the self attributed to Sense Data Solipsism will require revision. Let us take a closer look at Descartes's concept of the self.

In the *Meditations*, Descartes no sooner concludes that he exists than he goes on to ask what he is. His reply is that he is a thing that thinks, which reply he glosses as "a thing that doubts, understands, affirms, denies, is willing, is unwilling, and also imagines and has sensory perceptions."[4] He finds himself to be identical with this thinking being, a view for which he gives convincing support with the following series of rhetorical questions:

> Is it not one and the same 'I' who is now doubting almost everything, who nonetheless understands some things, who affirms that this one thing is true, denies everything else, desires to know more, is unwilling to be deceived, imagines many things even involuntarily, and is aware of many things which apparently come from the senses? Are not all these things just as true as the fact that I exist, even if I am asleep all the time, and even if he who created me is doing all he can to deceive me? Which of all these activities is distinct from my thinking? Which of them can be said to be separate from myself?

The thinking of the self constitutive of each of these activities is, on Descartes's construal of the matter, something substantially different from anything sensuous or corporeal or spatial; thinking is something nonsensuous, noncorporeal, nonspatial. Despite present-day impatience with talk of ethereal entities, Descartes's characterization of thinking must be judged much more plausible than one might at first suspect. Consider a few examples. When I look out the window and see hats and coats moving about in the street below, I know that the coats cover people, and not machines. Yet what is my knowing? It is certainly not something sensuously present in the experience. To borrow a well-borrowed image from Wittgenstein, if God were to look into my mind, he (or she) could not tell from anything *sensuously* present that I see men, or know that the hats cover men. The same is true of my intention if I go out into the hall to get a drink. I am aware of where I am going and what I want, as is shown by the fact that I could immediately tell anyone who asked. Yet neither my intention nor my awareness of it are sensuously present in the experience. Anyone looking into my mind and rummaging through its sensuous contents would find neither. Certainly there are many sensuous clues to be found in my experience: the dryness in my throat, my determined gait, the direction in which I am moving, perhaps a fleeting visual image of a water fountain. My intention might well be guessed from these, but it could not be known as it is by me.

Descartes's view of the nature of thinking rests upon precisely such an experiential base. This fact comes out at any number of points where he discusses thinking. In his search for the self in the second half of the *Second Meditation*,[5] Descartes finds the self or 'I' that exists in all one's thinking to be a somewhat puzzling entity in that it cannot be pictured in imagination. Consequently, he approaches it indirectly by way of its activities. Taking as an example the perception of a piece of wax as the same wax throughout its changes, Descartes argues that his perception is a matter of understanding, a matter of "purely mental scrutiny," rather than of vision or touch or imagination, and that things are perceived "by the mind alone." He makes a similar point with regard to his perception from his window of men in the street, since in fact, he actually sees only hats and coats. In the *Sixth Meditation* he takes great pains to distinguish pure understanding from imagination, and speaks of the mind as turning toward itself and its own ideas in understanding, whereas in imagining it turns toward body.[6] Descartes becomes quite impatient with Hobbes's failure to grasp the distinction, and Hobbes's assumption that an idea must be an image and that consequently there can be no idea of God.[7] The nonsensuous nature of thought is brought out again in answers to objections where Descartes defines thought as anything of which we are immediately aware and gives as an illustration of an idea or thought the idea one has when one understands the words one is saying.[8] Thought in this case is identical with the meaning the words have for oneself and, as such, is not something sensuously present in the experience.

The nonsensuous thinking must be the doing of a nonsensuous being. Descartes spells out the point more fully in a letter to Father

Mersenne (July 1641) in which he states an idea to be anything in one's mind when and in whatever way one conceives of something. The thinking being that thinks the thoughts is of the same immaterial and nonsensuous nature as the thoughts themselves: it cannot be imagined or represented by an image; it has neither color nor odor nor taste nor anything corporeal—and yet, it is quite conceivable and is indeed that through which anything is conceived.[9]

Now, will Descartes's conception of thinking bear up under scrutiny? As noted, thinking encompasses a wide variety of activities for Descartes. In the *Principles*, Descartes divides thinking into two modes: *perception*, which includes "sensory perception, imagination, and pure understanding," and *volition*, which itself apparently comprises two groups of phenomena, on one hand, such things as "desire" and "aversion," and on the other, "assertion, denial and doubt."[10] We shall have to examine all three groups to test Descartes's claim that thinking is conceivable apart from anything bodily. For reasons that will become apparent later if all goes well, it is best to begin with yet a fourth group, that of emotions and feelings.

Descartes terms emotions and feelings "passions of the soul," and classes them with perceptions. The particular location Descartes attributes to such perceptions involves a mistake heavy with consequences. On Descartes's account of perception, sounds and colored shapes are referred to objects in an external world; pains, hunger, warmth are referred to the body, while, curiously enough, joy and anger are referred to the soul itself.[11] Such a view is untenable. An appeal to the introspective evidence immediately places feelings in the body along with pains, hunger, and warmth, and not in some vaguely conceived additional entity termed "the soul." Descartes, to be sure, is not alone in his assessment, since feelings are often viewed as a nebulous mental accompaniment to one's particular involvement in the world, something on the order of a pervasive and subjective atmosphere enveloping and permeating events. The widespread espousal of the view would seem due largely to the fact that one's attention is generally centered on something out in the world, if not some person, then some task to be accomplished; it is not focused on bodily feelings, which as a result, become part of an ethereal, mental accompaniment to one's particular involvement in the world, something on the order of a pervasive, background atmosphere enveloping and permeating events. Undoubtedly, if the contrary was the case, and one's attention was focused intently and constantly on one's feelings, then the light and sound of the world would take on the role of atmosphere.

Feelings are primarily a specific state of the tactile-kinesthetic body and become atmosphere through inattention. To convince oneself that such is the case for any putative atmosphere, one need only cast a quick introspective glance at one's tactile-kinesthetic body. The point is most readily substantiated in the case of emotions. Hence, let us briefly consider what might be found with regard to one such emotion, anger, and flesh out the matter from there.

When one is in the throes of a vigorous rage, a furtive glance at one's feelings encounters a wealth of newcomers on the normally benign scene of one's tactile-kinesthetic body: a choking, seething throat, congestion in the face, a tingling in the scalp, a coursing thumping in temples and chest, a tension in the brow and round the eyes, a tightness in the thorax and shoulders, a churning in the abdomen, shaking in the knees, and gripping in the toes. Each of these various feelings is a modification of the tactile-kinesthetic body. Each occupies a certain, vaguely-defined volume of tactile-kinesthetic space; each has a location with respect to the others—is adjacent to, between, or distant from the others. Each is more than a qualitative presence; it is a certain state of tension of the tactile-kinesthetic complex, which also becomes, since one is always involved in some situation in the world, a mode of activity of a certain kind, a certain dynamics. The explosive energy and agitation of anger is very different from the welling enthusiasm and expansive grace of joy, the shrinking paralysis of fear, or the pained and lethargic obliviousness of grief. Anger is a complex spatiotemporal structure of feelings, tensions, and dynamics. These various elements make up the substance of the anger and likewise the substance of the felt body at the time of the anger. For this reason, it is nonsensical to ask where one is angry—not because anger is nowhere, but because it is everywhere throughout one's body.

Admittedly, the tensions and dynamics are not the sole constituents of the anger. There is also an awareness of grievances, an awareness of the person (or situation) toward whom (or which) the anger is directed. The anger is also in part a modification of one's mode of reasoning, as also of one's mode of perceiving, in that one's seeing and hearing are altered by the tactile-kinesthetic commotion. Nevertheless, the feelings are a necessary constituent of the anger, necessary in the sense that without them, there would be no anger. If the feelings and dynamics specific to anger were removed, the remaining state of the body would qualify rather as indifference or calm. Being angry entails having certain types of feeling, and entails behaving with a certain felt dynamics. Short of the tactile-kinesthetic feelings, the dynamics specific to the felt anger, one would not be angry.

The claim that the feelings specific to any emotion are an indispensable constituent in the emotion, is quite forcefully presented by William James. Says James: *"If we fancy some strong emotion, and then try to abstract from our consciousness of it all the feelings of its bodily symptoms, we find we have nothing left behind,* no 'mind-stuff' out of which the emotion can be constituted, and that a cold and neutral state of intellectual perception is all that remains."[12] Illustrating his point with the emotion of fear, he argues as follows: "What kind of an emotion of fear would be left if the feeling neither of quickened heartbeats nor of shallow breathing, neither of trembling lips nor of weakened limbs, neither of goose-flesh nor of visceral stirrings, were present, it is quite impossible to think."[13] The conclusion drawn by James is that there is no such thing as a disembodied human mood, emotion, or affection.

It is difficult not to endorse James's conclusion. In the case of love, for instance, the bubbly lassitude, the warmth, the tingling delight and rapt fascination, each pervade one's body and may be characterized as modes of the tactile-kinesthetic body. Similarly, the awe and delight experienced in watching a sequence of graceful movements is not some ethereal mental aura to the event; it is a lightness centered about one's eyes and radiating through one's body, a captivation of one's gaze that rivets attention so strongly to the movement as to lead one to forget to breathe. It would be quite possible to run through a multitude of less passionate affective states in turn—surprise, disgust, curiosity, disappointment, pride, sympathy, boredom, contentment, excitement, interest, irritation. Each may be found in the same way to be primarily a particular mode of the tactile-kinesthetic body, a specific complex of localized feelings, tensions, and activity that could with time and patience be described in detail, and distinguished from other affective happenings.

It is important to note that the spatially extended feelings are the substance of oneself, the person who is angry. When one declares, "I am furious!," one does not regard oneself as a mere thinking being, an intellect that happens to have at its disposition a tactile-kinesthetic body which is furious. One identifies with the seething, volatile configuration of tensions that defines the tactile-kinesthetic body (illuminated, of course, with awareness). Its inclinations are one's own inclinations, its agitation, one's own agitation. When one ceases to identify with the tensions and dynamics, one ceases to be angry and becomes a spectator to fast-fading feelings.

The case is similar with any other emotion. To be in love is to have feelings of a certain sort, to identify with their warmth and energy. If a tactile-kinesthetic body were merely something an incorporeal thinking subject had at its disposition, then one would be divorced from the being who was in love. The appropriate description of the situation would be not that one was in love, but that one's body was. Similarly, one would not be curious or excited or uneasy. One would simply happen to be conjoined to a body that was curious or excited or uneasy. One would have at one's disposal, as it were, a body charged with feeling—whether rage or terror, delight or despair—like a ship with engines throbbing and an immaterial pilot at the helm.

Descartes is, of course, not completely unaware of the implausible conclusion to which his metaphysical dualism leads. He recognizes that the relationship of the self to affectivity is not a mere extraneous one when he characterizes the union of a thinking self with its body as a "very close" one, an "intermingling" and "a substantial union," or again when he denies that the soul is in the body like a pilot in a ship.[14] Nevertheless, if the implications of declarations of the sort are not traced out and endorsed, they amount in the end to a mere paying of verbal homage, a vain attempt to placate the difficulty with soothing phrases. The root of the difficulty is that an allegedly immaterial and incorporeal self is found to identify itself with corporeal affectivity. Inasmuch as it does so identify itself, it cannot be simply an incorporeal thinking being. Descartes's account of the self is in contradiction with affective experience. He fails to see the contradiction, of course, because he incorrectly locates feelings in the soul and hence is able to ignore their tactile-kinesthetic and corporeal nature.

THE CORPOREALITY OF THE SELF THAT WILLS

Let us turn our attention now to the willing, which Descartes classes as one of the two modes of thinking, and more specifically to the willing more directly related to action, the willing characterized by Descartes as desire and aversion. Descartes's account of such willing has two serious and apparently irreparable flaws, one having to do with action proper, the other with motivation. Let us consider first what is unflawed in his account.

In *The Passions of the Soul*, Descartes characterizes volitions as actions rather than passions on the grounds that "we experience them as proceeding directly from our soul and as seeming to depend upon it alone."[15] Certainly, as Descartes maintains, willing is inconceivable without thinking.[16] In fact, there are several reasons for finding thinking to be an indispensable constituent in any volition. To begin with, willing is never a mere undirected impulse; it always involves some awareness of the situation or environment, and of a goal or expectation. Furthermore, as Descartes remarks of wanting and fearing, it is accompanied by an awareness of itself;[17] in any intended action, one is always aware of what one is doing, even if only marginally. In addition, it may include value judgments as to what is good or bad. Descartes lays a great deal of stress on this latter feature. In *The Passions*, he characterizes such value judgments as the "proper weapons" of the will in its struggle with the passions, and argues that to fight passion with passion is the sign of a weak soul.[18] The point gets him into some difficulty, and in an earlier letter to Father Mersenne (April 1637?), we find Descartes attempting to answer reservations with regard to his classification of willing as a mode of thinking, and to his accompanying rationale, *"il suffit de bien juger pour bien faire,"* ("to do what is good it suffices to see what is good").[19]

In any event, on Descartes's view, willing must involve something more than an intellectual operation of evaluation or judging. On the topic of the source of mistakes in judgments, Descartes argues, plausibly enough, that error can occur because "the scope of the will is wider than that of the intellect";[20] instead of restricting judgment to what is understood, assent or denial is proffered in cases where the truth is not clearly and distinctly perceived. The will, according to Descartes, has "the freedom to direct itself without the determination of the intellect."[21] In particular, this freedom allows it to be possible to be aware of some obvious good and yet not pursue it, or worse still adopt some other goal. In a letter to Father Mesland (May 1644?), Descartes explains the failure to do what one clearly sees to be good in terms of one's ability to direct one's attention elsewhere.[22]

It is true enough that to characterize willing as an intellectual operation alone would be a distorted interpretation of the introspective evidence. The directing of attention is one of the more basic operations of the will, yet one that introspection does not find to be a specifically intellectual operation. A shift of attention, for instance, from the print on a page to an unusual sound or to a protesting foot consists of a change of focus, a reorientation of the perceived world round some quite different center. Such a reorganization of the actually perceived world is not an intellectual operation at all. It is essentially a restructuring of a spatial complex. It certainly involves thinking in that the unusual noise or foot discomfort is recognized as being a certain type of phenomenon and, moreover, one that awakens certain expectations. Nevertheless it hardly appears to qualify as a solely intellectual operation.

Now, the further element in willing posited by Descartes, the element in virtue of which it is more than an intellectual operation, turns out to exist in name only. When giving a definition of thought in his answers to objections, Descartes takes pains to draw a distinction between an operation of the will and the voluntary movement that follows from it. The movement itself is not a thought, Descartes points out.[23] The distinction is a necessary one for Descartes to draw since movement belongs in the sphere of extended being rather than that of immaterial thinking. However, the distinction between willing and doing is ultimately undefendable. The reason, simply stated, is that there is no such distinction to be drawn; there is in fact no such thing as a willing that is not a doing.

Once again, let us consult the experiential evidence. A meticulous survey of the contents of experience turns up no act of willing per se. It may come across a number of processes prior to the execution of action, a desiring or longing, a choosing from among possible courses of action, a resolving to act at some particular future time, or a nursing of one's determination. Yet willing cannot properly be equated with any of these, since prior to the actual performance of an envisaged action, one is always free not to act. There is only a willing if there is a doing. Yet, if willing takes place only when doing does, it is difficult to see how the willing can be separated from the doing. To be distinct from the physical activity of the action, willing has to be the intentional and motivational component of the action. Yet any such intentional component may conceivably be indistinguishable from the intentional component of an experience where no action takes place. The sole apparent difference between an experience in which there is intent without action and one in which there is intent with action is simply the presence of the activity that constitutes the action: the appropriate tactile-kinesthetic commotion, perceptual changes and monitoring, and so on. Consequently, the alleged willing that is supposedly something more than the intention and other than the activity, is nowhere to be found in the picture. There is no such thing.

The second point of difficulty for Descartes's account concerns the feeling element in any desire. It is certainly true, as Descartes maintains, that awareness or thinking is an indispensable constituent in any desire, whether it is a matter of deciding or of doing. A desire is never a mere undirected impulse; it always involves some awareness of the situation or environment, and of a goal or expectation. It should immediately be added, however, that when the relevant experiences are introspected, they are found to contain not only cognitive and perceptual elements but also an affective element as well. The affective element may be very complex and involve not only motive, various feelings, and emotions but determination and energy. The movement effectuated clearly follows from these affective bodily elements as much as from the cognitive and perceptual ones. While the latter may be characterized as a form of thinking, immaterial and unextended, the affective element clearly cannot. Any feeling is some particular state of the tactile-kinesthetic body and, as such, must be rightly considered a form of extended or spatial being. The affective element that motivates one's decision, determination and action cannot rightly be characterized as unextended.

It should be emphasized that the affective constituent is not dispensable. In any willing (doing) there is an identification of the self with the affective motive. When one wills (or acts) out of anger, one identifies with the anger. When one wills (acts) out of curiosity, one identifies with the curiosity. Any of the multitude of affective states—boredom, malice, interest, playfulness, irritation, delight, disgust, fascination—is a mode of the tactile-kinesthetic body, and in acting from that affective state, one identifies with it.

Descartes's line of defence on this point is to draw a distinction between feeling and desire, the latter being understood apparently as a judgment of desirability. In a long letter to his friend, Chanut (February 1647) which treats of love, he denies that the bodily feelings of thirst are the desire itself.[24] The distinction being drawn comes out more clearly in Descartes's allusions to what he terms 'rational feelings', i.e., rational or intellectual love, joy, sadness, and desire, feelings that encompass the love of God and intellectual pursuits and that, Descartes claims, might be found in the soul even if it was not joined to a body.[25] Descartes ties these feelings to an appreciation of values, of good and bad, making them the effect on the soul of the contemplation of values. Yet whether it is a matter of the rational feelings or of bodily passions, it is no solution to identify the self with a value judgment and consider the affective resonance of the judgment to be an essentially superfluous item. Whether the feeling gives rise to the judgment, or the judgment gives rise to the feeling, or the two are inextricably intertwined, there is as much (or as little) call to eliminate one as to eliminate the other. A value judgment does not of itself constitute a willing (or doing). Even if the value judgment itself, independently of any feeling, were sufficient to bring about the action in the case of 'rational feelings', the same could not be said of the general run of activities. The latter all involve an identification of the self with some mode of the felt body—fear or interest, impulse or regret, an identification that is impossible within Descartes's account of the self.

THE CORPOREALITY OF THE THINKING SELF

Descartes's failure to appreciate the importance of the tactile-kinesthetic body extends far beyond his belittling of the role of affectivity in motivation. It permeates his account of all other modes of thinking, both the operations of affirming, doubting, and denying, which Descartes classes as forms of willing, and the properly intellectual modes of thinking—perception, understanding, and imagination. Let us look briefly at both these modes.

On the everyday view, attitudes such as assent, denial, doubt, or conviction require affective involvement, which is to say the participation of the tactile-kinesthetic body. The accuracy of the view is readily borne out by perceptual judgments in concrete everyday situations. Let us suppose one hears a peculiar sort of noise from the window, and thinks, "a bird." One's attitude may take a number of forms. It may be one of conviction equivalent to "That *must* be a bird." It may be more detached, a mere entertaining of an hypothesis, somewhat equivalent to "Maybe it's a bird." Then again, it might be an attitude of doubt or even of strong disbelief. In each case, the same two words might be uttered, although with a quite different tone of voice. Now, let us ask in what consists the difference in attitude in the various cases? The difference in attitude is not reducible to a verbal difference. The words, "a bird," could well be the same in each case. One might attempt to equate the difference in attitude with the difference in the tone in which the words are uttered, but such an account of the matter would be doubly mistaken. First of all, if one is thinking to oneself, the thought could well involve a sound or auditory image quite neutral in tone, or again, the thought could well be nonverbal and involve instead a visual image of a bird of the sort discussed earlier in chapter 9. In such cases there is no difference in tone of voice. Rather the difference between conviction, doubt, and mere possibility is quite clearly a difference in affective state: conviction is assurance, readiness to act, while doubt is hesitation and absence of commitment. A particular affective state is present, and it is what motivates any sincere tone of voice indicating belief or disbelief. Secondly, even in cases where tone of voice is a factor, it should be noted that the practice of using a certain tone of voice to indicate conviction, another to indicate doubt, is not a purely arbitrary convention. An emphatic utterance is appropriate as an indication of conviction precisely because it reflects the speaker's assurance, determination, and willingness to act, as opposed to the hesitation engendered by uncertainty, or to the absence of involvement specific to the mere entertaining of an hypothesis. Assurance, hesitation, and deliberation are all states of the tactile-kinesthetic body. If the state of the body were removed from the experience, there would be no conviction, no doubt, no hypothesizing, and hence no reason to adopt one tone of voice rather than another. No less than the emotions considered earlier, an attitude of judgment clearly and necessarily involve a tactile-kinesthetic body.

It is true enough that the above reflections leave out essential elements of the situation: the awareness of the evidence provided by the type of sound heard, one's knowledge of sound production, of environments and their possible residents, and so on. The belief or doubt or lack of commitment are obviously, to some degree, a function of the available evidence. It would be a mistake, however, to attempt to construe belief and doubt as essentially intellectual operations of evidence-evaluation, operations accompanied by affective overtones which are, in fact, dispensable. Descartes is quite right to class belief and doubt, assertion and denial, as modes of willing. In the average case, the adoption of belief is not a mere seeing of what the evidence is, or a mere evaluating of the likelihood of truth. It goes beyond the evidence; it is the embracing of an envisaged state of affairs, a treating of that state of affairs as fact, and doing so moreover on the strength of evidence that falls short of being compelling. The same is true of denial; it is a rejection that goes beyond a mere evaluation of evidence. The evaluating intelligence has finished its work once the likelihood of truth of the envisaged state of affairs is established. A pure intelligence has no cause to assert or to deny. Only a being endowed with feeling has any reason to leap beyond the evidence, whether driven by the exigency of action in the world or by any of a multitude of desires, hopes, and preferences. Only a tactile-kinesthetic body may believe or disbelieve, affirm or deny.

Feeling is operative, of course, not merely in the leap from evaluation to belief; often it so intrudes as to skew the evaluation itself. In the general course of human activities, evidence is more or less wittingly misread or distorted rather than considered impartially; certain considerations are belittled or ignored while others are accorded attention or emphasis. The range of emotions, desires, and fears capable of collusion in the distortion of evidence is more or less coextensive with the range of possible human feelings. They are not countered, as Descartes would have it, by pure value judgments but by a variety of other factors: respect for the truth and impartiality, a sense of fairness, or desire to be seen as impartial, for example, all of which are modes of affectivity. Both the deceiver (a dislike) and the watchdog (qualms about being fair) are feelings and hence modes of the tactile-kinesthetic body.

The more properly intellectual modes of thinking—perceiving, reflecting, imagining—also involve the tactile-kinesthetic body in a variety of roles. Among the more important functions are those of providing the motive for thinking, and providing the means for thinking, whether the energy or the vehicle. Any concerted thinking, any enterprise of inquiry or exploration requires a motive, and a motive involves at some level the tactile-kinesthetic body. Curiosity, for instance, is not a property of an immaterial, incorporeal intellect. The openness and directedness of the eyes, the eagerness or impatience to see, to feel, or to understand; the attractiveness of the object of curiosity; the mild wonder or puzzlement; or awe—these are all essential aspects of the curiosity. In their absence there would be no curiosity. Clearly too, all are locatable as specific modifications of the tactile-kinesthetic body. The same is true of anticipated delight or the enjoyment adherent to the exercise of one's thinking faculties. It is still more clearly true of the ambition or pride, desperation, or insecurity that might be prompting the performance from the wings. A pure thinking being would in fact have no reason to bother to think. It might contemplate ideas flushed up by the passing show, but it would be incapable of initiating any concerted thoughtful activity.

Serious thinking also involves a mobilization of resources, again a patently bodily phenomenon. The activity of thoughtful reflection is aptly captured in Rodin's statue *The Thinker*, which features a man seated and immobile, his chin cupped in his hand, his gaze vacant, his brow heavily cast. Quite obviously the statue is a representation, not of a pure spirit or bodiless thinking being, but of a mindful body in a pose and state of tension typical of concentrated thinking. If thinking were an activity specific to an incorporeal spirit, then what would Rodin's statue be a statue of? If it does not represent thinking, the only remotely plausible alternative interpretation is that it represents the activity of striving or of trying to think: the fixed gaze, heavy brow, and clenched jaw are all part of an effort to clear extraneous matters from the field of attention and hence allow the pure intelligence to engage in its characteristic activity.

Now, this answer is correct insofar as it places striving in the body. Any striving one does, including the effort required for serious thought, is some configuration of tactile-kinesthetic feelings located in one's felt body. Indeed, the very notion of a mental effort is nonsensical, if 'mental' is taken to mean 'nonbodily'. The point is easily verified by producing the alleged mental effort and subjecting it to an introspective clear-eyed gaze. The mental effort turns out to be some complex of tensions in the felt body. Making an effort, including an effort to think, is something a body does. Now this fact creates serious problems for the claim that thinking is the activity of a pure spirit. Since the body makes the effort, if a pure spirit does the thinking, then the striving and the thinking are the work of two distinct subjects. Surely this cannot be the case. The English expression "to think hard" is suggestive in this regard, but let us forgo the aseptic joys of linguistic dissection for the compromising toil of introspective excavation. The proposal is that the ostensible physical tension of thinking is to be construed as a trying or striving which the body makes to clear the terrain for the thinking of the mind. Yet the construal is mistaken in that it dissociates the effort from the thinking and makes the effort a feature of a body which a pure spirit has at its disposal. Effort is improperly construed as something alien to the self, akin perhaps to a muscular cramp. Effort is one's own doing. It is the measure of one's engagement in a particular course of action. It is the measure of one's merit, one's tenacity, one's sincerity, one's devotion—or alternatively, of one's demerit, one's stubbornness, malice, or vindictiveness. To view one's self as a pure intellect dissociated from all striving is no more warranted than to view one's self as a striving body dissociated from all intelligence. One is both, which is to say, one cannot be an incorporeal thinking being.

Finally, a word should be said on the vehicle of thinking, the perceptual processes, images, and words, that provide the structural support for thinking. Activities of various sorts are indispensable constituents in many of the processes of thinking. Bodily activity is required for the actual manipulation of objects, for the imagined transformation of a given perceived situation, for the exercise of the imagination. For instance, bodily movement, particularly eye movement, is indispensable to the planning of moves in chess, not only when the position studied is that of real pieces on a board, but when the board is called up in imagination and fleshed out with remembered verbal instructions. Verbal thinking itself requires the generation of verbal symbols. In general, the latter arise only concomitantly with various fluctuations of tensions in the throat, mouth, and lips, a point on which one may convince oneself by attempting to think verbally without any contractions of the sort. The important point in the present context is the very need for words and images to serve as vehicles for an associated meaning, the fact that thinking independently of any sensuous vehicle whatsoever is apparently unfeasible.

In sum, the purely intellectual activity of thinking is not a possible pursuit apart from a corporeal being. In itself, a purely intellectual activity has neither the motive, nor the energy, nor the vehicle necessary for its own thinking activity. A human intelligence bereft of a body would be an intellectual cripple. Certain sights could be familiar, certain collections of sounds or squiggles could have meaning. Yet for such an intelligence there would be no reason to inquire or pursue any question or issue, no energy to do so, no vehicle to act as support for any thought. No remotely plausible case can be made for identifying oneself with this derelict intelligence.

THE INVALIDITY OF *COGITO, ERGO SUM*

Descartes is clearly mistaken in his notion of the self as an incorporeal thinking being. Descartes's main argument for separating thinking from bodily being is that one may clearly and distinctly conceive of oneself as a thinking being independently of any notion of body or spatial extension. This claim is simply untrue. The thinking being which loves or spurns, which believes or denies, which desires to understand and strives to reflect, is a tactile-kinesthetic body and cannot be clearly and distinctly conceived to be incorporeal. While it is true that each of the acts of this thinking being contains an indispensable incorporeal thinking element—intention, goal, perception, cognition, and meaning—it is also true that it contains an indispensable tactile-kinesthetic one.

It follows that Descartes's favorite and better-known argument from the indubitability of one's own existence must also be unsound. Descartes argues that since his own existence remains absolutely certain despite his calling into question the existence of everything corporeal, he cannot himself be something corporeal. Only Descartes's mistaken conception of himself allows the argument to appear to be sound. Given a more adequate notion of self, one's own existence is no longer immune to doubt, and there can be no argument from the indubitability of such existence.

It follows as a further corollary that Descartes's well-known dictum, "I think, therefore I am," must be fallacious. Since the subject who thinks is a tactual body, the existence of this subject is no more indubitable, no more worthy of belief, than the existence of any other sensuous element in the flux of experience. If an ostensibly present sheet of paper cannot be said to exist—on the grounds that it may be an illusion or one of the constituents in a dream—then by parity of reasoning, the tactual body cannot be said to exist since it may equally be an illusion or a constituent in a dream. The thinking in which Descartes is indubitably engaged might well be, along with Descartes himself, an integral part of some unreal complex or world. Indeed, when in the *First Meditation* Descartes with a Moore-like gesture deliberately stretches out his hand, is attentive to the feelings in it, but nevertheless concludes that he may be dreaming, he unwittingly ruins his future claim regarding the reality of his own thinking processes. The feelings involved in his thinking and doubting have no better claim to be real than have the feelings in the hand whose claim to reality Descartes rejects. Hence, the word 'I' in the premiss "I think" refers to a thinking self which may be unreal. Since the conclusion "I am" is based on the premiss, the word 'I' it contains consequently also refers to a possibly unreal self. As a result the argument, *Cogito, ergo sum*, is more properly stated as follows:

Premiss: I, possibly a hoax, am thinking.

Conclusion: Therefore, I, possibly a hoax, exist.

If one assumes, as Descartes does, that the verb 'to exist' means among other things 'not to be a hoax', then the conclusion does not follow, since thinking is an activity like any other in which possibly nonexistent entities may engage. Conversely, if the conclusion did follow, it would be self-contradictory. It would state something of the sort,

Conclusion: Therefore, I, who am perhaps a hoax, am not a hoax.

It must be concluded, then, that the self of the radical skeptic who observes the remnant of the world remaining in the flux of experience, cannot be Descartes's thinking being but rather the more robust, thinking tactile-kinesthetic body of the Sense Data Solipsist. It is an interesting question why Descartes should have gone so far astray in his view of the self, even if the answer can only be conjectured. In part, perhaps he was captivated by the stark purity of a particular, intellectually satisfying, ontological scheme of the world to which he found the budding science of his day to lead, a scheme featuring two dissimilar substances, each clearly and distinctly conceivable, body or pure extension where mechanism reigns, and thought, an immaterial and incorporeal realm of freedom and rationality. The confusedly perceived everyday world with its sensuous qualities, including feelings generally, is relegated to the status of a mere confused representation in the mind—a representation that, as such, is ultimately unreal. On a more general level, the devaluation of feeling might be attributed to a male tendency to emphasize achievement and vision. It is significant that when Descartes discusses the body, that body is almost invariably the visual body. When he entertains the hypothesis of a malicious demon, he considers himself as "not having hands or eyes, or flesh, or blood or senses,"[26] which is to say, as a visual body, since blood is hardly a notable feature of a tactile-kinesthetic body. When he asks what he formerly thought he was, he remarks, "Well, the first thought to come to mind was that I had a face, hands, arms and the whole mechanical structure of limbs which can be seen in a corpse, and which I called the body."[27] The body to spring to his mind is certainly not the tactile-kinesthetic one, and it is hardly surprising that he should find himself conceivable apart from such a mechanical visual structure. The propensity to overvalue the visual and to neglect the felt is one to which male philosophers are perhaps particularly prone. As noted earlier, Hume fails to remark the presence of the felt body in the flux of impressions, and Wittgenstein has his solipsist equate himself with the experience of seeing. It would be hazardous to claim the propensity unique to the three philosophers mentioned.

It is a somewhat curious fact that a considerable number of the claims Descartes makes regarding the pure thinking being also hold *mutatis mutandis* for its rival, the thinking tactile-kinesthetic body. Instead of the indubitability of the existence of the thinking being with regard to the felt body, we find what might be characterized as the indubitability of the *phenomenal nature of the self.* It is not simply a matter of the self being what it appears to be, for such is the case for any phenomenon qua phenomenon. The important point is that the self cannot turn out to be in fact something other than what it appears to be. Such is not the case for other phenomena. The sun which appears to be a plump, red disk on the horizon may be judged on a more sophisticated view to be neither plump nor red nor on the horizon. One's own self, in contrast, cannot be divorced from what it appears to be. The affection one feels, the effort one makes, the conviction one experiences, each contributes to define who and what one is. None can turn out to be illusory in the way in which the plump, red sun is illusory—that is, turn out to be really quite different in characteristics despite appearances to the contrary. One's feelings, for instance, cannot turn out to be the illusory appearance of some other feelings; one's feelings of affection or involvement or grief cannot turn out to be in fact really disdain or reluctance or amusement. The reason is simply that one identifies with them, just as one identifies with one's goals, one's preferences, one's actions, one's thoughts. Any allegedly real self hidden behind the appearances would have to be another person, an alien, and not the person one is. Thus, even if one's tactile-kinesthetic body should turn out not to be real (perhaps along with everything else that is material), that felt body would remain an inalienable constituent of oneself. In point of fact, one identifies with the felt body involved in dreams, a point that surfaced in the discussion of dreams in chapter 3, in that one identifies with the residual reverberations of feelings and convictions which carry over from the dream into one's waking state. The phenomenal nature of the self is the grain of truth contained in the alleged certainty of one's existence. For this reason it might be stated as a revised version of *Cogito, ergo sum:*

I feel such, therefore I am such.

I think such, therefore I am such.

I do such, therefore I am such.

This revised form of the *cogito* should not be construed as the claim that one's feelings and goals may not turn out to be illusory in some metaphorical sense of being unfounded or unworthwhile. Nor should it be construed to imply that one's own motives may not be hidden, that one may not be acting on an impulse the source of which is unelucidated for oneself. Even less should it be construed to mean that one is always certain of one's feelings, or thoughts, or meanings. One is no more immune to error in this regard than one is immune to error with respect to what one actually perceives. The phenomenal nature of the self is an ontological matter, not an epistemological one.

Another and perhaps less well-known claim Descartes makes of the thinking self is that it is better known than corporeal nature. One might in parallel fashion make the claim that the tactile-kinesthetic self is better known than the visual or material one. Both the visual self and the material one are constructions incorporating little of the actually perceived data; they are physiological and social selves much further removed epistemologically than one's directly accessible body of feeling.

Not least of all, there is the somewhat ironic fact of a tactile-kinesthetic equivalent to Descartes's claim that the thinking being may conceivably exist independently of a body. The felt body may conceivably exist without the visual body and hence conceivably be separate from it after death or in some out-of-body experience. This very conceivability is what makes possible the Sense Data Solipsist's material separation of sense fields.

SPONTANEITY AND FREE CHOICE

One's freedom to do or not to do is experienced in all one's activities, mundane or momentous, habitual or concerted, ponderously deliberate or erratically spontaneous. It is experienced constantly, as constantly as one's incessant activities. It is most obviously operative in one's attention which is free to wander at will, go here, go there, flit from some colored shape to an imagined one, from an odor to a sound, from one's felt mouth to one's felt foot. It is operative in one's bodily movements, one's flexings and stirrings. One is free to wiggle a hand, a foot, or head, to wag it or not, to shake it or not, to pivot or jerk or twist it, to do some, all, or none of the preceding, to permutate, rotate, agitate, vacillate, or vegetate. Any account of the tactile-kinesthetic body or, more generally, any account of sense fields, would be seriously incomplete if it failed to mention this familiar spontaneous activity.

A quite straightforward reading of the experience of voluntary activity would characterize such activity as uncompelled. A voluntary action is never necessitated. It may well be pressured or constrained by some drive or exigency or passion, just as it might also be unconstrained or free of all pressures. Yet while feelings dispose, incline, and perhaps impel, they do not compel. In some cases pressures may be so great as to preclude certain otherwise possible courses of action—as when one is paralyzed with fear, or so deafened by noise as to be unable to reflect clearly. In no case, however, may it be rightly claimed that an action is necessitated or compelled by the pressure or constraint so that not performing the action is no longer an option. Actions performed under duress are nevertheless uncompelled: they could have not been performed, albeit perhaps at an exorbitantly high price.

Voluntary actions might also be described somewhat accurately as spontaneous, a characterization that reflects the fact that they are for the most part initiated with a surge of energy. The notion of spontaneity captures in positive terms what the notion of being uncompelled presents negatively. Spontaneous action is uncompelled, and uncompelled action is spontaneous. Both are optional in that they can be or not be.

There are severe enough mundane limitations on possible courses of action. A fairly obvious limitation is the need for a projected course of action to be physically possible. One is not free to fly about like a bird. The options of a prisoner are relatively limited while those of a paralytic are more limited still. A further serious limitation resides in the fact that for an option to be an option for oneself, one must be aware that it is an option. One cannot catch the bus if one does not know it is running. An option that is unknown ceases to be an option, just as does an option that is overlooked or forgotten. Certain perceived limitations, for instance, a poor self-image, may have the same effect by leading one to reject certain possibilities out of hand.

In point of fact, there are remarkably few genuine psychological barriers, as opposed to physiological ones. In this regard, some of the more dramatic illustrations of freedom sketched by Sartre are illuminating in their ability to bring out the implicitly known fact that no inner necessity either compels action or replaces the need for oneself to act. One illustration Sartre uses features Dostoyevsky's gambler, a man who has sincerely resolved not to gamble but who in the presence of the gaming table discovers the inefficacy of past resolutions and past prohibitions; he must conjure up anew the disastrous consequences of his gambling, make resolutions afresh if he is to tear himself away from the table.[28] Another illustration features a stroller, both horrified and attracted by a precipice, and anguished to realize that no prospect of annihilation, no instinct of self-preservation, compels his retreat from the edge of the cliff, and from the danger of self-destruction.[29] Yet another illustration features a tortured man who, despite the intensity and length of the suffering endured, could always have endured a few seconds more before begging for mercy.[30] In these various cases, no past actions, no future disasters, no present desires, instincts, emotions, or pain suffice in themselves to compel the performance of a particular course of action. The past resolutions and promises, the threat of family hardships, the fear of death, or the pain of torture is never so great as to compel one action or preclude another. The agent is never overwhelmed, carried along by an affective tide and so relieved of the responsibility of being the one to act. In each case, if there is to be an action, at some point the agent must simply act. The lack of any internal necessity sufficient of itself to produce an action is precisely what makes the action free. Whatever the nature of the motivation, whatever its strength, it may be espoused or not, followed or not; the course of action toward which it urges may be undertaken or not. There is a gap between motive and action; not doing the action is an open possibility, so that even when one espouses the motive by acting from it, it remains true that one could have chosen not to act on it.

If radical skepticism cannot endorse Descartes's account of the self, it must endorse the account of free will espoused by Descartes. The latter derives in straightforward enough fashion from the everyday experience of freedom. The derivation comes out clearly enough in the *Meditations* where Descartes states what he means by the will:

> The will simply consists in our ability to do or not do something (that is, to affirm or deny, to pursue or avoid); or rather, it consists simply in the fact that when the intellect puts something forward for affirmation or denial or for pursuit or avoidance, our inclinations are such that we do not feel that we are determined by any external force.[31]

The experiential base of this conception is explicitly affirmed in his reply to Hobbes's objection that the freedom of the will is simply assumed by Descartes and not established; Descartes impatiently notes that we experience freedom in ourselves every day and that there is no experiential difference between what is free and what is voluntary.[32] Appeal to experience is, of course, also the ground for Descartes's observations that judgment requires an operation of the will and not merely of the intellect (in cases where the evidence falls short of being a clear and distinct perception of what is the case),[33] and for his earlier-noted claim that the ability of the will to direct one's attention elsewhere is what allows one to avoid doing what seems best.

Descartes apparently finds the freedom to do or not as one pleases to be indubitable. In the *Principles* he declares that one knows nothing more clearly than the fact of one's own freedom.[34] He goes on to point out that even during the enterprise of methodical doubt one experiences one's own freedom—and thus comes close to giving a parasitism argument to the effect that the will is operative in the suspension of judgment constitutive of doubt and hence is a necessary condition of the skeptical activity of doubting. Descartes's main point, however, is the claim that, despite the supposition of a demon creator bent on deception, the fact of one's free will remains indubitable. The claim is a very interesting one. Unfortunately, Descartes does not spell out the reasons that justify the claim to his mind and so answer the question of why, after all, the demon could not deceive oneself with regard to one's free will. We shall have to do this for him.

Descartes's reason for finding one's free will indubitable is quite probably that to his mind the existence of the self is indubitable, and the self is identical with a free spontaneity. Even when the Cartesian claim of the indubitability of the existence of the self is dropped, it remains the case that one's self is identical with one's feelings, with one's thoughts, as also with one's spontaneity. Such is the phenomenal nature of the self: one identifies with one's phenomenal self, and can only so identify. It follows that any other being which one might be alleged to be, a nonspontaneous or nonfree being, for instance, is one with which one cannot identify; one is already identical with the phenomenal self, a self which is in fact spontaneous and free.

The result of this state of affairs is that a denial that one is free is nonsensical. Any such denial presupposes that one is something identifiable otherwise than as the spontaneity one is. Thus, to say that one is free is not simply to say that one must consider oneself to be free, that one must do so in order to act, or to think (or whatever); it is to make a judgment based on an ostensive definition, or more correctly, a descriptive analysis of the perceptually present entity that 'I' designates.

For this reason it makes no sense to claim that despite appearances, one has in fact some other nature or to claim one is really something else—that one is in fact a noumenal self behind the appearances and giving rise to an observed phenomenal one, or that one is really the complex and ever-active neural network which constitutes a living brain. The statement that one is this other entity ceases to be a statement about oneself, the subject with whom the entity is claimed to be identical. The statement may superficially appear to make sense, chiefly to a third person talking about the self of someone else, and who identifies the self in question with a perceived body. Yet as a statement about oneself, it is literally nonsensical. By definition the self is one's own familiar spontaneity. To equate this self with something else, and not realize that the resulting statement is meaningless, one must forget what one means by 'I', or, what amounts to the same thing, one must cease to be aware of who one is.

The point is relevant to present purposes. The spontaneous and uncompelled self is the self of which one is actually aware. It is the perceiving self of the terrain of the radical skeptic, and hence, it must be the self of the Sense Data Solipsist. This admission has far-reaching implications for both the skeptical problems with which we are concerned. Since the more direct relationship is to the problem of the continued existence of what is perceived, it is to this problem that we shall now turn.

CHAPTER TWELVE

UNOBSERVED EXISTENCE

THE PROBLEM OF THE
JUSTIFICATION OF INDUCTION

Introspective probing finds the terrain of the radical skeptic or Sense Data Solipsist to be quite structured: an ever-present, three-dimensional tactile-kinesthetic body with its immediate contacts, a roughly two-dimensional visual field directionally located with respect to the tactual field, and an enveloping sea of sound. One of the two skeptical problems we are pursuing concerns the rational warrant there may be to think that there exist any unobserved occupants in the spatial prolongations of the various sense fields. Both Ephemerata and Sense Data Solipsism claim that unobserved space is empty. Neither denies that the space structuring what is actually seen extends in various directions beyond what is seen or that the three-dimensional space structuring the tactile-kinesthetic body extends in all directions. Indeed, such a denial would be senseless, since it is inconceivable that space should come to an abrupt halt.

The commonsense claim is that objects for the most part continue to exist when unperceived. This claim is in no better a position evidentially than it was in chapter 2 where we judged it to be on par with the solipsistic thesis. As we saw, continued unobserved existence is a necessary presupposition neither of temporal succession nor of the reidentification of objects over time, and an inalienable component neither of our conceptual scheme, nor of public language.

On the bright side, the commonsense claim is in no worse position than its solipsistic rival. It was suggested earlier that Ephemerata Solipsism might with some plausibility claim the merit of making the lesser ontological commitment, which lesser commitment provides a sufficient reason for preferring it to any of its competitors; while other hypotheses posit the existence of various unobserved entities, the solipsistic thesis alone makes no extravagant ontological claims beyond those warranted by the evidence. The prima facie aura of plausibility to this line of reasoning soon dissipates under phlegmatic scrutiny. There is no obvious reason to think the world is the sparsest possible, that it either must conform or does conform to some model with minimal ontology. As one might put the matter, there is no particular reason to think either that the creator had to scrimp on building materials or that his taste in ontological matters runs toward desert landscapes. Thus, while, as solipsism maintains, the evidence does not support any claim for the continued existence of the ostensibly present, neither apparently does it lend any degree of support to the solipsistic hypothesis of empty space.

It might be added that the hypothesis of the emptiness of unobserved regions of space is but one possible hypothesis regarding the occupancy of unobserved places, as is also the commonsense hypothesis that the places continue to be occupied with their previously observed occupants. In point of fact, there are an indefinitely great number of possible hypotheses of which the solipsistic and commonsense theses are but two. The unobserved space might be occupied by Russell's kangaroos,[1] or by any of an ever-expanding proliferation of imaginable species of fauna and flora. In the absence of any cogent reasons for preferring one hypothesis to another, the only reasonable position to take is to suspend judgment on the issue pending the presentation of evidence that supports one of the theses.

The problem of unobserved existence is a particular instance of a more general problem of induction, the problem of the warrant there is for inductive inferences generally from observed occurrent regularities to unobserved ones. Thus it will not be amiss to survey briefly some possible solutions to the general problem before attempting to meet the particular challenge posed by Ephemerata Solipsism. Clearly the inductive issue of concern to us is one of warrant and not one of certainty, much less of entailment. As one might put the matter, there are three gaps between evidence and claim, a logical gap, an epistemic gap, and a warrant gap, but only the third concerns us. Consider the case where all of the individuals, a_1, a_2,...a_i, each having the property A, are also perceived to have the property B. Clearly it does not logically follow from the observed regularity that a further observed individual, a_k, with property A will also have the property B. Quite conceivably a_k, as well as all further instances of a's, might be non-b's. The logical gap in the inductive leap from perceived instances to unperceived ones could be filled only by converting all unobserved instances into observed ones. The reasonable course to take with regard to a skeptic who is pointing out a logical possibility, is simply to acknowledge that the skeptic is right, and to pass on to more interesting matters. The epistemic gap coincides with the fact that there is no apparent reason to claim on the basis of the observed individuals that it is known that a_k will have the property B. Since the concept of knowledge is a hopelessly confused one in this context, it is best once again to pass on. Our only concern is the warrant gap between observation and extrapolation, the question of exactly what support, if any, the alleged evidence or sequence of observed a's provides for the claim that further unobserved a's are also b's.

Now, it is widely believed that the observed regularity does provide some manner of support for the claim that unobserved cases are similar—so widely believed, in fact, that the proposition would undoubtedly carry a public opinion poll by quasi-unanimous acclamation. Furthermore, the claim that probability increases with the number of confirming instances seems a plausible enough claim to make. It would be extremely surprising, to say the least, if the contrary should prove to be the case. Nevertheless, it cannot be simply claimed to be self-evident that a first instance lends weight to the generalization, and that the weight increases with the number of instances. A claim of self-evidence in this context can amount to no more than a promissory note of analysis. The initial impression of obviousness vanishes when it is asked how the instances do lend weight, or can lend weight, to a generalization encompassing unobserved instances. How exactly does an encounter with white birds make it probable that the unencountered ones are also white? In the absence of any elucidation of the modus operandi of the weight-lending, it becomes questionable that any weight is lent or is even there to be lent. The skeptic's point is precisely that there is no apparent connection. The conclusion drawn by the skeptic, reasonably enough, is that the observed instances allow nothing whatever to be said about the unobserved ones. The task, then, is to show how the alleged support does in fact qualify as support and consequently makes the extrapolation from observed to unobserved instances more probable or more likely to be true than other possible hypotheses on the subject.

Clearly, if the evidence does provide support for the generalization, it does not do so in virtue of any necessary connection between the two properties involved in the generalization. As Hume observes, what are actually perceived are particular instances of concomitance, not necessary connections—or as Ayer reformulates the matter, "There is no such thing as seeing that A *must* be attended by B, and this is not just because we lack the requisite power of vision but because there is nothing of this sort to be seen."[2]

It is equally vain, as has been frequently pointed out, to look for a bridge between the observed and the unobserved in some general principle, such as a Principle of the Uniformity of Nature, or one that would at least guarantee that "instances of which we have had no experience must resemble those of which we have had experience."[3] Any such empirical principle could itself only be justified by experience in conjunction with a judgment of probability of the kind the principle itself is intended to justify.

A more promising approach is to make use of random sampling and inverse probability theory. Within such theory it can be shown to follow from various truths acceptable to rational skeptics that if individuals are selected at random from a set, then when the subset of selected individuals is sufficiently large, the subset may be expected to reflect rather faithfully the composition of the original set. The expectation is reasonable given that the chances of drawing a subset with a composition similar to that of the set are much greater than the chances of drawing the same subset from a set with quite different composition. To illustrate the matter, let us suppose ten individuals are chosen at random from an unknown group, and all ten are found to be female. A number of conclusions may be drawn about the composition of the group. It is unlikely that it is half female, half male, since the chances of drawing ten females at random from such a group are roughly less than 1 in 2^{10}, which is less than one in one thousand. It is even less likely that the group is a quarter female, and three quarters male, since the chances of drawing ten females at random from such a group are less than one in a million. Hence, there is little likelihood that males predominate in the group. Even on the supposition that the proportion of males is as high as one quarter, the chances of drawing ten females at random is less than one in seventeen. For this reason, the random drawing provides strong support for the hypothesis that most members of the group are female. The example suggests that if observations may be assimilated to a sample randomly drawn from a set of possible observations, then perhaps some sort of rational justification may be given for an inductive extrapolation from observed to unobserved instances.

The difficulty is to find a method of random selection that demonstrably yields random samples in a way immune to skeptical challenge. The usual methods of random selection can be shown to yield random samples only on the basis of empirical generalizations that presuppose the validity of inductive procedures. A very simple example of such a method is that of throwing a die, a throwing in which each face has apparently an equal chance of being the face facing up when the die comes to rest. The claim that random selections are effectuated in accordance with such a procedure presupposes unfortunately a good deal of empirical knowledge regarding the behavior of dice—the knowledge that they do not always come to rest showing the number 6, that faces do not turn up in a particular order, and so on. If inductive procedures are to be justified on the basis of random samples, the claim of randomness cannot itself be founded on generalizations that presuppose the validity of inductive procedures: the proposed justification would presuppose what it attempts to establish. A direct appeal to sampling methods employed to obtain representative samples in public opinion surveys, for instance, would be equally unfruitful. Such methods assume a good deal of empirical information, particularly with regard to factors likely to be relevant or irrelevant, and consequently presuppose inductive procedures. What is required is a presuppositionless procedure for effectuating random selections, one that does not presuppose the truth of any empirical generalizations.

One of the many principles advocated by Michael Slote, the Strong Principle of Induction, would, if defendable, provide the warrant required for drawing conclusions regarding unobserved instances from observed ones. Slote's principle, SPI for short, states that if in a given sample all a's are b's, and if a "careful, rational, thorough examination" discovers no reason to think the sample "unfair or biased," then it is reasonable to conclude that all a's in the total population are b's.[4] Difficulties immediately arise when it is asked how a sample can be known to be unbiased on the basis of an absence of reasons for thinking it biased. Clearly, a sample could be known to be a faithful reflection (in miniature) of the total population if the total population was examined and its composition determined—but in this case, the sample would become superfluous as a basis for an inductive estimate of that composition. When a population and a sample drawn from it are not directly compared, the sample can only be known to be biased or unbiased on the basis of generalizations from past samplings. Such generalizations themselves presuppose inductive procedures for their validation and hence presuppose what the principle was to establish. On the other hand, if nothing is known as to what factors make for unfair samples (and in this sense there is no reason to think the sample unfair), then it is hardly reasonable to conclude that the sample is a fair one; it could equally well be extremely unfair for all that is known about the matter. If SPI is applicable to the situation, it can only presuppose what it was intended to establish.

Henry E. Kyburg, Jr., also proposes a view that again, if it were defendable, would provide us with the required procedure. Simplistically stated, Kyburg's claim is that ignorance is a sufficient condition for randomness; if nothing in one's rational body of knowledge excludes randomness, then the conclusion to be drawn is that randomness obtains; otherwise stated, an individual is a random member of A both with respect to belonging to B and relative to a rational body of knowledge, if there is nothing in that body of knowledge to warrant the placing of the individual in some other reference class. Kyburg esteems in particular that if (per impossible) nothing is known of an individual except that it is a member of a set of a's of which a certain proportion, B/A, are b's, it "seems axiomatic" to treat the individual as a randomly chosen one and assign a probability of B/A to the hypothesis that it is a b.[5] Kyburg's principle is in fact a generalized version of the Population Indifference Principle (PIP) advocated by Simon Blackburn. The latter states that if an individual belongs to one of two equal sets, and if nothing is known (or is rationally believed or should have been discovered) to place the individual in one set rather than the other, then it is reasonable to accord equal confidence to each of the two possibilities.[6] Blackburn's PIP is Kyburg's principle in the particular case where B/A is equal to 1/2.

Now Kyburg's claim is that in the cognitive situation where nothing is known of the individual, a_k, it is at least reasonable to maintain that the probability that a_k is a b is B/A. Yet such a claim hardly seems warranted. If nothing whatever is known to indicate in which subset, that of the b's or that of the non-b's, the individual is to be found, then the conclusion to be drawn would seem to be merely that nothing is known. The fact that the proportion of b's among the a's is some known proportion, or some unknown but presumed specific proportion, in no way helps to determine whether any particular individual is in one subset rather than in the other. The individuals may be in whatever subset they please provided only that the proper overall proportions are preserved. As a result, it is difficult to see how the proportion of b's to non-b's among a's could in itself allow anything to be said regarding the probability that a particular individual is in a particular subset. If it were known in addition that the individual is one chosen at random from the total set, then it could be claimed that the probability of this randomly chosen individual being a b is B/A. Such is not the case, unfortunately. Nothing further is known about the individual, and as a result, nothing further may be cogently said.

THE IRRATIONALITY OF EPHEMERATA SOLIPSISM

It should be clear that a strong case could be made against skepticism with the help of a 'presuppositionless randomizer', that is, of a method of selecting at random which does not presuppose truths open to skeptical rejection. Consider a moment the thesis of Ephemerata Solipsism that objects cease to exist when unobserved by the solipsist. Let us suppose that a randomizer of the required sort is available and is actually being used to choose the times of observation by the solipsist. Let us suppose further that the solipsist chooses at random an observation time of one second from among ten possible seconds of observation, observes a particular place in space during that one second, and finds it occupied by some object or other. The solipsistic thesis, as distinct from the commonsense one, is that the occupant ceases to exist when unobserved. Hence, according to the solipsistic thesis, the occupant exists only during the one second of observation and ceases to exist during the nine other seconds. Now, if that one second is chosen at random, the solipsistic thesis comes down to the claim that, in choosing one of the ten seconds at random, the solipsist simply happens to choose the particular second when the occupant is present, rather than one of the nine seconds when the occupant is absent. The chances of such a choice being made are only 1 in 10. Thus, the truth of the solipsistic thesis is conditional on the occurrence of a somewhat unlikely event: that the solipsist should choose at random the one observation time in ten during which the occupant is present.

This unlikelihood increases with more prolonged periods of observation. Let us suppose that the solipsist chooses two times of observation of one second each at random from a stretch of time of twenty seconds, and each time the occupant is observed to be present. According to the solipsistic thesis, the occupant is present for merely two seconds of the twenty. The chances of precisely these two seconds of presence being chosen at random from the possible times are 2/20 x 1/19, or 1 chance in 190. For a thirty-second period of time with three observations, the chances of the three times of presence being chosen (those dictated by the solipsistic thesis) are 1 in 4,060. For two such thirty-second periods the chances of the exact times of presence being picked are less than 1 chance in 16,000,000. With further observations these chances decrease rapidly in inverse astronomical proportions. Thus, if we suppose a situation in which the times of observation are being chosen by a method of random selection and an occupant is observed to be present each time, the solipsistic hypothesis that occupants exist only when the solipsist observes them, is one that can be true only on the assumption of an extremely unlikely occurrence. Indeed, to speak of such an occurrence as 'extremely unlikely' is an understatement. With repeated observation the chances of the solipsist randomly observing places at precisely all and only those times when they have occupants according to his theory become one in billions of billions of billions.

Thus, if a randomizer were available for the choice of observation times, a very strong case could be made against Ephemerata Solipsism and against Sense Data Solipsism to the extent that the latter endorses the former. At the very least, it might be argued that an hypothesis that postulates the occurrence of so unlikely an eventuality is highly unlikely to be true. In contrast, the commonsense hypothesis that an unobserved occupant continues to exist would postulate the occurrence of no such unlikely event, nor indeed of any event even mildly unlikely. If the occupant is present at all times, the chances of choosing at random only instances in which the occupant is present are one chance in one. The occurrence of such an event could hardly be characterized as unlikely. In these circumstances, the commonsense hypothesis would have to be esteemed vastly superior to the solipsistic one. It would perhaps not be vastly superior to all other possible hypotheses regarding occupancy absences, although on the matter of its superiority much could be said. However, it would no longer have the solipsistic hypothesis as a serious competitor.

To be carried to a successful conclusion, the sampling argument requires a presuppositionless method of random selection capable of resisting the probes of a rational skeptic. The candidates considered above either presuppose certain empirical generalizations vulnerable to skeptical questioning or they make the questionable assumption that ignorance guarantees randomness. Since knowledge and ignorance together seem to exhaust the available possibilities, it is tempting to conclude at this point that we have reached a dead end, and that our problem has no solution.

Yet this pessimistic assessment of the situation clearly cannot be the last word on the matter. When thoughtfully considered in some concrete context, the thesis that objects cease to exist when one is unaware of them has a clear, resounding ring of absurdity to it. Why the feeling of absurdity? The question is not an idle one. If it were really the case that there is no reason to think that things continue to exist unobserved, then it would be merely a matter of dropping a perhaps cherished but unwarranted belief from one's repertory of beliefs. One has undoubtedly already done this sort of thing many times in the past, perhaps with regard to a childhood belief in the existence of ghosts in abandoned houses and monsters going bump in the night, perhaps with regard to the causal efficacy of wish-making or of marriage-ceremonies. In none of these cases did the denial appear preposterous. What is the source of the feeling of absurdity in the present case? If the skeptical thesis were in fact impossible to refute, it would leave us with a different and scarcely less perplexing problem on our hands, that of explaining why the thesis should appear so extravagant.

Let us attempt a different approach to the problem. What is it in a concrete situation that makes the existence of unobserved objects apparently so certain? To concretize matters, let us take a coffee mug sitting half-full beside me. What reasons have I for being so certain that the coffee remains quietly in my coffee mug when I look away? The immediate response is that the coffee is there each time I look—but what does this circumstance show? What guarantee does the observed presence give me that the presence continues when I am not looking? What reason have I to reject the solipsistic hypothesis that the coffee is not there continually, but only at those times when I look?

The answer that springs immediately to mind is that the state of affairs proposed by the solipsist would be too much of a coincidence. The important point here is that my looking is to all appearances quite fortuitous. There is no particular reason for my looking when I do; I just happen to look. My past glancings at the cup, I want to say, could have taken place at quite different times from the ones at which they did in fact take place; I looked at certain times and not at others, but I could very well have done otherwise. My freedom to look or not performs the function of a randomizer in the selection of the times of observation. The consequent fortuitousness in the observation times makes it highly implausible that the coffee should be present in the cup, as the solipsist claims, at all the very times and only the very times when I happen to look.

On reflection, however, a few reservations might begin to sprout. Perhaps the claim of the fortuitousness of the observations is too hastily made. Were not my past glances merely marginally monitored and incidental accompaniments of certain other events—the taking of sips of coffee, themselves triggered by vague promptings, idle spells, and so on? Surely it is presumptuous for me to maintain that I could very well have done otherwise when I was scarcely aware of what I was doing. Yet, while I may feel there is some obscurity in the situation involving half-attentive glances, I also feel there was nevertheless some degree of fortuitousness involved. The source of this latter conviction is my awareness of my capability with regard to casting fortuitous glances, a capability that carries over to some degree into less monitored activity. In any event, if claims free of reservations are required, they may be obtained readily enough through a more concerted exploitation of my talent for fortuitous glances.

Consider the following scenario and the sample of observations it yields. Making the mug and the issue of its contents the center of my undivided attention, I then set about to lie in wait, as it were, throwing sidelong and unexpected glances at the inside of the mug. Here, the unexpected glance is not one my mug does not expect; it is one I do not expect. It is a glance cast on impulse, and one that I do not know I am going to give until I give it. The glance is obviously not a totally unexpected event: I am, after all, the one to cast the glance and not a mere spectator of its occurrence; I do so voluntarily and with a clear awareness of what I am doing. I do so, however, in an unpremeditated way, without prior planning as to when the glance will be cast. Casting the glance is an option that is open, a possibility of which I am aware at each passing moment. At any particular time, it is something I can do as well as not do. As a result, when I look, it is also the case that I could also have not looked. When I do not look, it is also the case that I could have looked.

The faculty being marshalled here and put to service in the gathering of samples is the ability to choose: the freedom to do or not to do. Such freedom has an awareness of options as its necessary condition. It would be naive to claim that one is always free and to reason that, because one is free, whatever one does one could also have not done and, hence, that any of one's observations could also have not been. A possibility of which one is unaware ceases ipso facto to be a genuine possibility. Catching the boat is not an option for someone who does not know there is a boat. A person who knows but forgets is in the same situation. The person cannot choose and so may be accused of thoughtlessness, stupidity, of having suspiciously convenient memory lapses, of not caring enough, or of criminal negligence, but not of making the wrong choice. By the same token, one can choose to glance or not to glance at a coffee mug only if one is actually aware of the options. If one is absorbed in a book, the options disappear. If any moment is to be a possible moment of observation, there must be a clear awareness of the possibility of observing. For somewhat analogous reasons, there should be no prior decision as to when one will look or not look. Any decision is revokable, certainly, but it must nevertheless be revoked before the rejected options can reappear as genuine options. An absence of premeditation allows each passing moment to be a time when two possible options are present. Choosing on impulse and with undivided attention thus allows each passing moment to be one in which one can either do or not do, observe or not observe. The possibility of choosing to do or not to do might be termed *optional possibility* to distinguish it from other types of possibility.

If the skeptical claim that things cease to exist when unobserved is felt to be absurd, it is because one is vaguely aware that one's observations are representative of the situation that obtains. What is observed to occupy a particular location is a faithful reflection of what in fact occupies the location, and is so in virtue of the fact that the observations could easily have been made at other times. The observations were optional, that is, made with a degree of randomness, a degree varying with the circumstances and difficult to assess, but operative nevertheless in the choice of the times of observation.

Randomness is at its maximum when the two options of observing and not observing are kept continually in mind, and the choice to observe is simply made on impulse without premeditation. In these circumstances, each time considered is a possible time of observation, and can be elected or rejected as an observation time. Consequently, each time may be said to have a chance of being selected, where 'chance' is being used in a loose nonarithmetical sense. It is true of any time actually chosen that it could have not been chosen; it is true of any unchosen time that it could have been chosen. A selection made in this way maximizes randomness and hence yields optimum evidence against the solipsistic claim that objects cease to exist when unperceived.

The demonstration of the unlikelihood of the solipsistic claim is one that may be performed even by the more radical Sense Data Solipsist, the tactile-kinesthetic Cartesian subject immersed in a flux of ephemeral sensuous phenomena. Since for such a solipsist any claim of coordination between the visual and tactual fields is unwarranted, the observations are best performed tactually. Let us suppose that the test is being run with regard to the felt presence of an obstacle encountered by a foot when the leg is kicked forward from a bent position. A number of kicks may be given at quasi-randomly chosen times, that is, they may be given on impulse as the times of possible kicks flow by and are either elected or rejected. Let us suppose too that each kick encounters a resistance at a particular spot in tactual space relative to the tactile-kinesthetic body. Now what conclusions are warranted by these quasi-random observations?

The solipsistic hypothesis is the claim that objects exist only when perceived. In the present context, it entails the claim that a resistance is present at a particular point in tactile space only when it is felt to be there, i.e., only when it is encountered by a kick. Hence, the solipsistic hypothesis entails the claim that the times of the kicks coincide exactly with the times of the presence of the resistance. Since the times of the kicks are quasi-random, and could well have been other than what they were, in fact, the solipsistic hypothesis states what is in fact an extraordinary coincidence: the randomly chosen times of the kicks happen to be just those times when the resistance exists. The solipsistic thesis is eminently implausible. It is incredible that one should randomly happen to choose all those and only those times when the resistance exists. If the degree of implausibility is found insufficient, it may be augmented simply with a prolongation of the period of the kinetic sampling operation—or to vary matters, by an extension of the operation to other places in tactual space, through movements perhaps of arms, head, and torso. In all cases, the solipsistic thesis entails the implausible claim that the random observations happen to take place at only those times when obstacles exist. On the given evidence, no rational thinker could accept as true a thesis that entails such an unlikely state of affairs. The undeterred skeptic who seriously advocates the thesis of the nonexistence of what is unperceived, violates a fundamental rational principle, that of correlating likelihood of truth with strength of supporting evidence.

The present demonstration, unlike that sketched earlier, cannot be arithmetical. When times are chosen in quasi-random fashion, it cannot be meaningfully claimed that each time has a numerically equal chance of being chosen. Of each time it may be said that it could be chosen, just as it may be said that it could fail to be chosen. This situation gives each time 'a chance' of being chosen, but 'a chance' only in the sense that the particular time could be chosen. It could not be rightly claimed, for instance, if in a sixty-second period of time, four observations each of one second were made, that the chance of any particular time being chosen was one in fifteen. Each time could have been chosen, but there are no grounds for claiming that each has an equal chance with any of the others. In point of fact, there is no clear basis for assigning any numerical value whatever to the relevant chances. The irrationality of the thesis of Ephemerata Solipsism is no less evident, however, for anyone disposed to rational consideration of the evidence.

OPTIONAL POSSIBILITY AND RATIONAL BELIEF

The awareness of one's own freedom or of one's optional possibilities is at the root of the judgment that skeptical theses which deny continued existence are absurd and that objects in all likelihood continue to exist when unobserved. The judgment is based directly upon the awareness that the selection of observations is quasi-random in that different times of observation might very well have been chosen. Such awareness need not be verbal, any more than need be the correlated judgments of plausibility and implausibility. Indeed, from earliest infancy an awareness of the ability to do or not to do may well play a key role in nonverbal rational thinking. The random kicks of the prenatal infant are perhaps on this view not mindless releases of energy but more aptly seen as successful precursors of Dr. Johnson's celebrated attempt to refute Berkeley by kicking a stone. Be this as it may, the freedom to do or not to do is, beyond doubt, a natural talent possessed by all budding human beings and not one acquired only through proper grooming. Undoubtedly too, it is a faculty to some degree operative in any awareness of the world, and one to which appeal may be made to randomize observations of the world. The implicit awareness that the observations could easily have taken place at other times endows the observations with a degree of representativity, and warrants extrapolation from the regularities they exhibit. If each randomly made observation encounters the same phenomenon, there is no need of mathematics, much less language, to harbor the warranted suspicion that the phenomenon is also there unobserved at intervening times.

Although the demonstration remains to be traced out in detail, there can be little doubt that a randomizing spontaneity is an indispensable ally in the long epistemological trek from disparate sensuous fields with ephemeral occupants to the full-fledged material objects of the commonsense world. In this perspective, free will must be judged to be essential to any rational belief in the world of common sense. Without it, there is no warrant for assimilating actual observations to random samples and hence no warrant for thinking the observations indicative of what is not observed. To the extent that rational beliefs are based on random observations of the sort, they are pancultural; they are not relative to a particular scheme for classifying colors or shapes, nor to a particular system of oppositions, nor to metaphysical preferences for permanence over transience, or the contrary, nor to scientific paradigms. The ability to do or not do is part of a common human heritage, available to all species members independently of cultural grooming. It is hard at work well before the full impact of the latter on perceptual classification, and it provides the rudimentary structure common to all world views.

It is ironic that although Descartes in the *Meditations* speaks of free will as the faculty through which humans most resemble the divinity,[7] he quite fails to notice the crucial role played by free will in the epistemological construction of a nonsolipsistic world. The role played by freedom did not go entirely unnoticed by Husserl, although he failed to clarify in what that role consisted. Consider his following remark:

> Furthermore, the perception has horizons made up of other possibilities of perception, as perceptions that we *could* have, if we *actively directed* the course of perception otherwise: if, for example, we turned our eyes that way instead of this, or if we were to step forward or to one side, and so forth.... Everywhere in this connection an "I can and do, but I can also do otherwise than I am doing" plays its part.[8]

Such observations could easily be expanded into the above antisolipsistic line of reasoning.

It is perhaps worth opening a parenthesis in this connection to note that random behavior does not appear to be peculiar to humans to the exclusion of other living species. The biologist Jay Boyd Best in an article on behavior systems remarks that it is futile to attempt to guess what a rabbit will do when surprised at night in the glare of headlights; the behavior appears random in that the rabbit will sometimes not move at all, while at other times it will run directly away, or double-back, or run toward the car.[9] Best's assessment of the phenomenon is that such erratic behavior is perhaps the wisest policy for a stupid animal to follow. He finds worthy of reflection a curious conclusion reached by John von Neumann and O. Morgenstein in their theory of games: when an opponent is outclassed in all respects, a random strategy yielding unpredictable behavior is the only strategic policy that gives that opponent a nonzero probability of avoiding defeat. Natural selection might well have good cause to work in favor of randomized behavior. It could clearly have such cause whether it is a matter of a creature's behavior in the face of danger, or of observation geared toward warranted generalizations. In both cases, randomized behavior has distinct survival value. The point suggests that despite a wide divergence in their aims and methodology, Rationalized Epistemology and Naturalized Epistemology are not necessarily without points of contact.

On a straightforward reading of the experience of freedom, it follows that future actions may not be known. This ignorance with regard to future actions is not imputable to some limitation of one's cognitive abilities or sources of information. It springs from the fact that there is nothing to know, no present fact of the matter. If it is a real possibility that one may now do such and such a particular action or not do it, then it is not now true that one will do that particular possible action, any more than it is now true that one will not do it. This, of course, is the position advocated by Aristotle when he declares, "It is therefore plain that it is not of necessity that everything is or takes place; but in some instances there are real alternatives, in which case the affirmation is no more true and no more false than the denial."[10] Optional possibility implies absence of present truth.

The implication suggests a convenient means of defining optional possibility. Possibility is generally definable in terms of consistency. For instance, a logical possibility may be defined as anything consistent with the set of logical truths. An epistemic possibility is definable as anything consistent with the set of known truths. While an optional possibility might also be defined in this way, it is also definable as any proposition such that neither it nor its negation is now true. The Law of Excluded Middle (either P or not P) nevertheless holds between the two. For instance, it is an optional possibility that I shall get up tomorrow because it is now true neither that I shall get up nor that I shall not get up. Nevertheless, either I shall get up, or I shall not get up—and furthermore, it is now true that I shall either get up, or not get up.

That such a concept is not self-contradictory is seen from the fact that it is readily formalized. An appropriate system for the task is the Lewis System, S5, formed as suggested by Gödel by adding a primitive necessity operator, and suitable axioms and rules to the logic of *Principia Mathematica*.[11] The basic statements are tensed as in English. The primitive necessity operator may be replaced by a truth operator, T, since the intended interpretation of the operator is 'now true'. The intended interpretation of 'TP' becomes 'It is now true that P'. The logical equivalence of P and TP does not hold since it does not hold for the necessity operator in the system S5. The failure of equivalence reflects the fact that where P is a statement about someone's possible future action, P and TP are not in general logically equivalent. They are equivalent when the action is a present or past action, or when P concerns some natural phenomenon determined by causal laws, or when P is a logical truth. Distinctions of the sort could be drawn within the system if desired. Optional possibility, represented with a diamond, might be defined in the system as follows:

◊ P = $_{df}$ ~TP & ~T~P

On this definition, to say that P is optionally possible is to say that neither P nor its negation is now true. It is a theorem of the system that if P is optionally possible then so is its negation. Since it is a rule of the system that any logical truth is now true, it follows that logical truths are not optional possibilities. The Law of Excluded Middle holds between any statement of a future action and its negation. On the other hand, it is not a logical truth that either P is now true or that the negation of P is now true. All this is as it should be. The system thus captures the essential difference between statements about future actions and other statements indeterminate in truth value and for which Excluded Middle does not hold, e.g., vacuous statements.

On this interpretation of the system, the characteristic S5 axiom becomes the benign truth that if P is untrue now, then it is true now that P is untrue now. In A. Prior's proposed system S5 (with possibility interpreted as "true at some time," and necessity as "true at all times"[12]), the characteristic S5 axiom yields the contentious proposition that if it is true tomorrow that an agent will do a certain action tomorrow then it is true now that the agent will do that action tomorrow. The concept of an open future requires rather a system in which future truth does not imply present truth. The statement of a future action is one that is neither true nor false at present but that becomes true or false at the relevant time in the future.

FLESHING OUT THE SOLIPSISTIC WORLD

The conclusions warranted by random observations of tactual resistances are sufficient in themselves to refute Ephemerata Solipsism. They likewise refute certain tenets of the more radical Sense Data Solipsism. The latter doctrine denies the existence of causal regularities and other minds, in addition to the continued existence of what is actually perceived, and to boot throws in heavy doubts about the reality of the scraps of the world actually perceived. Consequently, we still have a long way to go in the epistemological construction of the commonsense world from the materials admitted by Sense Data Solipsism. The constructed world at this point encompasses no more than the areas of which random tactile-kinesthetic observations were made—and those areas only for the period of time of observation. Let us look very briefly at the sort of thing that might be done to expand horizons.

In the world of the Sense Data Solipsist the visual and tactile-kinesthetic fields form two contemporaneous worlds, directionally located with respect to each other but otherwise unrelated. The coordination of the two fields with each other presents a serious epistemological problem. Events in the visual field are situated in a certain direction relative to certain other contemporaneous events in the tactile-kinesthetic body. Yet as noted in the last section of chapter 10, such a relationship is nevertheless insufficient to lock the two fields together in one material system of common objects. On the face of things, there is no compelling reason whatever to claim that some visual phenomenon, such as a brightly colored surface, must belong together in the same material world with some tactual one, such as a hard smooth surface, as aspects of one and the same object. Indeed, qualitatively the two surfaces are strikingly different. In addition, the spatial systems of the two fields are structurally dissimilar in that one has but a shallow horizonal depth while the other is frankly three-dimensional. In these circumstances, what grounds are there to claim that the two fields form one spatiotemporal system in which particular visual items and particular tactual ones are so related as to be aspects of one object?

The answer is not immediately obvious. In point of fact, it may be recalled that a Sense Data Solipsist is a skeptic who, among other things, finds no grounds for any such claims and consequently declares sense fields to form distinct systems rather like concomitantly running moving pictures. The solipsist's conclusion is not wildly unreasonable. Certainly the color and sheen of the visual aspect of a particular object have nothing to tie them to the hardness and smoothness of its tactual counterpart. Similarly, the size of the visual aspect has nothing to relate it specifically to the size of its tactual counterpart. Only certain geometrical features such as shape, relative proportions, angles, and slopes, provide some grounds for coupling the two. An absence of corners and angles might provide a basis for associating a visual globe with a tactual one, just as an elongated shape with one pointed end and one capped end might be found to be the common ground of both a visual roof nail and a tactual one. Yet, the similarity is in itself a weak basis for an identification of the two items as aspects of one object. Similarities in geometrical features are rough-hewn rather than individually tailored, and they lose a great deal in translation from one sense medium to the other. This circumstance gives the similarities, at best, a status akin to vague circumstantial evidence. If it is assumed at the outset that to each visual object there is correlated a tactual one, then the similarities provide fair grounds for the correlation of a particular visual object with a particular tactual one, provided of course, that the objects considered are not too similar in structure to other objects in the field. The assumption that each object is so correlated is a sizeable one, however, and on the most flattering of estimates fails to qualify as overwhelmingly or even modestly weighty.

The randomizing capability of spontaneity, or one's freedom to do or not do, provides what is needed to remedy the awkward evidential situation. Consider the particular case of the identification of one's visual left hand and tactile-kinesthetic left hand as aspects of a single material object. The two share the same general orientation with respect to the tactile-kinesthetic body and, more importantly, bear certain structural similarities to each other: a somewhat flat main body, four aligned appendages, and a fifth opposable one. The structural similarity is such that if one were instructed to determine which item in one's tactual field is most similar in structure to one's visual left hand, undoubtedly on reflection one would come up with one's felt left hand, perhaps after some hesitation over one's tactual right hand. There is, of course, as matters stand, no particular reason to claim that one's visual left hand should be paired with anything tactual at all. Now, the situation changes dramatically as soon as one begins to move the left hand. To each movement of the tactual hand there corresponds a movement of the visual hand. These movements are structurally similar, a bending corresponding to a bending, a twist to a twist. They are also temporally correlated in that one is initiated when the other is, and stops when the other stops. The crucial feature of the movements is that they are initiated and stopped at will. No matter when one chooses to make a movement, both move. The choice of times of movement may be made quite at random, and yet the two movements continue to coincide. It is highly implausible that the coinciding should be coincidence. A visual movement of a certain kind occurs when and only when there is a tactual movement of a certain kind, and a tactual movement when and only when there is a visual one—whence the conclusion that, if there had been a movement of one, there would also have been a movement of the other. This intimate kinetic mirroring of the two similar structures is sufficient ground for considering the two to be one material object, or hand. More exactly, to be one hand rather than two disparate hands in two respective sensuous fields is to stand in precisely such an intimate mirroring relationship.

The linking of one's visual body to one's tactile-kinesthetic body is a necessary first giant step toward the coordination of the visual field with the tactile-kinesthetic field to form one material world. The similarities in shape and general topology between some visual object and its tactual counterpart are insufficient by themselves to warrant a correlation of the two. Once the visual hand is correlated with its tactual counterpart, there are good grounds for correlating objects, for instance, a visually grasped object and a contemporaneously grasped tactual one of similar topology. More generally, the correlation of the visual and tactual bodies furnishes good grounds for correlating any aspects of the environment contiguous to correlated parts of the body. The correlation of the two aspects of the one material body is at the same time a giant step toward the infusion of a genuine third dimension into the variously colored shapes in the quasi-flat complex of the visual field. One's felt body is already the three-dimensional center round which quasi-permanent visual panoramas may be found arrayed, somewhat in the manner of the auditory field. With the coordination of one's visual and tactile-kinesthetic bodies, one's experience of oneself as three-dimensional may serve as a model on which to interpret the visual observation of a progression of two-dimensional faces as the observation of the sides of a three-dimensional object.

The range of one's possible random observations is in one respect very limited at any particular time: one cannot now examine objects ten feet away, for instance, or visually examine hidden objects. Nevertheless, there exists the possibility of approaching objects too far away to be immediately felt, or of removing obstacles blocking the view of other objects. Possibilities of the sort bring the objects to some ill-defined degree within the range of possible observation and hence subject to generalizations extending in some degree to unobserved behavior. For instance, one's observations of one's car over the past twenty-four hours undoubtedly fail to qualify as a set of observations chosen at random from among the set of possible observations. Nevertheless, there remains some element of randomness to them in virtue of the spontaneity in one's activity, the fact that the activity could readily have been made different from what it actually was. As a result, one's actual observations are to some degree representative of the total set of possible observations of the car during a longer period of time and hence provide warrant for the permanence of the car over that period of time.

The causal regularities that were the object of Hume's solicitude find themselves in essentially the same evidential situation as that of continued existence. Observations of regular behavior of a certain sort may also be quasi random and, as such, provide warrant for the claim that the same behavior is manifested in cases of possible observation where no observation takes place in fact. The swinging of a pendulum observed at randomly chosen times to accompany the constant clicking heard may with warrant be judged to accompany likewise the constant clicking at times when the pendulum is not observed. A ball that is deformed whenever squeezed may with warrant be judged deformable, which is to say, that it would have changed shape if it had been squeezed. A dropped object goes invariably to the floor whenever observed, a fact that provides warrant for the belief that it does so whether observed or not. Random observations that find regularities in behavior thus give warrant for the judgment that such regularities hold at times when the possibility of observation is declined. Once again, in the reaching of a warranted judgment a key role is played by the randomizer, the free ability to do or not to do.

In actual practice the testimony of other people is one of the principal sources of information regarding objects outside the range of one's possible observations. Rational scruples, including those of the rational skeptic, raise the question of the warrant one has for lending credence to such testimony. The warrant that may be provided is obtained on precisely the same sort of grounds as in everyday life when warrant is felt to be needed. The fact that a person gives accurate testimony in cases where the testimony is checked for accuracy is itself plausible ground for thinking the person's reports to be accurate in cases where the accuracy is not checked, provided the cases of accurate testimony may reasonably be considered representative of the cases as a whole. In cases where random observations provide good reason to think that a certain object continues to exist unobserved during a given period of time, then the concurring testimony of another person as to the continued existence of the object is itself evidence of the reliability of the person's testimony. This evidence, in turn, provides support of sorts for the reliability of the person's testimony regarding phenomena that fall outside the field of one's own observations. Obviously, the greater the volume of testimony, the stronger the support in general.

THE REFUTATION OF MONOPSYCHE SOLIPSISM

After these very sketchy remarks on what is necessarily a considerably more complex process, let us turn now to one of our more official concerns, the answer that might be given to Monopsyche Solipsism. It will perhaps be recalled that the latter is a form of Ephemerata Solipsism that focuses uniquely on the denial of the existence of private experiences had by people other than the solipsist. Such solipsism might be more briefly defined as the denial of the existence of other minds, provided some vigilance is exercised regarding the ambiguities and confusing connotations of the word 'mind'. The Monopsyche Solipsist has no reason to deny the existence of the contents of minds where these are public items perceived by other persons—a blue sky, loud noise, or rough surface. Such items are all observable by the solipsist. The solipsistic denial applies only to private items perceived by others, items such as pains and emotions, strivings and desires, imaginings and dreams. The latter items coincide substantially with the tactile-kinesthetic bodies of others. Thus, to a considerable degree, a belief in other minds is a belief in the existence of other bodies, tactile-kinesthetic ones, that is. This belief is the one for which we must now attempt to uncover the warrant.

The belief that others do have private experiences would seem rationally defendable on either of two independent sets of considerations, one based on the testimony of others, the other on analogical reasoning. Before considering either, let us take a brief look at the epistemological situation in which one finds oneself with regard to one's own private tactile-kinesthetic feelings.

It is fairly obvious that what one may actually feel is confined very closely to the limits of one's own body. A particular solid outside one's body may be imagined to have internal feelings similar in nature to one's own internal feelings, but there is no known way in which one might manage to actually feel those feelings at the location where they putatively are or gain access to the location so as to determine whether there are feelings there or not. On the other side of the picture, much of what one feels is apparently never actually perceived by others. Strong support for this view is derivable from interactions with other people in as much as they often act as if they are ignorant of what takes place under one's skin and, furthermore, readily testify that they are in fact unaware of what is going on there. The discovery of the privacy of one's feelings, undoubtedly made by each of us at some early point in one's long epistemological trek, must have come as somewhat of a surprise. Taken at face value, feelings are as much a part of the world as anything else. The pain in one's foot, considered on its own merits, is as much a part of the world as the tight, pinching, black leather, or the warm, damp, pink solid that is the object of one's subsequent solicitude. It is odd that it should be private while the rest of the scene apparently is not, and particularly odd that the affective-kinesthetic features internal to one's body should be private while the tactile features of objects in the tactile-kinesthetic world are public.

It must be borne in mind that the epistemological terrain on which we are at present is but a few steps away from that of the Sense Data Solipsist. When philosophers, or people in science generally, state that tactile feelings of objects are equally private, they have moved to a more advanced epistemological level, that of the Representational Theory. This is the level at which may arise the skeptical question of whether another person sees the same colors as oneself, whether the person perhaps actually sees green where one sees red. Such questions cannot even sensibly arise in the present epistemological context. The softness of the leaves of a geranium, no less than the scarlet of its flowers or its distinctive odor, is out in the world along with the other person who looks at the flower, touches its leaves, inhales its ambient odor. To say that any of these items are private, one must ipso facto posit a private representation that has no spatial location in the world. On the other hand, to discover that feelings are private is not to take them out of the world; it is to leave them where they are felt to be, there within one's body, and to say simply that other people have no direct access to them.

Now, one of the pillars of a rational belief in the felt bodies of others is the testimony of these others as to what they are feeling. The warrant for thinking such testimony to be reliable is the same as the warrant one has for testimony with regard to anything of which one is actually unaware. This warrant may be considerable and, as such, provides solid support to the claim that other people have feelings. In addition, the testimony of other people with regard to their feelings may be very detailed and may resemble the description one would be tempted to give of one's own feelings in situations where the feelings are dynamically and structurally similar to the visible behavior of the other person. When the suggestiveness of the similar descriptions is combined with the judged reliability of the other person's testimony, the reasonable assessment is that the other person does indeed have feelings.

It might be noted that there is certainly as much warrant to accept another person's testimony regarding that person's private feelings as there is warrant to accept that person's testimony that one's own feelings are private—although the point cannnot be put to incisive use in the present context since a Monopsyche Solipsist need not attempt to show the privacy of the solipsist's own feelings. More germane is a point regarding the opposing claim that the Monopsyche Solipsist is constrained to make, that since people have no feelings, when they speak about their feelings they must be lying. Such a claim divides up testimony in an arbitrary way, some truthful, some deceitful with no particular reason for the line being drawn where the solipsist draws it rather than elsewhere. In addition, the tactile-kinesthetic field of other persons is also divided in any arbitrary way without reason. It is granted that people see, hear, and touch in a common world of public sights, sounds, and surfaces. Thus, allegedly other people are aware tactilely—say, of the smoothness, warmth, hardness, and weight of a particular body—but they are not aware affectively. Such a division of the tactile-kinesthetic world may look feasible when considered on the verbal level, but considered concretely, it is fraught with perplexing difficulty. An answer must be given to the question of which particular feelings in the tactile-kinesthetic complex are the ones to be deleted and which the ones to be admitted. Any perception of the roughness or warmth of an object involves feelings within the body, i.e., below the skin level of fingers, and so on. Any perception of hardness or resistance involves kinesthetic feelings also located within the body. How can the claim that another person has no feelings be squared with the fact of such perception? It is simply not plausible to claim that the person has kinesthetic feelings when the latter are occasioned by some exterior object but not when they are integral to some tactile-kinesthetic turmoil or self-initiated activity.

A second and independent argument in support of the thesis of the existence of other minds (or rather tactile-kinesthetic bodies) is based on an analogical line of reasoning. The analogical argument in favor of the existence of other minds is generally made to run roughly as follows: since certain forms of behavior on one's own part are invariably accompanied by certain feelings, it is reasonable to think that like behavior on the part of another person is accompanied by similar feelings for the other person. The use of an analogical argument of the sort to resolve the problem of the existence of other minds has over the years suffered considerable variation in popularity ratings. The successive waves of unpopularity coincide roughly with the successive waves of unpopularity that have broken over foundationalism, but they are undoubtedly also due to a large extent to multiple misunderstandings, in part, as to the strength of the case that may be made. As we shall see, the case is a very impressive one indeed.

A first point well worth noting is that analogical reasoning is not simply a form of reasoning trotted out by foundationalists to rid themselves of the problem of other minds. It is a form of reasoning frequently used in everyday circumstances with regard to the experiences, feelings, and thought processes of other people. When one stops to wonder what another person is feeling, the conclusions reached are based on the person's observed behavior in conjunction with one's knowledge of what one's own feelings are (or were) when behaving in like fashion. It is also used in any attempt to gain a deeper understanding of some creature quite different from oneself, any attempt to grasp, as it were, what it must be like to be that other creature. Analogical reasoning is indispensable to answering on a concrete level what it must be like to be a member of the opposite sex, for instance, or what it must be like to be a person steeped in some very foreign culture, or again, what it must be like to be a sheep (with the front half of one's head an olfactory kaleidoscope, one's curiosity limited to the issue of edibility, and one's predominant emotion terror). There is no essential difference between analogical reasoning in these cases and the analogical reasoning in the philosophical argument that purports to provide warrant for a belief in the existence of other minds. The point here is not that an argument from analogy is necessarily warranted but that it cannot with consistency be considered valid in everyday cases and invalid in the philosophical one.

In favor of the analogical argument for the existence of other minds, there are several important points to be made. First of all, the structure of the argument is often misconceived. To a large extent, the misconception itself springs from misconceptions about the nature of affective states. A feeling is wrongly likened to a sensation suspended through some mind-stuff—like cream in a cup of coffee. As noted in chapter 11, an emotion or mood or feeling is a whole mode of being of the tactile-kinesthetic body—a certain set of modifications and disturbances integrated into a general bodily dynamics. To be in pain is to have a torso tense and rigid, breath constricted, members agitated, mouth agape, and eyes closed or fixed. To be elated is to be light, buoyant, energetic, and flowing. Without its specific dynamics, the feeling would not be the feeling it is. It is precisely in virtue of the fact that each type of emotion or affective state has its specific dynamics that a piece of music may, through its dynamics, be heard as joyful, mournful, troubled, serene, agitated, or furious. In the same way, one recognizes in another person the dynamics of some particular type of feeling, although in this case with finer attunement since there are added structural details—peculiarities regarding stance, facial features, and limb postures. Having experienced feelings oneself, one recognizes the like dynamics, attitudes, and expressions in the visible body of the other person. One recognizes, for instance, not simply an erratic flow of constricted energy but a twisted mouth, bulging eyes, contracted hands, poised arms, heaving torso—a wealth of familiar tactile-kinesthetic details of the feeling.

The analogical argument has consequently a quite different structure from the one it is often attributed. It is not a matter of first having noted a constant conjunction of certain otherwise extraneous phenomena in one's own case, a conjunction of certain feelings and certain behaviors. The feelings in one's own case are feelings of felt behavior, which behavior is structurally and dynamically congruent with what one observes of one's visual behavior. The correlation of one's visual and tactile-kinesthetic bodies is the indispensable first step in the epistemological construction of a material world, one that receives continual corroboration but also could be made more extensive at any time should one choose to look into the matter. Thus, the correlation of felt behavior to visual behavior in one's own case is not an extraneous one of mere concomitance.

The analogical link between oneself and others is based on the observed structural and dynamic congruence of felt and visible behavior. It is claimed that just as one's own visible behavior is congruent with one's observed felt behavior, so another person has felt behavior congruent with observed visible behavior. The inferred fourth term in the relationship is a congruent tactual structure and, to repeat, not some extraneous element conjoined by mere concomitance. If the other person has any felt behavior at all, it should be congruent with the person's visible behavior. Otherwise, the person's felt behavior would be an independent tactile-kinesthetic performance, connected extraneously to the rest of the material world—like a tactual television set in the cosmic room; it would not be part of the mechanism, and like the beetle in Wittgenstein's box, it could as well be anything or nothing at all. It is not simply that the tactual performance would not in fact be connected with the rest of the world; rather, as a matter of principle, it could not be so integrated, since the dynamics of the different felt behavior would be incompatible with the dynamics of the public body, observed visually, auditorily and tactually. It is a mechanical impossibility, for instance, for a person to be laughing on the inside, grieving on the outside (even admitting that with appropriate mechanical constraints it is possible to achieve an approximation to such a state of affairs). To claim that another person has inner behavior different from outer behavior is to posit two conflicting behaviors instead of the two congruent behaviors experienced in one's own case.

Now, of course the Monopsyche Solipsist posits the absence of any inner feeling at all, and not the existence of an inner dynamics incompatible with the observed outer dynamics, simultaneously visual, auditory, and tactile. The situation is essentially the same, however. What is being claimed is that the intimate mirroring relationship experienced in one's own case is unique and is not to be found in the case of any other person. It is a very implausible claim that such a state of affairs should exist within the structured world, or world view reached with the admission of unobserved permanencies and regularities. In an orderly world, given the regularities in behavior and similarities between one's own behavior and that of others, it is highly anomalous that there should be such a huge difference in nature between oneself and others. To appreciate the enormity of the difference postulated by Monopsyche Solipsism, one need but review the role played by feelings, motives, strivings, convictions, tactual-visual coordination, and tactual three-dimensionality in the case of one's own activity and learning or, better still, simply the intimate relationship of the tactual-kinesthetic body to the person one is. Monopsyche Solipsism denies that any of this exists for others and claims that other people are empty shells whose antics unroll unsupported by these intimate inner workings. It is simply not plausible that such a state of affairs should exist in an apparently otherwise orderly enough universe. When the weight of this conclusion is conjoined with the above-mentioned considerations regarding the testimony of others, the evidence for the existence of other minds is nothing less than overwhelming.

CHAPTER THIRTEEN

THE REALITY OF THE WORLD

THE PROBLEM OF REALITY

An illusion may be roughly characterized as something that appears to be in a particular place but is not really there. The most striking feature of the average illusion is its apparent reality, the fact that it seems as real as anything nonillusory. The plump, red sun on the horizon, the bent spoon in a glass, the pastel shade of distant hills, the comet's tail on a moving object such as the glow of twirling embers in the dark, a disparity in the felt temperature of water for two hands—each is ostensibly embedded in a spatiotemporal system of real, everyday objects; each considered solely on its own merits has as much right as anything real to claim first-class citizenship in the world. How then does the item manage to get itself demoted in ontological status?

As a first approximation, it can be pointed out that in any everyday situation in which a perceived item is judged to be illusory, it is because some second different item has been accorded the occupancy of the spot apparently occupied by the illusory one at the time in question. Two items never occupy the same spot at the same time. The observation immediately raises the issue of the warrant there is to deny occupancy of the one spot to two distinct items. The only plausible justification there can be is the fact that two items are never observed to do so—that two hands, for instance, are never observed to pass through each other and hence never to occupy the same place. Insofar as a judgment of illusoriness presupposes one of single occupancy of places, it depends on a prior inductive inference.

With regard to the nature of the preemptive claim to occupancy, either of two very similar types of situation may arise. In one case the dictates of causal regularity put some posited item in the place of the ostensible occupant of that place. The ostensible occupant is said both to be the posited item and the way the posited item appears to be (e.g., both the sun and merely the way the sun looks at sunset), to be it and not to be it, but this perplexing state of affairs is not our present concern. The ostensible occupant is displaced (de jure, and not de facto) because it fails to conform to the general norms for characteristic behavior of things of its kind. Phenomena that are well-behaved and obey the established laws do not have their reality revoked. The behavioral norms are, of course, extrapolations from observed regularities. In a world view devoid of empirical generalizations and causal regularities, the most common reason for positing illusions would be lacking.

In a second type of situation two or more items are perceived in different perceptions to be in what is one and the same particular spot. The conflict may be between two reports—for instance, the smoky blue hill reported by a distant observer may conflict with the deep green foliage reported by an observer nearby. It may be a conflict between the perception of different sense modalities—a thumb seen double may be felt as single. It may be one registered by the same sense modality—water cold to a hand may be warm to a foot, or an item of one color to one eye may look another color to a second eye. In all these cases, there is conflict only in virtue of prior empirical generalizations, ones that provide warrant for the testimony of other observers, that dictate the coordination of two different sense fields into a single spatial system, or that place two different sense qualities of the same sense in a single location. Whatever the specifics of the illusion considered, it exists as an illusion only in a world view that encompasses regularities posited on the basis of inductive generalizations. In a world view devoid of such regularities, as for instance, that of the Sense Data Solipsist, the everyday distinction between illusion and reality would collapse.

An analogous situation holds with regard to dreams. As has been frequently observed, dream experience differs in a variety of ways from waking experience (and even the waking experience of an illusion). The key criterion for everyday dreamhood is nevertheless the inability of a sequence of events to fit into the larger spatiotemporal sequence of events in the waking world at the requisite point in such a way as to conserve the causal regularities of the system. If on waking, one invariably found that all available evidence and testimony pointed to the conclusion that there had occurred events in the waking world similar to the dreamt events, the very notion of a dream would have no application. Any individuals in the dream could reasonably be considered to be the waking individuals in person, at worst badly perceived. In the everyday world, causal regularities are incompatible with the incorporation of the dream events into the sequence of waking events. In addition, the evidence of these same regularities and permanencies bolstered by the testimony of others give good reason to posit the continuation of the waking world at the very time when the dream takes place—thus, making the dream doubly unwelcome as a constituent of the waking world. Warranted belief in the regularities clearly comes from inductive procedures. Consequently, in a world view resulting from a methodology that fails to countenance induction, a view such as Sense Data Solipsism, there would be no apparent reason not to consider dream events simply as peculiar stretches of reality. In the growth of a world view, illusions and dreams can only enter the picture after the positing of regularities and unperceived existence.

On the topic of causal regularities, it is perhaps interesting to note that the crucial feature of dreams is their lack of shared regularities, not simply with the waking world but with each other. Consider what one's attitude toward one's dreams would be if they were sequentially connected to each other so that the end situation in one carried over into the beginning of the next, and each time one awakened from a bad dream, one would be certain to find the same horrible situation again on falling back to sleep. The circumstance that one's dreams are private or subjective experiences unrelated to the real world would carry considerably less weight in one's attitude toward them. Or again, what would one's attitude toward dreams be if they were part of a larger dream incorporating the contemporaneous dreams of other dreamers—or better still, if they were part of a global dream world so related to the waking world that anyone who fell asleep in one world awoke into the other. Dreams could not be easily dismissed on the grounds that they were mere dreams.

Unreal World Solipsism attempts to draw a real/unreal distinction in a way both different from and additional to the way in which the distinction is usually drawn. As shown earlier, whether it is a matter of Phantasmata, Oneirata, Non-Sensa, or Demoniac Solipsism, the conceptual innovation is neither unfeasible nor nonsensical nor self-contradictory. The possibility envisaged with the distinction introduced is that the whole of the observed world is unreal, whether illusionlike, dreamlike, or sensationlike. The move takes obvious advantage of the fact that there is no criterion for reality as such, and that in normal circumstances what counts as real is simply what is not eliminated as unreal.

The various solipsistic theses make little or no attempt to justify their new real/unreal distinction by an appeal to fact. For the most part, the theses are merely theoretically possible hypotheses consistent with but unsupported by empirical data. This latter point is significant in that it marks a distinct difference between the real/unreal distinction as usually drawn and the distinction as drawn by the solipsist. In everyday contexts, the distinction is required (presumably) to accommodate empirical data, and the generalizations to which the data gives rise. In the case of the skeptic's distinction, no such claim can be made. For instance, the thesis that the observed world is a solipsistic dream is obviously based neither on the actual testimony of others, nor on the discovered failure of the world to fit into the requisite spot in some experienced waking world. A putative testimony-laden waking world enters the picture only hypothetically, which is to say, as that part of the solipsistic account that purports to explain how it is possible in principle to have evidence that the observed world is a dream. Furthermore, the thesis does not and need not attempt to gain plausibility by an appeal to the actual occurrence of dreams. If actual instances are to serve any useful purpose with regard to skeptical theses, it can only be the practical one of making the very notion of a dream a credible one. In a world in which no one ever dreamed, the notion of a dream might well be rejected outright as an absurdity.

Factual support is likewise absent for the other solipsistic theses. Impressive collections of instances of illusions are sometimes trotted out in an attempt to strengthen the skeptical case, but, as noted earlier, this cannot be validly done. An appeal to instances is useful to the skeptic, not to show that illusions exist, but rather to show that they are possible. An assertion of illusoriness inevitably involves a denial of the obvious, a denial that some particular entity is there where it ostensibly is. In view of the paradoxicality of the phenomenon, a passing acquaintance with illusions could be of invaluable assistance in lessening the strain placed on credibility.

In similar fashion, the Non-Sensa Solipsist's thesis—that the world is some private product of unknown origin—is undoubtedly made more credible by the prior spadework done by the Representational Theory of Perception. Our Cartesian solipsistic theses could in principle, however, dispense with the services rendered by any appeals to fact. They outline theoretical possibilities, make no assumption of the occurrence of like phenomena, and do not appeal to an accepted body of knowledge. The same cannot be said, of course, of all skeptical hypotheses. When Descartes's wily demon is replaced in present literature by a playful scientist manipulating electrodes on a brain in a vat, clearly some attempt is being made to make the skeptical thesis more plausible. In Descartes's day when witches were still burned, demons exorcized, and God was generally held to take a more active part in human affairs, the hypothesis of the wily demon was undoubtedly found to have an aura of plausibility it has since lost.

The issue raised by these Cartesian solipsistic hypotheses is that of the grounds or warrant, if any, that may be uncovered in support of the thesis of the reality of the everyday world as opposed to logically possible solipsistic theses which question or deny that reality. As we saw earlier, Cartesian solipsistic theses can be dismissed neither for failure to be meaningful nor for failure to cohere, nor for contradicting their own presuppositions. A rational foundationalist enterprise will presumably appeal to certain rational principles to achieve the desired end. What might these principles be?

To simplify matters, we might limit discussion for the moment to the question of illusions. The task is to uncover what grounds there may be for thinking that some particular thing such as a coffee mug, or better still, the visible face of a coffee mug, is really where it appears to be rather than only apparently there in the manner of a mirage.

One principle that would meet the requisite condition and furthermore do so in the most direct way possible is one on the order of what H. H. Price calls "The Principle of Confirmability." The latter, as originally formulated by Price, states roughly that the existence of a visual or tactual sense datum is prima facie evidence of existence or evidence that warrants a presumption of the existence of a material thing which really has the properties ostensibly displayed.[1] Such a principle would be excellent for our purposes since, as one might put the matter, if appearance warrants a presumption of reality, then it is reasonable to presume reality in the absence of further evidence and, ipso facto, reasonable to presume there is no illusion. Unfortunately, as Price points out, the principle is not self-evident and hence not immune to skeptical attack. Price's answer to the difficulty is to alter the nature of the principle slightly, to appeal to actual perceptual procedures and to claim that it is "indubitable" or "evident" that with increasing experience and specification of properties, "the existence of the material thing (merely accepted at first) becomes *more and more probable*"[2] While such a proposed solution echoes more or less actual practice with regard to everyday illusions, it is obviously quite unsatisfactory. As matters stand, it amounts to no more than a declaration of confidence. It remains to be shown that the alleged principle is not based on mere faith and does indeed incorporate truth-unearthing procedures.

Roderick M. Chisholm proposes a principle very similar to Price's principle in its original version. As Chisholm would have it, it is *reasonable* for a perceiver to believe (more reasonable than not) that there is something having a particular property, if the perceiver believes that he perceives something to have that property.[3] Yet if the reasonableness in question is prima facie reasonableness, the principle seems unfortunately no more self-evident than the one discarded by Price. Just as it is not clear why the sight of what is apparently the face of a coffee mug should be presumption-warranting evidence for the existence of a coffee mug, so it is no clearer why the sight of a mug should make it more reasonable than not that the mug is real rather than unreal in some way. To be convinced of this, one need only avail oneself of a mug of the appropriate sort, place it squarely in front of oneself, then on taking a hard look at it, ask oneself in virtue of what one may venture to claim that the ostensible presence of the mug makes what is seen more likely to be a real mug than an illusion. The mere mug-shaped presence suggests nothing whatever in the way of likelihood, whether a 95 percent likelihood of the mug really being there, a 66 percent likelihood, or one greater than 50 percent. It affords no grounds at all for any judgment of likelihood whatever, whether for or against the presence of a real mug. The matter rests there. To insist that in the given situation there are epistemic grounds for the claim that the ostensible presence is more likely than not to be real is to read one's own convictions into the evidence.

In a further variation on the above theme with regard to simple statements of reality, Pollock speaks of prima facie justified beliefs as beliefs that do not require evidence or reasons to be adduced in their favor, evidence and reasons being relevant only if they count against the belief.[4] Chisholm makes a very similar claim running as follows: "Our perceptual principles are instances of the more general truth: 'It is reasonable to trust the senses until one has positive reason for distrusting them.'"[5] Unfortunately, both positions (like the commonsense position of chapter 2) are based ultimately on an undefended claim to knowledge. Pollock argues in favor of there being a logical connection of some sort between statements of the kind "*x* looks red" and "*x* is red," on the grounds that otherwise the relation would be contingent and knowledge impossible. Yet such an approach simply begs the question at issue. One might analogously argue that there must be some logical connection between the existence of God and the existence of the world, since otherwise the relation would be contingent and knowledge of God impossible. What is required is elucidation of the connection, supposing elucidation possible.

UNREALITY AND PARSIMONY

In an attempt to find rational support for the commonsense view that the average well-behaved perceptual item is not a personal illusion, let us explore the distinction between simple perceptual judgments of appearance and the corresponding perceptual judgments of reality. It is fairly obvious that generally some sort of perceptual judgment of appearance is warranted by a perceived presence, although it is less obvious how that judgment might be expressed in the object-oriented medium of everyday language so as to provoke a minimum of protest. To keep matters from being obscured with verbal connotations, let us simply represent the judgment of appearance as P_0. We shall then let the corresponding judgment of reality be represented as P. The question is how the judgments, P_0 and P, are related or how they differ. Let us anchor the discussion in a concrete case such as the earlier-mentioned instance of a perceived coffee mug. It was argued that the ostensible presence of the visual mug-shaped form—the sense datum—seems insufficient to provide warrant for the claim that a real mug-shaped form is in fact present, or more likely present than not. In what way then does the judgment of the presence of a real mug-shaped form differ from the judgment of the presence of an apparent mug-shaped form?

The claim that a mug is real might in everyday circumstances, of course, mean any number of different things depending upon the context of utterance. In the present circumstances, the aim of the claim is to counter solipsistic doubts regarding the nonillusoriness of ostensible characteristics of the mug, and consequently, it does not concern everyday matters, such as the nature of the material of the putative mug or the question of whether anything could be encountered by passing a hand through the location of the thing. Nor does the claim impinge upon the Ephemerata Solipsist's question of whether the partial object has a far side. The claim concerns only the reality of what is actually seen, that is, the reality of the shining intricate shape with various color patterns and reflections on it. Thus, in the present context, to claim that the mug face is real is neither to specify any additional properties (unperceived ones), nor to predict the observation of certain phenomena in specific contextually assumed circumstances. The real mug and the apparent mug have exactly the same characteristics and properties, namely, those of the perceived mug. The two are in principle indistinguishable. They differ only in the fact that the apparent mug may be an illusion. Consequently, to claim that the apparent mug face is a real mug face is simply to claim that it is really there where it ostensibly is, as opposed to being only apparently there. This in turn is to say only that there is not something else (possibly empty space) really there where the mug apparently is. It is not to attribute any further properties to the mug; it is only to deny that there are any further occupants (or possibly empty space) in the place ostensibly occupied by the face of the mug.

Generalizing from the case of the mug, we may say then that in the context of a skeptical challenge, a judgment of reality, P, is simply a judgment of appearance, P_0, coupled with a denial that there is anything else (including empty space) really there but not actually perceived at the relevant site.

Now, a Phantasmata Solipsist states that in addition to the appearance there is some other item not actually perceived but really there at the relevant site. We might let 'G_i' stand for the complex property of having an illusion such that there is really something else at the relevant location. If we let 's' stand for the solipsist, so that '$G_i s$' stands for 'the solipsist is having an illusion', then a simplified version of the Phantasmata Solipsist's thesis, Q, might be represented as follows:

$$Q = P_0 \ \& \ G_i s \quad (1)$$

The rival commonsense position which denies that there is such a property may be represented as follows, where '~' means 'it is not the case that':

$$P = P_0 \ \& \ {\sim}G_i s \quad (2)$$

On a little reflection it soon becomes apparent that the 'Q' of statement No. 1 might equally well represent the thesis of some form of Cartesian solipsism other than Phantasmata Solipsism. With appropriate changes in the meanings of the predicate 'G' and the sentence 'P_0', the statement Q may be made to enunciate a simplified version of Oneirata Solipsism, for instance, in which 'P_0' represents some statement of a judgment of appearance, while 'G_i' represents the property of being asleep and dreaming in some further world at the time in question. With analogous changes, Q might be made to represent statements by the Demoniac or Non-Sensa Solipsist. With corresponding changes in No. 2, 'P' might be made to represent the rival commonsense position in each case.

The general commonsense position is to deny all the solipsistic theses, and hence to deny a conjunction of properties. This general position may also be easily represented in terms of the above conventions. To simplify matters, we might assume that there is a number, n, of possible forms of solipsism and hence a number, n, of possible relevant properties. Letting 'v' stand for 'or', the commonsense judgment of reality may then be represented as follows:

$$P = P_0 \ \& \ \sim(G_1s \ v \ G_2s \ v...v \ G_ns) \quad (2')$$

Now, the above account of the relative positions of solipsism and common sense puts a serious damper on any attempt to promote the solipsistic position on alleged ontological grounds. It was suggested earlier that a thesis of Phantasmata or Oneirata Solipsism could plausibly be supported with the claim that it involves a lesser ontological commitment than does its commonsense rival—that insofar as it postulates only the demi-reality of an illusion or a dream, it makes a more modest assertion. However, a claim of the sort soon pales under scrutiny. To claim that a thing is unreal is in fact to posit some further reality over and above the ostensible phenomenon, and this, on rudimentary arithmetical considerations, seems to entail greater ontological commitment. Oneirata Solipsism, for instance, posits a further world in addition to the presently experienced spatiotemporal flow of events, a world in which presumably the solipsist is asleep and might awaken at some time to confirm the thesis that the present world is but a dream. Clearly, such solipsism espouses an ontology less frugal than that consisting of the single world of the commonsense view.

Similar, although obviously less telling, evaluations may be made of the ontologies of our other solipsists who question the reality of the world. A judgment of unreality implies some further reality with respect to which the unreal is unreal: an actual occupant, a waking world, a deceiver, a cause of experiences. Without this further reality the allegedly unreal world is not unreal. Hence, any solipsist dealing in unreality necessarily espouses a more complex ontology than that of common sense. Indeed, even in the most favorable of circumstances in which this further reality is mere empty space, the ontological situation proposed is more complex and can hardly be convincingly held to involve a lesser commitment.

It may be found tempting to attempt to turn the point against the solipsist and to maintain that the solipsistic thesis is to be rejected on the grounds of its greater ontological commitment. Paul Moser does just this in a recent work, and gives as a reason against skeptical scenarios the fact that they posit "gratuitous items" and as a reason for preferring the commonsense position the fact that this position, "as ordinarily understood, does not posit items unidentifiable in experience."[6] Yet in point of fact, the question of ontological commitment is in no clear way germane to the present issue. This is because there is no clear relationship between ontological economy (or simplicity) and likelihood of truth. Why, one might ask, should the most frugal (or the least complex) model of the world be the most faithful model? There is no apparent reason why the world should be sparse and simple rather than profuse and complex; consequently, a thesis that portrays the world as sparse does not necessarily give the most accurate of possible pictures. Ontological economy may well have practical and even aesthetic value, but its connection with truth, if any, remains to be established.

Yet surely, it may be protested, this conclusion fails to recognize the clear superiority of the commonsense position. The latter proposes what might be characterized as a 'rational ontology', where 'rational' is given some sense opposed to 'gratuitous' or 'unfounded'. In contrast to its skeptical rivals, so the protest might go, it makes no unfounded or gratuitous claims regarding the furniture of the universe; it neither assumes nor postulates entities of any sort, real or unreal, entities for which there is no evidence, or more seriously, no reason. Consequently, it may claim in its favor that it confines its ontological census-taking to items acknowledged by all its competitors to be present in the world. Further, it may claim against its competitors that their less scrupulous theses, through their arbitrary conferments of unreality, implicitly if not explicitly make totally gratuitous additions to ontology. As one might put the matter more succinctly, only the commonsense position keeps ontology commensurate with evidence.

While the reasoning clearly has power to persuade, it embodies a certain confusion of ontological and epistemological considerations. What is being discussed is the epistemological status of the various views, and how well the views are commensurate with the evidence. As may be seen from statement No. 2 or No. 2', each of which renders the commonsense view in the present context, the commonsense position is more than a mere ontological endorsement; it is a conjunction in which one conjunct is a denial. The question is whether the denial is supported by the evidence. Clearly, it would seem not to be. It is true enough, on the other hand, that the solipsistic position involves an existential assertion which goes beyond what is actually observed (as is shown by No. 1), and which appears to be gratuitous. Yet surely on the matter of gratuitous claims it is irrelevant whether the claim is an assertion or a denial. The one no less than the other is a claim. Thus, while the commonsense position enjoys an advantage of some sort with regard to ontological commitment, it cannot be said to be rationally superior to its solipsistic competitors with regard to epistemological commitment. The latter, not the former, is what skepticism is all about.

For similar reasons, no fruitful use can be made of a further strategm or notion that might well surface at this point as a possible solution to our apparent impasse. The solipsist's gratuitous fabrications would seem, on the face of things, to be in flagrant violation of the *Principle of Parsimony*, or of Ockham's Razor, as it is termed. The prospects appear exciting at first peek, since the principle is a methodological one having to do with economy in explanatory postulates rather than in ontological commitment. As stated by Ockham, it runs as follows: *"Frustra fit per plura quod potest fieri per pauciora,"*[7] which is to say, "It is pointless to do with more what can be done with less." An apparently similar principle is implicitly used by Aristotle (for instance, in his rejection of the hypothesis of pores as "superfluous" or "futile" in the explanation of property modification[8]). On this interpretation the principle involved might be stated as the claim that it is pointless to adopt the conjunction of H_1 and H_2 as an explanation of some phenomenon, if H_1 alone offers as good an explanation. In these circumstances H_2 is superfluous, and consequently, its adoption is unnecessary. This is not to say that H_2 is false, but only that its incorporation in the explanation is gratuitous or without reason.

Now the various solipsistic theses that affirm the unreality of what is observed all clearly make some further posit which seems quite superfluous to the explanation of the observed data. Surely then, one might argue, the extravagance of their claims in some way contravenes the Principle of Parsimony. Unfortunately, however, this line of reasoning does not favor the commonsense hypothesis. Let us suppose for the sake of argument that the various hypotheses, solipsistic and commonsense, may be assimilated to explanations. In this case, the observed apparent presence is explained by the hypothesis of actual presence, just as it is also explained by the hypothesis of illusory presence. Yet the situation with regard to these hypotheses cannot be construed as a case that conforms to the above-mentioned model of the two explanatory hypotheses, H_1 on one hand, and H_1 and H_2 on the other. The only plausible interpretation of the situation favorable to common sense is one whereby H_1 states the fact of the apparent presence, and H_2 affirms the existence of some further real entity so that the further entity is a gratuitous addition in explaining the apparent presence. Unfortunately, by parity of reasoning, a similar argument could be used against the hypothesis of real presence proposed by common sense, since the latter hypothesis adds a denial. In both cases, it could be argued that the apparent presence is sufficient to explain the phenomenon (the apparent presence) and that any further addition is superfluous.

This conclusion fails to support even our original assumption that the commonsense and solipsistic hypotheses are explanations. In point of fact, it is doubtful that real presence (or illusory presence) constitutes any explanation at all of apparent presence. One can claim that the apparent presence of something is explained by the real presence of that thing only if one is thinking in terms of a causal chain of events terminating in the perceiving of the object. Such causal chains figure in the Representational Theory of Perception. On the epistemological level at which we are considering the matter, there is no question of a causal chain; there is only the apparent thing—ostensibly there, remaining exactly what it is, and no more or less ostensibly there whether judged to be real or unreal. The hypothesis of a real presence is not an explanation of the ostensible presence, since the hypothesis is simply a statement of that ostensible presence conjoined with the denial of any further reality. Putting the matter in terms of statement No. 2 above, since P is equivalent to a conjunction of P_0 with $\sim G_i$s, strictly speaking, P cannot be an explanation of P_0: the conjoined denial does not explain P_0, and P_0 itself could be considered an explanation of P_0 only as a degenerate case. For analogous reasons, of course, the hypothesis of an illusory presence does not explain the apparent presence. As may be seen from statement No. 1, it merely conjoins a further claim to the statement of apparent presence, a claim that is consistent with, but not explanatory of, that statement of presence.

LIMITLESSLY ARBITRARY HYPOTHESES

Our explorations so far give perhaps the impression of being fruitless and of leaving us with the problem with which we began still unsolved. Earlier, we found the net result of Moore's efforts to be at best the conclusion that the skeptic puts forth no cogent reasons in support of his thesis—a conclusion easily counterbalanced by the observation that no cogent reasons support the tenets of common sense. The impression is perhaps that we have advanced no further than Moore with our conclusion that the present renditions of both common sense and solipsism are gratuitous additions to the data. Yet such an estimate is precipitous. Several modest but distinct advantages enjoyed by the commonsense position over its solipsistic rivals lie awaiting discovery in the skeletal schemata of statements No. 1 and No. 2 above. One of these is that the epistemological impasse in which the rival theses are locked is a de facto endorsement of the commonsense position. Let us leave consideration of this particular point for the moment and concentrate on the second of these advantages.

Thus far, we have noted only that a solipsistic thesis and its commonsense rival, Q and P, differ in that the former asserts where the latter denies. Yet a second important difference between the two is suggested by their renditions in No. 1, and in No. 2 and No.2' above: whereas P in principle denies a number of skeptical hypotheses, each particular skeptical hypothesis asserts but one of these denied hypotheses. In the formulation No. 1, the particular hypothesis being asserted is indicated via the index, 'i'. Since 'i' picks out some particular one of a number of solipsistic theses, it immediately raises the question of why the thesis being asserted is not some other one of the skeptical theses. The assertion of one thesis (with index 'i') rather than another (the one with index 'k', for instance) appears arbitrary. Why this particular thesis and not some other?

The line of reasoning appears promising. Consider for a moment the skeptical hypothesis that the coffee mug of a few pages back is really a striped poached lobster. Such a hypothesis, like many another skeptical speculation, obviously has nothing to recommend it. Yet this particular thesis, if one may trust one's intuitions in the matter, is almost certain to have a poor popularity rating among skeptics. Its drawback is not merely that it strains credibility—most skeptical hypotheses manage this very well—but that it invites, or rather cries out for, its own rebuttal. The immediate retort it provokes is "Why striped?" or "Why poached?" The striped poached lobster envisaged immediately becomes but one possibility in a fast-proliferating population of hypothetical lobsters. Furthermore, if interest in color schemes should wane, then the question may arise of why the mug is really a lobster rather than something else. Why is it not really a crayfish or a hermit crab?—to mention but two other species of crustacean, and not to mention any of the thousands of other species in the class. The hypothesis in question is but one of an indefinitely great number of similar possible hypotheses. Of these countless hypotheses there is no apparent reason to prefer any one to any of the others.

Each has nothing to be said in its favor and, consequently, no more than what may be said for any of the others. In these circumstances, a claim that alleges the truth of one rather than that of another is quite unjustified and even irrational. Indeed, one might say that it attains a higher level of irrationality. It is not merely gratuitous, which is to say, unsupported or without reason. Nor is it simply arbitrarily chosen, since no better supported than its rivals. It is what might be termed *limitlessly arbitrary*, which is to say that it is no better supported than any of its rivals, the number of which may be increased without apparent limit or bounds. No rational thinker (and only a rational skeptic is of interest to us) can seriously assert such a claim, or refuse to see it as but one of an indefinitely great number of equally conceivable states of affairs.

A number of factors concur to yield this result. First of all, there is what might be termed the *Phenomenon of Unlimited Conceivability*, or PUC for short. Briefly described, the phenomenon is that of the apparently limitless number of hypotheses that may be conceived as alternatives to any detailed empirical hypothesis. Its phonetic analogue PUCK suggests the playful and limitless diversity possible in conceptual variation. To this phenomenon there must be joined the further fact that each of the conceivable hypotheses is simply conceivable. The latter fact places the indefinitely great number of conceivable hypotheses on the same evidential level of simple conceivability. Thirdly, there is the earlier-encountered *Rational Assertion Truism*, or RAT, that states a rational assertion is a function of evidence. Finally, from the conjoined efforts of the above three factors, there may be derived a further principle that might plausibly be construed as a specific negative version of Leibniz's Principle of Sufficient Reason. In deference to Leibniz, it may be called the *Principle of Insignificant Reason*, or PIR for short. The principle runs as follows:

> It is quite irrational to affirm any simply conceivable empirical hypothesis that is but one of an unlimited number of rival evidentially equivalent hypotheses.

The principle states what RAT yields in cases where PUC holds among merely conceivable hypotheses. PIR is in point of fact the rational principle that underlies Ockham's Principle of Parsimony and that gives the latter whatever rational warrant it has. It is rational to explain by less what is not better explained by more, not because God prefers shorter explanations but because the additional element—what remains when the less is subtracted from the more—plays a role that could equally well be played by any of an indefinitely great number of other hypotheses. Where H_1 adequately explains whatever it is that is to be explained, H_2 is but one of an indefinitely great number of further claims consistent with the data and conjoinable to H_1 to form explanatory hypotheses. H_1 is a better explanatory hypothesis than the conjunction, H_1 and H_2, because while both have the same explanatory value, the latter, unlike the former, involves the affirmation of a claim no more (and no less) warranted than any of an indefinitely great number of such claims. The ruling is not that H_2 is false, but only that H_2 is a gratuitous addition to the explanation.

PIR applies in just such fashion to our lobster thesis. The principle rules that it is irrational for a skeptic to contend that a particular coffee mug is a striped poached lobster. The skeptical claim is irrational in that it quite ignores the actual evidential situation, that is, it ignores the fact that the hypothesis envisaged is but one of an indefinitely great number of such hypotheses, no one of which on the evidence available to the skeptic is more likely to be true than any of the others. The skeptic cannot rationally affirm the truth of the claim. He or she may choose to believe the hypothesis but, in so doing, could not rightly claim to hold a rational belief.

THE IMPLAUSIBILITY OF DEMONIAC AND PHANTASMATA SOLIPSISM

Let us see how PIR might be fruitfully brought to bear against the related Cartesian solipsistic theses. The presence of the index 'i' in the formulation of the theses indicates that each of the various Cartesian theses envisages but one of several modes in which the world might be unreal. Furthermore, there is no particular reason to esteem one mode more likely than another to be realized. In particular, there would seem no cogent reason to claim that the world is, for instance, more likely to be a dream than an illusion or demon-perpetrated hoax. Yet while the point is well taken, it soon becomes clear that the number of distinct modes in which the world may be unreal cannot be multiplied without limit. Phantasmata Solipsism neglects to say anything about the real nature of the world behind the alleged illusion, just as Oneirata Solipsism has nothing to say on the nature of the alleged further waking world. As a result, PIR is not applicable here as it was in the case of the lobster illusion. It may be argued that there is no more reason to think any particular solipsistic thesis to be true than there is reason to think any of the others to be true. Any particular thesis is thus arbitrary to a certain degree, and the endorsement of any particular mode of solipsism may consequently be judged to be unwarranted on the evidence. The modern-day scenario of a scientist nursing a brain in a vat on Alpha Centauri is in contrast highly vulnerable to PIR, since one may reasonably maintain that Alpha Centauri is but one of an indefinitely great number of possible locations for a vat-dwelling brain. The Cartesian scenarios are far less specific about the nature of reality and, hence, far less vulnerable. In addition, even if specific forms of solipsism are slightly discredited, there remains nevertheless the general thesis of solipsism to refute, the thesis that the world is tied to oneself irrespective of its mode of unreality. Let us see if we may find some further support for a stronger verdict against solipsism, perhaps by way of some further point at which PIR may be more effectively applied.

That point in fact is not too difficult to find. It suffices to note the meaning of 's' in the sentence representing the solipsistic claim, '$G_i s$'. The egocentricity of the world involves a particular individual, the solipsist. The latter is the one who has the illusion, or who awakes to find it was all a dream, or who is being deceived by a demon. The reference to the individual solipsist introduces an arbitrary element into the solipsistic thesis. An awareness of this arbitrariness is implicit in the quasi-automatic rejoinder often addressed to solipsists to the effect that it is the solipsist, and not his or her interlocutor, who is simply one of the props in a world of which the other is the center. The underlying claim being tendered is that there is no good reason to appoint one particular subject rather than another to the position of hub of the universe.

In defense of what appears to be manifest partiality on the solipsist's part, the solipsist could, of course, reply that the ontological egocentricity of the solipsistic thesis simply reflects the manifest egocentricity of the epistemological situation. At least this is the reply a rational solipsist might well be inclined to give. The question to be asked then—and it is a question to be asked of oneself since, if solipsism is rationally warranted, it is rationally espousable by oneself—is the question of whether one has any rational grounds that militate in favor of the choice of oneself rather than some other self as hub of the world. On the supposition that the world one perceives is a dream, illusion, or hoax, what good reason does one have to think that the world is one's own dream, illusion, or hoax, and not that of someone else? What good reason (if any) does one have to embrace a solipsism with oneself, rather than someone else, as the dreamer or the person perceiving the vast illusion or the butt of a demon's hoax?

On reflection, it might be noticed that for Phantasmata and Demoniac Solipsism the question has somewhat of an edge to it. If the world is a hoax conjured up by a demon to deceive oneself, then one must exist. Likewise, if the world is one's presently perceived illusion, one must exist in order to do the perceiving. This circumstance suggests one reason that might be given for granting oneself rather than some other subject privileged status as center of the world: the certainty of one's own existence. For a fervent Cartesian, the Archimedean fixed point of solipsism will be, as for Descartes, the fact that one's own existence is indubitable while the rest of the world may be unreal. If the thinking subject indubitably exists despite the fact that the rest of the world may be a hoax or illusion, then there seems but one plausible answer to the question of whose world the world is: it is the world of the existing subject. It would hardly be plausible to claim that a particular thinking subject (oneself) indubitably exists, that the world perceived by the subject is of the stuff of a hoax or illusion, but that the hoax or illusion is the hoax or illusion of some other thinking subject. The indubitably existing subject would be in the absurd position of being part of someone else's illusion. Surely one must be oneself the most plausible candidate for the position in question.

This situation is transformed considerably by the conclusion reached at the end of chapter 11. Since the tactual body is integral to the perceiving subject, any impartial (rational) solipsist who declares the sensuous world to be unreal, must, by an involuntary self-referential manoeuvre, include himself or herself in the unreal world. To make an exception of his or her tactile-kinesthetic body would violate PIR since one might with as much reason make an exception of any of an indefinitely great number of items. The justification of the solipsist's choice of himself or herself as hub of the world cannot be the solipsist's allegedly indubitable existence.

Consider Demoniac Solipsism, the thesis that the world is the unreal conjuration of a devious demon bent on deceiving the solipsist. This scenario makes the claim that everything in the world is a hoax, everything except the demon, of course, and the individual the demon is attempting to deceive. Now who or what is this latter individual? It is the individual who doubts and denies, who is perplexed and appalled—which is to say, a tactile-kinesthetic body. This tactile-kinesthetic body integral to the thinking being is spatially contiguous to the world declared to be a conjuration of the demon. Is it plausible to claim that the felt body is real while the remainder of the world, felt, seen, and heard, is a hoax? To make an exception of the solipsist's tactile-kinesthetic body and to claim that this part of the world is real and is the subject for whom the rest of the world is a sham, is to violate PIR. It is to draw an arbitrary boundary separating real from unreal. Such a boundary might with as much reason be drawn at any of an indefinitely great number of other places. On the other hand, if the tactile-kinesthetic body were part of the hoax, the scenario would be senseless. The subject would then be part of the unreal world, or the hoax meant to deceive a subject. If the solipsist is part of the fabrication, whom is the demon attempting to deceive? There would be no real subject for whom the world was unreal or a hoax. Demoniac Solipsism must choose between a senseless thesis and a limitlessly arbitrary one. In neither case can a belief in such a thesis pretend to be remotely rational.

The situation is analogous for Phantasmata Solipsism. The latter makes the claim that nothing in the world is really there where it appears to be, that the world is a personal illusion. In all impartiality, the felt body and consequently the perceiving subject should also be considered to be part of the illusion. Yet if it is, then where is the subject for whom the tactile-kinesthetic body is a personal illusion? The answer can hardly be the tactile-kinesthetic body, since that body is part of the illusion; the subject would become an illusion for an illusion. Since the tactile-kinesthetic body is integral to the self, there is no other self to be the subject of the perception of the illusion. On the other hand, if an exception is made of the tactile-kinesthetic body in the general demotion of the world to the status of an illusion, PIR once again makes its appearance. Any such exception is an arbitrary decree, which is but one of an indefinitely great number of similarly arbitrary decrees, each with as much or as little warrant as the others. Phantasmata Solipsism must be abandoned by any rational thinker.

An analogous line of reasoning would also be effective against the remaining tenet of Sense Data Solipsism, the tenet that sense data are possibly unreal. The Principle of Insignificant Reason is apparently working havoc in the solipsistic host. It would be wise, however, to refrain from any precipitous rejoicing and sounding of trumpets. While the above line of reasoning is cogent enough against the mentioned variants of Unreal World Solipsism, in Oneirata Solipsism it encounters an obstacle of first magnitude. The latter claims that the world is but a dream one is having. Now, if that dream operates in the manner of everyday dreams, then the person dreaming is both the person consciously involved in the dream and the person in some quite different waking world, asleep at present but possibly awake at some future time. The unreality of the dream is not so all pervasive as to rule out its being unreal or a dream for a particular subject. In point of fact, in everyday dreams, some of the constituents of the dream are not unreal. The feelings of the dreamer are not unreal in the way the visual constituents of the dream are; they may be still present, reverberating when the dreamer awakes. The situation is presumably similar in the case of the dream envisaged by Oneirata Solipsism: the waking self is affectively identical with the dreaming one. The affective element that is continuous from one world to the other, need not, of course, be of a very violent or turbulent nature. In everyday dreams it is sometimes a mere mild curiosity or interest that dissipates on one's waking up. Whatever its nature, the affective element establishes a continuity of the dreaming self with the waking one. Indeed, even in the absence of affective continuities, memories and dispositions could provide sufficient grounds to warrant an identification of the dreaming self with the waking self. Thus, Oneirata Solipsism would seem to have little difficulty accommodating the fact that the tactile-kinesthetic subject may be part of the solipsist's envisaged sham.

A Phantasmata or Demoniac Solipsist cannot plausibly do likewise and claim that there is some further person who is identical in some manner or other with the solipsist's apparent self. As stressed earlier in chapter 11, the self is phenomenal in nature; the apparent self is the self in person. One identifies with one's feelings, even those of one's dreams, and that identification itself cannot turn out to be a mistake. The question of whether the self is identical with another self in a world other than the present one can be raised only if the envisaged identity is diachronic, i.e., only if it is being asked whether the self is identical with a self located at some date in time earlier or later than the time occupied by the apparent self. The self may in principle be synchronically identical with some unconscious body in some other world—the sleeping body of an Oneirata Solipsist or some entity envisaged by a Non-Sensa Solipsist. It cannot however be meaningfully identified with a conscious real person in any other concomitantly running world. A reservation might blossom at this point: if the Oneirata Solipsist may be part of a present unreal world, it might be asked, then why may not also the Phantasmata or Demoniac Solipsist? The answer is that an Oneirata Solipsist is diachronically identical with a real self of a later time. An illusion or demon conjuration in which the solipsist was part of the unreal world but diachronically identical with a real individual situated in some later real world, would differ from a dream in name only. The thesis propounding such a scenario would be identical with Oneirata Solipsism. Thus, it must be concluded that in view of the identification of the tactile-kinesthetic body with the self, and of the resolutely phenomenal nature of the self, neither Phantasmata Solipsism nor Demoniac Solipsism can be considered viable forms of Unreal World Solipsism. Thus also are dispelled the Sense Data Solipsist's doubts about reality.

THE IMPLAUSIBILITY OF ONEIRATA AND NON-SENSA SOLIPSISM

The remaining forms of Unreal World Solipsism, Oneirata and Non-Sensa Solipsism, escape any disastrous implications from the failure of Descartes's proof of his own existence. This is because the alleged real person beyond the mere appearances is some future individual. This future individual must be identical (diachronically) with the solipsist. A Chinese sage, Chuang Tzu, having dreamt one night that he was a butterfly, wondered whether he was now a butterfly dreaming that it was Chuang Tzu.[9] From the point of view of a solipsist, musings of the sort are admissible only if the butterfly is the solipsist with body renovated and redecorated. If the butterfly is an individual distinct from the solipsist, then there was no reason to speak of the dream as the solipsist's dream.

Let us return to our original question: What rational grounds has the solipsist (or oneself) to claim that the individual in the real world (the dreamer of Oneirata Solipsism or the perceiver of Non-Sensa Solipsism) is a being identical with the solipsist (or oneself) or with the solipsist's (or one's own) particular unreal tactile-kinesthetic body rather than being identical with the unreal counterpart of some other self, perhaps the neighbor's cat? What warrant is there for attributing the unreal world to the solipsist (oneself) rather than to some other self?

A number of reasons may well surface at this point. The Cartesian claim of indubitable existence has been rejected, but it was never the main source of solipsistic inclinations. The most persuasive reason, apparently, is that center stage is occupied by one's own tactile-kinesthetic body with its spontaneous movements, its moods and interests, by one's visual body, and by one's immediate tactual, visual, and auditory environment. One holds, one might be inclined to say, a privileged position in the world, which makes one the most likely candidate, if not the only likely one to be the hub of the world. Yet in what exactly does this privileged position consist? Let us try out a few possibilities.

What could be meant is that on an impartial look at the present world—at what is visibly present, felt, and heard—one's own felt body and one's movements play an ostensibly predominant role. Yet

such a view amounts to a surreptitious introduction of the Ephemerata Solipsist's view of the world in which the latter reduces to what
one actually perceives. This view was rejected in chapter 12. As we
saw, there is overwhelming reason to think that the perceived world
fleshes out in all directions beyond what one actually sees, feels, and
hears. This larger world does not have oneself as its center. To accord
oneself a privileged position metaphysically in the structure of that
world would be to fly in the face of PIR by endorsing but one of an
indefinitely great number of equally unsupported hypotheses.

What might be meant is that the world one perceives is a world
from a particular perspective. Despite the concession that the world
extends unperceived in all directions, the perceived world may be
argued to be nevertheless a world perceived from a particular point of
view. It is the world perceived from a certain position in space, and it
has oneself, the perceiving subject, at its center or perspectival focal
source. Now there is something to be said in favor of this assessment.
It is somewhat accurate with regard to the visual world, in that
objects may be hidden behind others, and objects do in fact occupy
less and less of the visual field as they recede further and further. The
auditory world also has some mode of perspective in that sounds
become fainter and fainter with distance. However, on the terrain of
the tactile-kinesthetic world, the notion of perspective has no application. As noted in chapter 10, tactile-kinesthetic phenomena generally
undergo no perspectival changes and have no focal center. The feelings in the hand are not felt from a point situated elsewhere—in the
head, for example. They do not become smaller or larger in function
of movements of the arm that vary with the distance of the hand from
the body. Nor are tactual objects outside the body perceived perspec-
tivally; when actually perceived, they are contiguous with the feelings
that constitute the body; when envisaged, anticipated, or intended,
they are located in a projection of the nonperspectival, three-dimensional space of the tactile-kinesthetic body. The lack of tactual perspective is highly embarrassing to the case a solipsist might wish to
make. The tactual world cannot be dismissed as unimportant or irrelevant; it is essential to any solipsistic world since it is par excellence
the world of the self; it is the only sense world necessary for the existence of a self (and indeed, for a solipsist both blind and deaf, the only
sense world there is). Yet it lacks perspective. What the solipsist must
claim rather is that the tactual world now actually perceived is limited to one's own body and to its contiguous environment. Such a
claim merely takes us back to the claims of Ephemerata Solipsism. It
might be added too that even in the case of what is visually per-

ceived, the fleshing out of the visual world makes other points of view possible. In a world of an indefinitely great number of possible points of view, it would be irrational to grant special status to one's present point of view rather than to any of the others.

A final reason that might surface for selecting oneself as the dreamer of a dreamt world is that no one but oneself could dream one's experiences. One has the impression that no one but oneself could experience one's own spontaneity without being that spontaneity and hence being oneself— whence it follows that one must oneself be the dreamer of one's experiences. Independently of its merits, such a line of reasoning is not one that a solipsist may safely pursue. The refutation of Monopsyche Solipsism found strong warrant for the claim that other selves exist along with their feelings, thoughts, and spontaneity. By parity of reasoning, it may be argued with regard to any of the various other selves proposed as candidates for the position of dreamer that no one but that self could dream that self's experiences. Consequently, it could never be the case that the whole world, including all the various experiences in it, was the dream of any particular self in that world. The most the solipsist could consistently claim to dream would be the world minus the experiences of others, and so could only preserve the solipsistic thesis by denying that other persons or organisms ever have experiences of spontaneity. As we saw in discussing Monopsyche Solipsism, such a denial is not rationally tenable.

In sum, the remaining forms of Unreal World Solipsism are chased into an impasse by their dogged nemesis PIR, or the Principle of Insignificant Reason. No significant reason can be offered for the claim that the world is the dream of one particular self, the solipsist, rather than that of any other of an indefinitely great number of such selves. Of the various reasons considered—the indubitability of one's own existence, the privileged position of oneself center stage in the world, the perspectival structure of one's perceptions, the inalienable privacy of one's spontaneity—none provides the solipsist with a reason sufficient to avoid the dictates of PIR. If the everyday assumptions of continued unobserved existence and of other minds are endorsed at the outset, then PIR provides the warrant for the everyday notion (encountered in chapter 2) that skeptical theses are to be dismissed as irrelevant. In any event, both remaining forms of Unreal World Solipsism, Oneirata Solipsism and Non-Sensa Solipsism, must plead guilty to a charge of being incalculably capricious or limitlessly arbitrary: there is no particular reason why the envisaged solipsistic world should be the personal world of the solipsist rather than that of any of an indefinitely great number of other selves. Each remaining form of the doctrine thus finds itself reduced to the status of but one of an indefinitely great number of like skeptical hypotheses, and so must be ruled by PIR to be no more (albeit no less) worthy of espousal than any of the others. The only course open for the remaining faithful few, if they are to qualify as rational, is to set aside their doctrinal and liturgical differences, renounce their specific identities, and issue a vaguely worded joint proclamation on the unreality of the world, one that specifies nothing regarding the mode of unreality.

Thus rational Unreal World Solipsism must lose itself in a simpler, less esoteric creed, the skeptical doctrine that the world is unreal in some way or other, a doctrine that is silent on all points of detail regarding the alleged unreality. This conclusion is based neither on considerations of coherence and fit nor on broad empirical generalizations as to the nature of the world. It relies purely on the perceptual given together with rational principles of evidence. No epistemological self—neither the astronomer with his sophisticated probings into past millennia nor the gargantuan tactual presence in the flux of experience—can hold a rationally warranted solipsistic belief.

THE PERMANENT POSSIBILITY OF UNREALITY

Nothing in the above discussion demonstrates the reality of the world. While the solipsistic thesis of any particular solipsist is shown to be one of an indefinitely great number of possible hypotheses, there remains the possibility that the world is nevertheless unreal in some way or other. Indeed, it seems we find ourselves at an epistemological impasse: there is apparently no valid argument to establish (or even make more likely than not) the thesis that the world is real rather than unreal in some way or other (or the contrary). To alleviate the discomfort perhaps occasioned by such a conclusion, a few reflections are in order.

First of all, the failure to turn up a general demonstration—or even a proof of likelihood—of the reality of the world may well prove to be a blessing. A demonstration of the reality of what one perceives would preclude the possibility of the perceived item being a mere representation and not the thing itself in person. It is difficult to see how one could procure a firm demonstration that the world is real without thereby closing (for better or for worse) the door on the Representational Theory of Perception. By the same token, of course, the door would be closed (for better or for worse) on a variety of interesting religious cosmologies.

Another helpful reflection focuses on a circumstance that might be characterized somewhat grandiloquently as the *Self-Identity of the Unreal.* Briefly stated, the fact in point is that anything unreal, like everything else, is what it is. The threat of being unreal does not make an item any less the item it is. If a shiny enamel shape is an illusion, it is no less a shiny enamel shape. A surface that refuses to budge under pressure from one's hand, although labeled perhaps an illusion, is no less obdurate a surface. Similarly, the prospect that the world is perhaps a dream that will cease at some future date does not make the present or past world any less what it is or was. A 16-billion-year dream nevertheless lasts for 16 billion years. A dreamt pain, no less than a psychosomatic one, is not made less painful by being tainted with unreality. A hero in a dream who must live through all the various experiences and perform the various feats in virtue of which he qualifies as a hero, is no less a hero for the fact that it all took place in a dream. As noted earlier in chapter 3, if a line of reasoning is rational, then the reasoning is not made less rational by the fact that it takes place in a dream.

What could lead astray here is the pejorative import of notions such as 'a mere dream' or 'a mere illusion'. In everyday circumstances, to say that something is an illusion or a dream is to say that it lacks certain properties (e.g., weight or durability) and that it is without the usual causal effects on other events. Yet, as is brought out by statements No. 1 and No. 2 of some pages back, a given phenomenon remains neither more nor less what it is whether considered simply as appearance, or demoted to the status of illusion, or promoted to that of reality. What is in the balance is not any perceptible characteristic of the phenomenon but rather the issue of whether there is anything further than the phenomenon, a reality with regard to which it is unreal. As one might put the matter, unreality is not something less than appearance; it is simply appearance that is mere appearance with respect to some further reality. Similarly, reality is not something more than appearance; it is appearance for which there is no further reality with respect to which the appearance is unreal.

A final helpful consideration is the one mentioned earlier, that the epistemological impasse in which the commonsense and skeptical theses are locked is a de facto endorsement of the commonsense position. Statements No. 1 and No. 2 above construe the commonsense tenet of reality as an appearance claim coupled with a denial of any further reality and the solipsistic claim as the same appearance claim coupled with an affirmation of some further reality or other. On the available evidence, both the commonsense denial and the skeptical affirmation are gratuitous additions. The rational course to follow in these circumstances is to confine assent to the appearance claim and withhold judgment on the issue of reality or unreality. The course is rational in that it attunes assent or belief to the available evidence. The resulting position is undoubtedly an abandonment of the commonsense view, but it is not an abandonment of the ontology of that view. The inventory of the contents of the world as given by P_0 is the same as that given by P. On the skeptical concept of unreality, the apparent is qualitatively indistinguishable from the real. Consequently, an account of what is apparently the case differs from an account of what is really the case not in the characteristics asserted but only in the broader possibilities admitted. The former account allows for the possibility of some further reality in addition to the appearance, while the latter account denies any such further reality with regard to which the appearance is unreal. Such a willingness to envisage the possible unreality of things is of course foreign to the commonsense view. It is, as one might say, an undogmatic version of common sense.

The de facto advantage enjoyed by common sense should not be underestimated. It would be a mistake to complain that since everyday objects have given way to everyday appearances, skepticism has triumphed over the plain everyday virtues. No form of Unreal World Solipsism has been established or even supported. All such theses have been left in limbo as logical possibilities bereft of supporting evidence, and that is where they must remain. Center stage is occupied by apparent objects, the observation of them and the investigation of their properties and relations. A suspension of judgment as to the ultimate reality of the apparent world has no effect whatever on epistemic inquiry. An investigation into the whereabouts of a missing cup, the dietary preference of scorpions, or the antics of volcanoes, is quite unaffected by the hypothesis that the whole world (including the cup, the scorpions, and the volcanoes) may be in some manner unreal. The various bugbears conjured up by the skeptic play no role in these investigations—or rather, can play a role only at the price of becoming verifiable or falsifiable like other empirical theses. What makes the Cartesian demon hypothesis, for instance, difficult to refute is precisely the fact that it leaves the natural course of events in the world exactly as it would be if there was no demon. In the absence of any derivable repercussions from the skeptic's envisaged real world, the apparent world continues its course unperturbed and continues to enjoy the rights of any first-comer, including the right to be the only known occupant until forcibly dislodged. The sole practical consequence of the epistemological impasse is to keep the issue of reality open, a consequence that in principle should make common sense less dogmatic than is its wont.

The above investigations raise as many questions as they answer. They provide strong support for belief in the existence of the everyday world to the limited extent that belief in certain rival solipsistic theses has been found to be irrational. A staggering amount of work remains to be done if the endorsement of the main tenets of common sense is to be assessed for rationality. The criterion of fit or coherence awaits satisfying analysis. The numerous steps leading from the world of the radical skeptic to the everyday world must be traced out and assessed in detail. The rationality of both logical and mathematical truth must be seriously investigated. The blurry line between the pancultural given and what is culturally added needs to be mapped out in detail.[10] The challenges remaining would be largely sufficient to keep the combined analytic skills of the trained philosophical community out of mischief for a full generation.

NOTES

CHAPTER ONE: CARTESIAN SOLIPSISM

1. René Descartes, *The Search for Truth* in *The Philosophical Writings of Descartes*, Vol. 2, tr. John Cottingham, Robert Stoothoff, and Dugald Murdoch (Cambridge: Cambridge University Press, 1984), 408.

2. Immanuel Kant, *The Critique of Pure Reason*, tr. Norman Kemp Smith (London: Macmillan, 1958), 34, note a.

3. René Descartes, *Meditations on First Philosophy* in *The Philosophical Writings of Descartes* Vol. 2, tr. John Cottingham, Robert Stoothoff, and Dugald Murdoch (Cambridge: Cambridge University Press, 1984), 13.

4. *Ibid.*, 14–15.

5. *Ibid.*, 12.

6. *Ibid.*, 53.

7. Descartes, *Search*, 407; *Meditations*, 12–13.

8. Descartes, *Meditations*, 26–27.

9. *Ibid.*, 21.

10. *Ibid.*, 13.

11. David Hume, *A Treatise of Human Nature*, ed. L. A. Selby-Bigge (Oxford: Clarendon Press, 1960), 188.

12. Bertrand Russell, *Human Knowledge* (London: George Allen and Unwin, 1948), 343.

13. Ludwig Wittgenstein, *Zettel*, ed. G. E. M. Anscombe and G. H. von Wright, tr. G. E. M. Anscombe (Berkeley: University of California Press, 1967), 75, par. 427.

14. Descartes, *Meditations*, 19; David Hume, *An Enquiry Concerning Human Understanding*, ed. Eric Steinberg (Indianapolis: Hackett, 1977), 16–25.

15. Hume, *Treatise*, 188.

16. Plato, *Theaetetus*, 158b.

17. Cicero, *Academica*, tr. H. Rackman (London: W. Heinemann, 1956), 2. 16. 49; 2. 27. 88.

18. Plato, *Phaedo*, 65a.

19. Cicero, *Academica*, 2.25.79.

20. Charlotte L. Stough, *Greek Skepticism* (Berkeley: University of California Press, 1969), 17; Sextus Empiricus, *Outlines of Pyrrhonism*, tr. R. G. Bury (London: W. Heinemann, 1933), 1.14.77.

21. G. S. Kirk and J. E. Raven, *The Presocratic Philosophers* (Cambridge: Cambridge University Press, 1957), 342, 423, 233.

22. Cicero, *Academica*, 2.6.18; 2.13.40.

23. Sextus, *Outlines*, 2.7.199; 2.6.185.

24. *Ibid.*, 1.7.11; 1.10.15.

25. *Ibid.*, 2.15.204.

26. Aurelius Augustine, *On the Trinity* in *The Works of Aurelius Augustine*, Vol. 7, tr. A. W. Haddan (Edinburgh: T. and T. Clark, 1873), 256.

27. Descartes, *Meditations*, 12.

28. *Ibid.*, 16.

29. *Ibid.*, 27.

30. Hume, *Treatise*, 139; *Enquiry*, 27.

31. Peter Unger, *Ignorance* (Oxford: Clarendon Press, 1975), 13ff.

32. Hume, *Treatise*, 139.

33. See Joseph Almog, "Naming Without Necessity," *The Journal of Philosophy*, 83:4 (April, 1986), 230.

CHAPTER TWO: THE CLAIM TO KNOW

1. G. E. Moore, "A Defence of Common Sense," in *Philosophical Papers* (London: George Allen and Unwin, 1958), 32.

2. G. E. Moore, "Certainty," in *Philosophical Papers* (London: George Allen and Unwin, 1958), 227.

3. G. E. Moore, "Proof of an External World," in *Philosophical Papers* (London: George Allen and Unwin, 1958), 146.

4. J. L. Austin, *Sense and Sensibilia* (Oxford: Oxford University Press, 1964), 114–115.

5. Anthony Quinton, *The Nature of Things* (London: Routledge and Kegan Paul, 1973), 186–187.

6. John L. Pollock, *Knowledge and Justification* (Princeton, N.J.: Princeton University Press, 1974), 29–30.

7. G. E. Moore, "Four Forms of Skepticism," in *Philosophical Papers* (London: George Allen and Unwin, 1958), 224; "Certainty," in *Papers*, 250.

8. Descartes, *Meditations*, 14, 15; Peter Unger, *Ignorance* (Oxford: Clarendon Press, 1975), 20; Moore, "Scepticism," in *Papers*, 224.

9. Descartes, *Meditations*, 13.

10. Unger, *Ignorance*, 21.

11. Robert Nozick, *Philosophical Explanations* (Cambridge: Harvard University Press, 1981), 201.

12. G. E. Moore, "Hume's Philosophy," in *Philosophical Studies* (London: Routledge and Kegan Paul, 1922), 161.

13. Moore, "Scepticism," in *Papers*, 225.

14. Alvin I. Goldman, *Epistemology and Cognition* (Cambridge: Harvard University Press, 1986), 55; Peter Klein, *Certainty: A Refutation of Scepticism* (Minneapolis: University of Minnesota Press, 1981), 170; Douglas Odegard, *Knowledge and Scepticism* (Totowa, N.J.: Rowman and Littlefield, 1982), 65; Nicholas Rescher, *Scepticism* (Totowa, N.J.: Rowman and Littlefield, 1980), 38; Nozick, *Explanations*, 199.

15. Rescher, *Scepticism*, 167–168; Odegard, *Knowledge*, 32–38; Klein, *Certainty*, 135, 177; Richard Rorty, *Philosophy and the Mirror of Nature* (Princeton, N.J.: Princeton University Press, 1979), 112, 311.

16. Fred Dretske, "Epistemic Operators," *Journal of Philosophy*, 67 (1970), 1007–1023.

17. Klein, *Certainty*, 37–38.

18. See Nozick, *Explanations*, 201, 204; Alvin Goldman, *Epistemology*, 56; Robert Audi, *Belief, Justification, and Knowledge* (Belmont, Calif.:

Wadsworth, 1988), 79, 145; Dretske, "Epistemic Operators," 1016 ; Colin McGuinn, "The Concept of Knowledge," in *Midwest Studies in Philosophy*, Vol. 9, ed. Peter French, Theodore Uehling, Jr., and Howard Wettstein (Minneapolis: University of Minnesota Press, 1984), 542. Klein espouses a closely related view in his defence of a Defeater Consequence Elimination Principle in *Certainty*, 95.

19. For such an attempt, see McGinn, "The Concept of Knowledge," 542.

20. Audi, *Belief*, 77, 145.

21. J. L. Austin, *Sense and Sensibilia* (New York: Oxford University Press, 1964), 118–119.

22. Moore, "Common Sense," in *Papers*, 44.

23. Moore, "External World," in *Papers*, 149.

24. Audi, *Belief*, 151.

25. See Odegard, *Knowledge*, 101; Alvin Goldman, *Epistemology*, 61–62.

26. Pierre Bayle, *The Dictionary Historical and Critical* (London: 1937), Vol. 5, 614. The quote is given by Richard H. Popkin, "Berkeley and Pyrrhonism," in *The Skeptical Tradition*, ed. Myles Burnyeat (Berkeley: University of California Press, 1983), 381.

27. George Berkeley, *On the Principles of Human Knowledge* ed. G. J. Warnock (London: Collins, 1962), 74.

28. This revokability is, of course, what makes so difficult the circumscription of a class of irrelevant hypotheses.

29. Peter Unger, *Philosophical Relativity* (Minneapolis: University of Minnesota Press, 1984), 46–54.

30. Unger, *Relativity*, 51.

CHAPTER THREE: THE LACONIC RETORT

1. Ludwig Wittgenstein, *Philosophical Investigations*, tr. G. E. M. Anscombe (Oxford: Basil Blackwell, 1963), 135, par. 477.

2. Ludwig Wittgenstein, *On Certainty*, ed. G. E. M. Anscombe and G. H. von Wright (New York: Harper and Row, 1969), 37, par. 287.

3. Moore, "Defence," in *Papers*, 44.

4. David Hume, *An Enquiry Concerning Human Understanding*, ed. Eric Steinberg (Indianapolis: Hackett, 1977), 27, 109–111.

5. Rescher, *Scepticism,* 85.

6. *Ibid.,* 84–85.

7. A. J. Ayer, *The Problem of Knowledge* (Marmondsworth, Middlesex: Penguin Books, 1956), 36–40.

8. *Ibid.,* 75, 81.

9. Rescher, *Scepticism,* 27, 29, 49.

10. *Ibid.,* 40.

11. *Ibid.,* 137, 79, 36.

12. *Ibid.,* 53–54.

13. Ayer, *Knowledge,* 118–129.

14. Klein, *Certainty,* 150.

15. *Ibid.,* 93,94.

16. Bertrand Russell, *An Outline of Philosophy* (London: George Allen and Unwin, 1927), 278.

17. Unger, *Ignorance,* 126–127.

18. Ayer, *Knowledge,* 75; see also 81.

19. Frederick L. Will, *Induction and Justification* (Ithaca: Cornell University Press, 1974), 90.

20. P. F. Strawson, *Individuals* (London: Methuen, 1959), 34.

21. Plato, *Protagoras,* 171.

22. Hume, *Treatise,* 268.

23. Bertrand Russell, *Human Knowledge; Its Scope and Limits* (London: George Allen and Unwin, 1948), 195.

24. Oliver A. Johnson, *Skepticism and Cognitivism* (Berkeley: University of California Press, 1978), 59.

25. For some further discussion of the point, see A. A. Johnstone, "Self-Reference, the Double Life and Gödel," *Logique et Analyse* 93 (March 1981): 35–47.

26. John Locke, *An Essay Concerning Human Understanding,* ed. Maurice Cranston (New York: Collier Books, 1965), Bk. 4, Part XI, 355.

27. Wittgenstein, *Certainty,* 49.

28. Arthur C. Danto, *Analytical Philosophy of Knowledge* (Cambridge: Cam-

bridge University Press, 1968), 170; Guy Robinson, "Scepticism about Scepticism II," *The Aristotelian Society,* Suppl. Vol. 51 (1977): 252; Norman Malcolm, *Dreaming* (London: Routledge and Kegan Paul, 1959), 112; "Dreaming and Scepticism," in *Philosophical Essays on Dreaming,* ed. Charles E. M. Dunlop (Ithaca: Cornell University Press, 1977), 124.

29. Malcolm, *Dreaming,* 51–52.

30. Wittgenstein, *Certainty,* 49.

31. William Boardman, "Dreams, Dramas and Skepticism," *Philosophical Quarterly* 29 (1979): 227.

CHAPTER FOUR: THE APPEAL TO PERCEPTION

1. Otto Neurath, "Protocol Sentences" in *Logical Positivism,* ed. A. J. Ayer (Glencoe, Ill.: The Free Press, 1959), 201.

2. Michael Williams, *Groundless Belief* (New Haven: Yale University Press, 1977), 23, 179.

3. Austin, *Sense,* 138.

4. Will, *Induction,* 112.

5. Richard Rorty, *Philosophy and the Mirror of Nature* (Princeton, N.J.: Princeton University Press, 1979), 113.

6. Descartes, *Meditations,* 19.

7. Price, *Perception,* 3.

8. Roderick Firth, "Sense Data and the Percept Theory," in *Perceiving, Sensing and Knowing,* ed. R. J. Swartz (Garden City, N.Y.: Doubleday, 1965), 211.

9. *Ibid.,* 212.

10. Moore, "Sense Data," *Studies,* 173.

11. John L. Pollock, "A Plethora of Epistemological Theories," in *Justification and Knowledge,* ed. George S. Pappas (Dordrecht, Holland: D. Reidel, 1979), 99.

12. H. von Helmholtz, *Treatise on Physiological Optics,* Vol. 3, ed. J. P. C. Southall (New York: Dover, 1962), 6.

13. Firth, 'Sense Data," *Perceiving,* 231.

14. Aaron Gurwitsch, *The Field of Consciousness* (Pittsburg: Dusquesne University Press, 1964), 88–89.

15. Aaron Gurwitsch, *Studies in Phenomenology and Psychology* (Evanston, Ill.: Northwestern University Press, 1966), 238–239, 189–206.

16. Firth, "Sense-Data" in *Perceiving*, 221.

17. Austin, *Sense*, 112–124.

18. *Ibid.*, 142.

19. *Ibid.*, 113.

20. John L. Pollock, *Contemporary Theories of Knowledge* (Totowa, N.J.: Rowman and Littlefield, 1986), 61.

21. Quinton, *Nature*, 190.

22. Willard Van Orman Quine, *Word and Object* (Cambridge: MIT Press, 1960), 2; Wilfrid Sellars, "Empiricism and the Philosophy of Mind," in *Science, Perception and Reality* (London: Routledge and Kegan Paul, 1963), 131: Michael Williams, *Groundless Belief* (New Haven: Yale University Press, 1977), 34.

23. Williams, *Belief*, 35.

24. Laurence BonJour, *The Structure of Empirical Knowledge* (Cambridge: Harvard University Press, 1985), 78.

25. BonJour, *Structure*, 30–33.

26. Willard Van Orman Quine, *From a Logical Point of View* (New York: Harper and Row, 1963), 20–46.

27. Willard Van Orman Quine, *Philosophy of Logic* (Englewood Cliffs, N.J.: Prentice Hall, 1970), 100.

28. Hilary Putnam, "Analyticity and Apriority: Beyond Wittgenstein and Quine," in *Midwest Studies in Philosophy*, Vol 4, ed. Peter French, Theodore E. Uehling, Jr., Howard K. Wettstein (Minneapolis: University of Minnesota Press, 1979), 436.

29. Quine, *Word*, 67.

30. Keith Lehrer, "Coherence and the Racehorse Paradox" in *Midwest Studies in Philosophy*, Vol. 5, ed. Peter A. French, Theodore E. Uehling, Jr., and Howard K. Wettstein (Minneapolis: University of Minnesota Press, 1980), 190.

31. Paul R. Thagard, "The Best Explanation: Criteria for Theory Choice," *Journal of Philosophy* 75 (February 1979): 79.

32. *Ibid.*, 86–90.

CHAPTER FIVE: EPISTEMIC PARASITISM

1. Wilfrid Sellars, "Phenomenalism," in *Science, Perception and Reality* (London: Routledge and Kegan Paul, 1963), 89.

2. Immanual Kant, *Critique of Pure Reason*, tr. Norman Kemp Smith (London: Macmillan, 1953), 244–247.

3. Edmund Husserl, *Ideas Pertaining to a Pure Phenomenology and to a Phenomenological Philosophy*, First Book, tr. F. Kersten (The Hague: Martinus Nijhoff, 1982), 185.

4. Barry Stroud, *The Significance of Philosophical Scepticism* (Oxford: Clarendon Press, 1984), 228.

5. Kant, *Pure Reason*, 59.

6. Wittgenstein, *Certainty*, pars. 167, 94, 83, 211, 403, 105.

7. *Ibid.*, pars. 53, 56.

8. *Ibid.*, pars. 103, 425, 628–630, 657, 662, 674.

9. *Ibid.*, pars. 407, 6, 3, 23.

10. *Ibid.*, pars. 18, 243, 484, 245.

11. *Ibid.*, pars. 32, 17, 301.

12. *Ibid.*, pars. 117, 119.

13. *Ibid.*, pars. 199, 215.

14. *Ibid.*, pars. 37, 464, 10.

15. *Ibid.*, pars. 346, 519, 391, 163, 337, 371.

16. *Ibid.*, par. 341; see also par. 115.

17. *Ibid.*, pars. 492, 419, 150, 157, 79–81, 257, 155.

18. *Ibid.*, par. 370.

19. *Ibid.*, pars. 167, 143, 538.

20. *Ibid.*, par. 212.

21. *Ibid.*, pars. 143, 94, 93, 279.

22. Stanley Cavell, *The Claim of Reason* (Oxford: The Clarendon Press, 1979), 236.

23. Martin Heidegger, *Being and Time*, tr. John Macquarrie and Edward Robinson (New York: Harper and Row, 1962), 249.

24. *Ibid.*, 250.

25. *Ibid.*, 191–193.

26. Charles B. Guignon, *Heidegger and the Problem of Knowledge* (Indianapolis: Hackett, 1983), 195.

27. *Ibid.*, 38.

28. *Ibid.*, 169.

29. Heidegger, *Being*, 213.

30. Moore, "Certainty," *Papers*, 248–249.

31. Quinton, *Nature*, 153–155.

32. W. V. O. Quine, *The Roots of Reference* (La Salle, Ill.: Open Court, 1973), 2–3.

33. *Ibid.*, 2.

34. Willard Van Orman Quine, "Epistemology Naturalized," in *Ontological Relativity and Other Essays* (New York: Columbia University Press, 1969), 83.

35. Sextus Empiricus, *Pyrrhonism*, 1. 14.

36. Quine, *Word*, 2.

37. Michael Woods, "Scepticism and Natural Knowledge," *Proceedings of the Aristotelian Society*, New Series, 80 (1980), 242–243.

38. *Ibid.*, 242–244.

39. George Berkeley, *The Principles of Human Knowledge*, ed. G. J. Warnock (London: William Collins Sons, 1962), 74.

40. Benson Mates, *Skeptical Essays* (Chicago: University of Chicago Press, 1981), 99–153.

41. Berkeley, *Principles*, 71.

42. *Ibid.*, 74.

43. Mates, *Skeptical Essays*, 102–103; Stroud, *Philosophical Scepticism*, 228–229.

CHAPTER SIX: THE CHARGE OF MEANINGLESSNESS

1. Wittgenstein, *Investigations*, 47, 19.

2. John Wisdom, *Other Minds* (Oxford: Blackwell, 1956), 2.

3. W. T. Stace, *The Theory of Knowledge and Existence* (Oxford: Oxford University Press, 1932), 67.

4. A. J. Ayer, *Language, Truth and Logic* (London: Victor Gollancz, 1946), 129–131.

5. Ludwig Wittgenstein, *The Blue and the Brown Books* (Oxford: Basil Blackwell, 1964), 65.

6. Ludwig Wittgenstein and Rush Rhees, "Wittgenstein's Notes for Lectures on 'Private Experience' and 'Sense Data'," *The Philosophical Review* 77:3 (July 1968), 300; Wittgenstein, *Investigations*, 103.

7. Wittgenstein, *Blue Book*, 59.

8. *Ibid.*, 45, 46, 59, 65.

9. *Ibid.*, 54.

10. Wittgenstein, *Investigations*, 90.

11. Wittgenstein, *Investigations*, 120; *Blue Book*, 55.

12. Wittgenstein, *Blue Book*, 54.

13. *Ibid.*, 60–63.

14. Wittgenstein, *Blue Book*, 71–72; *Investigations*, 121.

15. Wittgenstein, *Blue Book*, 66–69; *Investigations*, 122–125.

16. Hume, *Treatise*, 252–253.

17. Wittgenstein, *Investigations*, 121.

18. *Ibid.*, 137.

19. Wittgenstein, *Certainty*, pars. 294, 296, 608.

20. Wittgenstein, *Investigations*, 89.

21. Austin, *Sense*, 10.

22. Don Locke, *Perception*, (London: George Allen and Unwin, 1967), 128.

23. Quine, *Word*, 3.

24. Wittgenstein, *Zettel*, par. 571.

25. O. K. Bouwsma, "Descartes' Skepticism of the Senses," in *Philosophical Essays on Dreaming*, ed. Charles E. M. Dunlop (Ithaca: Cornell University Press, 1977), 60, 61.

26. J. L. Austin, "Other Minds," in *Philosophical Papers* (Oxford: Clarendon Press, 1961), 55.

27. Austin, *Sense*, 70, 77.

28. Gilbert Ryle, *The Concept of Mind* (London: Hutchinson, 1949), 213, 223, 232.

29. Austin, *Sense*, 15, 16, 19.

30. Mates, *Skeptical Essays*, 124.

31. Wittgenstein, *Certainty*, par. 56.

32. Gilbert Ryle, *Dilemmas* (Cambridge: Cambridge University Press, 1954), 94.

33. Austin, *Sense*, 11.

34. Wittgenstein, *Investigations*, 33–39; Austin, *Sense*, 120.

35. Arthur C. Danto, *Analytical Philosophy of Knowledge* (Cambridge: Cambridge University Press, 1968), 187.

36. Thompson Clarke, "The Legacy of Skepticism," *The Journal of Philosophy* 69 (November, 1972): 766–769.

37. Clarke, "Legacy," 766.

38. Stroud, *Philosophical Scepticism*, 267.

39. Hilary Putnam, *Reason, Truth and History* (Cambridge: Cambridge University Press, 1981), 12–16, 51.

40. Anthony L. Bruechner, "Brains in a Vat," *The Journal of Philosophy* 83 (March 1986), 148–167, in particular, 156.

41. See Bruce Bower, "Family Feud: Enter the 'Black Skull'," *Science News* 131:4 (January 24, 1987):8–59,

42. Putnam, *Reason*, 14–21.

43. *Ibid.*, 18–19, 22–25.

44. Hilary Putnam, "Meaning and Reference," in *Naming, Necessity, and Natural Kinds*, ed. Stephen P. Schwartz (Ithaca: Cornell University Press, 1977), 124; *Reason*,19.

CHAPTER SEVEN: CARTESIAN SEMANTICS

1. Wittgenstein, *Investigations*, 217.

2. Brian Loar, *Mind and Meaning* (Cambridge: Cambridge University Press, 1981), 1.

3. Wittgenstein, *Blue Book*, 65.

4. For a statement of Objectualism, see Joseph Almog, "Naming Without Necessity," *The Journal of Philosophy*, 83:4 (April 1986), 220; Howard Wettstein, "Has Semantics Rested on a Mistake?," *The Journal of Philosophy*, 83:4 (April, 1986), 198.

5. W. V. O. Quine, "Quantifiers and Propositional Attitudes," *The Journal of Philosophy*, 53:5 (March 1956), 179.

6. A. A. Johnstone, "Self-reference, the double life and Gödel," *Logique et Analyse*, 93 (March 1981), 35–47.

7. John R. Searle, *Intentionality* (Cambridge: Cambridge University Press, 1983), 204, 205, 214.

8. Putnam, "Meaning," in *Naming*, 124; *Reason*, 18.

9. Michael Devitt and Kim Sterelny, *Language and Reality*, (Cambridge: MIT Press, 1987), 69.

10. Putnam, "Meaning," in *Naming*, 120–123; *Reason*, 18–19, 22–23.

11. Putnam, *Reason*, 23–25.

12. Devitt and Sterelny, *Language*, 52.

13. Akeel Bilgrami, "Realism without Internalism: A Critique of Searle on Intentionality," *The Journal of Philosophy*, 86:2 (February 1989), 64.

14. See notably Hilary Putnam, "Is Semantics Possible?" in *Naming, Necessity, and Natural Kinds*, ed. Stephen P. Schwartz (Ithaca, N.Y.: Cornell University Press, 1977), 102–118; Saul A. Kripke, "Naming and Necessity," in *Semantics of Natural Language*, ed. Donald Davidson and Gilbert Harman (Dordrecht, Holland: D. Reidel, 1972), 259, 316–318.

15. John Locke, *An Essay Concerning Human Understanding*, ed. John W. Yolton (London: J. M. Dent and Sons, 1961), Vol. 2, 60.

16. John R. Searle, "Proper Names," in *Readings in the Philosophy of Language*, ed. Jay F. Rosenberg and Charles Travis (Englewood Cliffs, N.J.: Prentice Hall, 1971), 218.

17. Kripke, "Naming and Necessity," 317; Nathan U. Salmon *Reference and Essence* (Princeton, N.J.: Princeton University Press, 1981), 66–67.

18. Kripke, "Naming and Necessity," 315–317.

19. Kripke, "Naming and Necessity," 318.

20. Hilary Putnam, "Is Semantics Possible?," in *Naming, Necessity and Natural Kinds*, ed. Stephen P. Schwartz (Ithaca, N.Y.: Cornell University Press, 1977), 105; Kripke, "Naming" in *Semantics*, 314, 319–321.

21. Wittgenstein, *Investigations*, 37.

22. Kripke, "Naming and Necessity," 279.

23. Keith S. Donnellan, "Proper Names and Identifying Descriptions," in *Semantics of Natural Language*, ed. Donald Davidson and Gilbert Harman (Dordrecht: D. Reidel, 1972), 374.

24. Kripke, "Naming and Necessity," 278.

25. *Ibid.*, 277, 279.

26. Hume, *Treatise*, 256.

27. Kripke, "Naming and Necessity," 288, 289.

CHAPTER EIGHT:
CONCEPTUAL AND LINGUISTIC PARASITISM

1. Quine, *Word*, 3.

2. Strawson, *Individuals*, 106.

3. Barry Stroud, "Transcendental Arguments," *The Journal of Philosophy* 65 (May 8), 251.

4. Garrett L. Vander Veer, *Philosophical Skepticism and Ordinary Language* (Lawrence, Kansas: The Regents Press, 1978), 198.

5. Stroud, "Arguments," 255–256; Jeffrey Tlumak, "Some Defects in Strawson's Anti-Skeptical Method," *Philosophical Studies* 28 (1975), 263.

6. Wilfrid Sellars, *Science, Perception and Reality* (London: Routledge and Kegan Paul, 1963), 89.

7. Strawson, *Individuals*, 41.

8. Sellars, *Perception*, 189.

9. Wittgenstein, *Investigations*, 93, 117.

10. David Pears, *Wittgenstein* (London: Collins, 1971), 147.

11. Wittgenstein, *Investigations*, 92.

12. *Ibid.*, 100, 102.

13. *Ibid.*, 95.

14. *Ibid.*, 207.

15. Wittgenstein, *Blue Book*, 65.

16. Andrew Oldenquist, "Wittgenstein on Phenomenalism, Skepticism and Criteria," in *Essays on Wittgenstein,* ed. E. D. Klemke (Urbana, Illinois: University of Illinois Press, 1971), 401.

17. Wittgenstein, *Investigations,* 580.

18. S. Coval, *Scepticism and the First Person* (London: Methuen, 1966), 75–80.

19. Kant, *Pure Reason,* 245.

20. *Ibid.,* 34.

21. Peter F. Strawson, *The Bounds of Sense* (London: Methuen, 1966), 129.

22. Strawson, *Individuals,* 35.

23. *Ibid.*

24. A. C. Grayling, *The Refutation of Scepticism* (La Salle, Illinois: Open Court, 1985), 105.

25. Strawson, *Individuals,* 87–116.

26. *Ibid.,* 99 note.

27. *Ibid.,* 101, 104, 106, 109.

28. *Ibid.,* 106.

29. Grayling, *Scepticism,* 97–98.

30. *Ibid.,* 98.

31. Stroud, "Transcendental Arguments," 251.

32. Strawson, *Individuals,* 103.

33. *Ibid.,* 95 note.

34. *Ibid.,* 81–84.

35. A. J. Ayer, *Language,* 125; *The Foundations of Empirical Knowledge* (London: MacMillan, 1940), 142; *Knowledge,* 199; *The Concept of a Person and Other Essays* (London: MacMillan, 1963), 117.

36. Edmund Husserl, *Ideen zu einen reinen Phanomenologie und Phanomenologischen Philosophie,* Zweites Buch, Husserliana Vol. 4, ed. Marly Biemel (The Hague: Nijhoff, 1952).

37. Strawson, *Sense,* 100.

38. Descartes, *Meditations,* 54.

39. René Descartes, *Objections and Replies* in *The Philosophical Writings of*

Descartes, tr. John Cottingham, Robert Stoothoff, and Dugald Murdoch (Cambridge: Cambridge University Press, 1984), Vol. 2, 113; *Principles of Philosophy* in *The Philosophical Writings of Descartes* tr. John Cottingham, Robert Stoothoff, and Dugald Murdoch (Cambridge: Cambridge University Press, 1984), Vol. 1, 195.

40. Descartes, *Objections*, 124. For the French, see *Oeuvres et Lettres de Descartes*, ed. André Bridoux (Paris: Gallimard, 1949), 294.

41. Rorty, *Mirror*, 24.

42. Descartes, *Oeuvres*, 911.

43. Hume, *Treatise*, 257.

44. Strawson, *Sense*, 100.

45. *Ibid.*, 101.

46. *Ibid.*, 100.

47. *Ibid.*, 104, 105, 107, 109.

48. Price, *Perception*, VIII–IX.

49. Richard Rorty, "Strawson's Objectivity Argument," *The Review of Metaphysics* 24 (1970/71): 207–244.

50. Rorty, "Strawson's Argument," 235.

51. Wittgenstein, *Investigations*, 88.

52. Sellars, *Perception*, 339, 168.

53. *Ibid.*, 355.

54. Rorty, "Strawson's Argument," 234.

55. *Ibid.*, 219.

56. D. C. Stove, *Probability and Hume's Inductive Skepticism* (Oxford: The Clarendon Press, 1973), 68–69.

CHAPTER NINE:
THINKING OUTSIDE PUBLIC LANGUAGE

1. Wittgenstein, *Investigations*, 91.

2. *Ibid.*, 81.

3. *Ibid.*, 117.

4. John Kekes, *A Justification of Rationality* (Albany: State University of New York Press, 1976), 212.

5. Wittgenstein, *Investigations*, 81.

6. *Ibid.*, 92.

7. *Ibid.*, 94.

8. Anthony Kenny, *Wittgenstein* (Harmondsworth, Middlesex: Penguin Books, 1973), 192.

9. Saul A. Kripke, *Wittgenstein on Rules and Private Language*, (Cambridge: Harvard University Press, 1982), 7 et seq.

10. *Ibid.*, 68.

11. Wittgenstein, *Investigations*, 31.

12. Kripke, *Wittgenstein*, 21.

13. Wittgenstein, *Investigations*, 93–94.

14. *Ibid.*, 117–118.

15. *Ibid.*, 86.

16. *Ibid.*, 147.

17. *Ibid.*, 93.

18. Sellars, *Perception*, 160.

19. *Ibid.*, 161–162.

20. Wittgenstein, *Investigations*, 109–110.

21. Sellars, *Perception*, 131–132, 157.

22. Nelson Goodman, *Ways of Worldmaking* (Indianapolis: Hackett, 1978), 6.

23. Michael Williams, *Groundless Belief* (New Haven: Yale University Press, 1977), 102, 112.

24. Nelson Goodman, *Languages of Art* (Indianapolis: Hackett, 1976), 77.

25. Rorty, *Mirror*, 182.

26. *Ibid.*, 183–186.

27. Wittgenstein, *Investigations*, 148.

28. Edmund Husserl, *Experience and Judgement*, ed. Ludwig Landgrebe, tr. James S. Churchill and Karl Ameriks (Evanston, Ill.: Northwestern University Press, 1973), 88.

29. Jean Piaget, *La Naissance de l'intelligence chez l'enfant* (Neuchatel, Switzerland: Delachaux et Niestle, 1968), 273–274.

30. Jean Piaget, *La Construction du réel chez l'enfant* (Neuchatel, Switzerland: Delachaux et Niestle, 1967), 26, 31, 47, 61.

31. Rorty, *Mirror*, 187.

32. *Ibid.*, 186.

33. Edward Sapir, "Conceptual Categories in Primitive Languages," *Science* 74 (1931), 578.

34. Benjamin Lee Whorf, "Science and Linguistics," in *Language, Thought and Reality* (Cambridge: MIT Press, 1957), 213, 214.

35. Thomas S. Kuhn, *The Structure of Scientific Revolutions*, Second Edition (Chicago: The University of Chicago Press, 1970), 150.

36. Hans-Georg Gadamer, *Truth and Method* (New York: Crossroad, 1984), 401.

37. Donald Davidson, "On the Very Idea of a Conceptual Scheme," in *Inquiries into Truth and Interpretation* (Oxford: Clarendon Press, 1985), 189, 198.

38. Maxine Sheets-Johnstone, "Thinking in Movement," *Journal of Aesthetics and Art Criticism* 39 (Summer 1981), 404; see also "Hunting and the Evolution of Human Intelligence: An Alternative View," *The Midwest Quarterly* 28:1 (Autumn 1986), 9–35.

39. Berkeley, *Principles*, 55.

40. H. H. Price, *Thinking and Experience* (London: Methuen, 1953), 74.

41. Jonathan Bennett, *Rationality* (London: Routledge and Kegan Paul, 1964), 86–89.

CHAPTER TEN: THE GIVEN

1. Husserl, *Ideas*, First Book, 57.

2. William Lyons, *The Disappearance of Introspection* (Cambridge: MIT Press, 1986), 93.

3. Von Helmholtz, *Optics*, Vol. 3, 6.

4. *Ibid.*

5. Maurice Merleau-Ponty, *Phenomenology of Perception*, tr. Colin Smith (London: Routledge and Kegan Paul, 1962), 100.

6. Aristotle, *De Anima* 423ª 19–21.

7. Hume, *Treatise*, 252.

CHAPTER ELEVEN: THE SELF

1. Descartes, *Search*, 412.

2. Descartes, *Meditations*, 7.

3. *Ibid.*, 54.

4. *Ibid.*, 19.

5. *Ibid.*

6. *Ibid.*, 50–51.

7. Descartes, *Objections*, 126–127.

8. *Ibid.*, 113.

9. Descartes, *Oeuvres*, 902–906.

10. Descartes, *Principles*, 204.

11. René Descartes, *The Passions of the Soul* in *The Philosophical Writings of Descartes*, tr. John Cottingham, Robert Stoothoff, and Dugald Murdoch (Cambridge: Cambridge University Press, 1984), Vol. 1, 337, 338.

12. William James, *Principles of Psychology* (New York: Dover Publications, 1950), Vol. 2, p. 451.

13. *Ibid.*, 452.

14. René Descartes, *Discourse on the Method* in *The Philosophical Writings of Descartes*, tr. John Cottingham, Robert Stoothoff, and Dugald Murdoch (Cambridge: Cambridge University Press, 1984), Vol. 1, 141; *Meditations*, 56, 160.

15. Descartes, *Passions*, 335.

16. Descartes, *Principles*, 211.

17. Descartes, *Discourse*, 127.

18. Descartes, *Passions*, 347.

19. Descartes, *Oeuvres*, 750.

20. Descartes, *Meditations*, 40.

21. Descartes, *Objections*, 260.

22. Descartes, *Oeuvres*, 934–935.

23. Descartes, *Objections*, 113.

24. Descartes, *Oeuvres*, 1018.

25. Descartes, *Passions*, 356, 361; *Oeuvres*, 1018.

26. Descartes, *Meditations*, 15.

27. *Ibid.*, 17.

28. Jean-Paul Sartre, *Being and Nothingness*, tr. Hazel E. Barnes (New York: Philosophical Library, 1956), 32–33.

29. *Ibid.*, 31–32.

30. *Ibid.*, 403.

31. Descartes, *Meditations*, 40

32. Descartes, *Objections*, 134.

33. Descartes, *Principles*, 204.

34. *Ibid.*, 205–206.

CHAPTER TWELVE: UNOBSERVED EXISTENCE

1. Russell, *Knowledge*, 343.

2. A. J. Ayer, *Probability and Evidence* (New York: Columbia University Press, 1972), 4.

3. Hume, *Treatise*, 89.

4. Michael A. Slote, *Reason and Scepticism* (London: George Allen and Unwin,1970), 119–120.

5. Henry E. Kyburg Jr., "Randomness and the Right Reference Class," *The Journal of Philosophy* 74 (September 1977), 503–509.

6. Simon Blackburn, *Reason and Prediction* (Cambridge: Cambridge University Press, 1973), 126.

7. Descartes, *Meditations*, 40.

8. Edmund Husserl, *Cartesian Meditations*, tr. Dorion Cairns (The Hague: Martinus Nijhoff, 1973), 44–45.

9. Jay Boyd Best, "The Evolution and Organization of Sentient Biological Behavior Systems" in *Biology, History and Natural Philosophy,* ed. A. D. Breck and W. Yourgrau (New York: Plenum Press, 1974), 37–78.

10. Aristotle, *On Interpretation,* 19ª 17–20.

11. K. Gödel, "Eine Intrepretation des intuitionischen Aussagenkalkuls," *Ergebnisse eines mathematischen Kolloquiums,* 4 (1932), 39–40.

12. Arthur N. Prior, *Past, Present and Future* (Oxford: The Clarendon Press, 1967), 21.

CHAPTER THIRTEEN: THE REALITY OF THE WORLD

1. Price, *Perception,* 185.

2. *Ibid.,* 188.

3. Roderick M. Chisholm, *Theory of Knowledge,* (Englewood Cliffs, N.J.: Prentice Hall, 1956), 45–46.

4. Pollock, *Knowledge,* 31, 39–45.

5. Roderick M. Chisholm, *The Foundations of Knowing* (Minneapolis: University of Minnesota Press, 1982), 23.

6. Paul K. Moser, *Knowledge and Evidence* (Cambridge: Cambridge University Press, 1989), 163.

7. William of Ockham, *Summa Logicae* 1. 12. In *Opera Philosophica et Theologica, Opera Philosophica I,* (St. Bonaventare, N.Y.: Franciscan Institute Publications, 1974), 43.

8. Aristotle, *On Generation and Corruption* 1. 8. 326ᵇ, 7–28.

9. Chuang Tzu, *Basic Writings,* tr. Burton Watson (New York: Columbia University Press, 1964), 45.

10. For a phylogenetic approach, see Maxine Sheets-Johnstone, *The Roots of Thinking* (Philadelphia: Temple University Press, 1990).

INDEX